Skaidrite Rita Sparks

Best Wishes,
Rita Sparks

From Flames to Freedom:
FAITH RIDES THE RAILS

Latvian Refugee Girl's WWII Odyssey
To Destinations Unknown

Unless otherwise noted, Scripture quotations are taken from the King James Version of the Bible (Public Domain)

Photos of Martha Cook Building and song texts with permission of the Martha Cook Board of Governors

Photos from the "Salzburger Museum Augusteum Jahresschrift 1944/1955 by permission of the Salzburg Museum

Cover Design by:
Linards Lācis
UrbanPicture.lv

© 2012 Skaiddrite Rita Sparks
All Rights Reserved.

No part of this publication may be reproduced, stored in a retrieval system, or transmitted, in any form or by any means, electronic, mechanical, photocopying, recording, or otherwise, without the written permission of the author.

First published by Dog Ear Publishing
4010 W. 86th Street, Ste H
Indianapolis, IN 46268
www.dogearpublishing.net

ISBN: 978-1-4575-1531-6

This book is printed on acid-free paper.

Printed in the United States of America

CONTENTS

Introduction v
Preface..viii
Author's Note xiii
Dedication xiv
1   Train to Eternity, 1989...1
2   Jelgava Christmas, 1938 6
3   November Train Ride, 1917—The Bolshevik Revolution............13
4   Abysmal Journey: Novocherkassk to Riga, 1920..........................17
    ❖   The Years of Wine and Roses 19
    ❖   The Golden Years..21
    ❖   Red October, 1917 23
5   God Bless Latvia, 1918..26
6   Destination Station Riga, 1920 29
7   A New Family Begins, 1927 31
    ❖   At Home in Jelgava 33
8   Tatiana and Karlis 35
    ❖   The President's "Friendly Invitation", 1935 37
9   And Baby Makes Three 41
10 Nomads on the Move...45
    ❖   Blooming Spring—"Ziedoņi"...47
    ❖   Days of Shadow and Darkness..51
11 Home at Last on Valņu Street in Jelgava.......................................56
12 The Bright Summer Days, 1939..66
13 By the Beautiful Baltic Sea...69
14 Big Sister, 1940 76
15 The Russians Are Coming!..84
    ❖   A National Day of Mourning, 1941.......................................87
16 In the Shadow of the Iron Cross, 1941...92
17 The German March Continues, 1942...97
18 Dreams and Jelgava Turn to Ashes, 1944...................................108
19 Refugee Life Begins..113
    ❖   Family Torn Apart 118
    ❖   Leaving Riga, 1944...120
20 First Homecoming to Latvia, 1989...122
    ❖   Control by Fear and Intimidation 125
    ❖   Love and Tears 127
    ❖   Fellowship, Love and Tears Remain...................................129

	❖ Happy Memories	133
	❖ Where is My Home?	137
21	Train Destination Unknown—Farewell to Latvia, 1944	140
22	The Russians are Coming Again—Knittelfeld, 1945	152
23	Shalom, Judenburg	154
24	Millennium Journey 2000— Back to the Past Century	162
25	The Salzburg Experience, D.P. Camp Glasenbach, 1946	166
26	Living in a Microcosm, or Civilization Restored	174
27	School Days in Glasenbach	182
28	The Hills are Alive with the Sound of Music	188
29	Farewell, So Long, Aufwiedersehen, Good-Bye, 1948	193
30	Parting is Such Sweet Sorrow	202
	❖ In Munich Lies No "Hofbrauhaus"	204
31	SS Marine Flasher—Crossing the Atlantic, 1948	208
32	New York, New York—What a Wonderful Town	214
33	The Land of Milk and Honey	216
34	Michigan, "Land of Cowboys and Indians"	226
35	Blood Sweat and Tears	231
36	Home Sweet Home, 1951	244
	❖ A Trip Back to New York	256
37	Hail to the Victors Valiant	260
	❖ University Lutheran Chapel	263
	❖ "The Big House"	268
	❖ The Martha Cook Building	272
38	In Pursuit of Happiness	278
39	Epilogue	294
APPENDIX I		305
References		306

INTRODUCTION

"THE SEEDS OF IMPATIENCE"
By Skaidrite Rita Sparks, 1974

    The little towhead was impatient...
She did not understand why her people could not resist
The red militia who came in the quiet of the night.
The fearsome men who arrested her young friend's father.
"It isn't fair, do something!" she cried for the victims bound for Siberia.
The mother soothed her child and said:
"Our small country cannot fight the weapons of masses,
But larger, democratic lands will come to our aid,
We shall be free again. Be patient, my child..."
    A year went by, the little girl was impatient...
She wanted someone to fight the heartless persecutors,
The heartless men with rifles who marched her Jewish friend to her grave,
The SS men, whose bullets riddled the Star of David.
"It isn't fair, these men are wicked!" she cried through her tears.
The mother soothed her child and said:
"No men are wicked, only their intolerance is evil,
Justice will be done someday. Be patient, my child..."
    But the young girl did not learn to be patient with injustice...
"It isn't fair", she cried when asked to spy on her parents and friends.
In school she would not chant "Heil Hitler" or raise her hand in a salute
To honor the Fascist dictator who spoke of his superior race.
    "It isn't fair, those bombers are killers", cried the terrified girl
Over the lifeless bodies of a woman and children lying in the rubble.
Her mother tried to soothe her child and said:
"Those silvery eagles are American planes, fighting for freedom.
They will protect us from harm and bring justice to the world.
The war will soon be over. Be patient, my child..."
    The young teen was impatient...
Anxious to see the Statue of Liberty guarding the Land of the Free,
Where all men are equal, liberty and justice are rights given to all.
    In the land of opportunity, impatience was her ally.
Quickly she mastered another new language and new customs.
She was free to learn and hasten to the top of her class,
Free to be able to help and mentor others along the way,
Free to fight injustice with quiet determination.

The idealistic coed was impatient…
Impatient to dream the still impossible dream
That all men would be accepted as equals in true brotherhood,
Not just tolerated with condescension or bigotry,
   "It isn't fair", she cried in protest
Against the men who would not give shelter to her friend;
Why were white men afraid of his dark colored skin?
The friend consoled her with patient resignation,
"These men are blind from prejudice cultivated for over a century.
Our time has not yet come. Be patient, my friend."
   The little girl learned to be patient as she hid in the cold trenches.
She learned to be patient on the long journey fleeing from home.
From death, she learned the value of life and found meaning for existence.
Men's hatred for men taught her to love.
She learned to cope with adversity and not to panic in chaos.
Danger became a challenge to survive.
Time was precious, every minute in life counted.
From suffering she learned compassion for the less fortunate.
Music, laughter, and song became her allies in fighting fear and gloom.
In the piles of rubble she saw the impermanence of material things and
Discovered the healing grace and constancy of God's love.
She lived among strange peoples and developed a longing to understand them.
She looked beneath their multi-shaded skins to find their hearts.
In varied tongues she learned that prejudice is not in men's souls, it is taught.
   She studied patience for twenty more years—
She can differentiate between true patience in bearing burdens that cannot change
And situations where patience is worn as a virtuous mask covering

- ❖ *a lack of sensitivity to people's needs*
- ❖ *an absence in fortitude in correcting wrongs*
- ❖ *an excuse for low initiative and imagination*
- ❖ *tolerance of mediocrity and unjust authority*
- ❖ *imperturbable apathy with corruption.*
- ❖ *I am impatient when …*
- ❖ *showing concern for people*
- ❖ *standing up for my convictions*
- ❖ *trying to fight unkind deeds and innuendos*
- ❖ *not giving up when hurdles seem insurmountable*

The above poem was written in response to a colleague at Oakland University in Michigan asking me why I was so impatient in attempting to fight injustice and always trying to right the wrongs in this world. My childhood experiences were the garden germinating these seeds of impatience—impatience with men who try to take the world away from the hands of God and seize it with their own iron grip so that they can rule by weapons and fear.

PREFACE

*"Going Home, Going Home,
I am going home...."*

But where is my home?
For nearly a century, my life and that of my Latvian ancestors has been shaped by endless patterns of trains running on railroad tracks with frequent switches to far and unknown destinations, new trials in strange lands with new opportunities, and always a series of painful farewells, parting hugs, and tearful good-byes. There were no satellites and GPS systems during World War I and II to direct homeless refugees to their destinations. Yet God always knew the route he had charted for his children and had his angels, often in the guise as people, guide us through all danger as promised in Psalm 91:11 *"For he shall give his angels charge over thee, to keep thee in all thy ways. They shall bear thee up in their hands, lest thou dash thy foot against a stone."*

God in his mercy always provided unceasing spiritual strength to our family. Psalm 91 was my mother's confirmation verse at St. Nicholas Church in Jelgava, Latvia. The minister who chose the verse for her must have been guided by divine inspiration to choose a text that states, *"A thousand shall fall at thy side, and ten thousand at thy right hand; but it shall not come nigh thee"* (Psalm 91:7). Thousands did indeed fall during World War II while our family was spared even at times when dead bodies lay scattered like grotesque broken or dismembered dolls around us. My parents demonstrated a strong faith in God and indefatigable endurance in facing major evil forces determined to destroy not only our nuclear family, but also the entire Baltic region of Estonia, Latvia, and Lithuania. All we could rely on was God's mercy and the good will of strangers who, disregarding their own risk, often extended a helping hand to the refugees who had lost everything as a result of the perils of war and the atrocities committed by the invaders acting under the pretense of being "liberators".

Volumes of history have been written about the horrors of Nazism and the Holocaust, but relatively little has been understood about the horrors of Communism. The world has caught only brief glimpses of the sufferings experienced by the peoples of the Baltic countries before the collapse of the Soviet Union in 1991. America and the peoples of the free world honor and commemorate the victims of 9/11 when terrorists destroyed the New York City World Trade Center in 2001 and some 3000 innocent lives were lost. But the world hardly knows that Latvians throughout the world still commemorate the anniversary of 6/14 though over seven decades have passed since the night of horror in 1941 when over 15,000 innocent people, the country's elite, were rounded up like cattle and shipped to the frozen Gulag of Siberia where thousands died from torture and starvation. This day of infamy is largely unnoticed by the world and the evil deeds inflicted on a nation are not widely recorded and publicized as a significant historical event to be remembered. Even less information is recorded in history of the bravery and suffering of refugees driven out of their home countries by war. Thousands of Latvians, Lithuanians and Estonians became stateless refugees and were scattered throughout the world to live in exile because our native countries were occupied by the Soviets and no longer existed. Thousands of children experienced their childhood being blown away by the storms of war.

It is important to repeat the truth again and again at every opportunity so that "history does not repeat itself" in new generations. Yet, evil events do happen even today. The suffering inflicted on the children of World War II has been repeated with other war-traumatized groups. Children still wander homeless like the Lost Boys of Sudan did in fairly recent history. Almost daily we see pictures of emaciated children crying for food. Victims of present-day civil and religious wars in the Mideast and Africa are still crying for freedom and there are refugee camps throughout the world and the United States where people have become homeless and living under deplorable conditions due to natural disasters. I hope that families and children traumatized by homelessness and all the inhumanities of war or disaster can emerge as survivors and will not think of themselves as worthless victims and second-class citizens, but rather as children of a God who will not forsake them. God sometimes presents himself in unique ways that we may not visualize or understand, but he is always near.

Full steam ahead as tracks diverge to unknown destinations.

My story reconstructs the turmoil that comes into the life of a girl being torn from her sunny early childhood, much like strong winds tear a kite from a child's tiny hands, to be catapulted into the shadow of mass slayings and living a life of constant terror. In my family history, puffing steam engines[1] pulled long lines of boxcars along railroad tracks and wove a harsh, repetitive pattern for my ancestors, my life, and that of thousands of other Baltic children who rode the rails or were tossed about on the stormy seas. When viewed within the context of the entire Latvian refugee experience, my life as a displaced person was not unique but it speaks of a generation of children robbed of their childhood and cast into a state of fear, poverty and homelessness.

My immediate family history spans two world wars, three continents, several seas and the Atlantic Ocean. For three generations, when Latvia ceased to exist, we were uprooted and tossed about like pawns in the power struggles between the Communists and the Nazis while the leaders of the free world chose to look the other way because it was not politically expedient at that time to protect small countries from being devoured by powerful dictators. Deprived of our homeland and our birthright, thousands of citizens from the Baltic countries were deported to Siberia. Later others were forced into German labor and prisoner of war camps, always hoping to find their way home again. For the majority of those who were deported, displaced, or dispossessed, the dream of coming home again never came true after the Soviets took over Latvia. "Going home" took on the symbolic meaning of the old spiritual on which the Largo in the New World Symphony by Antonin Dvorak is based—"Going home, going home" to an eternal rest.

Refugee trains only ran one way; there were no round-trip tickets for us. As the years have been galloping by, new generations replaced the old. The huffing steam engines, that pulled the trains of our destiny along miles of glistening tracks, have been replaced by new streamlined diesel, electric, and even jet engines. The energy that powered the trains in our family history was of political origin. The world needs to understand the true historical forces that were the basis for Eastern European citizens having to leave their homes to be scattered throughout the world during World War II.

There have been many special moments, relationships, and unique wartime experiences in my life that had a significant impact on the kind of person I am. My parents who instilled Christian faith and values in me certainly laid the foundation for my character. Their love and spiritual strength showed me how to rely on God and to face life without giving in to despair. Not only have all these experiences shaped my character, beliefs and outlook on life, but they have, also had a profound effect on shaping the personalities and sets of values acquired by my children and their children as well. My children reflect a kaleidoscope of ancestral genes from Latvia, Germany, England, Estonia, Sweden, Russian Georgia, and America. My grandchildren are an even more complex potpourri with bits of France, Poland, Ireland, Wales, Scotland and Native American to make them truly of international origin. Claire, our great-granddaughter, adds yet another pleasant Dutch treat to the ancestry formula. But their story is yet to develop.

My book is written so that my children and their offspring know the forces that formed their heritage and can envision God's saving grace in their lives. The world is full of evil terrorists and we do not know what the future will bring, but we have God's promise that *"Thou shalt not be afraid for the terror by night; nor for the arrow that flies by day; nor for the pestilence that walks in darkness; nor for the destruction that wastes at noonday."(Psalm 91:5-6)*

The unresolved question that remains after the refugee years and all the beautiful places where we have lived since coming to America is the soul-searching issue of *"Where is our home?"* As a naturalized citizen of the United States, I am no longer "stateless". Yet, after more than six decades in America, I am often regarded as a foreigner; I still get curious inquiries about my nationality and country of birth when people hear my name. Likewise, when I visited my home country, a well-meaning Latvian lady on the streetcar in Riga started a conversation with me saying that she enjoys welcoming "foreign travelers" to Latvia. Sadly, I seem to be regarded as a foreigner in both of my "home" countries.

There is a beautiful sentimental Latvian song called *"Nekur Nav tik Labi kā Mājās*[2] or "Nowhere is it Good like at Home" with music written by the popular Latvian composer Maestro Raimonds Pauls and words by the well-known songwriter, drummer, poet and publisher, Guntars Račs. The lyrics and nostalgic tune aptly describe my feelings for my homeland for nowhere else have I been welcomed as warmly as each time I returned to the land of my birth. The song's refrain translates as follows:

Nowhere is it good like at home,
Nowhere are you as warmly awaited,
Nowhere have I felt any better,
And nowhere will be better than home.

The first two verses pose questions of whether there is anywhere on earth where meadows are as brightly blooming, birds so sweetly sing, girls laugh and dogs bark as happily. Having the nickname of Kaija, or Seagull, I identify most with the third verse:

"Nekur nav tik labi kā mājās,
Vai kaut kur jūra tā šalc?
Nekur nav tik labi man klājies,
Vai liedags vēl kaut kur tik balts"?

> *Nowhere is it good like at home,*
> *Does the sea murmur anywhere more?*
> *Nowhere have I felt any better.*
> *Is the beach as white anywhere?*

My eyes get misty whenever I hear the song, much like we in America feel sentimental over the song *"America, the Beautiful"*. I believe most Latvians living away from their original homeland feel equally nostalgic when they ponder the question "where is my home", but with family roots of several generations established in our new homelands, it is extremely difficult to leave everything again to return to Latvia to start all over again as a stranger in my own homeland. I will always call the peaceful city of Jelgava where I first came into the world my "home", but in my heart I know that for me home has taken on the meaning of a spiritual place rather than something made of boards and mortar which have no soul of their own.

The unknown destination of "Home" becomes less important when God is the conductor on the journeys of our life. The ultimate home destination in Heaven promised by God is yet to be. As a teenager living in refugee camps in Austria, I imagined myself as the seagull in the German song *"Möwe Due Fliegst in die Heimat"* and tearfully vowed to return to the Baltic shores when the stormy days were over. Now, when I am overcome by a longing for my native homeland, I am comforted knowing that my soul needs no geographic home. I get solace and a clearer focus on my final destination from the words of the old hymn by Thomas Rawson Taylor, "I'm But a Stranger Here"[3].

I'm but a stranger here,
Heaven is my home;
Earth is a desert drear;
Heaven is my home:
Danger and sorrow stand
Round me on every hand;
Heaven is my fatherland,
Heaven is my home.

AUTHOR'S NOTE

The stories in this book are all true. Memories of my childhood, the images I hold in the recesses of my mind of parents, grandparents, and significant events are generally formed by my own life experiences. In the 21st Century, *"Back to the Future"* still exists only in the fantasy world of movies. Technology has not as yet developed a means to transport me back into some era predating my own birth over seventy years ago. My train for time travel into the past is called "memories". Thus, my mind's eye can only visualize my ancestors as they were from the time my own relationship with them began. My children know my past only through brief glimpses as I recall for them some memory from a long-ago childhood. These memories may have become clouded through the passage of years but the people are real and as recorded in the images of my mind, conversations with family members, entries in my childhood diary kept by my mother, notations of residences in my father's Latvian passport, photo albums, and my own notes recorded in childish handwriting in a wartime log and a teen diary. The people and events are all based on actual experiences and people as I remember them. The conversations are paraphrased from the stories told to me by my parents and aunts and my own vivid memories. This is the story of my Latvian, albeit multinational, multicultural family from the shores of the River Don in Novocherkassk, the Sea of Azov in Western Russia to Latvia on the Baltic Sea, to the port of Hamburg on the North Sea, across the Atlantic to America, Nyack on the Hudson River, and to the Great Lakes State of Michigan—all one-way travel, mostly by rail to destinations unknown.

DEDICATION

This book is dedicated to all the children who have been deprived of their childhood by the trauma of war, disaster, abuse, or neglect and are searching for a place called home. I hope and pray that children traumatized by inhumanities that have separated them from their loved ones and made them homeless and dispossessed refugees living in constant fear and deprivation can emerge as survivors. Even when subjected to atrocities, children should not think of themselves as worthless victims and second-class citizens, but rather as precious children of a loving God who will not forsake them.

My survival can be credited to God's grace in giving me courageous and loving parents who shielded my sister and me from danger and showed strength when the winds of war threatened to blow our world apart. Their reliance on God's mercy kept us from giving in to despair in the face of enemy inhumaneness. Their unwavering trust in God taught us not to be afraid but to be thankful for each day in our lives. The love that Kārlis and Tatiana Gedrovics bestowed on our family allowed us to feel secure, loved, and at home, no matter how frightening the circumstances or humble the dwelling.

1

TRAIN TO ETERNITY, 1988

As the blustery November wind rattled the bare beechnut tree branches against the bedroom window, I sat cocooned in the predawn darkness and listened to my father's uneven raspy breathing. The only glimmer of light in the room came from the miniature Christmas lights strung on the small potted fir tree on the dresser across from the bed. Kārlis Gedrovics had always loved Christmas and I had brought the tree to his home in Ann Arbor so that he could enjoy its twinkling star-shaped lights during the Advent season. Perhaps the doctor who prescribed hospice care was right and my father's heart was too weak to keep on beating no matter how fervently we wished to keep him in our family circle. If it was God's will for him not to see yet another Christmas in the midst of our family, then we must let go so that he can join his ancestors in celebrating the birth of Christ with the heavenly hosts. I sat upright on a straight chair relying on its hardness to keep me awake after a long day at work as an administrator at Hutzel Hospital in Detroit. My younger sister Mudite Sipols and I were taking turns in keeping the nighttime vigil to give our mother Tatiana a few hours of rest during our father's long battle against his failing heart.

Kārlis' generous and loving heart had been faithfully beating since his birth on October 13, 1903. Over his eighty-five years his once-strong body had endured the ravages of two world wars and famine. A strong faith in God and a determination to protect his wife and daughters gave him strength to do hard labor so that the family would survive despite the loss of our home and all belongings in our native country Latvia. Bolshevik and Nazi occupation forces in Latvia had dealt our family a heavy hand, separating parents from the grandparents, the aunts, and the uncles, and scattering them throughout three continents. But Kārlis and his wife Tatiana Gedrovics, with the help of God, had managed to keep their nuclear family intact through all dangers. Would death now wield the final blow to take the loving father from the family?

The old man broke the silence by deep moaning and mumbling in his sleep. He tossed restlessly despite me gently stroking his hand in attempts to soothe his anxiety.

"*Papuk, what is wrong, are you in pain?*" I asked using the familiar Latvian word for "Daddy".

"*No, I must hurry. You must get me to the train station before the train leaves. They are waiting for me.*"

Perhaps the medicine was causing hallucinations or the old man was having a nightmare.

"*Papuk, you must have had a dream. Everything is quiet. I am here with you and you can go back to sleep.*"

But Kārlis was not to be quieted, "*Please take me to the train station so that I can get my ticket right away.*"

"*It is three o'clock in the morning, Papuk. The ticket office is closed. Why don't you rest for a bit and we can talk about the train again in the morning?*"

"*Kaija,*" Kārlis responded using my childhood nickname, "*You do not understand. I can see the light of the train engine and I can hear its whistle. I must get to the train right now. They are waiting for me.*"

"*Who is waiting for you, Papuk?*" I whispered though I knew in my heart what the answer would be. I could almost feel the presence of the spirits surrounding my father's bed in the darkened room although only the candles on the Christmas tree were casting their shadows in the mirror on the dresser.

"*My father, my mother, my brother, and my two sisters. They are all waiting for me. They are waiting so I can help them gather the potatoes from the fields before they freeze. We need food for the long train ride.*"

A chill seemed to sweep over the room. In my mind I could also hear the train whistle that I had heard so often when my father took me along on train rides from the railway station in Jelgava where he worked. Now the whistle was calling the old railroad man for his last ride. Some people who have near-death experiences talk of going through a bright tunnel of light as they enter eternity. It appeared appropriate that the man, who had spent many years of his career on the railroad, would be taken on his last voyage by the night train.

Kārlis missed the train that night. He got on the last train to join his sainted family the next day on November 30, 1988 while Mudite was keeping the night vigil at his bedside. Over the years while he lived in exile in America, Kārlis had always dreamed of returning to his homeland and that his family would be waiting for him at the railroad station. That was not destined to happen while he was still alive, but he certainly must have been greeted with joy by his jubilant family in eternity. A year after his death, the Soviet regime was beginning to crumble. My mother and I carried out his wish and visited Latvia for the first time after forty-five years. We had a sentimental reunion with Kārlis' one remaining sister Zelma and her family but the warm feeling of "home" seemed to have been overshadowed by an oppressive aura of Soviet enmity.

I would regret that I was not at my father's bedside to say the last good-bye, but I was assured that he boarded the train in peace knowing the love his family had for him. During our last conversation while I was reassuring my father that the train would still be there after he rested, I asked him if he knew that he was very much loved. His face lit up with a bright smile and he answered in Latvian with conviction, "Ak jā!"

"We will always have your love in our hearts, Papuk. Mīlestība nekad nebeidzās, love never ends. Our love will go along with you into eternity. Now you must rest for the long journey home."

Though tears were pressing against my eyelids, I tried not to upset him by crying. I just wanted him to be certain that he was loved. I could not bear to say good-bye, there had been too many good-byes in my life.

Finally my father settled down for a fitful sleep, often murmuring that he must return home to help his sisters harvest the fruit and potatoes. As his agitation subsided, I tried to gain peace from the quietly glimmering star-shaped Christmas tree lights casting a soft glow on the room. I was glad that I had brought the small fir tree to my father's bedroom at Thanksgiving so he could share in the Advent of the birth of Christ one more time before hearing the "All Aboard" for his final journey to his eternal home. After living forty-five years in exile away from his beloved homeland Latvia and his relatives, my father was finally going home to join his parents and siblings in their eternal home.

"Goin' home, goin' home, I'm a goin' home.
Quiet-like, some still day, I'm jes' going' home.
It's not far, jes' close by,
Through an open door;
Work all done, care laid by,
Goin' to fear no more."

My father had lived with fear through much of his life. From his fear filled boyhood days during World War I, worrying over the safety of his wife and children during the Russian and German occupations of Latvia during World War II, to the fear of the unknown in crossing the ocean to the strange country of America, Kārlis' life had been filled with fear and tension. The constant fear and ongoing tension had probably contributed to the heart attack that damaged his generous and loving heart. Yet, both my parents had used their fear as an opportunity to worship God and to rely on His grace. Eternal peace would come this Christmas and my father would have no more fear. The old spiritual *"Going Home"*[4], set to the music of Antonin Dvorak's Largo from the 9th Symphony, popularly known as the *New World Symphony,* continued to float through my mind as I listened to my father's labored breathing.

At times when I am really happy, overwhelmed with sadness, or facing some critical decision, it seems that some appropriate song emerges from my subconscious to express my feelings. Latvians always enjoy singing when they get together in good times and in times of sorrow and this singing heritage manifests itself within me as well. When I was little, I liked a Latvian folk song called *"Kas Tie Tādi, Kas Dziedāja.."* or "Who are they who were singing without sunshine in the night?" The plaintive song gives the answer that those were all orphan children, subjects of a harsh master. I asked my mother how these orphans could be singing when they were so sad and mother explained that songs lift our spirit and give us an outlet for voicing our feelings and emotions. The symbolic solution for these orphans was the sun rising at dawn to dry their tears. The *"Going Home"* lyrics by William A. Fisher filled my thoughts and gave me comfort this November night as my father was preparing for his journey to the new world where his departed family and friends were waiting with the Lord.

"Mother's there 'spectin' me,
Father's waitin' too;
Lots o' folk gather'd there,
All the friends I knew,
All the friends I knew.
Home, I'm goin' home!"

Content knowing that he would soon be going home, my father's face filled with peace as he slept. I remembered how he always looked so peaceful in his sleep. It almost seemed like he had a slight smile on his lips now and the pallor of his face gave him an ethereal angelic look. My mind was racing with memories of the life we had shared and how I had always felt safe in the care of my parents. Our roles were reversed now. Once my chubby little fingers had felt secure encircled in his strong hand as we went for walks along the banks of Lielupe (Big River) in Jelgava. When I expressed fear that I might fall into the river through the expansion cracks in the bridge, my father promised he would never let me go and his hand would hold me tighter. When the hissing steam from the train engines threatened to engulf me at the railroad station, my father assured me he would never let go of my hand lest I fall off the platform unto the tracks. Sitting at his bedside, I now held his frail hand in mine, hoping to give him assurance that my love would carry him over the bridge he now had to cross. But I would have to let go when the Lord called him. In the silence of the room, I could hear the strains of Dvorak's 9th Symphony played in my mind by an invisible orchestra leading my father to a New World as I started to feel the overwhelming pain we would face in losing him.

Nothin' lost, all's gain,
No more fret nor pain,
No more stumblin' on the way,
No more longin' for the day,
Goin' to roam no more!
Mornin' star lights the way,
Res'less dreams all done;
Shadows gone, break o' day,
Real life jes' begun.
There's no break, there's no end,
Jes' a livin' on;
Wide awake, with a smile
Goin' on and on.
Goin' home, goin' home, I'm jes' goin' home.

It was comforting to know that my beloved Papuks got to celebrate Christmas early and closed his eyes for the last time by the light of the glistening candle lights. Christmas has always occupied a special place in my memories of childhood Christmas celebrations with my family in our homeland Latvia. Then I was still called by my christened name Skaidrite, or the nickname Kaija I had chosen for myself, and not the substitute name Rita that foreign tongues in later years found easier to use. The melody of my father's favorite Christmas carol *"Es Skaistu Rozīt' Zinu..."* or *"Lo, How a Rose is Growing"*[5] also began floating through my mind. Perhaps *"one perfect flower here in the cold of winter and darkest midnight hour"* would open its petals to welcome him when my beloved Papuk will be brought *"into the bright courts of heaven and into endless day."* Tears filled my eyes and a lump rose in my throat as strains of more beloved Christmas carols came floating back from my childhood as I kept my lonesome and sad night vigil and recalled happy family festivities from a long ago..."Silent Night, Holy Night"...

2

JELGAVA CHRISTMAS, 1938

"Oh Come Little Children, Oh Come One and All"...

Winter scene in Latvia

Christmas as experienced by a three-year-old child in the midst of a loving family is full of magic and surprises. In Latvia, nature usually makes Christmas even more beautiful by covering the earth with a soft thick blanket of white snow. Long icicles, shining in the sunlight like the finest crystal, decorate tree branches and hang from the eaves of the houses, sometimes almost reaching the mounds of snow on the ground like giant glass stalactites. The winter sun reflects from the icicles in the colors of the rainbow and endows them with a likeness of the most precious glistening diamonds. Should an icicle break from its roots, it often transforms into a wonderful popsicle treat for a child. Sometimes the icicles grow so long as to almost reach the ground from the roof. Ignoring the warnings of their parents that the huge icicles could break off and pierce their bodies, the children delight in trying to knock them loose and let their imaginations transform the ice spears into sabers for fencing matches.

In 1938, Christmas was still anticipated as the sacred church festival celebrating the birth of Jesus, unmarred by Communist denial of religious holidays and the commercialism that surrounds Christmas in the current millennium. The air was filled with the pealing of church bells, the melodies of traditional Christmas carols, and the fragrance of pine trees and real candles burning on the Christmas tree. From the wood-burning stove in the kitchen floated the sweet aroma of the traditional "Piparkūkas", or gingerbread cookies that I was helping my mother bake. My mother said that her little Kaija's cheeks were as red as the bright apples we planned

Christmas 1938, Four Generations: Great-grandmother Tigulis 72, Omi Asja 48, Mother Tatiana 26, and Skaidrite 3

to hang on our tree. I was so excited I could hardly stand still in anticipation of the family visit with my great-grandmother and grandmother and the gifts I would receive from Father Christmas.

"*Kaija, your big blue eyes sparkle so much from joy, maybe we will not even need candles on the tree,*" my mother remarked. I ran to the mirror to see if my eyes really looked like the dancing candle flames, but I only saw my usual reflection. I was really happy though, like my mother had observed.

My mother, a devout Christian woman educated as a teacher, wanted her daughter to learn at an early age that Christmas was not just about cookies and getting presents but, most important, for celebrating the birth of Christ and bringing love to others by sharing the blessings God had bestowed on the family with children who were poor, orphaned, or neglected. Tatiana explained that even a small gift could bring joy to the heart of a poor child and bring a ray of sunshine and warmth into the cold grayness of poverty.

When mother asked which of my things I would like to take to church to donate for the poor children, I chose the brand new mittens my mother had just made for me. Our family lived very frugally and I did not have many things to give away, but I thought that at least an orphan could be warm wearing my mittens if there were no parents to keep the child warm. I always felt bad for all the little orphans remembering the old folk song about orphan children singing without sunshine in the dark of the night. After we finished baking the cookies, my mother and I walked hand in hand to the St. Nicholas Lutheran Church one block from our home. I presented my favorite blue mittens to the young associate minister, Rev. Gulbis.

"*I would like to give my mittens to a poor and needy child to keep the hands warm this winter*", I said rather timidly and with a little regret over giving up my new mittens.

"*But won't you need them to keep your hands warm?*" questioned the minister.

"*No, I still have my own Mamīte (Latvian diminutive for mommy) and she can make me another pair. Give mine to a child who has no mother.*"

Having made the donation, mother and I headed home across the churchyard to our own cozy apartment. The charitable mission was accomplished and Tatiana reminded her impressionable little daughter how blessed it was to help those in need. Little did I know that a surprise lay in store for me the following day.

On the day of Christmas Eve, my mother and I were busy in the kitchen finishing preparations for the Christmas dinner when the custodian from St. Nicholas church appeared at the door and asked if he could see the little Miss Skaidrite Gedrovics who had visited the church the previous day. He presented me with a small package and an envelope. When the package was opened, a bounty of sweets, nuts, cookies, and a small figurine of the Baby Jesus spilled out. The envelope contained a beautiful Christmas card with a message, *"A young orphan child is filled with joy because she now has warm mittens that you provided for her. She wishes you a blessed Christmas."*

The surprise made me jump for joy thinking that I had made the right choice and some poor child had actually cared enough to thank me for the mittens. I was not aware that Rev. Gulbis had made the kind gesture to impress upon me the joy that comes from giving. I read in my diary years later that my mother's eyes had filled with tears of joy and humility that day. She gave thanks in her heart that God had enriched her simple lesson through the sensitive and considerate minister who impressed upon her little daughter that good deeds are rewarded. The Rev. Gulbis continued his faithful ministry even after Latvia ceased to exist after WWII. The kind minister became the founder of a Lutheran church for Latvian immigrants in Caracas, Venezuela and spread God's word in the far-off continent of South America.

The Bible tells us to *"Train up a child in the way he should go: and when he is old he will not depart from it" (Proverbs 22:6).* The events of childhood are long remembered. Because young minds are receptive and retentive of memories, youth is an ideal time for instilling values in children. I would never forget the lesson I learned from my mother about sharing with orphaned, poor and neglected children. All of my adult life, I have volunteered to work on projects to help the children in care of the Lutheran Child and Family Service of Michigan (LCFS) agency. Eventually I became the President of the State Auxiliary (LCFSA). Every year when the Auxiliary prepares Christmas presents for the children, I vividly remember my first charitable donation. I am delighted that my mother instilled in me the joy of giving, especially to the least of God's children. In 2006 I was honored as "Lutheran Woman of the Year" for my volunteer work with needy children and families but the real honor and thanks were due to my dear Mamīte, the Lord, and the kind Rev. Gulbis that long-ago Christmas.

In the old bygone days of Christmas homes were not aglow with commercial decorations. The only decoration in the Latvian home was a fresh fir tree, an evergreen gift from nature. The tree was decorated just before Christmas Eve with pinecones, nuts, shiny red apples and real wax candles to be lit on Christmas Eve when the family gathered to sing carols and to await a home visit by Santa Claus, also known as "Father Christmas". It is noted in the diary where my mother kept track of "my little life", as I called it, that some of the red apples seemed to disappear along the bottom layers of the tree branches as some little person could not resist the tempting aroma of the fruit.

During the Advent weeks children rehearsed diligently to be ready to greet Father Christmas with a song or a poem recited especially for him in appreciation for his visit and to show what good children they had been. I was always excited when preparing my little performance and helping put candles into their shiny star-shaped clips.

"Papuk, will you listen to my poem again? I want to make sure it is perfect for Father Christmas."

"Bravo, that was beautiful. I am so proud of you", said Kārlis lifting his first-born high into the air after I repeated my poem.

" Kaija, I am certain Father Christmas will think you are a very good little girl and will bring you some presents".

"I hope you do not have to work this Christmas Eve, Papuk, so you can be here when Father Christmas comes!" I remembered with disappointment that the previous Christmas my Papuks was called out to work just before the arrival of Father Christmas at our house. I really wanted all of us to be together so I could make everyone proud of my recitation and to have Father Christmas acknowledge that I had indeed been a good girl.

But, alas, just after the candles on the tree were lit dear Papuks would again be summoned to hasten out to cover some important duty at the Jelgava railroad station where he worked as a paymaster. He would don his sheepskin-lined olive winter coat and off he would rush. Invariably, there would be a knock on the door a few minutes later. Father Christmas carried a burlap bag filled with gifts on his back and he was dressed in a wooly sheepskin coat with olive lining. He had a long white beard so soft it was like cotton batting. His blue eyes were kind and shiny just like my father's. I greeted Father Christmas with a curtsey and trepidation. In a deep voice he asked if I had been a good girl deserving a gift. If I had misbehaved, I knew, as all children did, that Father Christmas would leave a switch made of birch branches for naughty children. My parents could use the switch on my behind just in case I misbehaved!

"Yes, I am always a good girl and I have learned a poem for you", I said in a timid voice. By the time I had recited the poem perfectly with my cheeks glowing hot by the light of the candles, the room was filled with the aroma of melting wax and the smell of incense, as an occasional pine needle got singed in the flames of the candles. Father Christmas put his head back and gave a hearty laugh.

"Well done, little one!" and he presented me with special gifts from his bag and admonished me to be sure to obey my parents and behave at all times. Then he hurried away, no doubt to visit the other children in the family and the neighborhood. A little while later Papuks would return from work.

"Papuk, did you see Father Christmas out on the street? I am so sad you just missed him. I waited for you to come home before I open my present."

"Sorry, honey. Maybe I will not have to work next year. Let's see what he brought my big girl."

Skaidrite, Christmas 1938

Usually the presents were quite modest and utilitarian. That year when I was nearly four, Father Christmas brought me a big porcelain doll. She had the most beautiful face with blue eyes and long brown hair and black eyelashes. The eyelids closed when the doll was lying down. The doll's hair was real and I very carefully brushed and combed it and learned to braid it. Pink ribbons to match the pink ribbons on her lacy white dress adorned the doll's hair. Although my parents could not afford such an expensive imported doll complete with her own navy blue doll carriage, Christmas was a time of magic and sharing by the family. Father Christmas and his elves had connections that became known to me only years later. Kārlis' cousin Anna Rasins was married to a wealthy book publisher in Riga. They had a daughter named Ilona who was eight years older than I. Ilona had decided that she would be one of the helping elves and offered to share one doll from her bountiful collection to bring joy to her little cousin. And what a joy it was! Surprisingly, Kārlis' sister, Olga, also seemed to get inside information from Father Christmas and she bought a beautiful navy blue doll carriage for her little niece. A miniature sewing machine that could really sew was a present from my parents. I was so happy that I could learn to sew and help my mother make some clothes for my doll. These were the most memorable gifts I had received in my short childhood and I treasured them until the violence of war swept over the country and our family lost nearly all possessions. I could not save my beautiful doll or any other toys.

Two more years passed before it dawned on me that having to work on Christmas Eve was just a pretense so that my father could assume the role of Father Christmas. It was the coincidence of the sheepskin lining in my father's coat and Father Christmas' coat in reverse that gave away the secret. What girl would not be delighted to know that her own father was her "Real Father Christmas"? From then on I thought of my father as a blessing in disguise. Christmas was even better after that, but nobody knew then that by the time I was nine, war and oppressive dark political clouds would sweep over the country ending the celebration of Christmas in Latvia for fifty years. For the Gedrovics family there would eventually be another Santa Claus across the Atlantic Ocean in New York City to restore the gift of Christmas when I was already a teen-ager.

To this day, I think I am the only person besides my mother who knew that my father's true identity was that of Father Christmas for all the children in the Gedrovics family. My sister Mudite was only four when Christmas came to an end in Latvia and she has few memories of her homeland. Fifty years later, when I visited my three cousins in Latvia, they recalled the jolly Father Christmas who had brought them presents. However, during the decades that the Communists did not allow Christmas to be celebrated in Latvia, they had never learned from their mother, that her brother Kārlis was the real Father Christmas. The Soviets replaced Father Christmas with "Old Man Frost" so that children could still celebrate the winter holiday without religious connotations.

Jelgava Railroad Station 1944

Until 1944, Kārlis Arturs Gedrovics, when he was not delighting children as Father Christmas, took on his other identity as an accountant for the railroad in Jelgava, Latvia. In this capacity he brought joy to me by often taking me along to help him "work" at the Jelgava station or along for train rides when he had to make trips to stations in other cities. My mother wrote in my diary that inevitably, whenever the railroad station came into view during our walks, I would insist that we go to "work in station". Being quite headstrong, I would not accept any excuses from my mother for continuing the walk and would stomp my feet in my determined way until we would stop to visit Papuk at work. My beloved railway station was heavily damaged during World War II bombings, but its basic facade was rebuilt true to the original construction plans. When I brought my family for a visit to Latvia in 2009, the train station was the main point of interest I wanted to share with them in Jelgava. The old clock atop the building had been replaced in its landmark position. However, it seemed that the train platforms were not nearly as high and foreboding as they had appeared to a little girl when I held my father's hand as the steam engines came to a hissing halt at the station. As I stood on the platform reminiscing with my two sons, I wondered was it just sunlight dancing on the windowpanes or was it perhaps really the spirit of my father waving to his grandsons from his office window on the extreme left of the second story? I had spent so many hours in the office with Papuk as I filled pages and pages of blank paper with scribbles, official rubber stampings and dreamed of

Jelgava Railroad Station 2009, 65 years later

working at the railway station when I grew up. My father always made me feel so special when he allowed me to "work" in his office. These precious memories will live on forever.

Whether it was the attraction of the click-clack sound of the rails and the eerie train whistle, destiny, fate, or what I eventually recognized was God's plan–railroads figured prominently in the pathways that generations of my family would follow across the continent of Europe from Russia to Latvia, then to Austria, and eventually in North America.

3
NOVEMBER TRAIN RIDE, 1917
THE BOLSHEVIK REVOLUTION

Snowflakes obscured the sky as the drafty World War I Era passenger train chugged westward along the tracks through the bleak Russian countryside. The steam from the locomotive froze suspended in the air and shrouded the lead cars in an eerie fog. The damp November air chilled the tired and hungry passengers. November certainly was not a choice month for anyone to be traveling over the frozen tundra of Russia in unheated cars. Nothing in the solemn faces of the traveling families indicated a holiday mood. The men were talking in hushed undertones. This was an uncertain time and anything that a person said might be reported to the Soviet secret police. The men's worried expressions and furtive glances to constantly check who might be watching appeared to be characteristic of persons on the run from persecution. Women with pale tired-looking faces and dark circles under their eyes were huddled with children of various ages. The usual chatter and banter of children was absent on this journey. The oppressive silence was only broken by an occasional cough or whimper.

Kārlis Gedrovics, 14, and his sister Zelma, 16, huddled in one of the drafty cars. In hushed tones the parents, fifty-year-old Kristaps and his forty-nine-year-old wife Olga, recalled how just two years ago in 1915 they had left their home in Latvia and made the same train trip eastbound. Then they were full of hope to make a better living in Russia for their five children and to escape the oppression of Latvians by the wealthy German landowners. During World War I, as the German army occupied most of the country, thousands of Latvia's approximately two million residents left home as refugees to work in Russia as most of Latvia's industry had also been moved to Russia. Opportunities to find work and fair wages were plentiful both in agriculture and industry.

Kristaps Gedrovics

Kristaps was born in 1867 and was one of five children of a Latvian farming couple, Kristaps and Grieta Gedrovics. He had two brothers named Robert and Theodore and two sisters named Otilija and Paulina (Aunt Līna). Aunt Līna inherited the family farm when their father died in 1910. In the 1930's, Līna deeded the farm in the township of Livberze to her brother's youngest son, Kārlis Gedrovics. Kristaps and his wife Olga met while they both sang in a church choir in Jelgava.

In Kristaps, Olga found the steadfast friend and protector she had yearned for during her traumatic youth when she had to learn to be on her own at an early age. Olga was born in Estonia in 1868. Her mother was also named Olga and was an Estonian. Her father was a wealthy aristocrat of German origin. Mr. Gutmanis worked as a museum director and was able to provide the best of private schooling for young Olga. In 1879, when Olga was only eleven and her brother Leopold just a one-year-old baby, their mother died as did the father shortly thereafter and the orphaned children were invited to live with relatives in Jelgava, Latvia. One of the relatives was a minister, the other a farmer. The children were taken in to live with the farmer in the country. Shortly their circumstances took a turn for the worse and Olga was to regret moving to the farm. Since Olga only spoke Estonian and German, she was always being yelled at and called stupid because she had a hard time communicating in Latvian until she taught herself and her brother the language. If losing their parents and living in a foreign country was not enough trauma, the relative turned out to be abusive and forced both children to perform hard labor. Little Leopold was made to work herding cattle before he was even old enough to go to school and Olga had to do housework instead of furthering her education. Leopold's health deteriorated having to work outside in all sorts of weather and he became ill. Olga, who was just in her early teens, walked the 20 kilometers from the farm to Jelgava to find other work so she could support herself and her brother. A baron took pity on Olga and offered her a room and work on his estate. Olga worked for the baron ironing fine linens in the laundry. She was allowed to keep her little brother with her and she started home schooling him. However, Leopold remained frail and never recovered his health. He eventually did marry but his wife left him shortly after their beautiful daughter, Merse, was born. Leopold died at an early age and Merse was raised by three of his nieces. She married a man named Eglis but no other information about her is known.

Olga Gutmane Gedrovics

It was a blessing for Olga to meet Kristaps. Not only did they share the common interest of singing in the choir, but she also saw in him a kind and gentle man who could provide her the security she had lacked for so long. One can only imagine how protected Olga, who was less than five feet tall and weighed around ninety-five pounds, felt when she was encircled by the strong arms of the powerfully built red-headed Kristaps. God blessed their union with five children.

Their first-born daughter was born in 1892 and was named Olga after her brave mother and grandmother. Olga worked as an Assistant County Prosecutor. Marta, born in 1895, worked as a bookkeeper for the Jelgava Railroad administration. Brother Voldemars (Voldis), born on July 31, 1898, enrolled in the Naval Academy at age fifteen. After graduation, he joined the Latvian Merchant Marine and sailed many seas and oceans as a ship's helmsman. In those days Latvia exported goods to countries throughout the world and its ships sailed all the oceans, stopping frequently in ports in the Caribbean and Africa. The youngest daughter, Zelma, born in 1901, inherited her parents' musical talents and became a piano teacher. The youngest son Kārlis Arturs Gedrovics was born on October 13, 1903. Kārlis' Latvian baptismal certificate contains the Bible verse *"Blessed are they that hear the word of God and keep it"* Luke 11:28. Throughout his life, Kārlis remained faithful to God's word and firmly believed that he could always rely on God's grace in all circumstances.

Brothers Kārlis 2, Voldis 7

From the time they were little boys, Kārlis and his brother Voldis both dreamed of becoming sailors and sailing over the Baltic Sea to distant lands. Olga was very protective of her youngest son Kārlis. She absolutely forbade him to join his big brother on the seas. Whether she had a premonition or whether she was guided by the trauma she experienced as a young girl without a provider, Olga insisted that Kārlis stay in Jelgava so that the parents would have at least one son who would care for them in old age. As fate would have it, it would be up to him eventually to become the main provider for the entire family when illness, death, and wars tore apart their lives once more.

Even as the train chugged westward back toward Latvia in 1917, it was up to Kārlis to gather food for his sister and parents. When the family had left Latvia hoping to find more lucrative employment in Russia, Kristaps and Olga had to make the heart-wrenching decision to split up the family. In 1915 the two eldest daughters Olga and Marta were employed and Voldis had joined the Merchant Marine. Hoping that the family could be reunited after the parents found work in Russia, Kristaps and Olga took only their two youngest children and a few meager possessions with them as they headed across the tundra dreaming of a better future for their family. But this was not to be.

Political changes were underway that would carry them back two years later even poorer than before. In 1917 the Bolshevik forces overthrew the government of Czar Nicholas II and the Communist Regime took over. All industry and land was taken over by the Lenin government and the Latvians who had come to Russia in hopes of a better life now found themselves persecuted by the Communists. The brutal reign of terror of the Bolsheviks as well as the famine that took over Russia resulted in the majority of Latvians selling all their possessions to pay for the trip home after the 1917 Revolution.

The train ride from Russia to Latvia lasted several weeks. The food that Olga had brought along for the family was long gone and the haggard look that comes from starvation was on everyone's face. But the family never talked much about the hardships they had endured. They were best forgotten. Only when Kārlis was on his deathbed talking about having to catch the train to join his family did he relate vignettes of how he had scavenged for food to fight starvation.

The train they were riding on had no dining car, no heated cabins. Often the trip would be interrupted as the train stopped to refuel or the tracks were repaired as a result of being torn up during the war. Occasionally there were frozen potato fields near the places where they stopped. Most of the crops had already been harvested, but now and then one could find some leftover frozen potatoes in the mounds of frozen black dirt and snow. It was too risky for adults to venture into these government-owned fields, but usually nobody bothered children as they scampered to find a few remaining potatoes. Thus, it became the responsibility of Kārlis and his sister Zelma to jump off the train when it stopped and to quickly gather anything edible they could find. One can only imagine how chilled the teen-agers' fingers must have been trying to dig the frozen potatoes out of the frigid ground with their bare hands. Fear must have been in their hearts but their empty stomachs urged them to find food for the family. Perhaps these experiences during World War I made them stronger in spirit and determination to be able to face more hardships during World War II when Kārlis and Zelma had to protect their own children during grueling long train rides into an unknown future.

The Gedrovics women in 1918: Mother Olga & Zelma in front, Marta & Olga in back

The Gedrovics family saga was repeated over and over among the thousands of Latvian families riding similar trains westward toward Latvia. Fleeing the terrors of the Bolsheviks, the girl whom Kārlis later married also rode the rails from Russia with her mother and brother after the Bolshevik Revolution. God planned their separate paths along the same train route to Latvia to perhaps cross and meet years later.

★★★

4

ABYSMAL JOURNEY: NOVOCHERKASSK TO RIGA, 1920

The bottles of vintage wine were all gone now, slurped up by the Bolshevik Commissar whose taste buds, dulled by excesses of vodka, would not recognize and appreciate the fine bouquet of the aged premium reserve collection from the bountiful grape harvests in the Caucasian region. What cruel irony had taken control of her life, thought the young Asja Petrovs, cuddling her children Tatiana and Adrian close to her to keep them warm as the dilapidated train slowly chugged westward through the night and the cold Russian autumn. Once she and her handsome Georgian husband had enjoyed sipping delectable wine from shining crystal and silver goblets. Now she did not even have drinking water for her and her children and her mind was filled with dread and panic not knowing if her beloved husband Theodor Petrovs was dead or alive. Ruthless Bolshevik troops had invaded their home sometime during the Russian Civil War that raged through Novocherkassk 1917-1920 and dragged away the nobleman who had been a supporter of the Czar. Following Red October of 1917, the Novocherkassk region had been the center of fighting between the White Army of the Don Cossacks and the Bolshevik Red Army that overthrew the Czar. By 1920, all of the Czar's supporters either had been killed, arrested, or had fled into exile.

Asja still trembled in fear and revulsion as she recalled that dreadful night when she herself had been robbed, stripped, and raped and left with no documents or money. For months after her husband was hauled away and imprisoned by the Bolsheviks, Asja had been desperately trying to find out if her beloved Theodor was still alive. Day by day as more landowners and nobility were rounded up in freight trains and sent to Siberia or executed, her fear for the safety of her children grew. The few gold coins from the Czarist reign she still had hidden were no longer legal tender. Only the exquisite wine collection her husband had inherited from his wealthy father had any bartering value. Asja started trading the wine for food and other necessities for her children. In time she dared to approach some unscrupulous official in the new Communist government who was willing to take the prize wine as "blood money" in exchange for new documents so that she and the children could flee back to her parents in Latvia.

If life had not dealt them such a cruel blow, one could almost find dark humor in the unusual way the wine collection had risen from "the grave" to give them life! When Theodor's father died, his extensive property holdings were left to his two remaining children, Theodor and his sister named Olga. Although Theodor knew his father was a wine collector, no sign of such a collection was found initially as they looked over the estate. At some later date, when Theodor went down into the family mausoleum, he found several caskets lined up along the wall in the depths of the catacomb and not what would be the usual burial places inside the walls. Upon opening the caskets, he found dozens of bottles of hundred-year-old wine. As fate would have it, neither he nor Asja would have the pleasure of sipping this exquisite wine.

Bottle by bottle the priceless wine collection had been depleted in bribing an official of the People's Council in the City of Novocherkassk to procure copies of birth certificates recorded in the Ascension Cathedral Army Church so that travel documents and new passports could be issued for Anna Asja Tigulis Petrovs, age thirty, and her two children Tatiana, age eight, and Adrian, age five for the long train ride to Latvia.

Now Asja, known by her middle name, and her children Tatiana, and Adrian were finally on the grueling month-long train journey back to Latvia. The children, though cold and hungry, were not aware of the immenseness of the tragedy that had befallen them. They were unaware of Asja's shattered dreams of a bright future when she had taken the train to Russia following her graduation from the University in Riga to start a career in teaching French and German languages to the Russian aristocracy. How bright the future had looked for the vivacious young woman who spoke Latvian, German, Russian, and French. The language skills opened doors for her that she could have only imagined in her wildest dreams. Asja was on top of the world when she was invited by one of the Czar's army generals to tutor his children in French. Living among aristocrats, Asja was privileged to see the Czar and his family entourage riding in carriages past her street. The Czar had five children–Olga, Tatiana, Maria, Anastasia, and the heir-apparent Alexei. Tatiana was the most beautiful of the Czar's daughters and when her own precious daughter was born, Asja named her Tatiana after the noble princess in hopes that she would grow up to resemble the princess in her beauty, intellect, and regal bearing.

Now the future looked dark and lonesome though Asja thanked God she still had her two dear children. Tatiana and Adrian were her dearest treasures. They were nearly all that was left of her rich life with her beloved husband, their beautiful home, the high society that had filled their days with fun and glamour, and the sunny days and rich soil in the Caucasian Mountain Region that produced a bounty of fruit. Asja had stashed a few secret material treasures when they left their home and not even the children knew of their existence. If her plan worked and she managed to fool the Bolshevik guards, who repeatedly searched the meager belongings of the refugees for valuables, there was still hope she would have something left to start life over again in Latvia. They had already been thoroughly searched when they got on the train, perhaps they would be left alone now, she hoped.

Hunger was their constant companion. Asja had to ration their meager food supply to make it last through the long trip. As the journey seemed unending, the portions became smaller and smaller to make them last. During one meal, as Asja pulled some slices of bread from the food basket to feed her children, one of the soldiers appeared in front of them.

"Open the basket! Let me see what you have in there!"

"Please, there is just bread for the children and some rolls I baked to take home as a gift to my parents", answered Asja as fear gripped her heart. Now they would find out her secret and she would probably be hauled away.

"Mmmm, home baked rolls. I want to taste one", and the guard reached into the basket and popped the sweet roll into his mouth.

Asja silently prayed while the guard chewed the roll. Before they left their home, she had filled some of the yeast rolls with some precious stones, rings, and gold coins. So that the rolls would all look alike, she had distributed the jewelry randomly among the rolls.

"Please Lord, let this be an empty roll."

"Ochin khorosho (Very good), you are an excellent baker!" exclaimed the guard as he tipped his hat and moved on satisfied.

A bright and shiny ten ruble gold piece, featuring the Tsar Nicholas II image, minted in 1899, was hidden in one of the rolls. Asja never allowed herself to spend the gold piece, but kept it until the end of her life as a memento of her husband Theodor. She bequeathed the precious coin to Skaidrite, her first granddaughter, who has kept the gold piece among her treasured mementos.

Asja thanked the Lord that once again they had been spared. The roll had been one of the empty ones. Tears rolled down her cheeks partly from relief that her secret cache was still safe but mostly they flowed from dark despair. How could life be so fickle? One day she had been on top of the world and now she had to fear for their very life. Would she ever see her husband again? How had they arrived at such a desolate state? It was as if a bolt of lightning had flashed and destroyed the lifestyle they knew.

THE YEARS OF WINE AND ROSES

Skaidrite's great-grandparents, Jānis Tigulis and Lote Stein

Anna Asja Tigulis was born in Riga on March 23, 1890. Throughout her lifetime she preferred to use her middle name, Asja. Her father was Jānis Tigulis, son of Ernests Tigulis, a Latvian of Swedish origin. Her mother was Lote Stein, the daughter of Juris Stein and Anna Balode. Jānis worked for several years as a supervisor at a German Baron's estate. He learned the trade of a stonemason after the German estates were nationalized after World War I. Lote, who married Jānis when he was nineteen and she was seventeen, was the money manager in the family. Every month she put 120 Rubles into an account for tuition for her children to obtain higher education.

Lote firmly believed that an educated person should have the command of several languages. Both her daughters were fluent in Latvian, Russian, German, and French. In addition, Asja learned Spanish while living in Chile. The ability to speak foreign languages was passed on to Asja's daughter Tatiana as well as her granddaughter Skaidrite. Tatiana learned to speak five languages and Skaidrite learned four.

The Tigulis family was blessed with four children. Asja was the firstborn. Her brother Juris followed her. Juris died at the early age of twelve from an intestinal infection. He had become severely debilitated by a bout of typhoid fever that left his digestive system very fragile. The doctors had prescribed a bland diet. However, the boy really craved the coarse black farm bread that was his favorite. Thinking a little piece of bread could not hurt, his mother relented and gave Juris his treat only to have the coarse bread rupture his intestines and lead to the boy's death. Sister Zelma was born November 15, 1898. She worked as a German language tutor and bookkeeper. Zelma married Jacob Rutendarzs at age 21. They had one son, Ilmars, born in 1929. The Tigulis youngest son Rudis worked in an ammunitions factory. In 1941, when the Bolsheviks exterminated or exiled to Siberia thousands of Latvians for no valid reason, Rudis went to work one morning and never returned home. He disappeared without trace as had many others perceived to be the "Enemy of the USSR". One can hardly imagine the heartbreak Lote felt losing both her sons. Her granddaughter Tatiana recalls that Lote cried for days following the disappearance of Rudis. Her two daughters would later experience the same heartbreak losing all their male offspring in the prime of their lives.

In 1910, following graduation from the university, Asja obtained a much-coveted position as language teacher in Russia. In this position Asja had the opportunity to meet several dignitaries and aristocrats. One of the generals in the Czar's Army employed Asja to tutor his children in French. General Orechow and his wife Olga Petrovs were delighted with Asja and included her in family gatherings. It was at one of these celebrations that Asja met the brother of Olga Petrovs, the handsome nobleman Theodor Petrovs.

Theodor Petrovs, or Fyodor Fyodorovich as he was known in Russian where the patronymic, or father's first name is used instead of the surname, was the son of a wealthy landowner from Georgia. The father, also named Fyodor Petrovs and his Georgian wife had twelve children. The father owned vast areas of land covering an entire township and the family could well afford to live in luxury. Wealth, however, would not let them escape the grips of tragedy. Early in the twentieth century when miracle drugs were not prevalent, death was merciless and cast its shadow widely wiping out the young and the old. Ten of the Petrovs' children died from tuberculosis and only the oldest daughter Olga and her brother Theodor survived. Olga continued to live in high society after she married General Orechovs, who was one of the Cossack officers in the Czar's Imperial army.

Theodor graduated with high honors from the Don Polytechnic Institute with a degree in Civil Engineering. He had been one of the top students in his class and upon graduation the Czar bestowed on him the title of nobility. Theodor was successful in his work as a civil engineer in developing an irrigation system for the vineyards in the foothills of the Caucasian Mountain region. When Theodor met Asja and asked her to marry him, his mother was bitterly opposed to the union for reasons that could only be interpreted to be snobbery. She deemed that no commoner like the Latvian girl Asja was good enough for her son, the nobleman. She refused to recognize the fact Theodor was not a nobleman by virtue of his birth but had acquired the title based on his higher education, something that Asja also possessed. Furthermore, Asja was a Lutheran and in Russia only the Orthodox were recognized as "Correct Believers". Nevertheless, Theodor and Asja were married in the Russian Orthodox Cathedral and settled to live in the best neighborhood on the hills overlooking the city of Novocherkassk on the Don River, which connected through the Sea of Azov to the Black Sea. Theodor's professional expertise and accomplishments and the title nobility allowed him and his bride Asja to enjoy the benefits of a privileged class in society. Their home, managed by several servants, was on a choice site near the west triumphal arch.

THE GOLDEN YEARS

Novocherkassk[6] (New Cherkassk) was founded in 1805 on the elevated bank of the Aksay River (the right arm of the Don) as the new administrative center of the Don Cossack army after the Starocherkaskaya (Old Cherkassk) was inundated by the annual spring flooding of the Don River and its tributaries. The Cossack cavalry was a privileged military unit that fought for political and social equality against dictatorships. Following the Bolshevik Revolution of 1917, the Don Cossacks of Novocherkassk fought against the Soviet armies in the civil war of 1918-20 until the Soviet government abolished the Cossack privileges. At the beginning of the 20th Century, Novocherkassk had grown from being a Cossack army town to an important industrial region after the Rostov-on-Don railway line connected it to the railway system of Russia. By the early 1900's Novocherkassk, with a population estimated at around 55,000, had also become an important center of education and culture. The city had a technical school, a theological seminary, a Cossack military school, a cadet corps, a school for surgeon's assistants, three male grammar schools, four female grammar schools, several secondary establishments, a Polytechnic Institute, a Veterinary Institute, a Drama Theatre, the Don Cossack History Museum and several art galleries. The city was known as the city of students and the Petrovs thought it was a fine place to raise a family.

Their firstborn child came into the world on January 23, 1912. She was christened Tatiana in her father's Russian Orthodox faith in the Ascension Cathedral Army Church, which was the dominant architectural feature of the central part of Novocherkassk. The parents named their daughter Tatiana after the Czar's most beautiful daughter. The princess Tatiana was fashionable and had the posture and attitude of royalty. Of the Czar's daughters, Tatiana was known to be the most religious and read the Bible frequently. She was also the leader among her siblings and took charge of everything. During World War I, the princess volunteered to be a Red Cross nurse.[7] Time would tell if little Tatiana Petrovs would possess the attributes of the princess as her parents had wished for their beloved daughter.

Teodors & Asja with Tatiana, age 3, 1915

When Tatiana was three years old, her dear brother Adrian was born in 1915. Like Tatiana, he had the most beautiful blue eyes framed by long black lashes. Until they were grown, Tatiana and Adrian would enjoy a friendly sibling rivalry and argue as to who had the biggest and most gorgeous eyes. Although Novocherkassk had a highly developed educational system, the Petrovs children were home schooled by a governess, as was common practice for children of the privileged classes of nobility. The governess not only performed the duties of a nanny, she was also responsible for educating the children, teaching them languages and social skills. By the time Tatiana was five, she could converse fluently in Russian and French, which was considered the dominant language of the upper classes in Europe.

One cannot imagine a more idyllic early childhood than what the Petrovs sister and brother enjoyed. Their intelligent minds quickly grasped the lessons taught by the governess. The rest of the day could be enjoyed frolicking on the hillsides and by the river or going to the vineyards where their father was designing irrigation systems. Their mother Asja enjoyed entertaining and their house was often the site for parties and dances. Little Tatiana would watch wide-eyed as the couples danced and the ladies swirled around in their glamorous evening dresses. Dancing came easy to Tatiana as she imitated the dance steps. Her curly hair bouncing to the beat of the music, she dreamed of one day dancing dressed as beautifully as a princess at an Imperial Ball. But for the most part, Tatiana spent her days in Novocherkassk being a precocious, lively, active "tomboy" going through the antics of a child.

The Petrovs large home, situated on a hill, had a wrap-around veranda with a long stairway leading down to the street. The shiny bannister along the stairway was irresistible to the girl who feared no obstacles. This would be an expedient way to descend from the porch rather than bothering to climb down the steps. It took but a few seconds for Tatiana to seat herself on top of the bannister and down she slid with a whoosh. Making a perfect landing was a lesson she had not yet practiced or learned, but four-year-olds do not worry about consequences when they attempt an athletic feat. When she hit the brick sidewalk chest first, there was a bump and a crack. The crack, as diagnosed at the hospital, was in her right collarbone. Ninety years later, Tatiana could still point out the depression left in her collarbone from her flight down the bannister. Tatiana's daring Georgian personality traits can easily be recognized in some of her descendants in the generations following her.

The golden days were all too brief. The Bolsheviks changed the history of the world in 1917. When Tatiana was five, her happy days of childhood ended with the brutal arrest of the father she had loved and idolized.

RED OCTOBER 1917

The cataclysmic forces that changed the world for Tatiana's family and millions of innocent people during and following the "Red October" Russian Revolution were originally not rooted in evil. Rather, like a glowing ember that can initiate a wildfire, a single misstep on a pile of rocks can bring down the side of a mountain in a rockslide, or an avalanche that needs but a sudden noise to start it escalating into disaster, so some well-intended plans of a few men turned into a deadly catastrophe that destroyed thousands upon thousands of families and entire countries.

The maneuvers that led to the 1917 Revolution started decades before with some small steps when Nicholas II ascended to rule the Empire of Russia. Being of a shy and sensitive disposition, the son of Emperor Alexander III of the Royal House of Romanov had received little grooming for assuming his imperial role at age twenty-six. Nicholas was so unprepared for the duties of a Czar in 1894 that he is reported to have tearfully said to a cousin, "What is going to happen to me and all of Russia?"[8] Had Czar Nicholas II been more in tune with the needs of his subjects, would there still be a Royal Empire in Russia? Instead, he proved unable to settle the political unrest that descended on his country during World War I, which found Russia unprepared for the attack by German and the Austro-Hungarian Empires. The idealistic Czar felt it was his personal duty to lead the Russian troops directly. However, the plan to thus motivate his troops took Nicholas away from his executive duties over domestic policies, which he by default left in the hands of the Czarina Alexandra. Alexandra was of German origin. The Russian people mistrusted her and were further disturbed by her close association with Grigori Rasputin.[9] The person of Rasputin was a mystery with many faces. Many people, including the

Romanov family, perceived him as a holy man who had healing powers. Alexandra relied on the mystic Rasputin to save the life of her only son and intended successor to the Czar, the Czarevich Alexei, who was a hemophiliac under constant danger of bleeding to death. As Rasputin had frequently been able through his hypnotic powers to calm the young Czarevich and stop his bleeding, Alexandra came to rely on him more and more in running the Empire as well. Not everyone shared her opinion. Rasputin's undue influence on the royal family was resented by the people as the government's inability to prevent famine during the war activity led to severe national hardship. Czar Nicholas was so preoccupied in leading his troops that he was unaware or chose to ignore public opinion. He apparently did not understand how distrustful the common people were of his wife and Rasputin until anger over Rasputin's influence and Russia's lack of success in the war effort led to Rasputin's assassination.

With Nicholas away at the front, his authority collapsed. In February, 1917 in the Old Julian Calendar, and March in the Gregorian Calendar, massive demonstrations broke out over food shortages and riots turned into revolution with many of the Czar's army turning into deserters. Nicholas II was forced to abdicate at the end of February thus ending the monarchy with no apparent successor.[10] Provisional Government was formed and the imperial family moved to exile in Siberia to protect them from possible harm. A Commission was formed to investigate all persons of influence in the Czarist Regime and everyone who had any connections to the Czar was arrested. Since the people arrested and questioned were never given a reason for their arrest and their families were left in the dark as to their fate, it is not known whether Petrovs was arrested by people in the Provisional Government or later by the Communist officials who were intent on purging everyone who was in any way connected to the Royal Family which was executed in 1918. The February Revolution was just the prelude to the October Revolution yet to come.

The Red October Revolution, or the Bolshevik Revolution, was instigated by the February events and exacerbated by the mounting frustration of workers and soldiers over their economic plight.[11] On October 23, 1917, Vladimir Lenin led his Bolshevik leftist revolutionaries in an uprising in Petrograd, the capital of Russia, against the Provisional Government. The Bolshevik Red Guard took over government facilities and the Czar's Winter Palace with little opposition.[12] With the fall of the Winter Palace, power transferred to the Council of People's Commissars. The Bolsheviks viewed themselves as representing an alliance of workers and peasants. The Hammer and Sickle became the symbols on the coat of arms and the red flag of the Soviet Union.

The October Revolution transformed what had started as a massive uprising of socialism to evolve into the totalitarian reign of Communism. With time the Revolution further evolved into a monster of global proportions with the hungry Russian bear just two decades later gobbling up surrounding countries to which the Bolsheviks had granted independence following World War I. But as things stood in 1917, the Bolsheviks gave the right of independence and separation from Russia to the nationalities formerly included in the Czarist Empire. The masses of people who had been living and toiling in Russia were allowed to return to their native regions, including Latvia. Trains carrying thousands of Latvians to their fatherland started their long journey homeward.

★★★

5
GOD BLESS LATVIA, 1918

During their long homeward trip from Russia, the Gedrovics family suffered not only from cold and hunger, but their very lives were still in danger. Following the October Bolshevik Revolution, Russia was thrown into turmoil of civil war with the former Czar's Cossack army members fighting the Red Bolsheviks.

At long last they reached the railroad hub of Jelgava and were reunited with their two oldest daughters Olga and Marta. Kristaps and Olga had to re-establish a home for their family and start their lives all over again, but this time they could do it as free citizens at last. After centuries of domination by Germans and Russians, Latvia was officially declared an independent country on November 18, 1918.

The joyous family reunion was soon darkened by the tragic news that their oldest son, Voldis, had contracted tuberculosis while in the Merchant Marine. Tuberculosis was a plague to be feared with no cure available at the time. Voldis died in the summer of 1919 on July 20, eleven days short of his twenty-first birthday and was the first member of the Gedrovics family to be buried on the family plot at Zanders cemetery in Jelgava.

Upon re-establishing his family in Jelgava, Kristaps Gedrovics opened his own small business and operated a meat stand at the farmers market. He also helped his sister Līna work the family farm, leased fruit orchards, and added a produce business selling the fruit and vegetables at the marketplace. Kristaps not only knew how to grow farm products, he also was creative in how the products were combined in meal preparation and did most of the cooking for the family. Kārlis, as the only remaining son in the family, was constantly at his father's side helping him work on the farm and at the market when he was not in school studying accounting. He particularly enjoyed planting trees. During the

Voldis 1918 in Merchant Marine uniform

summer Kārlis worked with Aunt Līna's second husband, Žanis Birznieks, the district forester, to learn about planting, pruning, and maintaining woodlots and fruit orchards. Kārlis planned carefully so that every acre on his aunt's farm in Livberze was put to the best use. The approximately 85 acres, or thirty-five hectares, not only supplied feed for livestock, but also encompassed golden fields of grain, a garden of berry bushes, and an orchard.

Kārlis carefully selected the varieties of apple trees he planted to assure proper pollination and an extended season for harvesting. Grafting was one of Kārlis' special talents from which originated delicious new varieties in his orchard. The first apples to ripen in the summer had white, nearly transparent flesh and were refreshingly juicy with an almost lemony taste. "White and Sparkly" was their name. Later on followed bright, red-striped apples with a rosy flesh and the aroma of strawberries. These were aptly called "Strawberry Apples". In addition to these especially exotic eating varieties, there were many varieties that ripened later in the season. In the spring the orchard was covered with a canopy of different shades of white and pink blossoms where the bees from the nearby hives were busy pollinating and also filling their honeycombs. During World War II much of the orchard was destroyed and no photographs exist to document its beauty. However, the scene of the apple blossoms reflected in the nearby pond, where on its banks a large willow tree was gracefully swaying in the breeze, remains forever burned in the recesses of Kārlis' oldest daughter's mind. The memory of the strawberry apples would come alive sixty years later as, almost as if by magic, Kārlis' daughter Skaidrite discovered this antique variety grown on Christmas Tree Farm near Northport, Michigan. It remains a mystery how the Strawberry apple variety grafted in Latvia traveled across the ocean to find new roots in Michigan.

At age twenty, Kārlis was conscripted into the newly organized Latvian National Army where he served the obligatory two years utilizing his accounting skills as the bookkeeper for his regiment. In 1925, following discharge from the Army, Kārlis returned to his parents' home in Jelgava. His sister Marta, who had been working for the Jelgava Railroad administration, helped Kārlis start his career working for the railroad. His initial position was that of

Kārlis 1925 in Latvian National Army uniform

ticket agent, later advancing to payroll master. After he was married and became my father, he gave me the privilege of seeing his ticket office. I was fascinated by the rows upon rows of colorful tickets arranged by railroad lines and hundreds of destinations in far-away places. I could think of nothing more fascinating than getting a ticket of every color and riding the trains until I had visited all the possible destinations, especially the capital city of Latvia—Riga. I had no inkling at the time of my wishful fantasizing that in just a few years I would be forced to ride a train under adverse circumstances to unknown destinations with no option to return home.

★★★

6

DESTINATION STATION RIGA, 1920

The final destination for Asja Petrovs and her children Tatiana and Adrian on their tortuous journey from Novocherkassk was Riga, Latvia. There the three weary refugees from the Bolsheviks were tearfully reunited with Asja's parents Lote and Jānis Tigulis and her sister Zelma. They were no longer to live the privileged life they had previously enjoyed, but they were safe in the bosom of family. Asja and her children joined her parents to live in their crowded apartment, which after the marriage of Zelma housed three families. The old grandparents were in charge of the children, Tatiana and Adrian, while Asja and Zelma both worked. Grandfather Tigulis with his mustache and dark looks resembled an old Viking. He was a strict disciplinarian with the belief that rules were to be beaten into children with a belt. Tatiana's streak of independence frequently made it difficult for her to sit, due to the welts on her behind following one of her imaginative pranks.

The grandparent's apartment was in a house on Kalnciema (Hill Village) Street in a residential area across the Daugava River from the center of historic old Riga. The children had fun climbing the old trees in the yard. They particularly enjoyed sitting in the canopy of the chestnut trees extending over the sidewalk running along their fence. Watching people walking by soon got boring, so Tatiana added some variety to their play. As people would walk under their perch, some water would suddenly drip upon the unsuspecting heads. Usually people would just look up without spying the mischief-makers who were responsible for sprinkling them. One gentleman, who had previously felt the mysterious droplets, took upon himself to carefully observe just where the water was coming from. Apparently, he had no sense of humor. He made the children come down and took them by the hand to ask the grandfather if he knew who these little rascals were and what they had been doing. Tatiana, who was the oldest, always received blame for any mischief and had to succumb to being lashed with grandfather's belt. From the time that it was forbidden to sprinkle by-passers with water, Tatiana changed tactics and used chestnuts to drop on people's heads. This seemed a less suspicious event under the chestnut trees, but they were eventually discovered again with the same consequences via the old belt.

Schoolwork had always been easy for Tatiana with a governess as her teacher. Tatiana spoke fluent French and Russian when she arrived in Latvia, but the Latvian children made fun of her as she did not speak their language. The transition from home tutoring to attending a public school did not come easily. Initially, Tatiana was put into the second grade where she was unwilling to abide by the rules she considered too constricting and boring. When the teacher asked her to recite a poem she was supposed to learn, Tatiana refused. She informed the teacher that the governess had allowed her to determine when she would recite or when she preferred to do mathematics. All too quickly the teacher informed her that there would be no more independent study and that Tatiana had to do as told. When the teachers discovered the level of Tatiana's knowledge, she got promoted several grades. For Tatiana's quick brain, the pace of learning still offered no challenge.

During an algebra lesson Tatiana was found to be playing chess. The teacher informed her in no uncertain terms that she was supposed to pay attention to the lesson at all times. Tatiana replied,

"I already understood the first time you explained. You keep repeating the same thing over and over again and that is boring. So I play chess to occupy my mind".

Immediately the teacher summoned Tatiana to the blackboard and asked her to solve a most difficult problem for which the steps toward a solution had not as yet been explained. She solved the problem perfectly without hesitation. This angered the teacher so much that Tatiana got sent to the principal's office, a place she often visited due to her rebelliousness against boredom. Tatiana eventually became so expert at playing chess, that she was later invited to join the all-male chess club in high school. During all her school years, Tatiana was always the top student scholastically in every grade she attended. Her grades in every subject were always fives, the highest possible grade in Latvian schools. This earned Tatiana the privilege of sitting next to the school principal when class pictures were taken. The seat next to the principal was always reserved for the best student in the class and Tatiana can be seen in that position in all her school photographs.

At report card time, however, Tatiana's mother was always disappointed to see that her daughter's grade in deportment was a three or a four—needing improvement. What an enigma the intelligent girl presented to her mother! Tatiana had been groomed by the governess and her parents to have impeccable manners and had always shown courtesy toward everyone. She had also been accustomed to setting her goals high. In public school the achievement goals were set at a level Tatiana considered to be mediocre and thus her boredom manifested itself in rebellious behavior at times.

By the time Tatiana advanced to the high school level, she found more challenges and excelled in every scholastic and extracurricular activity at the Lomonosov Gymnasium. A college preparatory high school in Latvia is called a "Gymnasium". In addition to speaking Russian, French, and Latvian, she also studied German and English. Tatiana also enrolled in classes to learn Esperanto, an artificial language devised in 1887 as an international medium of communication. Esperanto never reached the level of world acceptance, however, to become the universal language for all nations. Tatiana was popular among the students and her beauty, charm and wit won her the title of the Lomonosov Beauty Queen.

★★★

7
A NEW FAMILY BEGINS, 1927

It was not easy for Asja to raise her two children without her husband and to work to support them, although she lived with her parents in their apartment on Kalnciema Street. For ten long and lonesome years she did not give up hope that her beloved Theodor was still alive and that one day they would be reunited. Year after year she contacted the International Red Cross to try to trace the whereabouts of Theodor Petrovs, but there were never any news of him. The landlord who owned the apartment house where she lived had noticed Asja's plight. He also noticed Asja's beauty and her strong determination. Over the years Asja became friends with her landlord, Jānis (John) Berzins, but she avoided any romantic involvement still hoping to find her long-missing husband. Ten years after her husband was arrested and disappeared, Asja finally relented and had her husband Theodor declared legally dead and her marriage dissolved. Asja accepted Jānis' proposal and they were married in 1927.

Asja & Janis Berzins Wedding 1927

Asja's second marriage, 1927

Jānis Berzins, born September 29, 1887, worked as a bank manager in Riga. He and his sister Maria owned the apartment building in Riga on Kalnciema Street where Asja and her children stayed with her parents. Jānis and Maria lived nearby at an apartment building they also owned at 95 Mazā Nometņu Iela (Small Camp Street), named after the army quarters nearby. Jānis and his sister were both gifted with excellent voices. Maria was a voice teacher and Jānis often performed as soloist with several choirs. Both also played piano accompanying the voice students as they performed. Prior to World War I, Jānis Berzins studied abroad in Russia at the University of St. Petersburg. During these student days Jānis met one of the University's most famous, or notorious alumnus, Vladimir Ilyich Ulyanov, or Lenin, as he later became known. It is regrettable that Jānis was never urged by his family to relate stories about his encounter with Lenin, but Jānis only mentioned in passing that he had been present when Lenin made one of his fiery speeches on St. Petersburg Square. Jānis recalled that the audience became quite aroused and cheered when Lenin eloquently promised that he would bring about change.

From reading the biography[13] of Lenin, one can come to the conclusion that the best intentions of an idealist can go horribly awry. Lenin's father and mother were both teachers. From them, Lenin absorbed during his childhood a desire to learn and a commitment to improve the lives of the ordinary citizens. He hated the rule of the aristocrats and believed that the key to change was political action by the working classes. Although he did not start out as a revolutionary, he attempted to rouse the consciousness of the workers through agitation. After Lenin was expelled from the University of Kazan for creating student disturbances, he did independent study at the University of St. Petersburg where he passed law examinations. His law practice lasted only briefly before he devoted himself to revolutionary activities. Jānis Berzins' memories of Lenin were that he was a "hothead", whose campus debates were filled with sarcasm and scorn for the capitalists. History now bears witness of how Lenin's originally idealistic interest in revitalizing the Russian economy according to Marxist guidelines and improving the lives of the working classes created an even more dictatorial power. The theses that many initially perceived as the ranting of a hothead student would in time cast clouds of terror over entire nations and would cause generations of families to become refugees living under fear.

When Jānis Berzins married Asja Tigulis Petrovs in 1927, any memories of meeting Lenin had become too insignificant to talk about. Tatiana and Adrian now had a stepfather who provided them with a good home, education, and again allowed them to live in a circle of the culturally elite. In 1928, a new half-brother named Jānis, nicknamed Janka, joined Tatiana and Adrian. The birth of the second son, Andris, a year later ended in tragedy for the Berzins family. The nurse, who attended the birth, dropped the slippery infant on the floor. The resulting brain damage led to his death one month later. The infant Andris spent his brief life screaming unceasingly throughout the day and night. He never experienced the joys of growing up in a loving home. Though he was held and rocked constantly, he never stopped screaming and refused to be fed. When God called him to Heaven, Andris' tiny body resembled a yellow parched mummy. The accident was something the nurse regretted the rest of her life. She resigned from her position and for years thereafter kept visiting the Berzins home and in tears begged Asja for forgiveness. Though Asja pitied the nurse and did not blame her for the unfortunate accident, the nurse could never forgive herself.

Though the death of baby Andris caused pain, the Berzins family enjoyed a good life. The family was financially secure, which allowed the children to develop their talents. Tatiana learned to play the piano and had voice lessons. She also took dancing lessons and, while in college, performed on stage in dance groups featuring

Hungarian and Russian folk dances. Tatiana's natural agility and sense of rhythm helped her perform a Latin tango or Viennese waltz as skillfully as a Polish Mazurka, a Hungarian Czardas, a complicated American Charleston, or the Russian Kazačok, which required rapid athletic leaping in the air from a deep knee-bend position with arms folded across the chest.

Tatiana, 3rd from right dancing Czardas

Since Jānis Berzins loved music and was known in music circles, Tatiana often went with him and her mother to opera, concert, and ballet performances. The ballets written by Tschaikovsky were a family favorite, particularly "Swan Lake". Tatiana would come home after a performance and for days dance on her toes, repeating the movements dancing as a swan, doing pirouettes and being lifted into the air by her stepfather. Tatiana showed such promise as a ballerina that she was offered a scholarship to ballet school. Her mother, however, would not allow her daughter to study to be a professional performer as she considered any dancers clad in scanty costumes to be a person of low moral standards. Instead, Tatiana was advised to study to be a teacher. Tatiana studied mathematics and added English to her knowledge of languages. Following her graduation, she worked as a private tutor in mathematics, writing, and languages.

Life was good. Tatiana had a nice home, good friends, and two brothers she loved dearly. Brother Adrian was her dearest friend. Little Janka was fun to play with and Tatiana liked to help her mother with his care and to take the toddler for walks in the park. In 1930, when Tatiana was eighteen, Jānis Berzins was promoted to the directorship of a bank in Jelgava and the family moved there from Riga.

AT HOME IN JELGAVA

Jelgava[14], the provincial capital of Zemgale, is situated on a fertile plain rising only 12 feet above the sea level between the riverbanks of Lielupe (Big River) and its tributary Driksa. The name Jelgava is believed to have derived from the Livonian word, "jelgab", meaning "low place". The settlement of Jelgava began during the 10th century when the German crusading Christians built a castle atop an island in the Lielupe. During the Livonian Wars (1558-83) when Russia attempted to capture Livonia, the country that would later become Latvia, it was partitioned between Sweden and the Grand Duchy of Poland-Lithuania. Jelgava received city rights in 1573 and became the capital of the united duchies of Courland and Semigallia in

1578. The Duchy of Courland became so successful in the 17th Century that its seafarers established colonies in Africa and on the Caribbean island of Tobago where people with Latvian surnames can still be found today. Since Voldis Gedrovics was helmsman on ships sailing to many parts of the world, it is conceivable that he had also traveled to Africa and Tobago. In 1596, when the Duchy of Courland split, Jelgava became the capital of Semigallia, or Zemgale.

Over the centuries, Jelgava developed into a significant cultural and industrial center and an important railroad hub in Latvia. The city was seized by force and came under the rule of many large imperialistic nations throughout the years. As wars were fought and treaties negotiated, Latvia became the "plum" of the spoils of wars. Riga, being the only northern port on the Baltic that did not freeze over in the winter, and Jelgava as the most significant railroad hub, became the pawns in the battles as more powerful nations fought for control of access to the Baltic Sea. Ruling governments that at one time or another called Jelgava as its own were Germany, the Polish-Lithuanian Commonwealth, Sweden, and Imperial Russia. With the outbreak of the French Revolution in 1789, Jelgava was annexed by Imperial Russia during the partition of Poland. The castle on the banks of Lielupe became the residence of Louis XVIII before he became the French king. During the Napoleonic Wars, the city was occupied by Prussian troops and did not suffer significant destruction. During World War I, Jelgava was the battleground between Soviets, Germans, and Latvian freedom fighters and suffered greatly from the ravages of war. At the end of the war, Latvia gained its independence at last on November 18, 1918. Under Latvia's first President Jānis Čakste, and his successor Kārlis Ulmanis, Latvia thrived as many agrarian, educational, and economic reforms were instituted.

It was in the pleasant city of Jelgava, with its many historic churches, broad streets lined with mansions of the former German nobility, castle gardens, and chestnut-lined parkways along the Lielupe, that God's plan for the pathways of Kārlis Gedrovics and Tatiana Petrovs to intersect and merge came to fruition.

★★★

8
TATIANA AND KĀRLIS

Working at the railroad ticket office and helping his father run his produce green-grocery business did not leave much time for Kārlis to pursue leisure activities or for dating girls. Unaware of the plans God had for him, Kārlis spent his days working and being the dutiful son and caring brother. In 1930, a sudden attack of appendicitis landed his sister Marta in the Jelgava Hospital for surgery. As a loving and caring brother, Kārlis visited her in the hospital every day. Since her entire family and friends all resided in Jelgava, Marta had many daily visitors. Her hospital roommate was an eighteen-year-old girl who had recently moved from Riga and was studying at the Teacher's Institute.

Tatiana Petrovs, a slender brunette with beautiful expressive blue eyes, lay alone in the bed next to Marta's following her appendectomy. She had no visitors as her family was under quarantine due to her brother Adrian being ill with scarlet fever. Marta, feeling sorry for the young girl, urged Kārlis to visit with the lonesome girl, Tatiana. Kārlis, having a somewhat reserved and quiet personality, initially refused.

"*How can you suggest a twenty-seven-year old man approach a completely strange young girl lying in bed and dressed in a hospital gown? It would be simply improper!*"

Marta was not to be deterred in her matchmaking efforts. The next time her brother came to visit her in the hospital, she was ready to make proper introductions,

Tatiana in 1931, age 19

"*Tatiana, I would like to introduce you to my youngest brother Kārlis Artūrs Gedrovics. Artūr (the family preferred to use his middle name), meet Tatiana Petrovs.*"

Ladylike, Tatiana extended her hand in greeting. Being mindful of his manners, Kārlis had to return the courtesy and shyly took her slender hand in his. As he looked down on this girl, he was struck by the wisdom that reflected from the deep blue pools of her eyes, shaded by thick black lashes, and noted how her thick dark brown hair cascaded in shiny waves over her shoulders. Perhaps it was indeed the gentlemanly thing to do to entertain this lonesome child.

It was fortunate that this meeting came about in the days when it was accepted medical practice to keep patients in the hospital for a week or more following surgery. In the days that followed, Kārlis helped Tatiana ambulate down the hospital hallways and during their conversations he realized that within this teenage girl was indeed the promise of a fascinating woman. After Tatiana was discharged from the hospital, Kārlis continued to visit her at home where she lived with her mother, step-father Jānis Berzins, her brother Adrian, and her two-year-old half-brother little Janka who usually was Tatiana's responsibility to babysit.

As was customary in those days, young couples would spend a lot of courtship time going for walks. Tatiana's mother thought this was an excellent opportunity for baby Jānis to get some fresh air.

"Tāta, as long as you are going out for a stroll in the park, why don't you take little Janka along in the stroller? It really would be good for him to get some sunshine and fresh air."

"Mother, but I am going for a walk with Kārlis!"

"So much the better. You can take turns pushing the buggy!" There is nothing like a cute baby in a stroller or a handsome dog on a leash to attract attention during a walk. People passing by would comment on what a nice family they made or ask Tatiana and Kārlis how old "their" baby is. Tatiana was absolutely mortified that people would think she had a baby when she was not even married. She dreaded meeting any of her classmates lest they think that Janka was indeed her child. As was the custom, Kārlis did the proper thing and asked Tatiana's mother for her hand before he proposed. One day, when Tatiana came home from school, her mother announced that Kārlis had visited and she had given him permission to take Tatiana for his wife. Though she loved Kārlis, this was a surprise to Tatiana. The independent young lady was upset that her life had been planned without her knowledge or consent and she broke out in angry tears.

Yet, her heart eventually accepted the love that Kārlis was offering her for a lifetime. Kārlis gave Tatiana a sterling silver engagement ring with an oblong-shaped clear yellow amber stone. But the beautiful bride who was named after the princess Tatiana was not destined to have a lavish wedding with a beautiful gown, dancing, and a sumptuous cake. Tatiana's joy of finding a loving mate was marred by her stepfather's disapproval of Kārlis. Just like her mother Asja was thought to be undeserving of the nobleman Fjodor Petrovs by his mother, so Jānis Berzins thought the railroad clerk Kārlis to be beneath the higher social class of which Berzins, as a bank director, thought himself worthy. Jānis Berzins refused to pay for the wedding of which he did not approve. Twenty-six years later he would be remorseful over the decision not to support the marriage of his stepdaughter in any way when he had to seek shelter with Tatiana's family in America after he was left alone following the deaths of his wife Asja and son Jānis.

Bishop Reinharts, the same minister who had baptized and confirmed Kārlis, married Kārlis and Tatiana on September 5, 1931 at the St. Nicholas Lutheran church office. Tatiana chose to follow her spouse's Lutheran religion and converted from the Russian Orthodox faith. When a person is confirmed into the Lutheran faith, the minister chooses a Bible verse for each confirmand. The verse dedicated to Tatiana was Psalm 91, which, true to its intent, protected Tatiana and her family during their lifetimes as if truly they had been carried on eagle's wings to lift them out of danger. Following the simple marriage ceremony where the bride and groom placed plain yellow bands of gold on the fourth finger of the right hand according to Latvian custom, they were treated to a wedding dinner prepared by Kristaps Gedrovics for the entire Gedrovics clan at their home. There were no funds for a honeymoon journey, but Kārlis and Tatiana were happy to be alone together when a friend of let them use his country cottage.

Kārlis and Tatiana, September 1931 honeymoon

Though their marriage had humble beginnings, Kārlis and Tatiana felt happy and secure as they started their life together. Tatiana joked that she felt like she was married to a celebrity since her husband shared his first name "Kārlis" with the President of Latvia, Kārlis Ulmanis.

THE PRESIDENT'S "FRIENDLY INVITATION" 1935

The second President and Prime Minister of Latvia, Kārlis Ulmanis, was highly supportive of education and agriculture, having received a degree in Agriculture and Animal Husbandry from the University of Nebraska in the United States. Kārlis Gedrovics was proud of the fact that he had the same first name as the popular President. It is a custom in Latvia to celebrate a person's "Name Day". On the Latvian calendar, each day of the year is assigned certain common first names and these names are displayed on all calendars under each date. Each year on the designated day for the name, all persons who share that particular name celebrate their

Name Day much like people who are named after saints may celebrate their saint's day, i.e. all people named Patrick would have their Name Day on March 17, Valentine on February 14, etc. The celebration of a person's Name Day in Latvia is considered to be of more importance than ones birthday. People are not likely to know the date for all their family and friends' birthdays, but if one knows a person's first name, one is expected to make a special effort to remember the honoree with a card, flowers, or a gift.

January 28 is the designated Name Day for all men named "Kārlis" and Kārlis Gedrovics considered it an honor to share this holiday with the President of Latvia. In 1935, this day gained further national recognition. President Kārlis Ulmanis chose to proclaim his Name Day henceforth to be "The Day of Friendly Invitation" (Draudzīgais Aicinājums). The President asked that every January 28, instead of giving presents to honor his name "Kārlis", all citizens make donations to Latvia's schools and libraries to promote his goal of universal literacy. The nation responded favorably and the Day of "Draudzīgais Aicinājums" has been celebrated by Latvians throughout the world since January 28, 1935 to raise funds for education. It is customary for individuals, clubs, religious and fraternal organizations to hold dinners, dances, concerts, and all sorts of other fund-raising events around this date to benefit Latvian schools and libraries in Latvia and wherever Latvian communities exist in the world. On January 28, 1935, Kārlis and Tatiana were discussing how nice it was that his Name Day had been proclaimed a national holiday.

"*Tāta, how clever! Now you will not have to give me a present, but since you are a teacher, you can just give a gift to promote education in honor of me!*"

"*But I do have a special gift for you this day. I really would not like to give away my gift for you to education or any school. After all, I have been carrying it within me near my heart for the past nine months. I had hoped to present it to you today on your Name Day. I do not think any school or library would really accept our firstborn as a donation*", replied Tatiana smiling brightly.

"*You mean....*"

Kārlis face showed wonder, joy and also fear as he realized it was time for their first child to be born. January 28 would always be special as he was about to receive the precious gift they had been eagerly awaiting for nine months. The educational institutions of Latvia would prosper from the gifts they received in the name of President Kārlis Ulmanis, but God's gift of a child for Tatiana and Kārlis would be theirs to keep and love forever. Hand in hand the couple walked through the snowy streets to the nearby Red Cross Infirmary where Tatiana delivered their firstborn child. How they had anticipated and planned for the birth of their baby to make their union complete!

Kārlis was usually a man who did not display his emotions and did not get poetic in expressing his love. However, on Tatiana's twenty-third birthday on January 23, 1935, he had surprised her with a gift of a hunter green leather-bound diary for recording important events in the life of their baby. He dedicated the diary to their child with the following poem he had composed:

"My Child....
I would wish that your eyes would be
Of anger and hate forever free,
But bright and trusting
Reflect only sunlight and vernal spring.
Your Father"

The diary was preserved throughout all the moves, the battles and infernos of war, years of living in displaced persons camps, and the journey across the Atlantic Ocean to America. Without a doubt, this record is the most precious legacy Tatiana and Kārlis have left for their first-born child to treasure forever as a testament of the parents' priceless legacy of love. On her birthday, January 23, 1935, Tatiana recorded her feelings for the baby within her–still unseen and unnamed but bestowed with a mother's love that is unending.

"23 January, year 1935

We are awaiting you, our little one! Waiting as if for the first bright ray of sunshine, which with its gentle caresses wakes up nature, entices from the ground most gloriously colored blossoms, bringing along brightness and beauty. You are the child of our lofty and great love. Because of you, bright hopes and happiness blossom in our hearts. We are awaiting you with impatience and great longing. Who are you going to be, our darling, a boy or a girl? Whoever you will be, our love already belongs to you–the great, immeasurable love of parents for their child– a love that motivates a parent to put his life on the line for the welfare of the child. Around you revolve all our beautiful dreams of the future.

You, little one, will have to fulfill all the hopes we have for you. You will have to grow up to be a noble and good person, because you are the fulfillment of a great love. Oh darling, you still have not arrived in the world, but how precious and loved you already are. With your Papuks we both observe your development, follow every little move. Your first fragile movements grabbed our hearts and brought tears of joy to our eyes. So subtly, almost imperceptibly, you announced your coming alive. We did not know how to thank God for the great mercy He has shown in giving us you, our first child.

From the very first day, when we started awaiting your arrival, you became the focus of our lives. Our most noble thoughts, bright hopes, and rosy dreams became woven into a wreath symbolizing your future, our little being. With every step, performing every task, our first thought was about you. From the moment you gave us the first sign of life, we could not stop rejoicing about the great fortune, which like the brilliant sun, brightens our lives. Every little movement you make grabs our hearts. We are guessing with Papuks if it is your little hand or foot which so energetically lets itself be felt.

*Oh child! How inexhaustible is the love of parents. If you will be capable of appreciating it, then perhaps you will grant us equally lasting love. Your Mamīte tirelessly prepared your layette. Your clothes were hand made, sewn, crocheted and embroidered with bright flowers. Your mother wishes that her little child in snow-white clothing would look as shiny and bright as new snowflakes. All your shirts and bibs are beautifully embroidered. Seldom will there be another child with such a bountiful and beautiful layette. Papuks and I were guided by an unselfish love and did not spare money or **labor** in preparing for your arrival. Be loving and good also toward us, little soul, when we will be frail and helpless in our old age just like you are now, our darling.*

Dear Child! You have bound your parents even closer together now. Your parents always lived in love, faithfulness, and unity, but each followed a different religious faith. But with your creation you brought with you the belief that we all must be united in one faith so that the three of us would never be separable. Your being instilled the thought and your mother converted from the Russian Orthodox to the Evangelical Lutheran faith. The minister, confirming your mother, said this Bible verse: 'Mountains will retreat, and hills will tremble, but the Mercy of God will follow you all the days of your life.' You, little one, along with me received this blessing because I was already expecting you. My child let your life be led by these words also. If we will be strong in faith and put our confidence in God, then we will not stray from the path He has chosen for us. Faith has great power to govern our lives. Putting our trust in God gives us energy and strength and also true happiness.

In a few days, your bright, clear eyes, like shiny stars, innocently and openly will look upon the wide world full of wonders. Your father and I both believe that God's mercy will not retreat from us and that you will grow into a strong person and that throughout your life your eyes will retain the honest, innocent look of a child who can face the world and mankind with courage.

Your Mother"

As Tatiana had hoped and prayed, the daughter whom they loved with all their hearts even before they knew her would return their love throughout their lifetime. When the second daughter was born five years later, three people welcomed her into the family, as Skaidrite joined her parents in loving the precious little sister God had sent her. The bond of love that united the foursome provided strength to overcome the ravages of war that soon would threaten to engulf them and shatter their home, dreams, and family unity.

★★★

9
AND BABY MAKES THREE

My mother Tatiana writes in my diary that on Monday, January 28, 1935, 12:02 p.m. her newborn baby's cry seemed like the most beautiful and blissful music to the young mother's ears as I emerged from her womb and greeted the world with a loud protest.

"It's a healthy, strong girl", exclaimed the midwife delivering the baby.

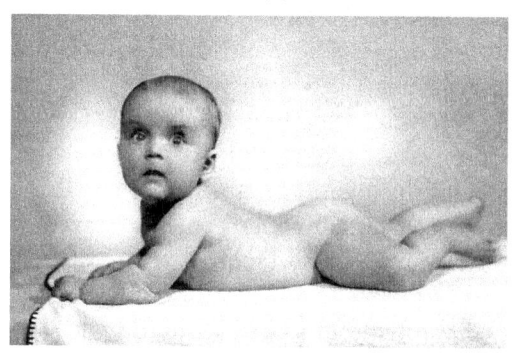

Weighing eight pounds and 20.5 inches long, I was indeed pronounced to be healthy. Tatiana was overjoyed to have her dream become joyful reality. Forgotten was the pain of the difficult delivery as my young mother at last got to see her firstborn daughter face to face. Tatiana writes that she looked at my tiny red and wrinkled face, so much like that of an old woman, but to her it was beautiful. Despite the wrinkles, she thought the resemblance to the baby's father, her dear husband Kārlis, was remarkable. Tatiana could hardly wait until Kārlis would arrive in the evening so she could present to him his daughter. In those days, fathers were not allowed to be present at the baby's birth and could only come during evening visiting hours. Kārlis had been instructed that he would be called at work when the child was born. Upon hearing the news, he sent a basket of white flowers to Tatiana and his daughter.

Baby Skaidrite, 1935

The white flowers were a symbol of purity for the name Skaidrite that Tatiana and Kārlis had chosen if their baby would be a girl. Kristaps, the name of Kārlis' father, was the name they had chosen had the baby been a boy. The name "Skaidrite" (the Latvian counterpart of the name Claire) stands for purity, brightness, clarity, and serenity. It was the parents' prayer when their daughter was christened on April 11, 1935 that she would grow up to be true to her name.

Wrapped in a white silk and lace coverlet with pink ribbons, a gift from Kārlis' sister Zelma, my godmother, I was baptized at the parsonage of Pastor Kraulis, the minister of St. Nicholas Lutheran Church in Jelgava. Godparents were Kārlis' sister Zelma and Tatiana's brother Adrian. Oblivious of the family surrounding me at this important event and unaware that a written record was made of my baptism in my diary, I snoozed through the ceremony. Only when the minister poured water on my head did I awaken with a bright smile and then drifted back again to dreamland. Pastor Kraulis offered the prayer that I would grow up to be a strong and good person who always walks on God's chosen pathways.

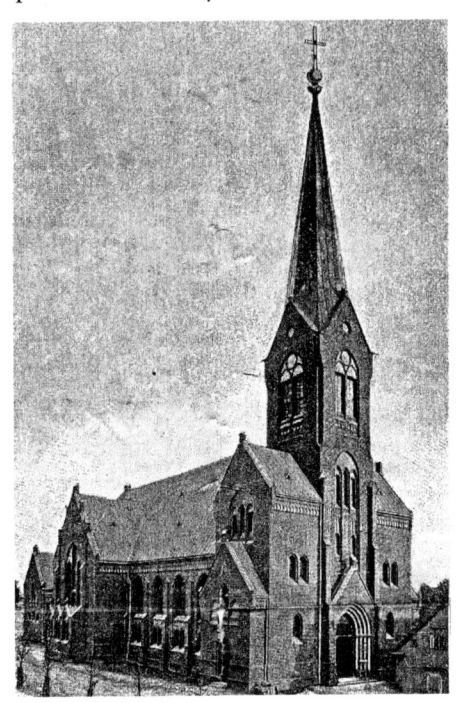

Tatiana wrote about the christening in her daughter's diary:

"My daughter, you looked like a tender new rosebud, just opening up to the sunshine at the dawn of life. Right now fragile and vulnerable, may you blossom brilliantly and may your gentleness and childlike sweetness encircle us as an ornate fragrant wreath"

The joy of the baptismal day, however, was also laced with tears. While I was received into the Kingdom of God through baptism at the dawn of my life, God in his mercy was ready to call my paternal grandfather home to Heaven in the sunset of his life. Kristaps Gedrovics was unable to witness the baptism as he lay on his deathbed at home with his daughter Marta at his side. In the spring of 1935 at the age of sixty-eight Kristaps was in an accident involving his wagon and team of horses. One of the horses apparently reared up overturning the wagon and in the process kicked Kristaps, fatally injuring his kidneys. Since kidney transplants were unheard of in 1935, the Gedrovics family had the agonizing experience of watching their beloved husband, father, and grandfather slowly dying day by day despite their unrelenting efforts to find doctors who could save him. Kārlis and his sisters Olga, Marta, and Zelma took turns staying at their father's bedside around the clock. They prayed that their efforts to keep him as comfortable as possible would somehow save his life. How devastated they all were not being able to keep death from taking their beloved father. But Death stood firmly at Kristap's bedside waiting to pull him from this world with her skeleton arms. Yet, confident in their faith, Kārlis and his father knew that death would have no victory. The victory would be God's because it was His will and might that determines when someone should be called to his eternal home. Kristaps' victory would be everlasting life.

Kārlis and Tatiana had promised my grandfather that they would take me to meet him for the first time immediately following the baptism. How excited Kristaps was waiting to see his very first grandchild. At every noise coming from the street, Kristaps asked that Marta look out the window to see if the baby had

St. Nicholas Lutheran Church, dedicated in 1909 and named after Czar Nicholas II

arrived. Despite the spring like weather, he gave instructions that a fire be built in the stove to make sure the baby would not be cold.

When Kārlis brought me to his father's bedside, Kristaps' eyes filled with tears of joy. As if on signal, I gave him one of my biggest smiles, bright as the rising sun at the beginning of a new day, while the grandfather's eyes appeared to dim with the evening dew. Kristaps grasped my soft little hand with his frail, trembling fingers and caressed it ever so gently. The grandfather wanted to bless his son's firstborn, but as he tried to tell me to grow strong in love, emotions overcame him and tears formed a hard lump in his throat before he could finish the blessing. Kristaps and Olga gave me a pair of beige-colored leather booties to wear when I took my first steps. I firmly believe that children recognize bonds of love from the time they are born. I must have understood the great love that my grandfather expressed during our first and last visit together. More than seventy years later I still treasure the booties among my keepsakes as testimony of the great love my grandfather had for me. Kristaps Gedrovics lapsed into a coma the next day and died on April 26, 1935.

Grandfather Kristaps at his produce stand

People would find it hard to believe that any infant at the age of two-and-a-half months can remember anything that happened. However, it has been documented before that an event during infancy somehow has left an indelible impression on a child's mind. Though nothing is written in my diary about the appearance of my grandfather on that day, I clearly remember the moment when I was brought to the old man's bedside. Perhaps it was energy currents in the emotion-charged air that forever printed my grandfather's image on my brain. I do not remember grandfather Kristaps as his image appears on family photos, but as a large man with gentle blue eyes and his head completely wrapped with a white bandage as his welcoming arms were stretched out toward me. Nobody paid any credence to this supposed memory. After all, everyone remembered Kristaps Gedrovics dying as a result of failed kidneys. However, in 1989, when I visited my godmother Zelma in Latvia, I asked my aunt if my grandfather had also had injured his head during the accident that damaged his kidneys and resulted in his death. I felt driven to know if the memory of my grandfather's bandaged head was real or some figment of the imagination.

"What a strange question! Your grandfather died due to kidney injury", aunt Zelma recalled.

"But now that you mention it, one of the horse's hoofs also put a gash in his head and his head was indeed wrapped in bandages. How could you possibly remember that?" Zelma asked in wonder. There will never be an explanation of this singular phenomenon, but along with a few other equally unusual memories, the moment of meeting my grandfather made a lasting recording on my impressionable mind.

Another indelible memory that dates back to my christening day is the fragrance of my favorite flower, Lily of the Valley. I have somehow always associated its lovely fragrance with nostalgic childhood memories. Strangely enough, it was a bunch of these white little spring blossoms that were the very first flowers I received as an infant on my baptism day from my father's cousin Anna Rasiņš. One can be sure that every spring, the fragrance of Lily of the Valley has been filling the air surrounding every home where I have lived. Every year since 1983 when the Sparks family purchased their NortHouse cottage in Ferry Township, clusters of the blossoms also poke their tiny fragrant heads through the grass and foliage in our woodland retreat.

★★★

10
NOMADS ON THE MOVE

*A*pril in the agricultural regions in Latvia was traditionally the moving month when farmhands entered new contracts and moved to live on the farm where they would be working for the next year. The day when the itinerant workers moved is called "Jurģi", or St. George's Day, which falls on April 23. Throughout much of Europe this traditionally was the day when farm hands paid rent to the landowners for the land they leased. Even after land was privatized and owned by individual farmers, the day continued to be the annual contract renewal date when workers became "free agents" to move to a new place before the work in the fields was to start.

My parents were educated professionals and landowners themselves and not considered to be in the class of itinerant workers. However, after the death of Kārlis' father and my birth, economic circumstances caused them to move from apartment to apartment frequently. They became economic nomads by choice rather than ethnicity or occupation and moved with greater frequency than the hired hands during the April "Jurģi" time.

Kristaps Gedrovics' injury and untimely death dealt a heavy financial blow to his surviving wife and daughters. Due to heavy medical expenses, loss of income, and business debts, the family was considering declaring bankruptcy. Kārlis vehemently refused to have his father's good name besmirched by having to declare his estate bankrupt. As a dutiful son, he took on his father's debts and vowed to repay them although his income left little to spare with a wife and daughter to support in addition to helping his mother with her expenses.

On April 12, 1935, the day after my christening, our family left our own little Catholic Street apartment, which my parents had so lovingly decorated while awaiting my birth. They left their little love nest and all their bright dreams and moved in with my maternal grandmother, mom's two brothers, and stepfather Jānis Berzins living on Kalpaka Street. Neither Tatiana nor Kārlis considered this move to be a sacrifice. Throughout their life, they both always put the best construction on everything. Tatiana describes their new room at her mother's apartment to be bright and sunny with a view of a nice garden where she would be able to take her baby for daily airings. Kārlis thought the arrangements would be perfect while he had to be away a great deal working and taking care of his father and his business affairs. Tatiana would have her mother close by to help take care of the baby and give her some respite.

Indeed the living arrangements worked beautifully. Although space was at a premium with Karlis, Tatiana, me, and all our belongings squeezed into one room, Tatiana enjoyed being with her mother and brothers again. Her little brother Janka, who was seven at the time, and her cousin Ilmars, age six, both adored "their baby" and kept me entertained most of the time. The boys marveled at my small fingers and could not get enough of holding my hand and playing with me. When I was three months old, my parents purchased my first set of wheels, a beautiful beige carriage where I could be taken for rides in comfort.

Tatiana lovingly recorded my development and growth in a diary she faithfully kept for the first five years. Apparently as a baby girl I was full of activity and vigor and did not like to be confined to a crib, carriage, or playpen. There was not a railing high enough that could confine me when I decided to explore my surroundings. At ten months I protested against any space limitations and climbed in and out of the crib and carriage. Perhaps having my boy-uncle Janka play with me speeded up the process of development. It is recorded that I said my first words at seven months, walked at eleven months, sang, danced, and loudly blew into a tonette on my first birthday, and was toilet trained by thirteen months. At eighteen months, I knew the names of all colors, could put together puzzles, and could count to twenty by age two. Apparently I had a keen sense of observation, which helped me learn to copy everything the adults around me did. It was not uncommon for me to help clear the table and put away dishes in their proper places before I was two years old. It really made me happy to be a little helper and I very carefully helped my mother do the dusting and to clean the kitchen floor.

But fate has its own agenda and does not follow the best-laid plans for raising a child in a peaceful and stable atmosphere. Regardless of their wishes, Tatiana and Kārlis were forced to pack up their belongings less than a year later to continue on the nomadic road again. On March 28, 1936, when I was fourteen months old, my mother's stepfather was transferred from the bank in Jelgava to take the director's position at the bank in Rezekne in the province of Latgale on the far eastern side of Latvia, 257 kilometers from Jelgava. The parting was difficult for all concerned. It seemed that there were always frequent farewells from loved ones. Tatiana would miss having her mother nearby for counsel and her mother and brother Janka had a hard time parting from their precious little Skaidrite. Kārlis and Tatiana faced the difficult task of finding another place to call their home. They needed a shelter at little or no cost, as Kārlis was still paying off his father's debts.

Through God's grace, Kārlis' good deeds did not go unrewarded. Pleased with her nephew's integrity in assuming her brother Kristaps' debts, Kārlis' Aunt Līna invited the Gedrovics family to live with her on the farm in the township of Livberze. She had been widowed and farmed alone with the help of a maid and hired hands. Līna deeded the farm called "Ziedoņi", or Blooming Spring, to Kārlis with the provision that she could live there for the remainder of her life. In Latvia farms are known by their names rather than a street address. "Blooming Spring" was a fitting name for Līna's farm. The many varieties of fruit trees and berry bushes Kārlis had planted on the farm with Līna's late forester husband, Žanis Birznieks, made a spectacular showing with pastel clouds of blossoms every spring. Thus, it was fitting that Kārlis, Tatiana, and I moved to our new home, Blooming Spring, on March 24, 1936, the week of the vernal equinox. Father did not mind having to take the train at dawn every morning to work at the Jelgava Railway station. By living on the farm there would be no rent to pay, which would help out the frugal budget. It would also be a healthy experience for the family. Kārlis hoped the fresh air and fresh food would bring color to the cheeks of his beloved wife and daughter.

BLOOMING SPRING, "ZIEDOŃI"

In April of 1936, when I was fifteen months old, my parents started a tradition at the farm in Livberze that would continue in the family from generation to generation. Kārlis held the belief that, in order for the family to be rooted in their new home, trees should be planted in honor of each member of the family and in memory of the people who preceded them. My father dug a deep hole in the rich black loam so that mother and I could plant a linden tree on each side of the driveway. According to my mother, I approached the task with great concentration, carefully pouring the soil with my little shovel around the roots of the tree. Afterwards I made sure my linden tree was watered daily from my little watering can. My father planted an oak for himself and my mother thought only an oak was befitting her big, strong, and generous husband, newly becoming a landowner. In all, we planted six linden trees and eight oak trees as a windbreak between the road and the farmhouse. The first linden tree was Tatiana's, then Kārlis' oak tree, next came my linden tree and after that an oak in honor of my late grandfather. The linden and oaks alternated, with the last and biggest oak tree being in memory of Aunt Līna's first husband, Mr. Hartman, who was the original owner of the farm. Kārlis and Tatiana each made wishes that the trees would grow straight, tall, and full. They could dream and imagine how in their old age they would sit under the trees and rest in the shade of the wide spreading branches. That dream was not to be. Our family would never see the trees reach toward the blue skies in their magnificent maturity. There would be no resting in the shade of the oak trees in Livberze. Yet, it must have been God's hand years later that pointed the way for me and my family to find a permanent home on another continent and across an ocean in a city named Royal Oak where two giant, ancient oak trees, as if the sheltering arms of ancestors, shade our home.

Somehow, the first tree-planting event took root in my memory. The tradition of planting trees on our new homesteads has continued since the spring of 1936 through three generations. I planted a mountain ash at my and my husband's first home in Madison Heights, and several at the NortHouse, just like Aunt Līna had in front of the farmhouse in Livberze. After my husband and I moved to Royal Oak in the spring of 1965, each of our sons planted a tree in our new yard on Magnolia Ave.

The tradition continued with the planting of thousands of pine trees in hedgerows and throughout our wooded property in Ferry Township. Hundreds of acorns from the oak trees in Royal Oak were gathered and planted in the woods surrounding the NortHouse to perpetuate the symbolic strength of the oak. Additional tree varieties our family introduced on the property were birch, conifers, apples, lilacs, and mountain ash so that the varieties that were native in my homeland Latvia would further enrich the existing American hardwoods.

Following the birth of each grandchild, a tree was planted in his or her honor. May those trees grow tall and strong and may they provide shade for generations to follow. At the time my father started the tree-planting tradition on our farm in Livberze, the family did not own a camera. However, the plantings on American soil have been duly recorded.

Arbor Day on Magnolia Avenue, Royal Oak 1966; Steven, David, and Andrew plant their trees

Grandson Shawn & Grandpa planting pines, 1996

Sparks Family Photographic Tree Planting History:

Rita, Steven, and Taffy planting 1500 pines, 1972 in Ferry Township

Daffodils planted on Doggie Hill, 1974

Planted in 1990, Latvian Chestnut tree blooms in son Steve & Kathy's yard

Lara planting Kārlis' Gedrovics currant bush cutting in Ferry Township 1999

Life on the Ziedoņi farm was full of wonder for an inquisitive toddler like me. The barn was the place that was always full of surprises. Whenever I was outside, my little feet would hurry on the pathway between the house and the barn to see all the animal creatures. There were always kittens in the barn and hayloft. I ran to catch them so I could scoop them into my arms and stroke their warm furry bodies. I only meant to hug the soft little creatures, but sometimes the kittens did not appreciate my tight squeezes and reciprocated by scratching my arm. The cute pink piglets were the funniest and I would squeal as loud as I could to imitate them. Occasionally, there were little orphan lambs to feed by bottle. Most of all I liked to help herd the cows into the barn. The young milkmaids who were responsible for the cows were amused by the pint-sized girl weighing less than thirty pounds having no qualms about getting behind the dairy cows weighing close to half a ton. The maids allowed me to help lead the cows to the barn for milking. I would slap my favorite black and white cow "Palma" on the hindquarter with some twigs and yell "home, home" to urge her to return to the barn.

When the cows returned to the barn it meant that would be milking time. Nothing tasted better than a foaming cup of warm milk that left a white mustache on my upper lip. Another favorite place was the chicken coop. In the mornings it was fun to help the maids gather the eggs and to giggle when the chickens clucked to announce the laying of an egg. Baby chicks with their soft yellow downy bodies were another wonder. Somehow being aware of the fragile nature of the baby chickens, I would talk to them in squeaky whispers. One day my mother found me with the chickens as I was quietly eating the grain and cottage cheese that had been laid out to feed the chicks. Perhaps I must have figured that if it was good for the baby chicks to eat, it must also be good for human babies. In like manner, much to the horror of my mother, I would be discovered patiently chewing on the dog's cache of bones. Nothing could be better than an "organic teething ring."

Stork family feeding time

Since both my mother and grandmother were skilled in speaking foreign languages, I showed promise of good multilingual skills in speaking to each of the animal species in their own language. Every morning I greeted the animals in their own native tongue: "Bow-wow, Meow-meow, Moo-moo, Oink-oink, Baa-baa. Anything that had wings was considered to be a bird and was addressed with a cheerful "Tweet-tweet". One winged creature was particularly fascinating. I had named it "BIG BIRD" and spent a great deal of time watching its activities. I tried my best to click my tongue almost perfectly imitating the clicking sounds made by the long beak of the big bird that lived atop a pole next to the driveway. Somebody had told me that the big white bird was the one who brought babies to mothers. When little white baby birds could be seen poking their little heads above the nest, I checked daily to see if the little birds had turned into babies.

Whether it was the stork who did indeed deliver the baby is not noted in my diary, but on August 1, 1936, a baby boy arrived at the home of my godmother, aunt Zelma. The baby was named Aris and the two of us became close playmates and good friends throughout our lifetimes, even after being separated for fifty years following World War II. By the time we were reunited, my little cousin had become Aris Lācis, M.D., Ph.D., an internationally known pediatric heart surgeon specializing in repairing congenital heart defects in infants and children in Riga. He is a well-known author and lecturer at medical schools and conferences throughout the world and is renown for performing the world's first successful stem cell transplant in an infant's heart in 2009. Aris jokingly comments that he learned everything from his "older cousin" when we played together as children.

When the haying and most of the summer work was done on the farm, Kārlis and Tatiana made the decision to move back to Jelgava. Although "Blooming Spring" had been a wonderful place to spend the spring and summer, commuting to work every day by train and working on the farm during the long summer evenings turned out to be a heavy load for my father. A new family of farm hands had also been hired and the small farmhouse did not have sufficient space to accommodate Aunt Līna plus two families. So, on August 3, 1936, the nomadic Gedrovics family of three packed up again and, with all our belongings atop a horse-drawn wagon, took the road back to Jelgava.

DAYS OF SORROW AND DARKNESS

Although their financial status was still stretched to the maximum, Kārlis and Tatiana prayed that they would be able to maintain a place they could call their own. This time, with the help of the farm income, albeit meager, our family moved into an apartment of our own at 41 Catholic Street (named after a church located on the street). Our apartment #23 was on the fourth floor, which meant there would be lots of stairs to climb, as elevators were not common in those days. My father would have to carry up loads of wood daily for the wood cooking and heating stoves. My mother had the task of making two trips each time we went out. She had to haul the heavy baby buggy up and down the stairs only to return for a second trip to carry an equally heavy, chubby me. Nevertheless, my parents were overjoyed to be in their very own little paradise. Tatiana decorated the apartment kitchen with her own hand-embroidered blue and white tapestries of the Seven Dwarfs who would in spirit help her run the household. One dwarf was depicted stirring a pot, another cleaning fish, yet another hanging up laundry. All the little workers had happy and smiling faces showing that work is to be enjoyed. It became a habit for me to say goodnight to each of the dwarf's images at night and then to greet them with a cheery good-morning at breakfast time. My mother's handicraft was so special to me that seventy years later, the tapestry with the Laundry Dwarf embroidered on it hangs in a blue frame on the bathroom wall in my home in Royal Oak.

With the cheerful faces from the tapestries smiling upon the family, Tatiana and Kārlis hoped that love would reign in their new home and that God would let peace dwell in their hearts henceforth. Yet, once again, fate held other plans to test their faith and strength. Our little family had only enjoyed the warm comfort of our new home for two months when tragedy struck putting my parents' hearts and minds into a whirlwind of despair.

The morning of September 30, 1936 dawned without giving hint of a dreaded omen. When Tatiana awoke, she found that Kārlis had already departed for work. Usually he read the morning newspaper at breakfast and left the paper for Tatiana to read after she and I had finished breakfast. On this morning the paper was missing. Thinking that perhaps Kārlis had not had time to go to the corner newsstand to pick up the paper, she got me dressed so we could run down to buy the day's newspaper. When my mother saw the headline on the front page, she let out a scream and started swaying as if the earth was slipping away under her feet. Sobbing, she barely had strength to gather me up in her arms to make it back up to the apartment before she collapsed. My father had indeed bought a paper that morning and had been equally shocked. He took the paper with him to run to work to tell his supervisor that he would be unable to work that day and ran back home hoping that mother had not somehow already heard the news during his absence. He got home just as she lost consciousness and collapsed in a heap on the floor. The doctor had to keep her under sedation for several days because of the great mental trauma she had experienced. The headline that my mother saw read as follows:

"SON OF REZEKNE BANK DIRECTOR DIES FOLLOWING SHOOTING".
Adrian Petrovs, age 21, died from a self-inflicted gunshot wound.....her dear brother, my godfather, gone from this world. There were no more entries in my diary for three months until January 1937, when mother finally could summon enough strength to write about the tragic event and summarize some of the highlights from the intervening months. Tatiana records her brother's death as follows:

"Oh life, dear life, how beautiful you can be, but also how horrible! But we must love life in all of its variations, all of its deviations. For the living must live and survive until God deems otherwise. Many magnificent trees grow and thrive in our fatherland's beautiful forests. Some are ancient and gray but still full of splendor. Other trees are young, fragile, just starting to grow. Yet all are equally wonderful, each with its individual identity. All are stretching their top and branches upward to meet the light and the sun.

Suddenly, a furious storm blows, swirling and raging, and without pity breaks one of the most beautiful young trees. It falls with but one groan and sinks into earth from whence he sprouted and received his nourishment only to sink down again to deteriorate. 'From dust you will come and to dust you shall return'.

Everyone is sorry for you, you fallen tree—broken in your youth and splendor although you could have still flourished and enjoyed the warm caress of the sun, which in its godliness is meant to spread its bright rays over everyone equally.

That happened on September 30th. His death was sudden and tragic...one bullet...one moan...and the young heart stopped beating...your mother's only brother's...Adrian's...your godfather's heart. The heart only had twenty-one years to beat. Now it is still, stilled for life. We will never know if this tragedy happened accidentally or on purpose. Only God in Heaven knows.

There was no note, not a farewell word. He was handling his weapon, apparently cleaning it. Whether it went off accidentally or with intent, we the survivors will never know. We should not examine it any further. May the dear departed brother rest in peace and let us pray that God gives peace to his soul.

My child, you no longer have a godfather, I have no brother. Let the pain cease! But there is so much sorrow over the dear boy's death. You are so fortunate, my little one, that you still do not understand life. Deep sorrow is still unknown to you and I pray that God will protect you from great heartache for a long time to come.

Yes, it happened on September 30, in the year 1936. Now it is already January 1937. Your mother gathered her strength to record this horrible event. And again there is such terrible sorrow and pain reliving the dreadful event. But it is said that time heals all wounds. Yes, the wound may heal and no longer bleed, but the scar will remain. Time cannot erase the scar or the memory".

Adrian Petrovs wearing University uniform, 1915-1936

Adrian Petrovs was a member of the National Guard and in that capacity had a permit to carry a weapon. On the day of his death, he had stood honor guard for six hours in dress uniform at a friend's funeral. When he came home he told his mother he was going to change clothes, clean his gun, and then rest. The rest remains shrouded in mystery. At first it was thought the death was possibly a suicide. The medical examiner, however, determined that the bullet had entered his left side and exited on the right. Adrian was right-handed. It was determined that the gun must have fallen and perhaps misfired as it would not be possible to purposely shoot with the right hand for the trajectory of the bullet to be from the left to the right.

April in 1937 became another "Jurģi" day as mother and I boarded the train for Rezekne to stay for several weeks with grandmother and mother's half-brother, young Janka and Mr. Berzins. Mother's stepfather always insisted he be addressed in this formal manner. This time the move was necessary for two reasons. Our family was still struggling to make ends meet and it would be less expensive for my father to live by himself in the city and just have one mouth to feed. My mother also still had a difficult time coping with the death of her brother Adrian. My Omi, Asja Berzins, was likewise in mourning. Having her daughter and granddaughter with her brought some sunshine and joy into her heart as mother and daughter consoled each other and I made both of them laugh over my antics. Everyone said that both mother and I seemed to thrive in Rezekne as everyone in the household was caring for us and making sure that we received plenty of nourishment, rest, and warm spring sunshine. There were several children in the neighborhood for me to play with and being with my loving nine-year-old uncle Janka again was a special joy.

Only one experience in Rezekne was terribly frightening and left a fearful impression on my mind. I had admired the storks at the farm in Livberze, or BIG BIRDS, and I had greeted them each day as friends. The BIG BIRDS in Rezekne were a different species altogether. One warm sunny day as I was playing in the yard, dressed in a bright red dress, I spied humongous BIG BIRDS in the yard and approached them to get acquainted. I was later told these birds were nearly the same size as the two-year-old girl trying to befriend them. Perhaps it was the swift movement of my red dress that excited the birds just like bulls are driven to frenzy by a toreador's red waving cape. Instead of letting me approach the flock, the largest male BIG BIRD came charging at me with his wings spread and a loud cackle in a foreign bird language I had never heard before: "Gobble, gobble, gobble"! Fortunately, my mother was nearby and heard the racket made by the charging BIG BIRD and her screaming, fleeing daughter and rescued me before the turkey could gobble me up or eat me as I imagined he would certainly do.

The two months in Rezekne seemed like a very long time for the family to be separated. At the end of May my father arrived to take his two girls home again. What a joyful reunion it was! I ran to jump into my father's arms and would not stop talking for a second to let my mother get a word in about our experiences. Reunited again and loaded down with farewell presents from the grandparents, we three were happy to take the long train ride home to our cozy little apartment. Home for the Gedrovics family was like a puzzle. You put the pieces together to make a home. Soon you take them apart again and put them in a box to be reassembled again later at a new location.

★★★

11
HOME AT LONG LAST ON VAĻŅU STREET IN JELGAVA

On June 12, 1937, all the pieces of the home on Catholic Street got put in boxes again for the Gedrovics family to move to a new apartment on Vaļņu Street 25, apartment 5. Vaļņu Street means Rampart Street. Historically, the city of Jelgava had been fortified with moats and ramparts surrounding city boundaries. The ramparts are still depicted on a schematic map drawn by a German artist, Julius Doering in 1845[15]. Apparently, when the ramparts were leveled as the city expanded, our apartment complex was built on the former site of the ramparts encircling historic Jelgava.

The Gedrovics apartment had four rooms and was located on the first floor. The living room in the front of the building faced a small park across the street with a children's playground and a huge sandbox. The kitchen, dining room, and bedroom faced the garden courtyard in the back. Sunshine constantly streamed through the big windows in the back rooms and I liked to watch how the bright rays streamed through the glass and danced on the shiny wood floor. I raised my arms high above my head and danced in the spotlight of the bright sun. My parents thanked God for their fortune in finding this beautiful new apartment and prayed that they may bathe in the endless warmth of the sun and let their bodies be filled with its energy, warmth, and joy. This was the apartment of their dreams. This was the place where they would put down their roots and raise their child in peace and happiness.

Vaļņu St. garden: Skaidrite on left, Elita in the middle 1938

The courtyard in the back of the apartments had a large sandbox for the children who lived in the apartments. A living hedge of fragrant lilacs separated the courtyard from the community garden that lay beyond. The lilac bushes cast shade on the benches placed beneath the spreading branches to provide a welcome resting place for the mothers while they watched their children at play. Another spot where we children liked to sit and play hide and seek was in the community garden. Sitting on the smooth clay soil under lush black currant bushes, fragrant with the sweet smell of the dark green leaves and ripening black berries hanging in dark clusters resembling ebony pearls, we could observe our mothers walking by. Not a sound would we make as the seekers looked for us in row after row of the huge berry bushes until our giggles bubbled over and disclosed our place of hiding.

Living on the first floor gave me freedom to express my true personality. No longer limited by four flights of stairs, I quickly learned how to open the door and the gate. In the blink of an eye, I would be out the door and run either into the garden or across the street into the park and disappear in the groups of children at play. My poor mother could never rest, always needing to have her eyes open so that she could run to catch her independent daughter who never hesitated to explore new places and meet new people. Whenever there was mention of going anywhere, I would be out the door and running ahead of everyone, not waiting to be led by the hand like other tots. The general store on the corner where Valņu Street began, one block away from the apartment, was a place I particularly liked to visit on my own. The store was a virtual wonderland for a child. Huge open barrels full of staples like flour, sugar, rice, macaroni, and nuts stood lined up like wooden soldiers against one wall. I particularly found the pickle barrel irresistible and liked to sniff the spicy fragrance of vinegar and spices. Occasionally, my mother would treat me to a pickle and I nibbled on the crunchy delicacy all the way home. Pickles still rank high among my favorite snacks. The glass-front display case along the other wall held butter, a variety of cheeses and luncheon meats, and large bowls of cottage cheese. Displayed on a shelf behind the counter were smaller glass containers filled with different spices, condiments, and several kinds of candy.

One day, when I was only three years old, I overheard my mother saying that she needed raisins for the dessert she was making. My father said that we should also pick up some candy. I recognized my chance to be helpful. I had gone to the store many times with my mother and I knew exactly how to shop. Before they could finish discussing when to go to the store, they heard the front door slam and I was well on my way running to the store. Apparently my mother tailed me at a distance. She did not want me to encounter any problems but she also did not want to stifle her daughter's independent spirit. Sure enough, into the store I went catching the owner by surprise. How could such a little child come to the store alone? My mother secretly watched the transaction from behind the door.

"Do you have any raisins?" the serious little shopper asked.

"How many raisins do you need?" asked the grocer, giving me the same serious and courteous service as if I were an adult.

"You don't have to count the raisins, just a couple of handfuls will be enough for my mommy to make the fruit soup", was the sure answer I knew from observing my mother. Receiving a nod from Tatiana behind the door, the grocer put some raisins in a paper sack and weighed them.

"Do you need anything else?" he inquired.

"*Yes, some candy, please*", I answered remembering my father's wish.

"*What kind of candy would you like?*"

"*Why, the somewhat tart kind, of course!*", I answered with conviction. "*They are green, with soft centers and are called Mayflowers. They are my favorite. I also need a bag of the candy called 'Gotiņas' (Fudge called "little cows"). Mamuks and papuks like them the best.*"

"*Do you have money to pay for all this?*" inquired the amused grocer.

"*No, just put it on my mommy's tab. She shops here all the time and will pay you next time,* " I answered, never lacking a solution.

When I returned from my first solo trip to the store, my parents praised me for getting all the right items on my own. They also gave me a serious lecture on how I always have to tell my parents when I go someplace so that they would not have to worry about losing their precious little daughter.

"*You both are so loving and sweet and take good care of me*", said the little wise one, "*but you do not have to worry about me going to the store. I know where it is and I can do it MYSELF!*"

Myself, or "PATE" in Latvian, became my modus operandi throughout my life. Whatever the task, I always preferred to attempt it on my own with little direction. Decision-making was something I practiced from a very early age. This trait would be helpful just a few years later when circumstances would force on me responsibilities normally assumed by adults.

Like the independent trip to the store taught me a lesson about the importance of telling my parents where I am going, another encounter at the store gave me a lesson in honesty. Shopping with my mother, I found some walnuts that were displayed in a big burlap sack. Since I was particularly fond of nuts, I begged my mother to buy some. Much to my regret, my mother had to refuse the request as nuts were an expensive imported delicacy and the family was on a tight budget. When mother and I returned home, I pulled three nuts out of my pocket where I had hidden them. Not being able to resist temptation, I had secretly taken them while my mother and the shopkeeper were not looking. I must have sensed that taking something without permission was wrong. When being questioned, I hung my little curly head low and admitted that I had secretly taken the nuts. The dishonest deed had to be rectified and a lesson in honesty taught. Back to the store marched mother and remorseful child and I had to admit my misdeed, give back the walnuts, and apologize to the storekeeper. The storekeeper was impressed by the lesson in honesty being taught and he further emphasized the importance of telling the truth by rewarding me with one of my favorite Mayflower candies to show that honesty is the best policy. The early lesson of not taking anything that does not belong to one and admitting ones mistakes remained ingrained in my mind forever.

Another time, my parents mentioned that it would be nice to have some luncheon meat for our supper sandwiches. Immediately, I said I would quickly run to the store to get some. My mother thought we could both go together, but again her independent daughter said: "PATE!" When asked how much luncheon meat I would buy, I answered, *"200 grams should be enough for one meal"*. Again, I was right, having observed my mother's usual shopping habits. When I returned from the store, my mother was surprised that I had bought Swiss cheese instead of meat. When questioned why I got cheese, I answered with self-assurance,

"They were out of luncheon meats. After all, we have to have something to put on the bread, so I got cheese."

My parents always marveled and told people about the keen power of observation, maturity, and self-assurance exhibited by their daughter at such an early age. Perhaps I was getting my knowledge from "auditing" and observing when my mother was tutoring her students at home. Desiring to be home to raise her daughter, my mother no longer wanted to teach in a formal school setting. Instead, she worked from our home as a tutor to preparatory school girls in mathematics, writing, and languages. I liked to pretend I was one of the students and always sat quietly like a little mouse and listened to my mother's teaching along with the much older girls. I always sat at a desk and pretended to be writing on my very own pad of paper. It was always fun to have so many young girls come to the house. I knew them all by name and was the darling of them all.

Tatiana and her students with Skaidrite in her lap, 1939

I observed which girls learned quickly and which needed explanations repeated over and over again. My mother was surprised by my ability to accurately assess the learning skills of her students. After each lesson, I would tell my mother which of the girls appeared to be smart and which had difficulties in learning. After one lesson, when my mother had to repeat the same thing several times before the girl she was tutoring could understand it, I remarked:

"It must be very difficult for you, Mamuk, to work with students who are not at all gifted. It is torture to just listen!" My mother found such an observation from a three-year-old to be quite remarkable.

My mother remembers me as being quick to learn. At age three, I had memorized six of my storybooks and "read" them word for word to my parents and whoever else was willing to listen. My mother would tease me and say that my tummy must be full of knowledge, as my little head could not possibly hold it all. There were times when my mother wished that her daughter would not be quite as smart and outspoken. When Aunt Līna was staying with our family in the city for a few months, my open comments offended the old lady. Noticing that the old aunt often used incorrect grammar when talking in a farm dialect, I blurted out,

"How incorrectly old-fashioned people talk!"

This offended the aunt so much that she refused to talk the rest of the day. She also offered the opinion that children should be taught to be quiet and not to speak unless spoken to. Not having had many experiences with older people, I later asked my mother if she would ever be as old and wrinkled as Aunt Līna. Mother explained that everyone after many, many years eventually becomes old.

"Well, I am sure that you will still be very pretty even with wrinkles and I will always love you".

That proved to be quite true. My mother would still possess her good looks, her blue, gentle eyes and her positive outlook on life in the tenth decade of her long and fruitful life. No matter what hard times life dealt Tatiana, she always put the best construction on everything. She taught both her daughters that life is good and is to be enjoyed.

Rain or shine, enjoyment and good times were in plentiful supply during my early years. There must have been some stormy days when it was not pleasant to enjoy the outdoors, but these times must be hidden far in the recesses of my mind. What surfaces when I recall my childhood is an endless summer with unending explorations. No matter what the weather, nature was always calling me outdoors. Going for a walk became a daily mantra. From the day my mother bought me a small umbrella, I considered it an obligation to go for a walk in the rain. One wonders if my mother was as thrilled as her little wanderer to hear the raindrops falling on our heads.

My beautiful mother at age 96 in 2008, one month before her death

Walk we did every day. Jelgava was a hiker's paradise with its river walks, parks, and Castle gardens. On weekends my father sometimes took me for a walk to the Jelgava Castle gardens situated on a picturesque island between the tributary Driksa River and across from the Lielupe Bridge over the "Big River". This was one time when I held on tightly to my father's hand.

Bridge over Lielupe

The bridge, called "Sky Bridge" or "Gaisa Tilts", seemed so high above the deep and wide river below. Though the expansion spaces between the sections of the bridge were probably no more than a few inches wide, I could see the rushing water below and was always terrified thinking my little body might slip through the cracks. But the frightening walk across the bridge was worth the beauty that lay beyond and I felt safe with my father holding my hand. Chestnut trees grew in abundance on the island and lined the pathways along the Lielupe. In the spring the trees were a fragrant cloud of candle-shaped clusters of white blossoms. In the fall the ground was always covered with shiny and smooth dark brown chestnuts, glistening in the sunshine like sparkling smoky quartz.

Outing in search of chestnuts, 1938

I always came prepared for these explorations. I carried a brown leather satchel over my shoulder. Quickly the satchel became filled with the brown nuts, which I treated like jewels. When we got home, my parents would help me to string the shiny chestnuts into strands of necklaces that I would proudly wear around my neck as if they were gleaming amber jewels. These jewels of nature were carefully stored in my toy drawer. Nobody happened to think about the consequences of storing fresh chestnuts in a drawer. Some weeks later, when I went to retrieve one of my jeweled necklaces, I was horrified to see white grubs slithering inside the drawer. The worms apparently had been inside some of the chestnuts. The beautiful shiny chestnuts were covered with a white film of mold and my treasured jewels had to be discarded. I was consoled knowing that there would be another bountiful harvest on the next outing.

November 18, Latvia's Independence Day, was a special time at the Castle garden. When I was three, I was allowed to stay up late on that one night to watch the fireworks above the river. The fountain in front of the castle was synchronized to music, as shimmering columns of water in wave-like patterns of changing colors rose into the air. In harmony with the musical fountain, fireworks were released to shoot high into the velvety black night toward the stars. This magic night when I saw the fireworks for the first time has not had its equal since then. Neither the fireworks at Disney World nor the 4th of July extravaganzas over the Detroit River and at the Straits of Mackinaw would hold the same thrill as that first time when the illuminated fountain and thousands of lights exploding in the sky filled me with awe and my little hands clapped in delight until they were sore.

Winter walks along the Lielupe were equally awesome, particularly when the ice began to break up, creating mountainous ice jams. Before my father and I would reach the river, we could hear the thunderous noise, as huge boulders of ice would crash into each other and spray icy fountains of water into the air. On sunny days the sight was simply grandiose when the mist above the icebergs was filled with sprays of water resembling crystals and diamonds.

Kārlis' at the Railroad ticket office

The route to visit my father's office at the Jelgava Railroad Station was also very familiar to me. I usually picked the railroad station as the destination when asked where I would like to go for a walk with my mother. On the way, I described various landmarks, which I remembered as well as any tour guide. There was always something exciting happening at the station. How enormous the black steam engines appeared to a little girl! I would stand at my father's side, tightly holding on to his hand, and watch the billows of steam hissing, rising, and almost touching me on the platform. At times a friendly conductor would let me stand on the steps of the coach as the passengers were boarding and let me collect the tickets. At other times my father settled me down at a desk in the payroll office and provided me with paper and rows of rubber stamps. The little payroll helper would labor diligently until every inch of the paper was stamped with various notations. How thrilled I was to be able to do such an important tasks for the payroll master. The best time of all was when my father had to go on an audit trip to another railroad station and I was taken along on some train rides if the distance to the next station was not too long.

The daily walks, when I explored Jelgava with my parents, must have charted a map of my beloved city deeply in the recesses of my brain to remain alive although nearly the entire city was consumed by fire and the winds of World War II blew my family to a different continent far across the Atlantic Ocean. Nearly seventy years later I revisited Jelgava with my husband and sons David and Andrew along with their families. Though most of the wooden structures had been consumed by fire in 1944, the Castle on the Lielupe River, the Railroad Station, and the familiar streets remained at their former familiar locations. Like a homing pigeon, I retraced my childhood routes and led my family along the remembered paths to the Railroad Station where I had spent many unforgettable happy hours with my father. The damage from the World War II bombing attacks had been repaired and the former walls of red brick had been reconstructed in yellow stucco, but the shell of the building with the clock at the top of the structure retained its old shape.

Skaidrite, Andrew & David at Jelgava RR station, 2009

Memories of the halcyon days of long ago came flooding over me as I stood on the platform with David and Andrew. I could almost hear the old steam engine chugging into the station as when I had stood on the same spot with my father. To the three-year-old, the platform had seemed so high and dangerously close to the billows of steam coming from the engines. With my tall sons at my side, the platform diminished in height and I felt peaceful having brought my family home to Jelgava, even if it was for just a day's visit. There were no steam engines in the station on this return visit, but a piece of cinder or ashes must have fallen into my eyes causing them to tear.

The most sentimental path during the family visit to Jelgava led my family and me to Vaļņu Street. The apartment house at number 25 had burned down in 1944, but the store on the corner of Mātera Street and Vaļņu Street # 1, where I had shown my independence in shopping as a toddler, stood like a fortress guarding old memories. Among the Gedrovics family photos is a picture taken in 1940 of my baby sister Mudite in a stroller and me in front of the old store. It would be another dream come true if we two sisters could someday visit this remaining monument of our childhood together and have another photo taken as a milestone in our family history. There were new windows in the building and it showed some cosmetic resurfacing changes, but the old steps still welcomed shoppers as they stepped through the corner door. In 2009, instead of being a general grocery store, the new marquee above the door proclaimed the name "Viss Dārzam", or "Everything for the Garden". Indeed, instead of bags containing staples and a counter full of sausages, cheese, and bread, there now were displays of garden tools, fertilizer and shelves filled with a great variety of seeds. I bought packets of sorrel seed hoping to coax them into sprouting and growing in American soil back home in Royal Oak. When the storeowner heard I had shopped at the store as a child and had brought my family on a sentimental journey home, she offered her parking space behind the store so that we could leave our car while exploring the neighborhood. Latvians certainly know how to show hospitality.

The old St. Nicholas church had never risen from the ruins and had been replaced by an apartment complex. However, the church park that ran along Vaļņu Street remained as in the days of old. Even the playground and the large sandbox where my friend Elita and I had spent many happy hours stood on the same spot across the street from where our apartment building had stood. The wood playground equipment that had burned had been replaced by modern metal and plastic structures, but the happy sounds of children still filled the air just like the voices that had drifted through the lilac bushes in front of our childhood home. Vaļņu Street seemed narrower than when the horse-drawn carriages had rumbled over the cobblestones, but the same old cobblestones still covered the street and in my imagination it felt as if I were walking along the yellow brick road through my childhood wonderland. But nobody can return to live in the past and the visit to Jelgava ended all too soon. Yet it allowed my family a brief glimpse into the magical places that forever will remain in my memories.

Skaidrite on playground in 2011. Building in back replaced burned home at #25. Windows behind her head are where family living room once was.

Another magical place our family often visited in my happy childhood days was the City of Riga. When I was four, my grandmother, Uncle Janka, and Mr. Berzins were transferred back from Rezekne to Riga, which was only a distance of forty-one kilometers, or approximately twenty-five miles from Jelgava. The Berzins family again lived on Mazā Nometņu Street 95 in the apartment house owned by Mr. Berzins and his sister Maria. Many were the times when my mother and I rode the train to Riga for a visit with my Omi. What a joy it was to be able to play with uncle

Janka again. At times we would visit my mother's aunt Zelma and her son Ilmars. Janka, age ten, and Ilmars, age nine, never tired of playing with me. I felt privileged to be able to play ball with them or engage in battles with the boys' toy soldiers. The only regret I had was that I did not have a bicycle so I could go riding with Janka and Ilmars. To prepare for when I was old enough to ride a bike, I would hold a stick in my hands whenever I went for a walk with my mother and grandmother. The stick was a substitute for handlebars which I practiced turning from one side to the other pretending I was riding a bike like the boys.

Being children, the boys and I occasionally engaged in mischief. When Maria Berzins, who was a voice teacher, was giving lessons in her apartment directly above where Janka lived, the three of us would imitate singing the scales with a chorus of "Aaaaaaaaa", "Eeeeeeeee", "Oooooooooo", "Uuuuuuuuu" until we collapsed with peals of laughter. Other times, we would quietly sneak up the stairs to the third floor and ring Aunt Maria's doorbell and then quickly run back down again to hide in grandmother's apartment #8 on the second floor. It did not take Aunt Maria long to figure out that the clicking noise on the marble stairs was made by the heels on the shoes of the little girl running to hide with her two boy accomplices in the apartment below. Being a "spinster lady", Aunt Maria did not find our antics amusing. When her forbidding, tall figure appeared at the door to talk to Mr. Berzins, we knew we were in for a scolding from the equally stern bank director who did not tolerate mischievous behavior.

"Bike ride" with mother and Omi 1939

★★★

12
THE BRIGHT SUMMER DAYS 1939

When summer came, the train rides were even more exciting with the promise of a destination full of adventure. At least one trip was planned each year to the farm in Livberze. When our family arrived at the railroad station, one of the farm hands was waiting with a horse and carriage to take us to "Ziedoņi". While at the farm, I was allowed to help the milkmaids herd the cows and to participate in haying when I used a little rake to gather the hay into stacks for drying. Now that I had attained the ripe old age of four, I also had the added privilege of being allowed to sleep overnight with my mother or father in the hayloft above the barn. With all due respect to such mattresses as the Serta "Perfect Sleeper", there really is no more comfortable place to rest than the fluffy piles of hay that allow one to be cocooned in its fragrant, though somewhat scratchy, mounds conforming to the body. Frequently, as an added bonus, there was a litter of kittens enjoying the comfort of the hayloft. The soft balls of fur did not mind being held in my arms. The soft purring of the kittens lulled me into dreamland as we cuddled in the hay.

Though farm work can be exhausting for grownups, for me every task was a new adventure. I always wanted to prove that I was a big girl and could be helpful. Whether picking black currants, shiny apples, or wild strawberries in the nearby woods, I approached each task with joy. The woods were also full of huckleberries. The only disadvantage in picking these was that everyone knew immediately whether more of the delicious berries went into the pail or my mouth by the color of my black lips and tongue.

Looking for mushrooms after a summer rain, which prompted the mushrooms to stick their heads through the carpet of moss and leaves, was a fun challenge. The big brown Portobello mushrooms were a prized discovery. Fried in butter, they were tastier than any steak. There were yellow mushrooms called "cock's comb" that also made a delicious side dish. Listening to my mother's warnings, I learned quickly not to touch the prettiest mushrooms of all. They were colored a bright red with white spots which I called "Freckles". Though beautiful, they were very poisonous and to be avoided completely.

The most magical of all summer nights was that preceding St. John's Day, a festival celebrated throughout Latvia on June 24, the Name Day for men by the name of "Jānis" and women named "Līga". Families, friends, and neighbors gathered for all-night partying and singing of "Līgo" songs. Favorite party venues were usually out in the country around a bonfire. Since the name John or "Jānis" is the most popular name in the land, persons by that name in nearly every household prepared to receive the numerous guests who pay a visit that night. For weeks before the event, the households were busy making home-brewed beer, a dark strong bock version for the men and a sparkling amber colored sweeter variety (much like hard cider) for the ladies. Even the children were allowed to have a small glass on this one special night. Ovens were fired up to bake loaves of black rye bread and "pīrāgi", white yeast rolls filled with bacon. The shelves in the kitchen held rows of clay bowls where the traditional St. John's cheese, made of farm cheese and caraway seeds, lay wrapped in layers of gauze while ripening for the big event.

On the morning of St. John's Eve, the ladies on the farm went out to gather flowers and oak branches to be woven into wreaths for everyone to wear as crowns on their heads that night. Daisies, cornflowers, and pink clover blossoms were formed into bright wreaths for the women, while oak leaves were intertwined into massive royal crowns for the honored men by the name of Jānis.

The rooms inside the farmhouse and the chairs for the honored Jānis' were decorated with fragrant boughs of birch branches. As evening approached, huge bonfires were lit to signal that the celebrations were about to begin. The celebrants would march from farm to farm singing traditional "Līgo" folk songs to greet all the Jānis' and asking for refreshments and hospitality from the hosts. The word "Līgo" has no direct translation. It is sung as a refrain to the traditional St. John's Day songs and describes a wave-like swinging or rocking motion of people singing. Since St. John's night falls near the summer equinox, the singing and dancing would last most of the "night" which actually is blessed with nearly twenty hours of daylight. I experienced the magic of this very special night again upon my visit to my homeland in 1994 with my mother and John (Jānis) Eglis, my mother's second husband, who celebrated his Name Day together with cousin Aris' grandson Jānis.

Then again in the year 2009, I fulfilled my lifelong dream to take my American family to visit the land of the ancestors and everyone got to participate in St. John Day festivities with the Latvian relatives at cousin Zigurds' farm and then continued the celebrating at cousin Aris' country home. The American girls all received flower wreaths to wear during the celebration.

Sparks girls with flower crowns at Cousin Zigurd's farm, St. John's Night 2009

Another tradition popular on St. John's Night in the country regions was to go into the woods in search of a rare blossom on the "Paparde" plant, or bracken plant, a large fern that is said to bloom only that one magical eve. If a young couple were fortunate enough to find the magical blossom, their wedding would be imminent that year. On one such St. John's Night, my father took me into the nearby forest to look for the

Paparde blossom. Although he knew we would not find the blossom since it was only a legend, I never forgot that enchanted walk in the forest. I felt so grown-up being allowed to stay up all night. The woods were filled with the strong fragrance of the white night violets blooming in abundance on the fertile soil and the song of nightingales floated through the dusky night air.

Occasionally we heard an owl hooting and my father joked that his daughter was also a little owl who stayed up all night. I responded by imitating the hooting of the owls. Perhaps I also acquired the nocturnal orientation of an owl that night, as all my life I have been more of a night person. From that night on, the owl became my favorite bird. Sometimes when I was very serious or pouted, my parents teased that I look like an owl. I did not mind being called that since owls are said to be smart and helpful. The magic of the "Līgo" Night, those happy childhood days spent at "Ziedoņi" farm, and the sunny barefoot days of summer on the amber shores of the Baltic Sea, remain brightly sketched in my memory as if they had happened just a season ago.

★★★

13

BY THE BEAUTIFUL BALTIC SEA

Along the thousands of miles of seashore in the world, there must be countless breathtakingly beautiful vistas that people have admired through the ages. But for a four-year-old girl the awe-inspiring endless expanse of the Baltic Sea, as glimpsed for the first time from an equally unending sweep of sand dunes, was an image of unparalleled splendor.

My grandmother, or Omi as she was called, had invited her daughter and granddaughter to spend a month with her and Janka at the one-room cottage she had rented at one of the seaside resorts collectively called "Jūrmala", or Seashore.

Although there are some 12,000 small rivers and 3,000 meandering lakes in Latvia, the name Jūrmala needs no explanation. When a Latvian speaks of Jūrmala, it naturally is the one and only, THE SEASHORE in the Riga Bay on the Baltic Sea.

I became quite impatient to see what the sea looked like as the train was taking my mother and me to the Seashore. Would it be bigger than the two rivers in Jelgava and some of the lakes we had visited on some previous summers? Would it be deeper than the pond on the farm in Livberze? The pond was a forbidden place where my mother had never allowed me to play by myself lest I would fall in and drown. I carefully listened as the train conductor called out the names of the Jūrmala resort towns at each stop...Lielupe, Bulduri, Dzintari, and Majori. When would we get to Dubulti, our destination? Finally, the conductor called "Dubulti". Sure enough, there was Omi and Janka waiting on the platform. As a child I was fascinated by the sound of the resort name "Dzintari"(Amber). I imagined it to be a lovely place for a vacation. Was the seashore covered with amber there? Pieces of the semiprecious stone amber, which is fossilized resin from the pines growing in the sand dunes by the sea, is often found by people walking on the seashore. According to God's plan, it was not meant for me to visit Dzintari until some sixty years later when world politics changed and Latvia gained freedom from Communist rule and the seashore was again opened for tourists.

The cottage where we stayed the summer of 1939 has faded from my memory. It could not have been much fun for everyone to be squeezed into one room. But what lay outside the confining walls of the cottage was truly paradise. Lush fruit and flower gardens surrounded all the cottages and cabins, just like at the big baronial homes. Our cottage had a hammock hanging between two linden trees where Janka and I spent hours swinging to our hearts content. Fragrant roses surrounded the cottage. A little further in the garden were gooseberry bushes with huge almost translucent green berries in great abundance. There was also a big hazelnut bush. I often sat inside the bush and, like a squirrel, broke the green outer shells of the nuts to get at the small round crunchy kernel inside.

When Omi and my mother had finished the morning chores, they prepared snacks and drinks to take to the beach and finally we were off! I had no idea where the beach was, but I ran ahead of Omi and mother anyway, following Janka who was lugging all sorts of beach toys along. Just one block away, we turned to go up a high sand dune. The virgin white pines growing in the white sand were taller than any of the trees I had ever seen in the Livberze woods. To a small girl, the trees seemed like giants reaching for the sky. The ground beneath the pines was covered with thousands of pinecones. The sea breeze made a rustling noise in the swaying tree branches and a refreshing pine scent permeated the air. It was a hard climb through the sand to reach the top of the dunes via the access path and my little legs got pretty tired. From the top of the dunes the view made me stop in my tracks. The view was astounding. There was no end to the sea or to the sandy shore. As far as anyone could see, the white sand and blue water just went on and on to the very edge of the earth! Huge waves white with foam were breaking at the edge of the water and the sound they made seemed equal to that of thunder!

Janka and I both ran and slid down the dune to reach the water. The sand made a squeaking sound when our feet ran over it. I rushed toward the breaking waves. I was unprepared for the force of the water rushing toward me and was knocked off my feet. As Janka helped me up, I was sputtering to get the water out of my mouth and laughing at the same time.

Tatiana, Kaija, Janka, Omi at Dubulti Seashore 1939

"Mother, Omi, somebody spilled salt in the water. It tastes like brine we use for pickling!"

The month spent on the beach was fun beyond compare. All day long I, as all little children did on the beach, ran around naked in my "birthday suit" to soak up the warm sunshine. With my arms spread wide in a wing formation, I ran into the sea time and again, pretending to fly like the seagulls that flew all around us. Omi cautioned me not to run too far. She said that with my very light blond hair, I looked just like the white bird "Kaija", or seagull in Latvian. I thought this was very funny and I laughed and flew around even faster and chanted in a chirpy voice:

"I am Kaija! I am Kaija!"

The nickname stuck. From then on I was called Kaija by my family with the given name Skaidrite used only for formal occasions like at school or on legal documents. Who could guess that two generations later in America, my son David would give the name Kaija to his Siberian Huskie? Steven, the oldest son, also mindful of his Latvian origins, named his amber colored Golden Retrievers "Dzintra" and "Skaija", the latter name being a combination of both Skaidrite and Kaija.

During the halcyon joyful summer of 1939, Janka and I splashed in the shallow water for hours, sending shiny sprays of crystalline water drops high into the air to make them sparkle like jewels in the bright sunlight. There were countless games played with beach balls, rubber rings that flew through the air like frisbees, and birch-bark boats to float over the waves. Within a few days, the sun had tanned everyone brown like Indians and bleached my hair to almost white. I thought that made me resemble the seagulls even more. It was hard to break someone named Kaija away from the sea.

Fifty years after I first fell in love with the Baltic Sea and when Latvia was free again from Soviet rule, I visited Jūrmala again with my cousins Aris, Zigurds, and Edite Lācis Paseiko, the children of my godmother Zelma. It is said that time changes everything, except perhaps the beautiful sea. Walking up the old sandy path over the dunes, the magnificent view was still the same. White pines stood straight and tall having survived half a century of gales and enemy occupation. The clean white sand still squeaked and made the same wavelike patterns as it drifted from one hill to another. The sea grass still waved in the breeze and the scent of pine and seawater filled the air.

Kaijas in Florida 1970

Nephew Tim Sipols, Edite, Tatiana, Zigurds, Kaija & Aris at Jūrmala 1989

The pitch still dripped from the pines and slowly sank into the soft sand. With time, the yellow droplets of pitch would become as hard as a fossil and morph into clear precious stones of amber. With all the changes brought by time, wars and disasters, the beautiful nature of the Baltic Seashore created by God has remained as steadfast as God himself throughout generations.

In 2001, like a seagull returning to its nesting grounds, I returned to Dzintari for the second time, this time bringing along my two granddaughters Jessica and Stephanie to experience the beauty of the Baltic Sea. They walked over the same sandy paths through the tall pine trees over the dunes, which I had climbed countless times in my childhood. The girls, like Kaija long ago, ran into the waves and played with balls and Frisbees with another Jānis from their generation. Experiencing the illusion of déjà vu, I watched my cousin Aris' grandson, Jānis Lācis, playing with the two girls just like I had frolicked with my Uncle Janka so long ago. This was history coming to life once more with the family from two continents reunited in a new era.

Jessica & Stephanie at Dzintari 2001

With my eyes turning misty as the gentle breeze caressed my face, the old seagull Kaija could see herself and her beloved uncle Janka frolicking among the young people to the sound of the ceaseless waves rolling up the amber shoreline. I did not dream at this time that, like a homing bird, I would once more have the fortune to return to my beloved seashore in 2009, this time bringing along my husband, two of my sons and their families to get acquainted with my homeland and its beautiful sea. This time handfuls of the beautiful white sand from the dunes found their way into the luggage of my daughters-in-law Laura and Suzanne, who took bags full of sand home as a physical reminder of their enchanted trip.

★★★

Photos from the Beautiful Baltic Sea

Marta, Olga, grandma Olga, Zelma at Jūrmala 1920's

Skaidrite and Norman at Dzintari 2009, reflecting on phantom image of Kaija and Janka at Jūrmala in 1939

Skaidrite and Dr Inga Lāce at Liepāju 2009

Shawn on Liepāja seawall 2009

Skulte Seashore 2009: Laura, David, Norman, Suzanne, and Andrew

Stephanie, Toms Jansons, Shawn, Andy II, Jessica at Vidzeme Shore, Skulte

Stephanie welcomed by Dr. Aris Lācis 2009 at Cēsis

Hands of Friendship Across the Sea; Stephanie and Leontijs Nočka 2009

David and Stephanie frolicking in waves at Dzintari 2009

14
BIG SISTER, 1940

*J*ust like our beautiful dreams fade at the break of day when our minds awaken to reality, so the carefree summer must come to an end as the days grow shorter and autumn mist hovers over the sea. When the 1939 summer holidays at Jūrmala came to an end, mother and I had to bid farewell to our idyllic days on the beach and to dear Omi and my beloved playmate, young Janka. Back in the city, although I had many "outside" playmates, I longed to have a little brother or sister to be at my side to make my family complete. I felt lonesome after being used to having Janka as a surrogate brother. My desire for a baby brother and sister had been particularly strong since January 8 when my cousin Aris had a baby sister named Edite delivered to his family. I particularly remembered the joyful event because Aris' father, Dr. Lācis, treated the entire extended Gedrovics family to a festive dinner to celebrate Edite's birth and baptism. The celebration took place at the Jelgava Hotel located at the Driksa Bridge, which we often crossed on our walks to the castle gardens. It was the first time in my life that I experienced eating in a luxurious hotel restaurant. We all got to feast on "Karbenāde", the delicious Latvian version of a Wienerschnitzel, my all-time favorite. Aris' father even insisted that I order a full dinner from the adult menu for this special occasion. Apparently Aris also remembered our all-time favorite meat dish and cooked it to welcome me at his seaside cottage when we first met after a long separation of forty-five years.

Hotel Jelgava on Driksa River

According to my logic, it was not right that Aris had a baby sister and all the joy of celebrating. I was the oldest of the Gedrovics children and should have had the honor first. Whenever our walks led past the Red Cross Infirmary where I had been born, I begged my mother to please go inside to buy another baby. When repeated urgings did not produce an affirmative response, I invoked a higher authority for my pleas:

"Mother, I know that the railroad Payroll Master wants more children. Let us get a new baby for him!"

My mother had to smile hearing such logic from her little daughter.

" Yes, I agree that another baby would add more happiness to our family, but we must wait until God sends one to us".

Now I knew exactly what action I must take to have my wish for a baby granted. I had to make my wishes known to yet a higher authority than my father, the Payroll Master. Every evening when I folded my hands in prayer, I added to my "Now I Lay Me Down to Sleep" prayer the most important supplication of all:

"God bless mother, father, and Kaija and please send us another baby soon".

God fulfilled my humble request. It is written in my diary that my mother's visit to the doctor confirmed that she was indeed with child. What happiness that brought to everyone! At last my wish would be fulfilled and there would be a baby joining me in my happy fairytale childhood world. I started planning for the arrival of my sibling. In all seriousness, I assured my mother that the new baby would not mean any additional work for her at all. Since I considered myself to be the instigator of the family addition, I promised to feed and help take care of the baby and that I would share my clothes and toys. Having overheard my parents discuss the economic implications of raising another child, I assured my father that he would not have to work harder to earn more money. I started a monetary fund of my own to save for the baby's arrival. If only finances were as simple as they are in the realm of childhood! Whenever we went to a store, I begged my mother for the santims, the Latvian equivalent of pennies, received in change. When asked why the money was needed, I responded:

"I have to save for some big expenditures I will have in the future".

My parents inquired as to what expenses I foresaw in my future. Having already priced the items I would need, I disclosed why I suddenly needed a source of income.

"When the baby comes, I will need to go to buy a bottle, a pacifier, and a rattle so I can take care of my little brother or sister. I hope we will get a little brother because we already have me as the sister."

I diligently guarded my little pile of change. The money was all meant for the baby brother or sister, never to buy a toy or candy for myself. If somebody needed to borrow a few coins, I kept track and insisted I be paid back. But as carefully as I guarded the money in the fund, a disaster struck and wiped out my entire savings. For me it was as serious as any sudden depression in the financial world and it taught me a valuable lesson about money management and responsibility.

One cold day in November of 1939, I was playing on a big pile of rocks in the back yard. A boy from another nearby apartment building came out to play with me. The boy, nicknamed Becis, was considered to be the neighborhood bully and was always getting into trouble. He challenged me to see which of the two of us could throw a stone the farthest.

"Bet a girl can't throw a stone as far as I can", goaded the mischievous Becis.

"*I am very strong*", replied the proud and independent Kaija as I pictured myself as a heroine, similar to the movie character Annie Oakley becoming popular years later with the song 'Anything you can do, I can do better'.

"*Alright, since you are smaller and a girl, I will let you go first*", Becis challenged, "*See if you can throw your stone as far as your neighbor's window just above you*".

I hauled back my arm and threw a baseball-sized stone as hard as I could, right through the double-paned storm window with the glass shattering in all directions.

"Bravo!" exclaimed Becis. "*You really can do it better than I can. Because you are so strong, I will let you throw my stone for me as well*".

I was really flattered. Big Becis, who was two years older and feared by all the younger children in the apartment complex, thought I was stronger and could throw better than he could. Glowing from the unexpected compliment, I took yet another stone from Becis and with great precision smashed the second window as well.

"*Ha! Now you will get spanked twice for breaking two windows, stupid girl!*" yelled Becis with a wicked laugh as he ran away.

Only then did I realize that I had been tricked by the mean boy's cunning plan. Sobbing, I ran home and told my mother of the disaster. Mother explained to me the seriousness of the misdeed and why one should never do something just to satisfy personal glory. Mother and I went to the neighbor's apartment and I had to apologize for the broken windows and for causing the inconvenience of the cold November wind blowing in through the now open windows. When my father got home from work, I got a spanking from him. Never before had I been spanked, as my parents did not believe in corporal punishment. Both mother and father must have agonized over whether to spank their daughter for the misdeed she had done in her innocent fall for Becis' subterfuge. However, they decided that a lesson must be taught about pride going before the fall. My parents explained that they love me very much but that bad deeds need to be punished. It surely tore at their hearts to see me cry as father spanked me, but the lesson took hold although it was learned the hard way. I never forgot the admonition about not following what others tell me to do if it does not seem right in my own mind. I never forgot that everyone should be responsible for his or her own actions. The window replacement cost the family the equivalent of five dollars, which was a great deal of money in those days. Part of the cost had to be covered from my savings that I had earmarked for the baby. While the spanking hurt only momentarily, losing the baby fund because of my own ignorance in not recognizing a scam artist, taught me the financial as well as moral consequences of my actions.

With the lesson taught, my baby fund soon got replenished as my parents miraculously found extra change daily. The second expenditure from the baby fund was for a present I gave to my mother on her 28th birthday on January 23, 1940. I surprised my mother with the gift of a green leather-bound diary, just like the one where my life's significant moments were being recorded. The diary for the baby was purchased entirely from my savings, but apparently my dear Papuks was able to buy it at a real "bargain price". He also always found extra change to supplement his daughter's generosity. I told my mother that it was important for the baby to have a diary also so that we both could read about our "little lives" when we got older and had children of our own. After the purchase of the diary, I immediately started saving again for the yet to be purchased bottle. My father renewed the fund with the addition of a shiny silver "Lats", or roughly the equivalent of two silver dollar.

During the time while we were getting prepared for the baby's arrival, a new bridge had been built over the Lielupe River. According to superstition, if a person made a wish the first time they walk across a new bridge, that wish would become fulfilled. My father reminded me to make a wish when we crossed the bridge for the first time on the way to the Castle Park and a walk along the river. When we got home, my mother asked what wish I had made. Since the wish was supposed to be a secret, I whispered it into my mother's ear so that nobody would overhear:

"I was wishing that, if everything goes well with this new baby, we would get a third child right away!" For some reason, I thought that three children make a perfect family. This formula was carried out successfully when my husband and I started our family.

It seemed that from the time I found out that I would indeed have a baby brother or sister, all my thoughts and activities revolved around the coming birth. I spent hours cuddling up next to my mother so I could feel the baby kicking. One day I filled my little pail with water and proceeded to wipe the wooden floors with a clean rag until not a speck of dust appeared on the shiny surface. I informed my mother that the apartment had to be made "sanitary" for the little infant so that no germs would make it sick. Indeed, my mother was surprised to find the floors wiped clean with even the corners and floor moldings carefully cleaned until they shone.

The new baby was due to be born around my birthday the end of January and I thought it would be the greatest present if the baby arrived on my fifth birthday which fell on a Sunday. In that case our new baby would also arrive in response to the President's "Friendly Invitation". That did not happen as I had wished. The baby was taking time to leave the safe and warm place within the mother, but I thought it was still the best birthday I ever had in my life because I was so excited anticipating the new baby. Mother baked the traditional pretzel-shaped birthday cake called "Klingeris" and decorated it with five red candles in star-shaped holders. Many relatives came to help celebrate and to feast on the cake and hot chocolate and brought many surprise presents including a little embroidery kit. I immediately began to embroider a bib for my new baby. The bib was made of a pale blue colored cloth on which was drawn a little girl with a balloon. I embroidered the outline of the drawing with carefully aligned running stitches in bright orange thread. The girl with the balloons was to symbolize the big sister welcoming the new baby. So neat and even were the small stitches that my mother marveled about the patience and skill of her five-year-old independent daughter. My mother made a mental note to preserve the bib as a memento of my love and devotion for the new baby just like she saved the baby layette she embroidered anticipating my birth. It was actually not unusual for a five-year-old girl in Latvia to be doing embroidery. Latvian girls are taught embroidery stitches at an early age so that they become proficient in making traditional Latvian handicraft items.

While the baby was eagerly awaited, I was worried about being separated from my mother while she would be in the hospital having the baby. Mother and child had never been apart for even one day since I was born. As we were discussing what a good time I would have with Omi and Janka in Riga, I remarked that it might be difficult for me to avoid shedding tears, as I would not be able to cuddle with my dear Mamuk for about ten days. But it was my mother who could not avoid the tears as she stood on the platform at the railway station and parted from her little darling daughter before my father and I boarded the train to go to my grandmother's place. As she waved good-by, my mother made the sign of the cross praying that God would protect her little one while we were apart. I raised my hand cocooned in a mitten and also made a sign of the cross toward my Mamuk to keep her and the baby safe.

Throughout our lifetime, my mother and I would always continue to make the sign of the cross whenever we parted so that God's grace would always go with us. Not only did my mother make the sign of the cross in parting from her daughters, many others were blessed with this sign of faith and love. In the years that followed, the same sign always followed all the loved ones in our family. My mother never ceased blessing any of her daughters, grandchildren, and great-grandchildren with the sign of the cross whenever they parted so that the angels of the Lord would watch over them. To this day, when I say my prayers at night, I make the sign of the cross in the directions of where my loved ones reside to keep them safe through the night. The image of my loving mother standing in the doorway with her arm raised, waving a farewell blessing with the sign of a cross, will always remain engraved on my mind.

Eight days after my 5th birthday, my father visited me in Riga and brought me some presents that my mother had made as a surprise for the little daughter she missed. Mother had crocheted new dresses for my dolls as well as a blanket for the doll bed and buggy. Now I could take my dolls, protected by the new warm blanket, outside even in cold weather. Then my dad put me in his lap and told me about the best present, I had a baby sister! Mudite Gedrovics was born on February 5, 1940. I was absolutely delighted to hear I had a baby sister and asked to be taken home immediately. However, there had been complications during the birth causing my mother to hemorrhage heavily and she had to remain in the hospital with the baby for almost another month. Realizing that my mother was too weak to shop for the baby, I convinced my grandmother to take me shopping for Mudite in Riga.

Omi and I rode the tram to the center of Riga to shop at the new and only department store in the country. I was used to shopping at the little general store on the corner of my street in Jelgava, but the experience of shopping at the Economic Department Store in Riga was almost overwhelming. There were bright shiny glass counters full of cosmetics, perfumes, and all sorts of fineries. The floors were made of marble, smooth enough for me to skate on with my patent leather shoes. There were elevators with brass doors and operators made the elevators rise and descend again just by moving a large handle. The biggest marvel was the moving stairway that carried people up and down by some sort of magic. My grandmother and I must have gone up and down this new self-propelled stairway, called escalator, dozens of times until I completely lost track of how many floors this enormous store had. Fifty years later in 1990 when I visited this famous department store again, I was surprised that the building seemingly had shrunk to only two floors! But to a girl of five, the store was enormous!

In the baby and children's department I bought a bottle, a pacifier, and a rattle entirely from my own funds. I had brought the little purse with my savings money to Riga. Until my grandmother took me to the department store, I hid the money under my pillow to make sure no robber would ever find the coins I had saved for the baby. Omi rewarded me for being such a loving and well-behaved girl by buying me a new pair of shiny black patent leather shoes. I insisted on wearing them right away to hear how the shoes clicked on the marble floors and to test how easily they would slide when I pretended to skate.

On the way home the two shoppers stopped at the big central farmers market to buy some lunch. Again, I was surprised by the enormous size of the market covering several city blocks and displaying food items not only from the farms, but also every kind of fish imaginable and sweet-smelling imported fruits like oranges and bananas which were not native to Latvia and were so expensive that they were bought only for special occasions. Having a new baby in the family certainly was a great reason to celebrate, so Omi bought a bright yellow bunch of bananas especially for me. Omi also splurged on a block of black butter made of hemp seeds from the plant of the genus Cannabis. This was a delicacy with the consistency of crunchy peanut butter and was absolutely my favorite spread on thick slices of fresh white bread. This delicious buttery spread, called "Kaņepu Sviests", much to my regret, is not readily available because hemp is no longer grown in sufficient quantities to produce by-products to be sold commercially.

When smoking the leaves of the hemp plant became a substance abuse problem, because marihuana has a euphoric effect on people, the hemp plant was outlawed along with other narcotic substances and the original buttery product made from the hemp seeds has nearly disappeared from the stocks of luxury delicacies in homes and fine restaurants. Apparently, there had never been any ill effects from eating the Cannabis seed butter, which was considered a rich and nourishing food even for little children when I was growing up. However, with the illegal use of marihuana, the good use of the hemp plant was significantly curtailed, but not before Omi and I celebrated Mudīte's birth with a lunch of "Kaņepu sviests". The euphoria we felt that day was from celebrating the birth of my little baby sister and the second granddaughter for Omi.

While I was staying with Omi on Mazā Nometņu Street, not only did I get to enjoy the delicious black butter with the unique nutty flavor, I also once again succumbed to the temptation of nuts, which my grandmother kept stored in a jar in a kitchen cupboard. This time it was almonds that I could not resist, however I did remember to ask for permission as I had learned from the incident with the walnuts at the corner store in Jelgava. Omi said that I could take two almonds so as not to spoil my appetite for dinner. I took this literally and over several days visited the nut jar several times, each time taking only two almonds as instructed. When my grandmother looked for the nuts when she was baking later that month, the nut jar was nearly empty. When Omi wondered what had happened to her supply of nuts, I admitted in all honesty that I had eaten them, but that I had listened and never taken more than two nuts at a time so that my appetite for dinner would not be spoiled! Apparently I had also learned how to rationalize in addition to being honest.

Finally, on March 3, Omi brought me back to Jelgava on the train for a joyous first meeting with baby Mudite. The baby was not much bigger than my big doll, but she was soft and warm and her skin had a wonderful fragrance, a combination of Nivea soap and baby powder. As a Big Sister I took my duties very seriously, according to notes in my diary. After Mudite was born, my mother no longer had time to write detailed entries in the diaries. My father jotted brief sentences on notepaper about each of his daughter's activities until the summer of 1941, hoping that mother would have time to expand on the entries later, but chaos of war prevented this task from ever being completed. Both diaries and the notes were among the family's treasured possessions that eventually made their way to the United States.

Father notes in my diary that at times when the baby was not being nursed, I fed her from the bottle I had bought and I continually checked if my baby sister had wet her diaper. I talked to my tiny charge assuring her that she would always have her big sister to care for her.

"Don't worry, Mudite, it is alright if you wet your diapers. I will change you and will not let anyone scold you."

I made true my promise and always shared my toys with my little sister. When I overheard my parents discussing how they would meet all their expenses, I, with a worried look clouding my usually happy face, pleaded with my parents,

"Please don't sell my baby to get more money! She will not need anything new. She can have any of my things."

On April 28, 1940, Mudite was baptized at St. Nicholas Lutheran Church. The godparents were Tatiana's mother Asja and her husband Jānis Berzins. When the minister asked if the godparents promise to raise the child in the Christian faith, I also answered in a loud voice, *"I DO!"*

Although I had good intentions, as a five-year-old I was sometimes lacking in mothering skills. On a sunny day in May when the garden was in full bloom and the fragrance of lilacs permeated the air, I was playing outside with my dolls. Mother brought Mudite outside and put her on a blanket for the baby to benefit from the fresh spring air. I was told to stay next to the baby while mother ran back inside to get a book. Thinking that my baby sister would enjoy a ride in the doll carriage more than just lying on the blanket, I removed my dolls from the carriage, picked up the baby, and tried stuffing her into the doll carriage. The doll buggy proved to be too small for the chubby baby. Mudite started to yell in protest to my attempt to stuff her into the cramped space and mother came running to rescue the baby. I was flushed from the exertion of trying to wrestle my sister into the buggy and got scolded even though my intentions had been good. Being independent is not always easy.

While my first attempt to take my sister for a ride in the buggy did not have any serious consequences, an outing with my mother and the baby in her stroller one month later proved to be of historic significance. Political winds changed the direction of our lives. Our pleasant walks to the beloved corner store were interrupted by the winds of war and subsequently terminated. Seventy years later we finally stood side by side on the same corner again when I joined Mudite and her family on their first visit back to Jelgava.

Mudite & Big Sister in front of corner store at #1 Vaļņu Street 1940

★★★

Skaidrite and Mudite return to Vaļņu Street in May 2011

15
THE RUSSIANS ARE COMING!

On June 17, 1940, my mother settled Mudite in her stroller and we went for a morning walk along Lielā Iela, the main street in Jelgava. We were completely surprised and unprepared for the arrival of foreign forces that would change our world forever. At first there was just a rumbling in the distance. Soon columns of tanks appeared from the direction of the bridge over Lielupe and clanked noisily past us in a seemingly endless stream. Soviet troops sat atop the tanks decorated with huge red stars and waved victoriously to the silent and frightened people lining the sidewalks of the street. Although I was too young to grasp the meaning of this invasion, I would always remember this frightening event. Even a small child could feel that the menacing tanks and the soldiers with rifles yelling in a foreign tongue did not come as welcome guests. As the sidewalk seemed to shake from the thunderous noise of the tanks, my mother told me to hold on to my sister's buggy and we hurried to get back to the safety of our home. This day was but a precursor of evil forces that would invade my world of innocence and introduce me to the feeling of living in fear. Just one summer ago I had pretended to be a carefree seagull frolicking on the beach. I somehow felt that I had emerged from my sheltered nest and entered a hostile environment that fateful day and now shared with my parents an uncertain future.

The invasion of Latvia by the Soviets came suddenly within days after the Germans invaded Paris. The world was only interested in the fate of Paris and Latvia's invasion was only briefly mentioned in international headlines. A pact signed by the Germans and Soviets in 1939, the Molotov-Ribentropp Pact, allowed Russia to occupy Latvia. Latvia was unprepared to defend its independence and President Ulmanis decided that it would be suicidal for the small country to oppose the mighty Red Army. Much has been debated about what the President should or should not have done to oppose the Soviets, but apparently Ulmanis believed that he would be allowed to remain in office and still retain some political rights in governing Latvia. However, President Ulmanis was deposed from office and Latvia was annexed by the Soviet Union. Kārlis Ulmanis was arrested and later died while imprisoned in Siberia. Within days of our walk, Soviet troops were everywhere in Jelgava. Although nobody could predict the outcome of the invasion, it turned out to be the beginning of a year of terror, or "Baigais Gads" as the Latvians call it.

Intimidation and fear were the weapons of choice used by the Soviets. Fear was driven into people by threats that they are being watched constantly for signs of opposition to the Soviet "Motherland". Nobody really knew who was to be feared, but fear was always lurking in the shadows. I was attending kindergarten at this time. One day an intimidating official visited the kindergarten class and instructed the children to be sure to report to their teacher any suspicious acts or conversations among their parents and family members that would imply that they do not like the Soviets. He stressed the fact that the children must be obedient first and foremost to the Soviets who were there to help Latvia. If any family member did not understand this, then it was important that the children report this so that the parents could also be "educated". He also urged the children to join the Pioneer Youth organization, explaining that they were like good Boy and Girl Scouts, only they would be wearing red bandanas to honor the Soviet flag.

Instinct, which over the years proved to be a reliable people evaluation tool for me, signaled that the official visitor was not to be trusted. I told my parents about this encounter and we discussed that parents instruct their child on what is right and wrong according to God's word written in the Bible. I was told that it was not right for anyone in the family to spy for a foreign government, which had taken our country's freedom away from us. My parents also taught me that there is a difference between a country's government and its people. I learned that while the Communist government had evil intentions in subjugating the Latvian people, the Russian people themselves were basically good people.

Skaidrite and Ljusha 1941

Some of the neighbors on Vaļņu Street next to the Gedrovics' apartment were forced to vacate their homes to make room for the Russian officers and their families. The Russian officer's family that moved in next door had a little daughter, named Ljusha, about two years younger than I. Ljusha's mother seemed to be a loving and caring mother and she asked my mother for permission for Ljusha to play with me so that the little girl could learn the Latvian language. Remembering how difficult it had been for her to be accepted by the Latvian children because she was unable to speak the Latvian language when she first came to Riga from Russia, my mother gladly agreed to help Ljusha become assimilated. We played together daily and at first communicated, each in a different language, but with a common understanding that children seem to share.

One near mishap occurred as I tried to communicate in Russian while playing at my new friend's apartment. Only the emphasis being placed on a different syllable and a lengthened vowel sound separate the meanings of the words of "write" (pe-sat') and "urinate" (pee'-sat). As I repeatedly thought I said that I needed to void, Ljusha kept bringing me pencils, paper, crayons and a pen for writing. I was urgently fidgeting from one foot to the other before my need to use the bathroom became evident. It is not known whether little Ljusha ever learned to speak fluent Latvian. By March 1941, I was speaking fluent Russian much to my parents' amazement. Perhaps I was a more apt student of languages than a teacher.

I found the Russians neighbors warm and friendly, a family as nice as my own. Perhaps other people had different, less favorable, experiences with the occupying army. There were many anecdotes floating around in 1940 about the lack of intelligence and social manners among the Soviet troops though the same could have been said about my experience in learning Russian. One story making universal rounds was about a Soviet officer who was complaining to his landlord about the inconvenient bathroom fixtures. Apparently, every time the officer would push the handle to fill the bowl for washing his face, the water would rush out with a flush. Not used to modern plumbing, the officer did not know the difference between the toilet and the washbowl. Other stories circulated about the Soviet wives who appeared at a grand officers ball clad in nightgowns the Latvian sales clerks as a prank had sold to them instead of ballroom finery. It is interesting to note that in the 21st Century it is actually fashionable for formal gowns to resemble slips or scant nightgowns. But though people joked and went about their business, there was always the undercurrent of fear present. One never knew who might be watching and who might betray their neighbor for a price.

The initial fear brought on by the invading tanks abated as I played with my friends. My best friend in the apartment complex was a dark-haired Latvian girl with beautiful brown eyes. Her name was Elita Krasts, or Lita for short. Lita was four years older and already in the third grade. Lita also had become the older sister with the birth of her baby brother, Edgars. I practiced writing the alphabet while Lita did her more advanced homework in incomprehensible subjects like fractions. I was certain that I would never be able to master such complicated homework. While Lita was in school, there were other younger children in the apartment complex or Ljusha next door to keep me company when I was not busy playing with baby Mudite. All the children had learned that there is safety in numbers and we all stuck together as a defense against Becis who continued to plague everyone with his tricks.

Yet, though the children played, they were not free of the uneasy feeling that one day, their parents might get taken away by the Soviets for some unknown reason. It was not unusual for people to suddenly disappear, never to be seen again. One day Soviet officials summoned my mother, who had a good command of the

Russian language. They tried to persuade her to work for them. Mother refused the offer saying that she needed to stay home with her two daughters. After hours of intimidating interviewing, the official remarked that no doubt my mother was refusing to work for him because she must be a German spy under the cover of being a German language teacher. Never lacking an appropriate response, my mother stated that perhaps he should also consider that she might be a Soviet under-cover agent spying on him, since they had just spent hours conversing in fluent Russian. The clever response made the official somewhat wary and he allowed my mother to go home to her daughters. By the time she arrived at home, it was already dark outside and I was nearly hysterical from fear. I had been anxiously waiting for my mother's return and was in tears thinking that the Soviets might have imprisoned her. Mother was never summoned again after that one long questioning. Thousands of others were not that fortunate. Siberia awaited them.

A NATIONAL DAY OF MOURNING

On the 14th of June 1941 was the dawning of the darkest day in Latvia's history when the Soviets carried out the mass deportation of 15,424 Latvian men, women, and children to Siberia[16] where over a third of them died from cold, starvation, and torture. This "ethnic cleansing" of alleged "foreign social elements" to the Soviet Regime, wiped out 0.79% of Latvia's citizens. Among these "harmful elements and enemies of the Communists" were 1610 children who had not yet attained the age of seven and 741 elderly people. The youngest of the deported was an infant boy born that fateful June 14 at the railroad station from which his parents were being deported in cattle cars. Seven decades later, Latvians still commemorate June 14 as a national day of mourning, The 6/14 date can be considered the counterpart of 9/11 when Americans remember the evil act of terrorism that destroyed the World Trade Center in 2001 and some 3000 lives were lost. The whole world is aware of 9/11, yet nobody but the Latvians weep for the souls lost on 6/14. If the statistics of this mass deportation are considered proportionately to a country's population, the over 15,000 Latvians would equal some eight million Chinese if that country's population is assumed to be one billion people, or over one million Americans of the total 1940 U. S. Census population. Yet, nobody in the Western world objected to this mass crime against humanity, not wanting to damage relations with the Soviet Union. This initial mass deportation of innocent people who suffered and died in the Gulag forced labor camps in Siberia is poignantly expressed in a poem written by Professor Emeritus Valters Nollendorfs of the University of Wisconsin.[17] Currently Professor Nollendorfs is the Chairman of the Board of the Occupation Museum Association of Latvia and Director of External Affairs of the Occupation Museum located in Riga.

"They came in the darkest time in the night,
They took us out of our beds, our homes, our land.
They herded us into cattle cars behind bars,
They gave us no food and no drink,
They drove us towards living death.

Lucky the child, the elder, the sick who died quickly
and was left by the wayside;
we, who were left, were to die slowly
in the barbed wire islands of the Gulag.

We no longer were humans, we were numbers;
We were driven to work without rest, without bread;
hunger was our brother, death our sister;
our bones were stacked like logs on the frozen tundra."

Only a few, years later, could traverse the miles
toward home that no longer was home;
only a few returned, broken or saints,
who had gone through hell and survived.

The Jelgava District lost six hundred and ninety-three of its best citizens at predawn that June morning. The apartment complex on Vaļņu Street 25, where the Gedrovics family had lived so happily, did not escape the heavy ominous sound made by the heavy black boots of the NKVD men, as they marched through the gate and the cobblestone passage next to our apartment. They came with no warning and marched up the stairs of the rear building in the courtyard to round up a young man the Soviets considered to be a criminal against the State. Their intended victim was a family man whose "crime" was that he worked as a prison guard. Anyone in a civil service position was likely to be included on the list of the people to be eliminated.

Fate sometimes plays ironic games. The arrested man in our apartment complex was the father of my archenemy, the naughty Becis. Although Becis had been a menace to all the children living in the apartment complex, I cried when I heard the news that Becis had lost his father. It was unbearable to think that my own dear Papuks could have also been taken away. By the grace of God, my father's name was not on the first list of the purge victims. My friend Lita's father who was a policeman was also spared during the first wave of the purge but he later found out that his name was on a subsequent list. The Soviets could not complete all the intended deportations when they had to retreat from Jelgava not long after the initial day of horror. Of course, having a naughty son was not the reason Becis' father was deported, but I thought it was a terrible punishment for the boy's cunning and misdeeds. The father was not guilty of any known wrongful acts. He was arrested because of who he was, an ordinary citizen working for the city government. All those eliminated were the country's leaders and best. The inhuman roundup of people and their treatment as cattle extended even to children, among them infants and newborns. The day after the night of horror when we had been awakened by the noise made by the raiding party and the screams of the victim and his family, I went along with my mother to visit Becis and his mother to express our condolences. I actually felt pity for my former tormentor. His eyes were red from crying and he looked like a frightened little boy mourning the loss of his father. Perhaps the boy's tough personality would serve him well in the future now that Becis had to assume the role of the man of the house. There was hardly a household in Latvia that did not mourn someone who had been a victim of the brutality on that dark summer night that would live in infamy.

Since then, June 14, annually, is considered to be a day or mourning by Latvians throughout the world. Since 1991, when Latvia regained its independence, the deportation is being commemorated with special events throughout the land and a monument to the repressed people was built near the Riga railway station. The 1941 Deportation is depicted in graphic exhibits at the Occupation Museum in Riga where all the somber events of fifty years of occupation bear witness to the relatively unknown Latvian holocaust perpetrated by the Soviets. Dr. Nollendorfs, a former WWII Displaced Person now residing back home in Latvia, has made a significant contribution in preserving the true history of Latvia and the tragedy that befell Latvia and its sister Baltic States of Estonia and Lithuania. In a festive ceremony in 2011, Dr. Nollendorfs was presented the Latvian government's highest honor for his efforts in furthering an understanding of Latvia's history throughout the world and his unselfish work in promoting the future vision for the Occupation Museum[18]. In 1997 Prof. Nollendorfs was also decorated with the President's Three Star Order for his contributions to the national interests of Latvia.

Following the June 14, 1941 deportation horror, fear hug over our once peaceful town although the sunny skies gave no warning of the coming storms. Everyone lived in constant fear that they could be sent to Siberia any day, since people were disappearing without trace all the time. My mother's uncle Rudis went to work one day in 1941 and never came home. He disappeared without a trace. There was the feeling of being constantly watched and any friend or neighbor could turn out to be a betrayer. But for the Gedrovics family there was still the promise of a bright day in the future, which we all awaited with great anxiety. The only bright side to the Soviet occupation of Latvia held the promise of an exciting event we could only have imagined in the wildest of dreams. Sometime in July a most astounding visitor from Russia was expected to visit our family. Early in 1941, my mother's stepfather Mr. Berzins unexpectedly came to visit his stepdaughter Tatiana and told her he was bringing news that she better hear sitting down.

As Tatiana waited with anxiety, Mr. Berzins somberly asked her,

"*Tāta, how would you feel about having two fathers?*"

"*But my father is dead and I only have you, how could I have two fathers?*" asked the puzzled Tatiana.

"*Theodor Petrovs has contacted your grandparents Tigulis in Riga. He has been released from prison and is alive. Now that Latvia is considered a Soviet State, he was allowed to make inquiries about his long-lost family.*"

Tatiana was overjoyed. I vividly remember how my mother rushed out into the yard where Mudite and I were playing, gathered us in her arms and with joyful tears running down her cheeks exclaimed,

" *Your grandfather is alive! My father is alive! Praise the Lord!*"

Many letters and photographs were exchanged between my mother and her father. He asked his daughter to write in detail about his son-in-law and the two granddaughters he was anxious to meet. There was, of course, no possibility of the Petrovs family ever to live together again after so many years. Tatiana's mother Asja, having presumed Theodor to be dead, was married to Jānis Berzins. Likewise, her father, not being able to find out what had happened to his wife and children, had married a widow by the name of Alexandra who had two grown children. Suddenly, Tatiana had acquired a stepsister, Marochka, and a stepbrother, Oleg, who was a pilot in the USSR Air Force. For Tatiana and her family, the joy of finding her father alive compensated for all the difficulties they were facing as a result of the Soviet occupation.

At Easter in 1941, a package arrived from Novocherkassk. Grandfather Petrovs had sent goodies for his daughter's family. The package was filled with exotic dried fruits native to the Caucasus Region–apricots, plump raisins, bananas, figs, and dates–all expensive imported delicacies in Latvia. The best Easter gift of all was the promise that Fyodor Petrovs would come to visit us all in July. Everyone speculated about how wonderful it will be to meet the dear man who for years had been presumed to be dead. For Theodor and Asja, the reunion would be bittersweet as each was married to someone else now. Being assured that he would not be replaced as husband and father, even Mr. Berzins was looking forward to meeting the man who had been Asja's first husband. I could not wait to meet my new grandfather and was happy that I would be able to speak with him in Russian. Maybe sometime later our family could all travel to Novocherkassk to visit the city where my mother was born! Summer was coming; all would be bright!

Even after the tragedy of June 14 overshadowed the country, hope for the family reunion remained in our hearts. But, once again fate showed her dark side. Within a week of the mass deportation, Soviet planes started flying in mass formations over Latvia. It was said they were carrying bombs to stop the approaching German armies invading Poland and approaching the Baltic countries. As I looked up at the Soviet planes with the red star on their wings, I wondered if any of them were piloted by my grandfather's stepson Oleg. Surely my grandfather would have told Oleg that we lived in Jelgava and he would keep his bombs from hitting us! With the invasion by Germany so close, one wonders why the deportation of the thousands of Latvians to Siberia took place. Why were the Soviets still trying to "clean the country" of people they suspected to be enemies of their State when they were about to lose the land they had invaded? Were the deportations an act of revenge for Latvians not welcoming the Soviets during the time of their occupation, or did they simply need more manpower in their slave labor Gulags in Siberia? Who can understand the minds of warring dictators? People are but pawns of politicians who engage in wars to occupy countries rather than liberating its people.

Escaping Jelgava 1941; Aris, Edite, Skaidrite all dressed in white, Mudite in dark dress partially obscured in front.

German army troops occupied Jelgava on Sunday, June 29, 1941 while the families of Karlis Gedrovics and his sister Zelma Lacis sought shelter at the farm in Livberze until the skirmishes were over. Mudite and I and our cousins Aris and Edite, thought the farm outing was for pleasure even though we had all left the city rather suddenly, riding in a farmer's truck. I thought it was unusual to be going to the farm wearing our Sunday clothes. How would we keep our white shoes and stockings clean? We did not know that Soviet and German planes were engaging in dogfights in the air over Jelgava and that the rumbling we heard in the distance was the sound of war and not thunder. The concept of war and its consequences was too overwhelming for children to grasp, but the tentacles of war had reached out once again to prevent the Gedrovics family from ever being reunited with grandfather Petrovs whose fate would remain forever unknown.

★★★

16

IN THE SHADOW OF THE IRON CROSS, 1941

The yearlong nightmare of Soviet occupation ended on June 29, 1941 when trainloads of German army personnel chugged into the Jelgava railroad hub and soldiers on foot marched behind the advancing tanks and cannons. They brought with them forceful winds that changed the political climate. Fate rode in with the roaring war machinery and showed once again that she was in control. The people had no say in their future. Life, like a silent black river, flowed on and carried everyone along with the stream. Anchors and oars were powerless against the strong current. The black iron crosses replaced the hammer and sickle. The menacing dark cloud of suspicion that people had lived under still hung over the land. There was no longer the dread of night raids by the Soviet Secret Police, but the "Geheime Staatspolizei" (GESTAPO), as the Nazi Secret Police was called, had murderous plots of its own. The German Army was disciplined, well groomed, and it marched to new rousing tunes of victory, but to the Latvians the words were still foreign. The drummer was different, not one of their own.

The summer of 1941 in Jelgava started with the blue skies overcast with foreboding clouds of war and change, without the cheerful brightness of joyous "Ligo" songs for our family. The long-awaited train carrying my grandfather would never leave for Latvia. Only trainloads of German soldiers were arriving at the Jelgava railroad terminal. The concept of war and its ominous consequences was too overwhelming for a child to understand, but it was clear to me that somehow the long tentacles of war had reached out to prevent my family from being reunited with my grandfather. German occupation terminated all contacts with anyone in Russia and mother lost all contact with her father for the second time, never to hear from him again. Only the love that was renewed remained in our hearts and I often thought of the grandfather whose love had brought me happiness if for only a few months.

In retrospect, it seems that my childhood ended in 1941. Nearly every child has had the unfortunate experience of having the wind lash out to tear a balloon or a kite from a child's grasp to blow it out of reach to some distant unknown place in the skies. The child may cry over the loss but soon the lost toy is forgotten and replaced by other toys and games. The loss of a childhood can come as suddenly as a gust of wind whirling away a kite, only a childhood can never be recovered and the effects of its loss can alter dreams and entire lifetimes. War has a way of robbing children of their happy years of security and making them face the darkness of reality instead of engaging in games of pretend. Life did go on after World War II made the peaceful county of Latvia into a battlefield. Certainly there were moments of pleasure within my loving family, but the memories that remain of the war years after 1941 are all tinged with sadness, loss, and vignettes of traumatic circumstances over which nobody had control. My mother and I did return for a visit to Omi's cottage at the seashore, this time taking little Mudite along. Yet, this time in 1942, even the sunny summer interlude was tinged with a frightful incident as if it were an omen of things to come.

One morning when we started out on the usually pleasant climb over the dunes to reach the seashore, Mudite was cheerfully skipping ahead when suddenly a huge fierce dog resembling a wolf, perhaps a German Shepherd darted out from the cluster of pines. Ferocious growls and fierce barking mixed with the crying of the terrified toddler overpowered the sound of the sea as the animal took off after little Mudite. Before the dog could do any harm, I rushed forward and started beating it with a stick I had picked up, and mother ran screaming toward the battle site. Whether it was from the blows the big sister inflicted or all the screaming that filled the air, but the dog ran back up into the pines. The pleasant day was ruined nevertheless as everyone was too upset to continue on to the beach. Mudite was so traumatized that she feared dogs for many years to come. Whether the ferocious animal was a German Shepherd or perhaps a Russian Wolfhound, the incident turned out to be symbolic of the hostile forces that arrived suddenly and eventually took over Latvia and prevented the family from visiting their beloved seashore for half a century.

After the mass deportations of Latvians by the Soviets and the irretrievable loss of mother's father for the second time, death claimed another victim from the Gedrovics family. My father's oldest sister, Olga, had been fighting tuberculosis for some twenty years since she contracted the deadly bacillus from her brother Voldis. In her youth she had been engaged to a seaman who served on the same ship as Voldis. The young man could not face marriage to someone who had an incurable disease and broke the engagement. At times the disease had been in remission following stays in sanatoriums and various treatments and drugs. Olga continued working as an assistant prosecuting attorney whenever her health allowed but she never married.

In the fall of 1941, Olga lost her fight for life, as her lungs no longer responded to the gas inhalation treatments. It was hard for me to comprehend how one of my favorite aunts could die at the relatively young age of forty-nine. Just the year before, Aunt Olga had been at St. Nicholas church when Pastor Krauklis baptized Mudite. Now I was attending my first funeral at the Zanders Cemetery in Jelgava and listening to Pastor Krauklis give the eulogy. Everyone was dressed in somber black. With a black veil covering my grandmother Gedrovics' face, I could not tell is she was crying when her daughter Olga's casket was lowered into the grave next to her son Voldis and her husband Kristaps. But my grandmother looked so forlorn and small, as if grief over losing the second of her two oldest children had made her shrink into a bundle of sorrow.

Tears were stinging my eyes as I picked up a handful of sand and lightly scattered it over the coffin wishing Aunt Olga a peaceful sweet slumber, "Saldu dusu", until she awakens in the presence of God. I would miss the aunt who never failed to bring some oranges when she came for a visit. Aunt Olga doted on her brother's and sister Zelma's children and she always seemed to know what my favorite fruit was or what toy my young heart yearned for. Sixty years later I returned to the Cemetery again with my cousin Zigurds. The Gedrovics family plot looked the same as I had remembered. There was still the small white picket fence around the plot and a bench stood along the graves where a visitor could rest while visiting departed loved ones. Only the marble headstone, that my father had purchased for his father and brother with the **GEDROVICS** name prominently engraved, was missing from the site, most likely falling into the hands of wartime plunderers. Grandmother Olga Gedrovics and her daughter Marta were also buried at the site, but circumstances had not allowed anybody from my immediate family to be present at their funerals since the war had carried us far away from Latvia.

It is said at funerals, "*Oh death, where is thy sting? Oh grave, where is thy victory?*"(*I Cor. 15:55*) Christians believe that the victory belongs to God who grants resurrection and everlasting life. Yet, for the Gedrovics family, although some of their loved ones had been called to their heavenly home with God, war claimed a different victory in robbing the family of togetherness and the opportunity to comfort each other with love during times of sorrow. But the sorrow that filled the hearts of the Gedrovics family was just a prelude of the devastation and death that was to follow in Jewish families when tens of thousands of Jewish people throughout lands occupied by the Nazi war machine were claimed by the unforgettable Holocaust.

THE SILENT DEATH MARCH

The arrival of the German military forces in Latvia in June 1941 put a temporary stop to the mass deportations of Latvians to Siberia, but the destruction of thousands of innocent people did not end. This time the victims were people of the Jewish faith. It was Adolf Hitler's devious plan to destroy Jewish life and people with non-Aryan blood. His "Endloesung", or final solution, for a genetically perfect race was to populate the world with blonde, blue-eyed people of Nordic descent.

To distinguish the Jews from the Aryan population, an edict was issued in August of 1941 that all Jewish men, women and children were required to wear yellow badges[19] in the shape of the Jewish star with the word "Jude" printed on it. The star made the Jews marked people with whom contact and business dealings were to be avoided.

The killing of Jews in Latvia was carried out in two phases. The first phase, when the rural population of Jews was liquidated between July and October, was done quietly and did not attract much attention as

The Star of David badge identifying a Jew.

disappearances were isolated and did not occur in noticeable mass marches. The second phase of the execution swept through the cities. The largest mass seizures of the Jewish people occurred in the Riga and Liepaja regions, but also included Jelgava. The process was carried out with stealth and under a great pretext or relocating the Jewish families to a baronial estate complex. During one of our family outings when we were out enjoying one of our regular walks, we saw a procession of people wearing the yellow star silently marching by. There were men, women, and children in the group. All were nicely dressed as if they were out for a Sunday stroll. There were mothers with infants and toddlers in their arms and fathers and grandparents carrying their belongings in suitcases, as all walked slowly with their heavy burdens. Two boys were being pushed in a stroller. What seemed peculiar was that uniformed men with rifles surrounded the procession. Their shiny black boots pounded menacingly on the pavement and they wore red armbands with a strange-looking black cross in the middle of a white circle. The stern look on their faces gave no indication of any friendliness. These SS men were driving the people as if they were animals in a roundup. I instinctively felt an unknown fear enter my body as though some evil spirit had cast a deadly spell on the procession. Shivers ran over my body and I could not look at the faces of these men carrying rifles. They looked evil and different from other soldiers I had seen marching in parades. Why were these people wearing the Star of David herded like cattle if they were only to be peacefully relocated to different living quarters in an estate? A little dark-haired girl, carrying her doll, waved as she passed in front of me. We smiled at each other, neither being aware of death being the destination of the cataclysmic march. My mother sensed the true purpose of the march and could not hold back the tears for the mass of innocent victims. One of the Nazi SS troopers approached her and menacingly inquired,

"*What are you crying about? Do you want your family to join the march?*"
Many hours later machine gun fire was heard from the direction of the wooded area toward which the procession was heading. The executions were done by specially-trained, rapidly deployed, Nazi military murder squads called "Einsatzgruppen" at mass grave sites where people were told to leave their belongings and outerwear before they were machine gunned to death. The image of the little girl with the doll still haunts me to this day. Why...? Why would the man named Hitler with dark black hair and mustache and rumored to be of Jewish blood himself want to develop his "super" race of only Aryan people and ruthlessly execute Jewish people? Though the mind of a six-year-old could not fully comprehend how to distinguish Nazis from the identity of German people and Communists from Russians, I learned early in life that individual people are unique and not the stereotypes created by political forces.

Throughout my life I have continued to accept people and their culture on their own merit without prejudice and have fought for people's equality in my personal relationships as well as my professional life. However, while I consider myself not to be prejudiced against people of any nation, I do not think I can ever forgive the Nazi and the Bolshevik executioners of masses of innocent people. I wept when I visited the Menorah Holocaust Memorial on the beach in Liepaja in 2009 as I remembered the little girl with the doll in the death procession in Jelgava. I also wept when I visited the Occupation Museum in Riga. Executions of masses of innocent people will never make sense to me.

★★★

Plaque at the Holocaust Memorial in Liepaja actually translates "My eyes overflow with tears, like water from the rivers."

17
THE GERMAN MARCH CONTINUES, 1942

After the sorrow and horrors of 1941, the coming of spring in 1942 brought a little ray of sunshine, though very briefly, into my life. I had the pleasant experience of being chosen to dance in my first-grade musical play about plants and flowers being awakened by the warm rays of sunshine. Though I would have preferred to star as the bright orange sunshine or the graceful white lilies opening their buds in springtime, my acting talents were thought to be better suited for the role of an onion. Clad in a drab yellow costume and black stockings for the earth-covered roots, the onions danced and twirled along with the orange carrots and red radishes, extending their green shoots toward the sun. The onions must not have brought tears to the eyes of the audience, as the applause the little actors received was as loud as that which the beautiful flowers received from the parents attending the play production. Walking home from the performance, the happiness of being a budding actress was erased by flashes of a sharp pain shooting through the lower right side of my abdomen.

There was no celebration to mark my debut into stardom. Instead I was hospitalized for an appendectomy. I promised my mother I would be brave and not cry while being left alone in the big hospital ward with dozens of other patients. Wanting to be sure that I had the best of care, my mother persuaded the most prominent surgeon in Jelgava, Dr. Dargevics, to perform the surgery. Everyone in the operating room was astounded that the renowned surgeon had taken on such a simple surgery for this little child. The nurses were speculating that I must be some person of prominence! I concurred since I thought of myself as a budding star of the theatre. The surgery went well and Dr. Dargevics was so skillful that no scar shows where he did his incision. The chief surgeon left my post-operative care in the hands of his young assistant, a Dr. Bumbieris. The name translates to Dr. Pear and I had to giggle every time Dr. Pear came to check on my progress. The doctor was quite handsome and very kind and I was quite impressed by him and followed his directions to the letter.

My post-surgery instructions were to walk as much as possible. It was up to me to walk down a long hallway to the restrooms with nobody available to assist me after the first time I was shown how to navigate the long corridors. I was only seven years old, but I thought I must look like a bent over little old lady, as I slowly made the long walk while pressing my hands over the incision site. In those days the hospital stay lasted six days. Although I missed my family when they had to go home after each visit, I managed not to cry though my lips were trembling when I said goodnight to my mother. Then on the third day of the hospitalization, my father's cousin, Anna Rasins, brought a children's book her husband had published so that I could read while recuperating. The title of the book was *"Modris' and Mudite's Wonderful Adventures"*. My little sister's name in the title of the book brought a wave of homesickness that overwhelmed me and a torrent of tears broke loose. The book was enjoyable though, sort of a Latvian version of the "Nancy Drew" series.

A horse-drawn carriage was hired by my parents to bring me home from the hospital. Ordinarily, riding in a carriage would have been a great treat. The ride home from the hospital turned out to be torture. The steel-rimmed wooden wagon wheels bounced on the cobblestone Vaļņu Street jarring the carriage and its occupants. With every bounce, pain shot through my abdomen, yet I just pressed more firmly on the incision and did not say one word of complaint so that I would not appear ungrateful for the surprise carriage ride my mother had arranged. It was good to be home, though there would be little joy and sunshine in the days and years to come.

The remaining three years of German occupation all run together in a grey blur. Few happy events were permanently recorded in my memory during this period. The one happy and noteworthy event of 1942 was the birth of the third child in the Lācis family. On November 5, 1942, a son named Zigurds joined brother Aris and sister Edite to give grandmother Olga Gedrovics a total of five grandchildren and three cousins for Mudite and me. What a happy childhood the five cousins expected to have, all living in the same town and frequently visiting each other. Nobody could guess at the time Zigurds was born, that soon the families would be separated and the cousins would not see each other for half a century. Zigurds, nicknamed Zigis, was a roly-poly happy baby, always greeting everyone with a smile. For his baptism, Aunt Zelma hosted a big party and served a most delicious torte for dessert. I could not get enough of the fluffy layers of sponge cake filled with the most delicious mocha cream filling. The excitement of the day and the rich cake soon got the best of my tummy as it refused to hold down the multiple helpings of cake. It was very embarrassing to become ill and throw up in front of all the guests and to leave the party early. The only consolation was that I got to ride piggyback on my father's strong back and shoulders as I felt too weak to walk all the way home. Somehow my father always had the strength to carry his children even when the walk was long. A seven-year-old could not have been a light load, but Papuks made the piggyback ride feel like a fun experience.

Most of the other remembered events are jumbled together, generally clouded by sadness and always fear. The Russian language I learned while playing with Ljusha was of no use with the Germans. Ljusha and her family had left in a hurry to go back to Russia. Everyone in school had to learn German. In America so much emphasis is placed on teaching "English as a **Second** Language" to immigrants and accommodating native languages in all aspects of society. In Latvia the occupying forces simply dictated what language I and everyone else had to learn next. In 1940,

I spoke Russian, from 1941 through 1948 the official second language I was taught was German, and in 1948 I had to suddenly transition to English without help from anyone except my mother's tutoring. In Europe it was unheard of that a country would be expected to provide translators to accommodate people who were not willing to learn whatever was declared to be the official language of a country.

My mother's knowledge of German not only helped me to learn the language in 1941, it was also the reason for my parents being designated to host four German railroad officials to acclimate them during their assignment in Latvia. The Latvian railroad employees were asked to take the German officials under their wing during their stay in Latvia, or perhaps to have the German officials watch their Latvian counterparts to avoid any sabotage of the railroad under this "friendly mentoring arrangement". Thus, four uniformed officers from the German National Railway became frequent visitors at the Gedrovics home. Just like my mother's humanitarian nature and Christian beliefs led us to welcome Ljusha's Russian family when they were far from their home, so the German railroad workers were also welcomed in our family's midst. Mother explained that the men were not to be stereotyped as the enemy responsible for invading our country. Instead they were railroad workers just like my father and that they must miss their families terribly while they were away in a strange country. These four men, who came from different parts of Germany and had been strangers to each other, became a close-knit quartet that often provided musical entertainment for the family. I can still picture the four men in their navy blue uniforms and remember the lyrics of the sentimental German songs they sang being nostalgic for their homeland.

The oldest of the men was a slight, grey-haired, grandfatherly looking, Hans Moritz. Perhaps he found solace in being with the Gedrovics family while he missed his family back home. Herr Moritz enjoyed eating roast duck. Although meat was rationed, he frequently managed to procure some ducks for my mother to roast and the whole family enjoyed the feast of "Duck a la Moritz". I hardly remember anything about the tall hulk of a man named Herr Ufer. He had a strong bass singing voice but looked very intimidating with his large frame and dark hair, somewhat resembling the American actor Brad Garrett, who had the role of Raymond's brother in the sitcom "Everybody Loves Raymond".

The youngest and handsomest member of the foursome was twenty-year-old Herr Goetze. He was an accomplished pianist and he and my mother usually took turns accompanying the singing group on the piano. Though I was only seven, I was a little flirt and I imagined that Herr Goetze would really make a handsome boyfriend for me when I got older. Goetze's musical knowledge was extensive. He played by ear and his repertoire included not only popular songs, but also opera and operetta music. One day he played a beautiful haunting melody and asked if my mother could identify it. When she could not place the beautiful tune, he surprised her by saying that he had composed the melody for her and called it "Tatiana". Fittingly, the piece was written in a minor key that suited the wartime mood. There was yet no written score for the melody that Goetze heard in his mind and played so beautifully. My mother asked him to write the score down for her and autograph it, but again fate thought otherwise. Goetze was commissioned to go to another assignment in Russia before he could visit us again. It was learned after the war that Goetze never made it back home to Germany, he was killed during some bombing raid on the railroad system and the haunting melody evaporated with the winds of war.

The gentleman who visited the family most regularly was Wilhelm Birke from the town of Halle on the Saale River in the Saxony region of East Germany. He was close in age to my father and also had two children whom he had to leave in Germany when he received his orders to serve in Jelgava. Birke almost became like a member of the family and he wanted to be called "uncle". "Onki Birke" was the name Mudite and I called him. He must have missed his own children Elsa and Hans very much. His loneliness prompted him to look at the four Gedrovics' as his surrogate family. Whenever he could, he brought food and other necessary items to help out. Onki Birke was very fond of the Swedish pancakes my mother often prepared for dinner. His appetite for the pancakes was insatiable and he consumed big stacks of them in one sitting. Mudite remembers watching in awe as Birke made mounds of the pancakes disappear. Nobody resented his big appetite as he generously provided many of the groceries for the Gedrovics family. Not wanting to waste any food presented to him, Wilhelm Birke ate everything set in front of him. We often had tomato salad with sour cream and dill prepared according to a favorite Latvian recipe. Birke ate the salad without complaint until he confessed after several months that tomatoes really did not agree with his digestive system. Whenever the need arose, Onki Birke was a willing baby-sitter for us girls. Sometimes he took the family on outings and was a lifesaver in obtaining transportation out of town for the family when Jelgava came under attack.

Strange, how some memories are brief and soon fade away, while others keep meandering through the cobwebs of the mind and linger on, suddenly to resurface as a melody from long, long ago. When the four railroad officers came over for one of mother's home-cooked dinners, the evening usually ended with everyone gathered around the piano in the living room. Goetze played the piano and seemed to know how to play all the tunes by ear. The other three men joined him in song, usually a sentimental song popular during WWII. Just like "Sentimental Journey" was a favorite of the American armed forces, the German favorite was the song "Lili Marlene", made popular by the sultry German songstress, Marlene Dietrich. I still know all the words of the song by heart seventy years later....

"*Unter der Kaserne, bei dem grossen Tor,*
Stand einst eine Laterne und steht sie noch da vor...."

The lyrics talk of a lantern under which lovers once stood and where they hoped to be reunited if they should meet again. Another frequent song was one called "Heimat, deine Sterne", which recalls the stars shining over the far away homeland.

The lyrics reminisce about beautiful starry evening hours when one dreams of the distant Fatherland. My parents, like the German railroad men, must have had many such nostalgic evenings during their refugee years in exile when they gazed at the stars filling the black velvety night sky and recalled the stars shining over Latvia. The evenings spent in fellowship and singing the familiar songs with the four Germans resulted in us all becoming friends. I vividly remember the lyrics and melodies of most of these songs permanently stored in my memory.

When my cousin Zigurds visited our family at our NortHouse cottage in Michigan forty-five years later, we took a walk one summer evening under a beautiful celestial carpet of twinkling stars. I spontaneously started humming the old German song about the stars over the homeland and, with tears glistening in my eyes, I told Zigurds about how I was imagining the same stars twinkling over Latvia and all the relatives so far away. Zigurds took my hand and promised that he would always remember the walk we shared under the stars in America. Whenever I long for my homeland and my relatives across the sea, all I have to do is to gaze at the stars and remember that Zigurds is looking at them also and that the stars will keep us close to each other. The symbol of staying united under the velvet carpet of shimmering stars is a sweet and sentimental allegory, if one can ignore the reality that stars are light years away from the earth. Sometimes it feels like my homeland is indeed light years away.

A favorite song Goetze sometimes played and sang especially for me was the "Song of the Lorelei..." It translates to "I don't know what it should mean, that I am feeling so sad...a fairy tale from ancient times will not leave my mind." During a dinner at the Bavarian Inn in Frankenmuth, Michigan, a soloist sang the song for me again decades later and brought back such sweet, albeit sad, memories. My happy childhood in Latvia did seem like colored pictures from a fairytale book from ancient times forever hovering in my mind. With each turn of the page in my mental book of memories, a familiar melody emerges from the sub-conscious, like the lilting song of "Vilya" from the "Merry Widow" operetta by Franz Lehar, which was another favorite of the railroad quartet. I found the song recorded on tape decades later and gave it to my mother as a memento of the halcyon days with the railroad men. Usually, those evening musicals of long ago ended with the same sentimental song refrain, which each man must have personally dedicated to some love he left behind in Germany. How melancholy and lonely these men must have felt as they sang this lullaby to their loved one so far away at home while they had to be away at war in a foreign land.

" Hoerst Du mein heimliches Rufen,[20]
Oeffne dein Herzkaemmerlein.
Hast Du heute Nacht,
Schon lieb an mich gedacht,
Dann darf ich im Traum bei dir sein.

Lass dich nur einmal noch sehen,
Zeig mir Dein liebes Gesicht.
Dann lösche aus das Light,
Mein Herz vergisst dich nicht
Schlafe, schlafe ein..."

Roughly it translates....
"Do you hear my secretive calling,
Open the chambers of your heart..
Have you on this night,
Already thought of me with love,
Then I may be with you in a dream.
Let me see you once more,
Show me your lovely face.
Then turn out the light,
My heart will not forget you.
Then go to sleep, go to sleep..."

Sometime during the German years, mother became ill with typhoid fever. Her lengthy hospitalization created a problem regarding who would take care of us girls. Papuks was obligated to go to work. Sometimes grandmother Gedrovics came over to babysit. I liked these times because grandmother made the most delicious fried potatoes for lunch. Though I do not have the recipe for the ingredients that made grandmother's potatoes so special, I did get to taste the family delicacy again in Latvia when cousin Edite and her daughter Ilze prepared it when I visited them in 1990. The recipe must have been passed down from grandmother Olga to her daughter Zelma and then down to granddaughter Edite. I could never quite replicate it. Some recipes are better remembered than duplicated.

For the most part, Wilhelm Birke took over the task of taking care of my sister and me while our mother was hospitalized. Being a senior member of the German railroad men, he enjoyed more fringe benefits and was able to take more time off from work. He cooked, washed, cleaned, and even darned our girls'

Mudite and Skaidrite 1942

socks. It seemed comical to see this uniformed German officer stitching up the holes in our white socks. Due to the typhoid, mother was under quarantine and visitors could only look at her through the hospital window. Our father and Birke took turns watching her and the nurses made jokes about which one was the real husband. The family was always grateful for the friendship and help we received from Onki Birke.

So often, fate reverses the roles people play. Some ten years later, when the Gedrovics family was already in the United States, Wilhelm Birke wrote to us asking for help. He had lost his wife and his health and was living alone in a convalescent home for retired veterans of the railroad service. He was in dire need of bedding and clothing since those items were in short supply in the Russian Occupation Zone where he lived. Onki Birke enclosed a photograph of himself. It was sad to see how time had taken its toll and sculpted his face with deep lines of sorrow. However, the old retired gentleman in the picture had never lost the proud stance of a German officer standing at attention and looking perfectly groomed in his railroad uniform. His friends Tatiana and Kārlis thankfully reciprocated his kindness to them during wartime and sent him packages with the needed items.

In 1942 as the WWII battles were taking place in the Eastern Front on Russian territory, everyone seemed to be glued to the radio. Every day father listened to news from the front and marked on the map how far the German armies had advanced. The German Summer Offensive of 1942 brought them to the Caucasus Region in July. There were reports daily of fighting around the River Don as Germans advanced through Novocherkassk and into the Caucasus Mountains. The city was occupied by Nazi troops from July, 1942 to February, 1943. Latvians generally cheered the German advances and the Soviet retreats eastward, hoping their Communist oppressor would be defeated once and for all. Yet, the heavy fighting which caused great destruction and a heavy loss of lives in Novocherkassk, brought dread into the heart of Tatiana. She could only pray that her father was not among the thousands of civilian casualties of the ceaseless heavy bombings of the area, but there was never any way to find out if Fyodor Petrovs survived the war. Every evening a somber mood descended on the household as reports of the fighting came over the radio and the impersonal voice of the newscaster brought the news down to a personal level.

I was still confused about how the radio knew what was happening on the Russian Front. Young Uncle Janka was a self-taught mechanical wizard at age fourteen. He was visiting the Gedrovics family during his summer vacation in 1942 and he explained to me that someone in Russia was talking into a microphone and that the voice was carried into the radio receiver. According to Janka, anyone could connect a microphone to a radio and make his voice come out through the speaker. Janka and I decided that we all had had enough of the somber news, the sad faces, and creased brows every evening. While father was at work one day, Janka ran some wires from a microphone he had hidden in the bedroom to the radio speaker in the living room. All day we two conspirators practiced an alternate radio program we would broadcast that evening. After dinner, as was his usual practice, my unsuspecting father sat down on the couch and turned on the radio which Janka had connected to the microphone. What Karlis and Tatiana heard was an announcement by Janka in a deep resonant voice that the battles in Russia were going so well, that the radio station had decided to run an alternate program of musical entertainment.

"Ladies and gentlemen, sit back and relax, and enjoy this nice summer evening as we bring you music by some new stars of Radio Latvia".

The broadcast started with Janka playing his trumpet while I held the microphone. A song that I had been practicing for school followed the trumpet prelude. Perhaps, if my singing talent had indeed been heard throughout the land instead of just in the Gedrovics living room, I might have had a career as a songstress. At least that was the thought passing through my vain mind. Unfortunately, I could not contain the giggles that crept into my song and the two musicians were soon "discovered" hiding in the bedroom as father came looking for us. Father was worried that his radio would never be in working order again after being rewired by Janka but he was told not to worry. The budding young mechanic promised to reconnect all the wires and the radio would be as good as new again. Everyone marveled that Janka had discovered that the radio had an alternate use as a speaker when connected to a microphone. At least for one evening, the family did not listen to the news but we all had fun speaking and singing into the microphone though the real news was that thousands of soldiers lost their lives on the distant front lines in Russia.

The respite from war news was brief, however. As the fighting in Russia accelerated, the news became bleaker and more foreboding. The most titanic battle of World War II was the prolonged battle around Stalingrad. The siege around Stalingrad from July to November 1942 saw major losses suffered by the German land forces. The fighting through the winter of 1943 was desperate for both the Germans and the Russians who were running out of food and ammunition. In December of 1942, the Russians managed to launch an attack to encircle the depleted German troops who were determined to hold Stalingrad at all costs. In all, the Battle of Stalingrad may have cost the Germans as many as one and a half million men killed, wounded, missing and prisoner, nearly a quarter of their strength on the eastern front. [21] The final Russian surge to recapture Stalingrad came in February of 1943 and with that the front started moving back westward.

As the war moved back closer toward the Baltic States, the Germans started preparations to defend their position in Latvia. It was hard to believe that the Germans were indeed retreating, but during the summer of 1943, the reality that war may threaten Jelgava again became evident right in front of the Gedrovics' apartment on Vaļņu Street. To prepare for entrenchment, the Germans dug up the entire St. Nicholas church park to construct an underground bunker. The park must have been the site of an ancient cemetery at some time in history. As the trenches were dug for the bunkers, hundreds upon hundreds of skeletons and skulls were brought to the surface. The bones and skulls were piled in huge piles for later disposal. Imagine being eight years old and having to go to school past the grotesque piles of skulls and bones in the pre-dawn darkness of winter. I had to run as fast as I could to get past this spooky site to reach the safety of my school several blocks away. In my fertile imagination, hundreds of eyes were focused on me from the hollows in the skulls and the bare bones of the arms were reaching out to capture me. On some mornings my friend Elita accompanied me and we would clutch each other's hand in a tight grip to get past the skeletons and the deadly stares of the hollow eye sockets in the skulls. On some mornings, a dog could be heard howling in the distance and the eerie sound made the ghostly scene even more terrifying. No Halloween display can evoke the terror exuded by real human skeletons. To a child, the piles of skulls were scarier than the approaching war.

When the school year ended in the summer of 1944, I felt most relieved that I would no longer have to make the early morning walk past the heaps of skulls and bones. I was also relieved that I had finished the second grade with flying colors. In all subjects I had received the highest grade of "5". Gone were the fears of earlier years that I would never be as smart as my friend Elita who knew fractions and grammar. My report card stated that I was being promoted to the 3rd grade in the fall.

What would fall be like with the storms of war already coming back to the eastern part of Latvia? Many people were leaving Jelgava for fear of the fighting coming closer and closer. Kārlis and Tatiana also prepared to move the family to the farm in Livberze temporarily, as the city and the railroad hub would be more likely to be the target of bombings. Expecting to come back when the war situation cleared up, we packed only the most important belongings. Yet, somehow some subconscious instinct or premonition must have given warning to my parents to pack for a longer journey. Kārlis built two wooden trunks with locks to hold our most treasured things. He built the boxes strong and solid to withstand whatever blows and rough roads fate had in store for them. One of these plain trunks has lasted for over sixty-five years and hundreds of tales about war and refugee life are hidden within it. I prize it more than any antique I could acquire.

Tatiana did not worry about taking along material things like silver, crystal, and china— they could be replaced. She took great care in packing all our documents, photographs, the girls' diaries, some of her handicraft, and the baby layettes she had saved for her daughters. One wonders how Tatiana and Kārlis in a very short time period were able to plan ahead so wisely. Perhaps their difficult journeys after World War I had prepared them for the instant decisions they had to make for the family's safety. Although it was summer, Tatiana and Kārlis had the foresight to take along their winter clothing and fur coats, including the shearling coat worn by Father Christmas. Somehow they also managed to take along several of their jars of preserved fruits and jams that proved to be vital as nourishment in days to come.

Mother also gave me the assignment to pack my most important things. The only things I took to Livberze were my favorite books, the porcelain doll with the real hair, a teddy bear, and a tiny tan fabric dog with black velvet ears. The tiny dog and bear were treasured because my mother had lovingly made them for me. At the last minute, I also packed a small fabric doll that Elita gave me as a parting gift. It was difficult for the two best friends, who were used to being together every day, to say good-bye to each other. Elita's father, a policeman, was aware that he would be sent to Siberia if he remained in Latvia when it was again occupied by the Soviets. The Krasts family left Jelgava for Liepaja from where they sailed to Germany on a ship with other refugees. This heartbreaking experience of having to part from someone I held dear was an event that would repeat itself over and over again throughout my life. But it was not an experience from which one learns how to cope with loss. No matter how many the partings, they never got easier. They were all painful, all full of sorrow and tears. The multiple partings filled me with an understanding that friendships and loving relationships can be torn apart without any recourse or warning, but that these relationships of even a short duration are treasured for a lifetime.

Elita gave me a small doll as a gift. The doll had brown eyes and hair made out of brown yarn. Elita thought this would remind me of her until we could be back together again soon. Both of us cried as we hurriedly hugged each other for the last time. Surely we would see each other again and walk to school together in the fall. Who would have thought that the next time we would see each other would be when both of us were already grandmothers over half a century later in Indianapolis in a strange land named America across several seas and an ocean. I was fortunate also to reunite with several other wartime pals many decades later on different continents.

Having to part from Elita was not the only painful good-bye I had to experience in the summer of 1944. The retreating German armed forces were taking along vital manpower from Latvia to Germany. Particularly needed were medical personnel. Karlis' sister Zelma was married to a prominent surgeon, Teodors Lācis. When Dr. Lācis got his orders to leave for East Germany, I had to say goodbye to my dear cousins Aris, Edite, and little Zigurds. Aunt Marta also left for Germany with the Lācis family so that she could help her sister with the three children. As the family was being torn apart, Kārlis decided that he would take his mother along with our family to join Aunt Līna in Livberze rather than have the frail grandmother face the long and difficult journey to Germany. Sometime in June of 1944, my father and mother, reasoning that the country would be safer than the city, took their two daughters and grandmother Olga Gedrovics to Livberze. At this time, I had no inkling that this farm stay would be different from the previous happy times I had spent at "Ziedoni".

Of course, I missed my cousins and Elita, but now I had all the animals again to keep me occupied and so many exciting places to show my little sister Mudite. Our family of four moved into the one bedroom in the small farmhouse where the tenant and his family had been living. The tenant's pregnant wife and mother moved their beds into part of the dining room. The tenant himself had to sleep with other hired hands in the adjoining granary. Grandmother Olga opted out of this crowded and chaotic living arrangement and went to stay with Aunt Līna on a neighboring farm.

"Ziedoni" that long ago, distant summer of 1944 was as full of sunshine and as beautiful as always. Though I was nine now, I still did not go near the pond, nor lean over the wooden walls of the deep well lest I fall in, but the rest of nature was just waiting to be explored. Little apples had formed on the trees in the orchard, which promised an abundant harvest. The milk from the old cow "Palma" flowed as sweet as ever as if it were really coming from the coconuts on a palm tree. The branches of the black currant bushes hung low under the weight of the berry clusters and still emitted their refreshing fragrance. Rows of smoked hams hung from the rafters of the granary filled with the delicious fragrance of flour and grain. Everything was as wonderful as I remembered from past summers. The only part of farm life that I did not like was going to the outhouse. For those who have grown up with modern indoor plumbing, an "outhouse" was a wooden hut built around a pit toilet. Somebody had warned me to watch out for the poisonous black widow spiders, which allegedly liked to spin their webs in the dark corners of the outhouse. Thus, having to visit the outhouse was always an unnerving experience for a girl who did not like any kind of spiders. It was essential to hurry and get the toilet visit over with in record time while my eyes were darting around on the lookout for the poisonous spider creature. Fortunately, I never saw anything but a few Daddy Long Legs, but I was sure the black widow spider was at least as big as my fist with even more tentacles than the fingers on my hand.

Most of July passed uneventfully. Father took the train or sometimes rode his bicycle to work in Jelgava, 15 kilometers from Livberze. Mother, Mudite and I stayed and helped at the farm. In the evening the three of us would start walking down the road to greet father as he returned home. Everything seemed peaceful. Perhaps the war would bypass our little corner of the world. Only the deep droning of the bomber formations flying overhead, instead of the graceful white storks of previous years, gave an indication that danger was in the air. Where it would strike was a question that would soon be answered. During the last waning days of July, something more deadly than the tentacles of a black widow spider reached out and gripped the hearts of everyone on the farm...Jelgava was burning!

★★★

18
DREAMS AND JELGAVA TURN TO ASHES

On that fateful day, July 27, 1944, Kārlis left Livberze for work a little earlier than usual. He wanted to stop and check if everything was all right at the apartment and to pick up some jars of preserves before he returned to the farm. Sometime late in the morning when mother and I were outside in the garden, we noticed tumultuous billows of dark smoke rising above the horizon in the southeasterly direction toward Jelgava. As the hours went by, the smoke clouds merged and grew into a solid high wall of dark smoke, tinged with fiery red. Someone ran over from the neighboring farm to say he had heard on the radio that the Jelgava Railroad complex had suffered a direct hit by Soviet bombers and that German troop trains, hospital, and refugee trains were in flames that were spreading throughout the city. Dear God, that is where dear Papuks is working! Please, don't let the flames engulf him! My mother must have been devastated by fear that the bombs had claimed her husband. Yet she found enough strength to assure my sister and me that our Papuks would be returning in the evening and that we would meet him on the road as usual. Though she must have been trembling inside, Tatiana assured her daughters that God would be looking after their dear Papuk because it was written in the Bible that God promises to help in all sorts of difficulties, "*When thou walkest through fire, thou shalt not be burned; neither shall the flame kindle upon thee.*" (Isaiah 43:2)

As evening came, the sky in the Southeast became redder and redder and reflected in the farmhouse windows like a spectacular sunset. But the sun does not set in the East! This reflection was cast by a colossal fiery hell that was devouring the entire city. I have never forgotten any details of that terrible day when the fiery wall of smoke and flames rose like a terrible omen that threatened to engulf everything in its path. Mudite and I went out with our mother to meet Papuk at the regular time, but nobody came toward us as expected. Minutes turned into hours as the greyness of twilight covered the land and the rosy waves of the fire rose higher and higher without ceasing. Still there was no Kārlis in sight. As it got later and later, we returned to the farmhouse to put Mudite to bed. As soon as the child had been settled in bed, mother and I returned to keep our lonesome, frightful vigil on the road. The image of Tatiana, dressed in a beige summer dress with a pattern of tiny red flowers scattered on the fabric, standing alone on the road will never leave my mind. Tatiana looked so lonesome and forlorn standing with her hand raised above her eyes looking for her husband in the smoky distance, as if her hand could shade her eyes from the fiery terror in front of her. I moved to be closer to my mother and silently slipped my hand into her trembling hand as we both waited and waited...

At last, toward midnight, a tiny figure emerged in the distance. As it got closer, we could see in the twilight of the summer skies that it was my father slowly walking toward us, pushing his bicycle beside him. We rushed toward him and held him in a tearful embrace. Slowly, the three of us made our way back to the farmhouse, our silhouettes framed by the fiery skyline that completely engulfed the landscape. Papuks was so exhausted that he could hardly speak. His face, hands, and clothing were covered with a grey mixture of soot, smoke, dust and the pallor that comes from a day of terror. The sadness in his eyes and an expression of extreme weariness gave indication of the horrors he had escaped. Although he had not eaten since leaving Livberze early in the morning, he was too traumatized to eat the supper mother had saved for him.

Little by little, Kārlis spoke of the total destruction that had befallen Jelgava that day. He had been in his office getting ready to prepare the payroll envelopes for the employees. In those days, employees received their pay in cash and not payroll checks. The bank had just delivered bags of money for the payroll and Kārlis had placed them into the walk-in safe. Without any warning from air raid sirens, there were suddenly Soviet bombers flying low over the railroad station, as Kārlis was coming out of the safe. On that day, the station was filled with trains. Some, filled with German troops, had just arrived and were unloading men and weapons to reinforce the front lines of battle. Several hospital trains, with the emblem of the Red Cross displayed on the roofs of the cars, were filled with wounded soldiers bound for hospitals in Germany. Trainloads of refugees fleeing from the Soviets also were lined up waiting for the signal to leave for Germany. Freight trains filled with ammunition were intermingled with the people transports.

Suddenly, bombers were flying so low over the station that Kārlis could feel the building shaking and the air was filled with the deafening sound of the airplane motors. The planes were zeroing in directly over the trains and a terrible whistling noise filled the air as bombs began falling with their deadly payload. The explosions shattered the trains, taking the lives of hundreds of people, and started fires throughout the station. Four trainloads with refugees were destroyed along with two passenger trains. When the bombs hit the ammunition train, the explosions were even more devastating. The sounds of the bomb blasts were mingled with the screams of men, as they tried to run with their uniforms wrapped in flames. For the wounded on the hospital train, the deadly bombs brought an end to their suffering. As glass, chunks of plaster, and shrapnel were flying through his office Kārlis took shelter in the safe constructed with thick walls of steel. He crouched there, surrounded by piles of money, for what seemed like an eternity until the sound of the airplanes faded into the distance. Carefully, Kārlis made his way toward the door of the safe when a horrible thought struck him. What if the door of the safe had locked shut from the violent concussion of the bombs that shook the station! He pushed on the heavy door with all his strength and inch-by-inch it opened wide enough for him to crawl through. He thanked God, that he had not been trapped in the safe to slowly suffocate.

Though the station itself had not been a direct hit, there were fires and dead bodies all around, as Kārlis was making his way through the rubble that surrounded him. He left so quickly that he did not take any of his belongings from his desk. Later, it struck Kārlis as ironic that he had not even taken his own payroll envelope. He could have escaped with bags full of money that had surrounded him in the safe and nobody would have known if anything was missing, as the fire eventually gutted the inside of the railroad station. But as the fire raged all around, Kārlis only thought of getting away from the explosions and fire.

Miraculously, his bicycle, covered with soot and debris, was still in the stand where he had left it in the morning. Kārlis jumped on it and started pedaling, but all he heard was the sound of tearing metal as all the spokes broke on the front wheel where the lock was still attached. In his haste to get away, he had forgotten to take off the lock that had been threaded through the spokes to secure the bike to a stand. At times of extreme stress, people sometimes do not make rational decisions. Instead of abandoning the now useless bicycle and fleeing as fast as he could, Kārlis half dragged and half carried it with him, making it harder to get around the rubble covering the street and sidewalks.

He must have been hoping he could fix the bicycle that had been his pride and joy and his primary mode of transportation. The bicycle was indeed a grand one. It was a deluxe model in its day and Kārlis took excellent care of it. The shiny black frame was accented with bright chrome wheels and trim. Built for long distance touring, the bicycle had ball bearings, a comfortable padded seat, and a luggage carrier over the back wheel. This was where I sat when my father took me for rides. There was a big chrome headlight in front of the handlebars for night visibility. It is the ball bearings that I remember well. My uncle Janka, always being interested in mechanics, had taken the bicycle apart one day for what he called "routine maintenance". When he put all the parts back together again, a small handful of the little balls was left over. Father scolded Janka for disabling the bicycle and for taking it apart without permission. The young mechanic and I both learned that the shiny balls had an important function in making the bike run smoothly and were not just a shiny decoration intended for play. No wonder that Kārlis lugged the damaged bicycle with him through the flames. He planned to stop at the apartment to pick up some extra spokes along with the jars of preserves.

The fire around the railroad station was spreading rapidly. Oil storage tanks exploded in the station's freight area. Fanned by the wind, flames were jumping from one wooden building to the next and within minutes, several blocks were engulfed in flames. Most of the buildings and apartments in Jelgava were constructed of wood. The flames were devouring everything in their path as if waves of flames were roaring out of the huge mouth of a fiery dragon. Kārlis could see that the streets leading to our apartment were already engulfed in flames, which were forging ahead faster than he could run. He had no choice, there was no way back to our beloved home. Sadly, he turned to hurry directly to his family in Livberze and away from the burning city. It was useless to look back. Kārlis did not know at the time that this would be the last time he would be in Jelgava, the railroad station he was so proud of, and the familiar streets where he had enjoyed pleasant walks with his family. It was not in his destiny to ever return to the city of his birth, but this was not a time for looking back, not a time for farewells. Kārlis hastened to join his family.

Intense fires devoured Jelgava as a series of attacks continued for four days. Not all the fires were caused by the initial Soviet bombing attack on July 27th. As the bombing took place, the German command had given orders to defend Jelgava at all costs. Latvian soldiers did most of the defense. When the German troops were later forced to withdraw from the city, they blew up all their warehouses and set fires as they retreated. On July 28th Russian tanks were approaching the city from the South. Heroic Latvian defenders with some help from German attack planes halted this attack. On the 29th of July the defenders of Jelgava repelled another attack from the East. A new attack started on July 31 as Soviet tanks and artillery advanced into the city. This time, a small number of Latvian airplanes provided much of the heroic defense, but the attacking forces invaded the city with an overwhelming superiority of tanks, heavy artillery and aerial support. Combat continued on a house-to-house, or rubble-to-rubble basis. On that day Moscow radio already reported that Jelgava had been "liberated". However during the first week of August, German infantry troops from Riga staged a surprise attack to regain the captured city where Soviet troops were looting any stores and buildings remaining standing. The Soviets retreated, not being able to withstand the sudden attack of many artillery, infantry, and tank troops brought in from other nearby cities. The German troops reestablished its stronghold in Jelgava for a few weeks, but it was impossible to contain the colossal fire, which leveled 90% of the city except for some brick and masonry walls of churches and public buildings. The dark wall of smoke could be seen surrounding the city by day and red flames danced on the horizon throughout the night. The Gedrovics family could only watch the red horizon from Livberze as the fiery conflagration devoured their possessions and future dreams. The sunny apartment on Vaļņu Street was no more as flames consumed all the buildings constructed of wood.

The stately St. Nicholas church must have suffered a direct hit by a

Rubble and mounds of ashes were all that remained of the apartments at #25 Vaļņu Street. 1880's water tower in background still stands at Horse Market.

bomb as it was completely destroyed and in later years was replaced by an apartment complex. Miraculously, the little corner store, where I had shopped as a little girl and where the photo was taken as I walked with Mudite in a stroller, remained standing as the only building within two blocks. In 1990 tears flowed as, overwhelmed by memories, I climbed the same steps to enter the old-time store. Constructed of brick, the corner store was the only building on Vaļņu Street to survive the inferno. Nineteen years later in 2009, my husband and I and our sons Andrew and David along with their wives Suzanne and Laura were able to follow up the same stairs in my footsteps to visit the still-standing store, which stood like a memorial to a long-ago childhood. No longer was it a corner grocery, however. Seeds and gardening supplies were featured in the space once occupied by barrels and sacks filled with food staples. Using the old rationale that you have to buy "something to eat", I bought packets of sorrel seed hoping to grow them into luscious green leaves for the making of some sorrel soup, another Latvian delicacy generally unavailable in the United States. As the family made its pilgrimage along the old familiar cobblestone pavement, very few of the other buildings on Vaļņu Street appeared familiar to me; only the park along the street still existed. Fortunately, the gruesome piles of skeletons, uncovered from an ancient cemetery during the building of a bomb shelter during the war, were long gone and again replaced by shrubs and grass. Amazingly, in the same spot, across from where the Gedrovics apartment had once stood, children were playing in a sandbox on the same spot where my playmates and I had once built sand castles. The only difference was that the sandbox was constructed of modern colorful synthetic material, whereas the old sandbox I remembered had sides built of weathered wood. Some apartment buildings built with brick and cement also still stood on the other side of the park.

Jelgava was rebuilt as a different city following the war with some of the old landmarks restored, but in the summer of 1944 there were no places remaining that the residents who survived the battles could call home. The city was a desolate field of rubble and ashes. Nobody really knew exactly what happened in Jelgava after the July attacks. Presumably most of the former residents who were still alive had left the city and got scattered throughout the world. There was nobody to contact. Again, our family had become nomads. This time there was no place where to unpack the puzzle to put the home back together again. All that was left of our home were the few items we had packed in a couple of suitcases and the wooden boxes my father had built. But what really mattered was that God had spared our lives and we still had each other.

★★★

19
REFUGEE LIFE BEGINS

Within a few days of Jelgava burning, billows of smoke sprang up in multiple places surrounding Jelgava as the Soviets accelerated the air attack on the depleted German troops. The country road running in front of "Ziedoni" had always been quiet with only an occasional farm wagon going by. In August, streams of refugee wagons going in a westward direction began passing the farm. There did not seem to be an end to the wagon trains as people displaced from Jelgava were joined by people from nearby farms. There were countless families who had been made homeless by the bombings and they were now going westward. Nobody had any definite destination in mind; everyone just wanted to get out of the way of the bombing and shelling by the advancing Russian troops. The wagons were piled high with various bundles and small children were sitting on top of the piles of belongings. Cattle, sheep, and pigs were herded beside the wagons. The trees and shrubs along the road became grey from the dust that was constantly being churned up by the wagon wheels. Even the darkness of night did not stop the refugee wagon trains going toward an unknown fate.

Although the fighting seemed to be coming closer to the farm, Kārlis and Tatiana did not think it would be wise for them to become homeless nomads by joining the throngs of refugees. The only refuge for them now was the country home at "Ziedoni". This was their land and surely the farm region would not become a war target. Even if the Soviets invaded all of Latvia again, it seemed best to stay put on their land where they had roots rather than fleeing to unknown places and unknown new dangers.

Sleep did not come easy for the Gedrovics family with the clatter of the wagon wheels, occasional sputtering of the horses straining from their heavy loads, and the mournful sounds of mooing cattle filling the night air. Among the wagon trains were also people on bicycles loaded down with whatever their racks could hold and many more persons pushing handcarts for want of better transportation. As I watched the caravans of people and animals going by, I could only wonder where all these people were coming from and where they were all heading throughout the day and night. Sometimes a weary family would pull into the yard at "Ziedoni" to let their horses rest in the pasture and to fill their water containers from the well. These unexpected guests were always very humble and polite, as if apologizing for their sudden status of having to beg for water and a brief respite from the grueling walk along the dusty road. The Gedrovics family felt fortunate that we had the farm to shelter and sustain us with food.

After the refugees came the legions of German soldiers retreating from the Eastern front and hoping to establish a stronghold when they reached Riga. When the German military first occupied Latvia in 1941, the troops had marched with bravado to a disciplined lively cadence often accompanied by patriotic marching songs. The soldiers had held their heads high, their uniforms were perfectly groomed, and their polished black boots rose and fell in unison in straight rows. Three years later in August of 1944, the retreating troops looked defeated and bedraggled. There was no song, no lively cadence. The uniforms were torn and dusty. Their once shiny boots were covered with mud and dust and the soldiers' heads were hanging low, as the bone-weary men shuffled by with defeat written all over their haggard faces.

The sound of explosions, anti-aircraft guns, and artillery fire kept coming closer and closer to Livberze. The flowering fields and fruit orchards suddenly took on the grim veneer of a battleground. What had seemed to be a safe place of refuge was becoming the front line of attacks. There was no remission at night as search rockets lit up the sky. To the children it all seemed unreal. We watched in wonder as the search rockets sent waves of light swirling in the sky and made it look like an Aurora Borealis. But the fieldstone house still seemed like a safe haven that could withstand any shelling. The window for escape to some place safer, if there indeed was such a place, was closed. Livberze was in the midst of the battlefield.

"We must make preparations for a shelter", Kārlis said to Jānis, the tenant farmer, after a particularly frightful night when the shelling and multiple fires were coming so close that it seemed like the fighting from the distant horizon had moved in on our once pastoral farmland. Jānis agreed. He also had been thinking of a safe shelter to harbor his wife who was expecting their first child any day. Listening to the conversation, I wondered why the men were worried about a shelter when the stone house seemed as invincible as any other place. The possibility of the thatch roof being hit by incendiary bombs was beyond my imagination.

"They will be here any day", father continued. I was puzzled as to who "they" might be. So many caravans of people had passed by. Who else was expected to come to pay us a visit? Soon it became apparent even to me as a child that the Russians were coming back and buildings were being bombed and destroyed along the way. Father and Jānis set to work digging a large trench in the field between the house and the pond. They reinforced the walls with logs cut in the nearby woods. Logs, covered with dirt and sod, formed a cover over the shelter, which looked more like a big ditch than a room to house ten people. A ladder made of boards led up to a trap door, which was camouflaged with sod and branches to look like small bushes. An upright stovepipe ran vertically up along one wall through the cover to provide ventilation in the pit. Wooden planks formed benches along the walls of the pit with just enough room for everyone to sit down. As primitive as the shelter was, it would have to hide and protect the Gedrovics family, Aunt Līna, Grandmother Olga, and the tenant family from the advancing Russian infantry. It still

seemed unbelievable that the farm would actually be in the direct line of attack. Surely, the fighting would soon blow over and we could resume normal harvesting again.

The shelter was barely finished when German soldiers rushed into the farmyard and ordered everyone to leave the house. They were appropriating it for their field hospital. The German headquarters had taken over the neighboring farmhouse. There was just enough time to take along emergency provisions. The fighting front had reached "Ziedoņi" and our beautiful summer retreat was captured and invaded. There was no place for the Gedrovics family and the tenant farmers to go but to the underground shelter. The hayloft above the barn would have been a fire-trap if a shell or grenade should hit.

Life in the trench shelter was miserable at best. If living underground started as an adventure for us children, being confined in the dark around the clock could make a person claustrophobic in a hurry. There was nothing to do but sit and breathe in the dank air while condensation dripped from the logs forming the roof. There was no light, no toys, no communication with the outside world, and no entertainment except the noise of the cannon fire and the flares lighting up the sky. It took extraordinary strength and resourcefulness for Tatiana and Kārlis to meet the challenges of keeping their children in the underground shelter for what seemed like weeks. To relieve the tension and the boredom, Tatiana would start some well-known hymn or folk song and then all would join in the singing. Latvians traditionally have been known as singing people. In good times and bad times, whenever Latvians gather, someone would start singing and everyone would add their voices to the chorus. The hymn my mother sang most often was *"Lord, Take my Hand and Lead me..."* asking God's help in choosing the right path to follow into the unknown. I would learn the words by heart in the coming months and years, *"Pie Rokas Ņem un Vadi, Kungs mani Pats..."*

It seemed that there was no end to mother's repertoire of songs and games that were familiar to both the children and adults. To draw attention away from the shells exploding around us, Tatiana came up with fascinating stories and word games. For toilet needs everyone had to use a large bucket which the men emptied outside when the shelling ceased periodically. Fortunately, the adults had had the foresight to bring along water, bread, butter, jars of jam, and some of the smoked hams from the granary.

With continuous shooting and shelling going on, it was too dangerous to venture above ground, especially in the daytime. On a couple of occasions, either the tenant farmer or my father did sneak out under the cover of darkness just before dawn to milk some of the cows grazing nearby. Everyone welcomed the warm milk to satisfy their hunger and to warm their bodies in the damp and chilly shelter. Surely the cows also welcomed the milking that brought relief to their bulging udders. Sometimes the shelling stopped briefly to allow a hasty run to the orchard to pick some apples. But the hasty milking expeditions came to an abrupt end when the neighbor across the road from "Ziedoni" was killed during one of his milk runs. Thinking it would be safe to venture into the pasture early in the morning, the farmer and his cow were hit by some shells or grenades and both were literally blown to bits. My father and Jānis crawled to look for the neighbor and I only learned that the farmer's body was never found. The details of the mangled body parts scattered in the field as a result of the direct hit were too gruesome for discussion.

It was impossible for me to keep track of time in the never-ending darkness of the shelter. Hours turned into days and days turned into night while we sat and sometimes dozed. The adults probably knew whether it was day or night and how many days and hours were spent underground. The sound of fighting went on and on. There were rumblings of machinery coming from the road and exploding shells overhead. One morning the trap door was suddenly ripped opened and Bolshevik reconnaissance soldiers were aiming guns into the shelter. They were shouting for everyone to come out for them to check if any German soldiers were hiding in the trench. Tatiana explained to them that there were only civilians hiding underground to protect their children until they are "liberated". Convinced that this woman speaking Russian must be on their side, the Soviet soldiers posed a further question,

"*Can you tell us where the Germans are? Which way did they go?*"

"*Nyet*", Tatiana responded with perfect coolness. "*We were sitting in the dark. You are the ones fighting the war. Should you not know where the enemy is?*"

The Russian advance patrol took off, not finding any German personnel on the farm, and everyone went back into the shelter as the fighting and shelling continued. Evidently the Germans must have won the subsequent skirmishes and recaptured the farmhouse. The next morning it was German soldiers who checked out the shelter to see if any Russian soldiers were entrenched there.

Whether the tension of being under attack brought on early labor nobody knew, but while everyone was still in the shelter, it became evident that the tenant's wife was about to deliver her child. Delivering a baby is not simple even in a hospital with experienced medical personnel in attendance. Assisting the mother to deliver her baby in damp and dark ditch with no supplies or instruments was traumatic for Tatiana who had no prior experience in midwifery. Fortunately, the baby came quickly without complications. She laid the child on top of the mother to keep it warm, but what to do with the cord still binding the baby to the mother! Nobody knew how to cut the cord, nor were any instruments available for cutting it. The only hope lay in getting help from the German medic at the farmhouse being used as field hospital. Tatiana and the tenant Jānis decided they would have to somehow get to the house. They did not want to risk running and getting hit by grenades like their neighbor. Inch by inch they crawled on their bellies until they reached the house. Tatiana tried her best explaining to the medic in German that a baby had been born in the shelter and that the umbilical cord needed cutting. She could not think of the term used for umbilical cord. She kept waving her arms as if pulling a string and said,

"Baby has string, baby has string. It needs cutting."

Somehow, the medic got the gist of the problem and some soldiers were ordered to take a litter to bring the mother and infant back to the house. The litter bearers managed to get the mother and baby back to the house without being hit. The medic had never delivered a baby either, but with my mother helping him, he thought he could manage cutting the umbilical cord. As they were leaning over the mother, a shell hit the house and a piece of shrapnel flew directly between the medic and Tatiana, missing both their heads by inches. Tatiana thanked God for protecting her and the medic as they were both helping the mother and the baby. She was convinced that it was God's hand or the hand of an angel that guided the shrapnel away from them. She kept the jagged piece of metal, measuring approximately six inches in length, as a sacred reminder of how God's hand works miracles. The shrapnel accompanied the Gedrovics family as a precious possession through all wanderings during the war years and across the ocean to the United States. It now resides with Tatiana's grandson Tim Sipols who has framed and preserved it as a sacred trophy.

As the fighting continued throughout August, it must have become apparent to the Germans that their weary and depleted troops would not be able to hold Livberze or any remaining strongholds in Zemgale with Jelgava and the surrounding towns already occupied by the Soviets. However, Hitler had given orders to hold the Baltic port of Riga at all costs. Along with any remaining German troops being ordered to make the last stand at Riga, the order was issued for all able-bodied civilians to leave Livberze to help defend Riga. The order was very clear–everyone was either to retreat along with the military or be shot as the Germans did not intend to leave any manpower behind for the Soviets.

Kārlis and Tatiana had no choice if they wanted to save their family from certain death. They decided to follow the order to evacuate to Riga as there they might still find refuge at the home of Tatiana's mother. Our family had to leave the farm in a hurry with little time to pack. It is amazing that my parents could make vital life-changing decisions in just a few moments while under great pressure. Somehow mother convinced the German officers to give back the farm horse they had appropriated so that the horse could pull the wagon with some of the family's most important belongings. As if having a premonition that this trip to Riga would be without a return, Kārlis and Tatiana again took only the two wooden trunks they had brought from Jelgava with their most important treasures, a couple of suitcases with the family's clothing, and enough food for the long journey along the back roads to Riga. The books and toys had to be left behind. I worried that my precious toys might get destroyed with the troops constantly running throughout the house. While the adults were busy loading the belongings into the wagon, I carefully wrapped my precious porcelain doll in the blanket my mother had made and packed it into a box along with a favorite book, a teddy bear, and the doll that Elita had given to me as a farewell present when we parted in Jelgava. The beautiful doll was all that I had left from my happy childhood and now I had to leave her as well. Taking care that nobody saw me, I carried the box up into the attic of the stone farmhouse and stashed it behind some rafters hoping that nobody would find my treasures in this hiding place until I could return when the war ends. It would remain forever unknown to me if somebody found my treasures for some other girl to enjoy or if they were destroyed during an attack. When my aunt Marta was able to visit Livberze several years after the war, only the fieldstone walls of he house were still standing. There was no trace of the roof, attic, or furniture remaining.

FAMILY TORN APART

At dawn on a cold and rainy day late in August, the wagon was loaded and ready to go. Little Mudite had a very high fever, having become ill during the cold and damp days in the trench shelter. To keep her warm, she was wrapped in a rose-colored blanket with a white pattern of flower vines, the same blanket that cocooned her on the way to the church in Jelgava for her baptism. The bundle with the sick toddler was carefully secured on top of the load, as she was too ill to walk or even sit up. Kārlis decided that his elderly mother would also ride on top of the wagon and wanted to help her climb up. At this moment Olga Gedrovics made a fateful decision that would haunt her children for the rest of their lives. The brave Olga, who as an orphan had raised her brother and had sustained her own five children through the hardships of World War I and widowhood, suddenly decided that at age seventy-six she would not become a refugee again. She and Aunt Līna had decided that they would stay on their own land no matter what the future held. Grandmother Olga ordered Kārlis to take her suitcase off the wagon and with anguished wailing pleaded with her son to hurry and leave with his family to keep them safe. She was convinced that nobody would shoot two old ladies if they stayed, since they were not able-bodied enough to help in defending Riga. As I gave her a last hug, I could feel grandma's frail body shivering under her coat, but she put on a brave face and ordered her son to leave with his family immediately. Grandma Olga's small figure, clad in a long black coat, slowly receded in the background. She stood in the rain and waved the last farewell to her son Kārlis and his family, as the horse pulled the wagon out of the muddy drive. It was a scene of utter desolation. The sky was dark and clouds were bursting with rain, as the family departed in tears. If Kārlis had known at that time that he would never see his mother again, perhaps the family's destiny would have taken a different twist. Would my parents have been shot and Mudite and I orphaned if Kārlis and Tatiana had also refused to leave their farm in Livberze?

It must have been an unspeakably traumatic decision for my father to decide between leaving his mother and saving his wife and children. Of course, at that time nobody knew that the parting, although painful, would be final. When Kārlis' sisters Marta and Zelma were taken back to Latvia in 1945 by the Soviets, who invaded East Germany where Zelma's physician husband had been ordered to work, they went to Livberze to look for their mother and brother's family. Someone gave them the news that Aunt Līna had died. Their mother Olga had been found in a traumatized state as she was walking alone along a country road carrying a suitcase. She was unable to tell anyone where her daughters and son were. When the suitcase was opened, it was found to be empty except for one photograph of her son Kārlis, apparently her only treasure. Olga was placed in an old people's home where she died alone before her daughters returned to Latvia. The image of his mother, walking alone with just his picture in her suitcase, broke Kārlis' heart when he received the news from his sisters a decade later after they found each other again with the help of the Red Cross. Kārlis and Tatiana placed a beautiful flower arrangement on the altar at St. Paul's Latvian Evangelical Lutheran Church in Detroit and had prayers said in memory of his departed mother. Kārlis never gave up hope that some day he might be able to be reunited with his sisters again, but he died one year before the Iron Curtain was lifted enough to allow people to return to Latvia without fear of being deported to Siberia.

On that dark rainy autumn-like day in late August of 1944, not knowing what God had planned for them in the future, the Gedrovics family trudged in the rain through the mud behind the horse-drawn wagon hoping to find refuge in Riga with Omi and Jānis Berzins. I remember feeling quite grown-up as I walked behind the wagon with my parents while my little sister rested on top of the bundles of what was left of the family's earthly goods. As a grown-up nine-year-old, I had been given the responsibility to herd the baby lambs and piglets we were taking along from the farm. These animals were later traded to farmers for milk and overnight shelter along the forty-kilometer route to Riga during the long, slow journey. The squealing piglets were quite a handful for me. With great frequency, the animals scattered and ran off into the woods or fields along the road. The piglets were quite adept at playing in their natural habitat in the mud while my boots were constantly sinking and getting stuck in the mud as I ran to catch the renegade piglets. The wind and rain whipped into my face as I rounded up the piglets. Soon my shoes filled with water and my coat became as covered with mud as the pig's underbellies while I struggled to carry them back to the rest of the herd. The family learned what the journey must have been like for Mary and Joseph on their way to Bethlehem. As in old Biblical times, there was "no room at any inn". Finding a place for the family and the weary horse to rest was a constant problem although in times of a severe crisis people generally were co-operative in sharing and helping each other. Firebombs had destroyed many of the farms along the way. At some others, the owners were themselves preoccupied with getting ready to flee and were unwilling to help others, or their farm was already filled with other refugees spending the night. The Gedrovics family felt lucky when we were put up in a barn or a hayloft by some old sympathizing farmer so we could dry out our wet clothing and rest during the cold nights.

After several days on the road, our family finally reached Riga on the first of September, but the safety of Omi's house was not meant to be. By the time we arrived in the city, Riga was also under aerial attack. There was a constant sound of air raid sirens and the whistle of bombs raining down on the city. Uncle Janka at age sixteen and his cousin Ilmars, age fifteen, had both been drafted to serve in the German civil air patrol. Both boys were sent for duty in Germany when it became evident that the Germans would have to retreat from Riga as well. I had always enjoyed staying in Omi's cozy and warm apartment. This time the family, along with all the other inhabitants of the apartment house, were crowded in the cold and damp basement, which served as a bomb shelter. There were no benches to rest upon like in the trench at Livberze. Everyone had to lie on the wet clay floor while the building shook as Riga was under air attack.

LEAVING RIGA, 1944

In October, the fall of Riga became imminent and again orders were given that all able-bodied people must leave Latvia for labor camps in Germany. Some Latvians decided to escape both the German labor camps and the advancing Russians by taking fishing boats across the Baltic Sea to Sweden. Among the refugees crossing the sea to Sweden were my father's cousin Anna Rasins, her husband, and daughter Ilona. My parents chose not to risk the dangerous voyage across the stormy sea and opted to take the travel passes for the last freight train of railroad workers going to railroad labor camps in Germany. This time there was no family mausoleum to hide Omi's treasures as there had been in Novocherkassk. The night before the train was to leave, everyone in the family was busy digging pits in the garden to bury Omi's silver, china, rolls of silk fabric, and furs in metal drums to protect the belongings from looters until the family could once again return to their home. But all the digging was in vain. The invading Soviet troops or local treasure hunters dug up all these countless "graves of treasures" that were buried in everyone's back yard. No doubt, Omi's family heirlooms still grace the homes of the invading looters. When it was time for the Gedrovics family to be loaded into the cattle cars that were to carry them to Germany, it was discovered that Tatiana's mother and stepfather were not included in the family pass. Having already suffered the traumatic experience of leaving Kārlis' mother behind in Livberze, Tatiana was determined to get a pass for her mother and her stepfather. As it was, we had already had a tearful parting from Omi's parents, my great-grandparents Tigulis, who refused to leave as they did not think they could survive the long, hard journey at their advanced age. Omi's sister Zelma decided to stay with the parents in Riga so that her son Ilmars could find her if he ever came home from Germany where he had been deployed with the civil air patrol.

With no time to lose before our freight train was scheduled to leave, my mother rushed up the hill to where the German Commander's headquarters was located.

She paid no heed to the armed guard stationed outside as he yelled, "Halt!" and rushed into the Commander's office to plead for a pass on the last train for her parents. The surprised commander asked the guard why this excited woman was rushing into his office without permission. The guard answered, "*Sie ist eine verrueckte Frau!*", she is a crazy woman. Impressed by Tatiana's passion, daring, and fearlessness, the Commander granted the passes for her parents to take the railroad workers train with only minutes to spare before the last train left Riga.

It was October 13, 1944. This was the day of my father's forty-first birthday. Kārlis' present that day was that his family was saved. Shortly after the train pulled out, Riga was invaded by the Soviets. Nobody on the train had even the slightest inkling that the passes for the train were irrevocably one-way. Hundreds of thousands Latvians left their homeland in 1944 and fled westward. Approximately 150,000 left by ship to Germany while some five thousand people in small boats risked their lives on the stormy Baltic Sea to flee to Sweden.[22] Our fateful odyssey, like that of my ancestors was by rail. At the time, everyone thought that Latvia would be free again after the war, but there would be no return trip back home to Latvia for most of the departing families. The beautiful striped burgundy-white-burgundy flag would not wave over Latvia for over four decades and by then circumstances would make it too late for most of us to start a new home all over again.

My dream of returning home was obliterated by still-existing nightmares of the fear-driven Soviet regime when my mother and I set foot on Latvian soil again in 1989. My fatherland welcomed us with fragrant spring blossoms and its natural beauty shone just like I remembered it, but the large contingent of Russian-speaking people and military forces in evidence everywhere made me feel like I was in hostile territory instead of my home country.

★★★

20
FIRST HOMECOMING TO LATVIA, 1989

When the Soviet regime let down some of its barriers and the breakup of its dictatorship began in 1989, people finally felt less afraid to visit Latvia though restrictions for tourist travel still followed very stringent rules. Though many brave souls had visited Latvia in some earlier years, still no tourist from the Western world was allowed to travel independently within the countries occupied by the Soviets. All travel had to be under the direction of the official Soviet government controlled INTOURIST agency. My nephew Tim Sipols was part of the orchestra of a theater group going to Latvia to perform the play "Tango Lugano" through a cultural exchange program. Though mother was still very much concerned about our safety in a Soviet-occupied country, my sister and I persuaded her to join Tim's INTOURIST group with me going along as her travel companion. At long last at age 77, she summoned her amazing courage again to carry out her and my father's wish to be reunited with his only sister after forty-five years of living in exile, separated from our extended Latvian family. I had become a fifty-five-year-old married woman and grandmother when I returned to the childhood dreams I had lost at the age of nine.

On May 9, 1989, after some complicated maneuvers to obtain the required passports and visas, mother and I left Detroit Metro Airport via Pan Am for New York JFK Airport. No porters were available at the airport to help us maneuver our great load of luggage. We each carried more pieces of luggage going back to Latvia than our entire family had taken out of the country in our hasty departure forty-five years ago. Since everything was in short supply in Latvia, we were bringing along all sorts of medicines requested by my aunt's family, clothing for everyone, cosmetic supplies for the ladies, toys for the children, and gifts for our hosts in addition to our personal items. If anyone had really checked our suitcases, we would have had to do a great deal of explaining about our multiple alleged ailments that the medicines were to cure. We had heard that Soviet Customs only allowed limited quantities of any item brought in for personal use. To reduce the number of like items in our suitcases, we decided to wear several layers of clothing when entering Soviet territory the next day and made sure that the medicine and cosmetics were distributed evenly among our many pieces of luggage so that nothing would be obvious in large quantities. The eclectic wardrobe I brought along ranged from children's clothing to dressy women's garments, and men's shirts and jeans in a wide range of larger sizes. My explanation for the larger sizes would have been the expectation that I might have a significant weight gain from enjoying the delicious Latvian food!

Apparently our flight across the Atlantic was to be as stormy as our initial coming to America. The morning brought pouring rain to last the entire day and our flight was delayed due to rough weather. Tim, who was getting his Master's degree at Columbia University and lived in New York City at the time, joined mother and me at the airport and we were able to change our assigned seats to be together, as many passengers missed the flight due to delayed connections. The overnight transatlantic flight was comfortable and we even got to lie down in the empty adjoining seats. This was perhaps the shortest night I had ever experienced. It got dark around 10:00 P.M. and with changing time zones, dawn began to rise an hour later. I opted out of watching the movie shown on the plane during the trip. It seemed that "A Cry in the Night" would just bring back memories of the many cries in the night that had filled the air during our long odyssey through military occupation, war, and endless days as refugees.

After a fifteen-minute stop on Swedish soil in Stockholm, our plane headed for Helsinki. My heart seemed to jump into my throat as the Baltic Sea finally came into my line of vision. Our flight plan required an overnight stay in Helsinki. A Union Tour representative working in cooperation with INTOURIST met us and thirteen other Latvians at the airport and efficiently got us registered at the "Tower" or Torni Hotel. We were assigned a beautiful modern room, which was furnished with down comforters on the beds and luxurious cosmetics in the tile bathroom complete with a bidet. At dinner our entire group was entertained with piano and violin music. Mother was rather exhausted after the long flight and wanted to rest, but Tim and I decided to sacrifice sleep so that we could see most of the important sights in Helsinki. We spent several hours in the afternoon, evening, and the next morning literally running from place to place to see this interesting cosmopolitan city and to sample its Scandinavian delicacies.

Invigorated by the excitement of the homeward journey, Tim and I climbed the one hundred steps to the Dom, the oldest Catholic Cathedral on top of the hill near the Helsinki University. The Helsinki Cathedral had a magnificent organ and we were anxious to compare it to the famous organ at the Riga Dom Cathedral. We enjoyed a beautiful view from the oldest Russian church with its golden domes and then headed for the Helsinki harbor with its famous open-air market. The stalls were filled with exquisite flowers, all sorts of high-quality fruit and countless varieties of seafood. The following morning we were treated to at a sumptuous Scandinavian breakfast buffet at the Torni Hotel. The buffet tables were overflowing with all sorts of cold meats, cheeses, baked goods, eggs, fresh and cooked fruit compotes, hot and cold cereals, coffee cakes, a variety of juices and beverages, and my favorites— herring in sour cream and cucumber salad with fresh dill! I really felt stuffed as I dressed for the ferry ride with multiple layers of clothing I was bringing for my cousins. I managed to wrestle into three T-shirts from American sports teams, a pair of slacks, two pairs of blue jeans, a sweater, a windbreaker, and a jacket. I hoped that I would be able to stay on the deck in order not to suffocate from heat and that my cousins would not laugh at my padded rigid look as I waddled off the ship looking like an overstuffed obese mannequin. At last we boarded the bus that took us to the Estonian ferry *Georg Ots for* crossing the Baltic Sea to Tallinn.

Mother and I crossing the Baltic Sea by ferry "Georg Ots" from Finland to Estonia 1989

During the three-hour trip on the ferry, we felt joy in seeing the waters of our beloved Baltic Sea glistening all around and caressing the boat with gentle waves. The dour faces of the personnel in the ship's dining room, however, gave us a glimpse of Soviet hospitality, or lack of it. It seemed that the INTOURIST agency had failed to make reservations for a table for our Latvian group of sixteen although lunch was included in the tour package. The headwaiter marched us to a table where a group of sixteen people were already seated to convince us that the table was already taken and we could not be seated. Being American citizens, we had learned to stand up for our rights. Our entire group then resolutely marched to the ship's information counter to resolve the problem. We were informed that we could only be served if someone in the group would sign the check as security that there would be reimbursement from Union Tours or INTOURIST. A correspondent traveling from Chicago signed the check and our group was served a delicious lunch at one of several empty tables in the ship's restaurant. According to Soviet logic, it seemed that no reservations were needed except for the one table for sixteen that the waiter showed us was already taken. Union Tours showed that they care for their clients and graciously refunded the cost of the lunch when our group returned to Helsinki to make up for the INTOURIST oversight in making reservations.

Our excitement mounted as the shores of Estonia emerged on the horizon. We felt a certain kinship with our sister country to the North. Almost home, but then we saw countless Soviet warships anchored in what we assumed to be a Soviet Navy base in Tallinn, the capital of Estonia. We were on our beloved Amber Sea and the dunes on shore were Baltic sand, but the joyous feeling of coming home was tempered by the evidence that foreign troops still occupied the Baltic countries and the red flag with the hammer and sickle still flew over our Latvia and its sister countries where the people lived in oppression and fear.

CONTROL BY FEAR AND INTIMIDATION

When our ship docked in Tallinn, luggage was unloaded first so that the Customs' dogs could carry out their duties of sniffing for contraband. Next, tourists with Soviet passports were allowed to disembark and only then were the Latvian "foreigners" allowed to find their luggage on the dock where porters had the suitcases arranged on their carts. People who had previous travel experience to Latvia had given us advice on the art of passing through Customs the Soviet way. If we showed American currency to the porter holding our suitcases, we would be directed to a "friendly" Custom's agent who would process us more expediently without searching the luggage. Mother was afraid to speak in Russian because she still feared of being identified as one of their citizens and arrested for defecting. She quietly slipped the porter two twenty-dollar bills for handling our luggage. Apparently the sum pleased him as dollars had high purchasing power for scarce commodities. He gave us the biggest smile and led us to a Customs agent who gave us the only other smile we would see on a Russian's face for the next two weeks. It seemed that people rarely smiled in a Soviet land. We were waved through to the next agent who carefully looked at our passport photos and then scrutinized our faces to make sure they matched the photos. Our names were then checked against a list of "Undesirable Persons" who were not to be let into the Soviet Union. We had a brief scare when the official who checked the list identified Tim as a possible suspect because of the rather common "Sipols" surname appearing on the list of undesirables. Another official cleared Tim when the birth data on the list did not match.

At last we were released to the area where our Latvian family members were waiting for us with armloads of flowers. They had all traveled for over three hours to Estonia to greet us. My oldest cousin Aris was delayed, but there stood dear Zigurds whom I had last seen as a little toddler with his arms open wide and his wife Sandra along with their daughter Agnes waving flowers. My cousin Edite was shedding cascades of tears just like mother and I. Her daughter Ilze, husband Normunds and little son Kristaps also embraced us with warm hugs although we had never met before, but the feeling of kinship and love filled us all. We were all overflowing with happiness over this reunion and were anxiously waiting for cousin Aris who was to be our official host and had the permits required for us to stay at his home rather than the INTOURIST hotel.

Our joy evaporated in just a few minutes when the controlling Soviet arm of the INTOURIST guide reached out to us and ordered us to get on her bus to Riga immediately. We informed her that we had permission to stay with Dr. Aris Lācis. The woman, Mrs. V., stuck to her guns saying that our names were on her list and that all people who obtained their entry visas through INTOURIST had to be on her bus and accounted for. Zigurds intervened and appealed to the Estonian INTOURIST representative at the airport. She had no objections to us waiting for the arrival of Aris with the proper permits. Mrs. V., the Latvian guide, however, was not at all sympathetic to our situation. She had our names on her list and she was not about to return to Riga without us on her bus. Apparently she feared being reprimanded for allowing some tourists to leave the tightly monitored and restricted group. Just as the bus was pulling out of the parking lot, we saw Aris and his wife Aija in their car going in the opposite direction. Mrs. V. refused to stop the bus so that the matter could be resolved.

I was furious with Mrs. V.'s actions and continued to argue with her that mother and I had every right to be with our family. Only Tim had made arrangements to register at the tourist hotel with the rest of the theatre group. We were informed that Tim actually was supposed to take a train from Tallinn to Riga with another guide to join the theatre group and that she was allowing him on her bus only "out of the goodness of her heart" so that our family could be together. Mrs. V. then made the announcement that all persons on the bus had to turn over their passports to her for registering at the hotel. I absolutely refused to relinquish our American passports to anyone, as Aris had already registered us with the Police Department as required if anyone housed guests in their home. Meanwhile my mother was literally shaking from fear and kept saying that we will be sent to Siberia for sure if I kept arguing with the guide.

I knew that I had to keep my arguments at a low level so that I would not be considered an enemy of the state. I "respectfully" informed the stubborn woman that she was ruining my cousin's plans for our welcome and that I was certain that she was acquainted with this famous surgeon who would not be pleased that she forcefully detained his special guests. My cousins had all driven to Tallinn from Riga for several hours to welcome us. Zigurds had informed me that Aris had planned a special surprise reunion dinner for us at one of Tallinn's best restaurants. The owner of the restaurant had come in especially to meet Aris' American family and had hired special waiters for the private party. All this was ruined through totalitarian bureaucratic illogical roadblocks put up by the INTOURIST guide. It passed through my mind that perhaps the special waiters the owner of the restaurant had to bring in were really some secret police required to make sure that none of us "dangerous enemies of the state" escaped with some top-secret Soviet recipes!

The INTOURIST bus stopped when we reached the Latvian border where a large wall made of stone had "LATVIJA" engraved in large letters. At this moment my anger over our "detainment" dissipated and tears began to flow as we were allowed to step off the bus to set foot on the soft Latvian sand dunes for the first time. However, Mrs. V. brought us back to the harsh realization that this was not meant to be a sentimental moment. We had stopped for a rest break under the cover of the pines. Rest areas with proper facilities were unheard of in Soviet Latvia at that time. Travelers had to take cover in roadside woods and brush to take care of their needs.

"Men go left into the pine woods, women go right. Watch where you step and be back on the bus in five minutes."

Mother and I managed to hurry further down the dunes so that we could actually touch our beloved Amber Sea and gather some of the white sand into small plastic bags we had brought along to take back to the United States as a sacred memento of our homeland. Mrs. V. had no control over the pines softly waving their branches to welcome us or to keep the waves from rushing to the shore to touch our hands as if to say "Sveiki". We also filled our cache of memories with the sweet smell of the linden trees and lilacs blooming along the roadside. People had changed during our long years of absence from the seashore, but the sea and its surrounding nature had remained constant and as beautiful as we remembered.

It was late in the evening when the bus finally reached the Hotel Latvija. Aris was waiting for us at the entrance. When Mrs. V. saw his face, she broke out in a big smile and extended her hand in the familiar greeting, *"Sveiki, Dr. Lācis!"* She informed my cousin that she had taken extra care in making sure his guests arrived safely! Of course she knew Aris as I had suspected, she just did not want to take the words of a stranger that he would be our host. What a pitiful society to live in where one is afraid to trust anyone's word and people suffer great inconveniences because of it. Mrs. V. immediately invited us to have dinner at the Hotel Latvija as her guests. We took her up on her offer as we felt she owed us for ruining Aris' plans. I had not anticipated how embarrassing it would be to walk through the luxurious dining room where other guests were dressed quite formally for the late evening dinner hour. Everyone turned around to stare at the group of us outrageously dressed Americans. The local female guests were clad in glamorous cocktail dresses while I looked overstuffed in my multiple layers of T-shirts and bulky men's jeans and jackets. Latvian women never wore jeans in those days. Vive la difference!

LOVE AND TEARS

At last we arrived at Aris' apartment where more family members were waiting to welcome us with armloads of flowers and a lavish table full of refreshments. Aris and Aija lived in a Soviet-built grey apartment house much like American tenement buildings. Although the building looked unkempt, their elegant two-bedroom apartment with a tiny kitchen was professionally decorated with wallpaper, oil paintings, shiny inlaid wood floors, and bookcases that took up entire walls. Latvians characteristically are lovers of books and one can find bookcases prominently lining the walls in nearly any home, no matter how small.

Everyone in the family was incredibly nice and warm and welcomed us like long lost prodigal daughters. The hugs and tears as well as the brandy were flowing freely making up for the forty-five years of separation. Perhaps living under the Soviets had hardened many of the people, but the love we had inherited from our mutual ancestors had kept our family ties strong and indestructible. There was so much catching up to do and we stayed up until dawn trying to fill the gap of the past decades. It was interesting to note the family resemblances in looks, sense of humor and personal characteristics exhibited by my cousins' families and my own sons. Though an ocean apart and never having met, the families living on both sides of the ocean shared interesting parallels.

We were all too excited to sleep and were up early the next morning. Aija, also a doctor by profession, was an incredible hostess and had prepared a sumptuous breakfast. Before we could start on the day's adventures, Aris had to go to the police station to report our arrival at his home. This time I was willing to give him my passport so that I could be officially registered at his residence. The main event for the day was the emotional reunion with Aris' mother, my father's youngest sister who is my godmother. She lived with my cousin Edite and daughter Ilze's family in an apartment house identical to Aris' just a few blocks away. Aunt Zelma was getting so anxious to see us that she started to call on the phone before we were even dressed for the day and had a chance to sort out all the gifts we had brought along. Aris teased that it looked like his apartment had been taken over by foreign invaders. Indeed every surface was covered with piles of gifts for the close to thirty family members and their in-laws we expected to meet.

Zelma was leaning out of the fifth-floor apartment window and waving to us when we walked into the courtyard of the apartment complex. Meeting my dear godmother was a breathtaking experience perhaps partly due to the five flights of stairs we had to climb or the excitement of a cherished dream becoming reality. Mother and I greeted Zelma with hugs and tears and it was a long time before any of us could speak as we were overcome by emotion. Although I had grown to be some three inches taller than her, Aunt Zelma held me in her arms and kept whispering, *"Mazā Skaidrite…Little Skaidrite…Little Skaidrite"*. When I gave her a golden cross as a gift, she immediately asked that I fasten the chain around her neck and announced that she will wear it always, especially when her time comes to meet the Lord. Aunt Zelma, my beautiful godmother, at age eighty-eight was also still very much interested in keeping up her appearance. She picked out an eyebrow pencil and some lipsticks from my cosmetics supply and asked that we apply the make-up to her face immediately so that she would look her best on the photos we took. Her great-grandson Kristaps was still clutching the little metal car I had given him the previous evening when we first met. Edite told me that he had insisted on sleeping in the jeans' outfit I had given him. The jacket had many pockets and three-year-old Kristaps said, *"Now I look like a real man"*. When I gave him a yellow slicker to wear in the rain, he quickly put it on and baring his teeth snarled, *"Now I will be a yellow wolf!"* Yellow wolves fascinated Kristaps at this age and "Yellow Wolf" became my nickname for him in subsequent years.

FELLOWSHIP, LOVE, AND TEARS REMAIN

The next few days were spent in a whirlwind of activity. My cousins tried to show us all the places that had been dear to us and all the places where their extended family lived. A feast awaited us at every home we visited. Though no supermarkets existed and the smaller specialty stores like bakeries, dairies, and meat markets were largely empty of supplies, my cousins had managed through personal connections to procure all the food for welcoming us. It was wonderful to feast on favorite Latvian home cooking utilizing natural ingredients. Sorrel soup, cucumber and tomato salad, potatoes flavored with dill, and pork or chicken cooked in a variety of ways were on nearly every menu capped off with magnificent tortes or custard puddings with fruit. It seemed that my cousins had compiled a list of my favorite foods from my old letters where I sometimes mentioned the Latvian things I missed the most. They had taken great pains of preparing the foods and desserts that had been my childhood favorites. If I mentioned any food that I had liked in my childhood, it appeared at the next meal! On one occasion I mentioned that I like "Šprotes" or Sprats sardines, which are a specialty product of Latvia. The next morning Edite presented a can of Sprats among the breakfast selections. After dinner the previous night, my dear cousin had walked through the rain to a store several blocks away to bring back the treat for me.

Strawberries were in season during our visit and huge bowls of the lush red berries greeted us with their exquisite aroma at every home. The taste of home-grown Latvian strawberries can only be described as heavenly. Their taste and aroma is superior to any strawberries grown anywhere else in the world. Perhaps it is the rich soil, the sea air, or the longer daylight hours that make the berries sweeter and more flavorful. I have picked fresh strawberries in Michigan, Florida, and California but nowhere have they been as grand as the ones grown in Aris' garden at his cottage in the seaside resort town of Saulkrasti and other Latvian gardens.

On our first outing Aris took us to the beautiful Jūrmala where we enjoyed walking along the seashore with all three of our cousins. Getting there was rather complicated due to Soviet regulations. People were not allowed to drive to certain seashore towns unless they received a special permit from guards at checkpoints on some roads leading to the sea. There was strict control over the number of vehicles that could be driven anywhere on the seashore. Even residents had to present their permits and state the reason for entering a controlled zone. The return trip was supposed to be along the same route so that the permits could be turned back in at the entry control checkpoint to make sure people did not remain in the beach area overnight. Allegedly the controls were in place to prevent traffic congestion in the protected dune area. To my suspicious nature it seemed that the controls were in place to keep people away from various navy bases and military installations. It was oppressive to realize how many restrictive Soviet rules people had to worry about. Aris had no difficulty in getting a permit to enter the beach area. He was known at the checkpoints because of his frequent trips for medical consultations. Fortunately we were not detained and had miles of the beach nearly all to ourselves.

The day was beautiful and sunny with puffs of white clouds in the blue skies. The sea, however, was not like I had remembered it. Instead of clear blue water all the way to the horizon and white waves breaking on shore, the Baltic Sea in the Bay of Riga looked cloudy and brown as if it no longer was alive. Signs at some beach areas warned of polluted water. I bent down to pick up a pebble to throw into the water, but Aris grabbed my hand and warned me not to pick up anything on the beach. Not only was some industrial waste being dumped into the sea, the fallout from the nuclear accident at Chernobyl had also reached the Baltic region. Some yellow nuclear particles resembling amber were dangerous to touch and could cause serious burns to the skin. No wonder we could see no bathers in the water on such a warm day. Instead of splashing in the water, it had become customary for people to promenade on the beach on Sundays in particular. Instead of wearing beach clothing, everyone was dressed in their Sunday clothes and formally walked along the packed sand as if on parade. We saw many Soviet officers and generals promenading on the beach dressed in parade uniforms and showing off rows of medals on their chests. I wanted to scream at these Soviet invaders who had robbed me of not only my homeland but had also managed to pollute even the beautiful sea. Fortunately the sea has returned to its grand state since Latvia's independence was re-established and people can again enjoy swimming in its waters.

Another day Aris drove through Riga on Brīvības (Freedom) Street and the Vanšu Bridge over the Daugava River to reach Zaslauki where my mother had lived with Omi and Janka. We found mother's girlhood home where she lived with her grandparents at 75 Kalnciema Street still standing though it looked sad with all the paint gone from the weathered wood siding. Gone were also the chestnut trees along the fence from which my mother and her brother Adrian had pelted passersby with chestnuts. We walked through the familiar streets to 95 Mazā Nometņu Street where Mr. Berzins and Omi's apartment house still stood. People still lived in the apartments that Mother was entitled to claim as the only living heir of the owners before the property was nationalized by the Soviets. I would not have recognized the building if the street number had not been on it. There were stains on the stucco walls, there was damage to the roof, and the flower gardens and shrubbery had disappeared from the large back yard where now only bare clay ground and weeds remained and cars were haphazardly parked everywhere.

The inside of the building had also been neglected. The shiny marble stairway where my heels had once made such a nice clicking sound had been patched or replaced by cement tiles, which felt dirty and sticky. An elderly Russian lady in a third floor apartment remembered my mother and was moved to tears to meet her again. She showed us the apartment where mother's aunt Maria had lived. The apartment was vacant at the time and, except for some crumbling plaster, had not changed from how I remembered it. Forty-five years ago it had been considered a contemporary apartment with modern plumbing, but now it seemed cramped and lacking today's modern utilities. All the apartments still had cooking stoves, hot water tanks, and heating units that used wood for fuel. The toilet tanks were fastened high on the wall and a chain had to be pulled to flush the toilet. It made me appreciate all the work that had been required for my parents and grandparents just to keep the family warm and fed day in and day out. Like in all the old pre-war buildings, there was no elevator and all the wood had to be carried up the stairs from the woodsheds in the back yard. All the tenants who had lived in the building for the past half a century under Soviet government management were used to the circumstances and stoically just considered the lack of central heat and hot water a part of daily living. For my mother and me came the sad realization that at our age we would find it difficult if not impossible if we had to return to her "homestead" to cope with all the labor-intensive home maintenance chores and the shortages in every conceivable category of goods and services. Even if mother would be willing to leave Mudite and me and our American families behind to claim her parents' apartment, her health would never allow her to manage the complicated daily living requirements on her own.

Jelgava, my hometown, was closed to tourist travel. However, I was not to be deterred by senseless regulations. We found a driver who was willing to take mother and me on a quick clandestine tour of Jelgava. He had grown up in the same town and was familiar with all the places of interest. As a Soviet citizen he was allowed to travel everywhere in the area without a special permit. He reasoned that if we were stopped for any reason, he would not be required to carry a passport. Thus, he saw no reason why mother and I would have to volunteer showing our passports. We just had to remain silent so that our "American accent" would not be noted if we allowed him to do the talking. Our driver cautioned us that we would only stop briefly at each point of interest and should not talk in order not to attract attention. The warning was not necessary, as I found it difficult to speak while my tears flowed freely all the time we walked in the footsteps we had left behind forty-five years ago.

Mother and I visited the Zanders Cemetery to pay respects to our departed family members. The family plot looked well cared for as graves in Latvia are constantly kept raked and planted with flowers. My cousins had retained an elderly lady to take care of the graves of our ancestors on a regular basis. The bench on the Gedrovics plot was still in place but the monument my father had put up when his father died had disappeared. Again it was time for tears as I remembered the painful image of my grandmother bent over in sorrow at her daughter Olga's funeral and the last memory of her as she stood in the rain and waved her final farewell to us as our family had to leave Livberze at the start of our refugee journey.

We drove by the Jelgava railroad station, which had been rebuilt according to its original plans. The windows and the clock on top of the building looked familiar, but the exterior of the building was made of yellow stucco material instead of the red brick I remembered. I silently thanked God for saving my father's life when the station was destroyed by the Soviets and also added a little prayer for my dear Papuks to look down from heaven to see mother and me returning to the family and places we had all loved.

Our last stop was on Vaļņu Street where our family had lived. Amazingly, my favorite corner store had survived the colossal fire that had leveled a great part of the city. The building sported new windows, but the entrance was exactly where I remembered it. The store now sold garden supplies instead of groceries. We could not go inside since we were not supposed to even be in town. The St. Nicholas church had been totally destroyed and had been replaced by apartment buildings, but the church park was exactly as I remembered it with the pathways where they had always stood. Lilacs still bloomed and children were playing in a large sandbox where I had built my sand castles in my childhood. Only now the sandbox was built of modern plastic material instead of the old weathered wood sides. Some additional playground toys also surrounded the sandbox. We knew that our apartment house had been consumed by fire, as had all the other houses on our block. Our house had been rebuilt according to the original architectural plans except for the front courtyard gateway, which had been replaced by wide entrance doors and no longer allowed access to the back yard. The building no longer housed apartments but was used as a kindergarten and pre-school. I felt as if I had traveled back into my past when I saw a girl looking through what had been our living room window. For just a brief flash it felt like I was looking at my own reflection in the glass.

We walked silently along the familiar paths, each of us immersed in memories. I was glad that the piles of human skeletons and the trenches dug for bomb shelters had long disappeared from view and that children's voices filled the air again. Careful not to speak too loudly, I mentioned to my mother that on the one hand some things like the cobblestone street, the old pathways and the sandbox had remained the same, but that familiar landscapes like the church had disappeared forever. Apparently my comment was overheard by a man I had not noticed sitting on one of the park benches. He stood up and addressed me directly in a loud voice.

"Let me tell you girl how the dirty dogs changed and destroyed our park where we played as children!"

The woman sitting with the man told him to hush up and not start any trouble. She was probably afraid that the man might say something critical of the controlling Soviet regime. We walked away in silence, afraid of getting involved in a conversation since we could be arrested for visiting a town that was off-limits to tourists. I kept wondering if the man who appeared to be of my age had perhaps been one of the boys from our apartment house. It would have been wonderful to chat with him about the past, but again the fear of Soviet might and dictatorial tactics stopped any friendly conversation that would have occurred in any free country welcoming back a returning daughter. Latvians still had to live in fear of saying anything in a public place that could be construed as being anti-government. Perhaps that was the reason for not seeing smiles on anyone's face and people not returning greetings. We silently returned to the car and mother and I again left Jelgava with tears in our eyes just like we had in 1944.

HAPPY MEMORIES

In the next few days Aris managed to take us on a whirlwind tour to visit his sons Aigars and Andis and their families in their apartments. Everywhere we went we were greeted with warm hugs just as if we had always lived together as a close family. The fact that we had been separated by an ocean for nearly half a century and had never met in person before did not seem to lessen the feeling of family kinship. The grandchildren were also very friendly and loving and greeted us as if we had always been their favorite aunts. It was delightful to watch how well behaved they all were and that they all were at an intellectual level well beyond their chronological age. Andis' daughters Liene and Zane performed little dances and recitations to welcome us. When we parted the children wanted to know *"When will we see you again?"* It was so difficult to answer such a simple question. It had taken us forty-five years to return to our homeland. Nobody could tell when the next time would be or predict whether the Soviet government would once again impose tighter controls on entering the country.

One more tearful reunion was in store for us as we were reunited with my mother's aunt, Zelma Rutendarzs, who at this time was nearly ninety years old. Great-aunt Zeļa as she was nicknamed was the mother of my beloved uncle Janka's cousin Ilmars. Again tears flowed as we embraced this dear aunt whose only remaining relative was my mother. Her only son Ilmars died shortly after the war in Germany after contracting tuberculosis in a POW camp. Aunt Zeļa lived with the family of the daughter of her dearest friend. When the friend died, the daughter Ausma Valtners and her husband Professor Arnolds Valtners and their daughter Dr. Anda Jansone accepted Aunt Zeļa into their apartment as a member of their family and treated her like a beloved grandmother. My mother reciprocated by accepting Ausma and Anda as our family members and had been sending parcels from the United States to fill some of their needs. The Valtners' lived on the eighth floor in a drab Russian-built behemoth apartment house where the elevator shook and rattled and frequently was out of order. The hallways of the building showed

Skaidrite and Great-Aunt Zeļa at Skulte, 1989

signs of vandalism, but inside the apartment was clean, tastefully decorated and contained several walls of shelves filled with books.

Aunt Zeļa had a very bright mind and a positive spirit and we spent many hours reminiscing together. I learned a great deal from her about my great-grandparents as well as my Omi's life prior to the Russian Revolution when she was married to Theodor Petrovs. Aunt Zeļa also shared amusing stories about my mother's childhood and the antics they participated in together. Apparently this aunt never lost the sparkle in her blue eyes or the joy of a child in her heart despite the tragedies she suffered. Anda's little daughter Elina apparently found Aunt Zeļa to be her best friend, co-conspirator and storyteller extraordinaire. More tears flowed as we had to bid good-bye to the dear aunt, the only remaining relative on my mother's side of the family. Aunt Zeļa tried to break up the tension of the moment by joking that we did not need to add to the moisture in the air as it was raining outside. She cautioned us to try to stay dry. When I mentioned that we would use our umbrellas, Aunt Zeļa laughingly remarked that she had not owned an umbrella for forty-five years. Apparently an umbrella was a scarce commodity in Latvia. Mother and I left our umbrellas for Aunt Zeļa. We promised that we would return to celebrate Aunt Zeļa's one-hundredth birthday but this was not in God's plan. She died from a head injury sustained in a fall just three months from the century milestone. Before we parted, Aunt Zeļa gave Tim a gift of one hundred rubles for spending money on the continuing portion of his trip to Moscow and an antique history book to read on the way. The Soviet regime saw to it that Tim would not be able to enjoy the generous gifts as the book and rubles were confiscated as "forbidden contraband" by Customs agents. Perhaps some trumped up reason could be found for not taking a Latvian book into Russia but where is the logic of not being able to carry the official monetary unit of rubles from Soviet Latvia to Soviet Russia?

Ausma and Anda took my mother and me to the Pleskadale cemetery, which was near where mother had lived with Omi on Kalnciema Street. It was very painful for my mother to return to this site where her dear brother Adrian was buried. The grave of Maria Berzins, the sister of mother's stepfather was also located nearby. Ausma had very thoughtfully brought along flowers so that mother and I could put them on the family graves. The Valtners family had continued to care for the graves throughout the years out of love and respect for Aunt Zeļa's family. The area surrounding the graves was planted with flowers and the gravel pathways were carefully weeded and raked so that they would not be marred by footsteps. This was a sentimental and sad pilgrimage to be reunited in spirit with loved ones who will live on in our hearts forever.

Another occasion that affected my mother and me deeply was a visit to meet Sandra's mother whom I only got to know by the endearing family nickname "Mims". Mims was in her eighties when we met and still sharp and with a cheerful heart as most of the courageous Latvian women who had survived untold tragedies. Mims lived on the fifth floor of an apartment house with a beautiful pre-war architectural design. The rooms had high coved plaster ceilings and large windows, but the building had been severely neglected by the Soviet government landlords and was in a state of disrepair. The elevators had long been vandalized and out of service. No light bulbs were in the light fixtures and we had to negotiate the stairs by feeling our way. It boggled our minds to imagine how an old person with arms full of groceries could climb five flights of stairs in the darkness as a daily trial. In contrast, Mims' apartment was neat and clean and was decorated with beautiful hand-made items and the usual large book collection that was evident in all Latvian homes we visited. In one corner of the small living room was Mim's pride and joy, her piano. She still played it daily. As her work-worn hands nimbly danced over the keyboard, she entertained us by playing several classical as well as folk tunes. The repertoire stored in her memory seemed to be limitless as she played without the need to read music scores.

We were welcomed as old friends and Mims and my mother seemed to bond instantly as they discussed common experiences from their youth, love for their families, and their love for music. I was deeply moved to observe this amazing woman who despite all the hardships of daily living still could be so gracious and show a genuine zest for living through her smile. The only inconvenience for which Mims apologized was the lack of water pressure at the end of the day in the upper floors. When all the people were home from work, the water pressure was too weak to reach the fifth floor. Some days there was no water at all. Mims kept the bathtub filled with the brownish water and had to dip from the tub with a bucket to obtain water for washing and flushing the toilet. I was in a state of wonder about the fortitude of women like Mims, Aunt Zeļa, and my own brave mother whose lives had taken infinite twists and turns under adverse circumstances and yet they had not lost their inner joy and viewed life as being full of possibilities. I was compelled to discourage my mother from even considering returning to live in the Berzins' apartment house she was entitled to reclaim. After all the hardships in her life, my mother was entitled to live out her days in the relative comforts of her home in the United States in the midst of her own daughters' families.

Some other excursions, not as poignant, were a joyful respite from all the tears and sadness of being reunited and then having to part again from loved ones. We spent a delightful day visiting the Open Air Museum with Zigurds and Sandra where historic buildings and craftsmen represent life in earlier times, much like Greenfield Village in Dearborn, Michigan. It was also a treat for the entire family to explore the ruins of the legendary Turaida fortress, which was in the process of being restored. Little Kristaps volunteered to lead me on an interesting climb on the massive walls made of stone for a spectacular view of the Gauja River in the valley below.

Riga, which is known as a cultural capital of Europe, is the home of a magnificent opera house and multiple major theatres. Aris made sure that we got to attend all the theatre and opera performances while we were his guests. One of the performances we attended was a modern rock version of the musical "Lāčplēsis", or

Bear Fighter, which was a modernized version of an old tale with political overtones about a Latvian warrior tearing apart bears, allegedly referring to the attacking Russian bears. Aris had managed to get tickets in the first row of the sports arena, which was the venue for the concert. The entire place was packed.

The next evening it was a treat to go to the Dailes Theatre to see the play "Tango Lugano" performed by the theatre group of Latvians from New York with Tim playing in the pit orchestra. The audience was very receptive of the visiting troupe and gave multiple ovations, hearty applause, and participated in singing at the end of the play. As it is customary in Latvia, many of the patrons brought armloads of flowers to present to the actors and even Tim and the orchestra members received several bouquets. Another delightful evening was spent at the Riga Opera House at the ballet performance of "Giselle". The interior of the Opera House is very ornate. The gilded decorations reminded me somewhat of the Fox Theatre in Detroit. The Opera House was scheduled to close for nearly a decade for a complete restoration to its original magnificence. Aris was surprised to hear that I had attended very few opera and ballet performances during my lifetime as such events are quite costly in America. In Latvia cultural and musical events are priced very reasonably to be within reach of the average citizen. It seemed to me that Aris and Aija attended concerts, opera, ballet, and the theatre at least once a week in Riga, the European capital of culture.

We also had the opportunity to hear the magnificent organ at the Riga Dom Cathedral. The organ was built in Ludwigsburg, Germany in 1883 by Walcker & Co.. The organ has 127 registers and 6768 pipes with the longest being ten meters, or roughly thirty feet, and the shortest thirteen centimeters, or just a little over five inches. A free organ concert can be heard every day at noon with major concerts always being a sellout. The Riga Dom was restored for use again as a cathedral in fairly recent history when the Soviet prohibition of religion ceased. For many years the government had designated the Dom and other churches for alternate uses such as sports arenas and storage facilities.

When Latvia regained its freedom, a great deal of activity ensued in restoring the old churches, though many of them were beyond repair and had to be rebuilt from the foundations. American church groups, sister Latvian congregations throughout the world, and private citizens provided much of the funding for the restorations. Mother and I visited the New Gertrude Lutheran Church in Riga and met Pastor Uldis Saveljevs who a few years later served as Pastor in the St. Paul Latvian Evangelical Lutheran Church in Farmington, Michigan. On the Sunday we visited the New Gertrude church, it was already packed with worshippers half an hour before the service. Though church worship had been outlawed for decades, the Holy Spirit did not cease working in people's hearts and they returned to the house of the Lord at the first opportunity. Mother and I felt humbled by Pastor Saveljevs' personal dedication and sacrifices in helping his congregation grow and flourish. He had sold his personal car to fund a new roof for his church. Despite the Communist stand against religion for half a century, Christianity was beginning to reawaken in Latvia. Between January 1, 1989 and the middle of May, Pastor Saveljevs had brought 255 souls into the church through the rite of Baptism, confirmed 53 youths, and married 43 couples. One hundred people were in the youth group with many of them planning to study for the ministry. Our encounter with Pastor Saveljevs proved to be of great personal significance to mother a few years later though we were unaware on that May morning in 1989 of God's plans for my mother's future.

WHERE IS MY HOME?

All too soon the time came when we had to part again from our homeland and our loved ones. We had to say our final farewells and return to America. The entire extended Lācis family participated in preparing a magnificent farewell party for us except for my dear cousin Aris. I had to say a tearful good-bye to him a couple of days earlier because he had to fly to Moscow the morning of the party to get an entry visa for London where he and a group of fellow physicians were invited to a professional conference. Again ridiculous stringent bureaucratic rules made it necessary for Aris to personally appear in Moscow on a Friday to pick up the visa for the Monday flight to London. According to rules, the visas could not be mailed or picked up anywhere except personally in Moscow. Aris called me from Moscow on the eve of the party and said he and the other doctors had spent the entire Friday sitting on the stairway waiting their turn to pick up the visas. Five minutes before closing time, Aris and another doctor were given their visas and the other doctors received denials and had to cancel the conference invitation. It is difficult to understand how government can have such gross disregard for professional people in making them travel long distances and have them waste entire days waiting only to receive refusal to attend a medical conference.

Andis, Aris' son who was a pediatric oncologist, came in the afternoon of the party to help his mother Aija with the preparations. He put up and set the table, made a salad and peeled mounds of potatoes for a "Rosols" potato salad. Aija had taken the train to the seashore in the morning to gather the fresh ingredients from her garden for the salad. Aris' other son Aigars, a hematologist, brought a delicious torte for the occasion. Mother and I helped with the preparations and felt like we are members of the family circle, all getting ready for some guests. It was easier to be in that frame of mind instead of thinking of us being the guests who are leaving. As we sat enjoying the pork loin, caviar and salmon sandwiches, potato salad, home-brewed liqueurs, pastries, and torte, Sandra started the tape recorder to play a collection of Latvian songs she had brought for background music.

When the first strains of the Latvian national anthem, "Dievs Svētī Latviju" (God Bless Latvia) began, someone rewound the tape to the beginning of the anthem, turned up the volume, and everyone spontaneously stood up and sang along. This was a courageous and patriotic act for us all to show allegiance to the free Latvia we once knew. The anthem was on the Soviet list of forbidden songs, but we all joined our voices despite the windows being wide open for the breeze to blow the melody of the hymn throughout the courtyard. All the young people had their eyes focused on my mother and me to see if we still remembered our national anthem. The national anthem is something that persons just do not forget over the years if they love their country and we joined in singing with tears in our eyes. At the end of the hymn we were told by one of the young men in the family,

"Now we know that you truly are real Latvian people!"

At last I was among people who recognized me as their own only to face the imminent farewell again.

The next morning Zigurds and Sandra came bringing large loaves of Latvian country bread for us to take back to America. Edite, Ilze, and Normunds also came bringing flowers. Edite was so overcome with the sadness of parting that she could not speak and just kept pressing her tearstained wet cheek against my equally wet cheek. Zigurd's daughter Agnes and husband Visvaldis brought bouquets of my favorite flower Lily of the Valley and Aija gave us armfuls of lilacs. Everyone presented us with parting gifts of special Latvian significance like photo albums, books, music tapes, ceramics, and handicraft items. Mother and I in turn emptied our suitcases of nearly all our clothing and shoes, which were in short supply in Latvia, and distributed the items among members of the family. Edite, who was as dear as a sister to me, was in great need of shoes and I gladly gave her mine and made the trip home in bedroom slippers. Since Latvia finally became independent again in 1991 and came out from under the yoke of Soviet oppression, the stores are as well stocked with goods as in any western nation and there is no more need to bring in ordinary consumer goods except for special gifts one wishes to give to the family.

We went back to the Hotel Latvija where we had to board the INTOURIST bus going to Estonia. Everyone in the family followed for the final good-by waves until the loving familiar figures could no longer be seen in the distance. On the return trip to Estonia the guide Mrs. V. was a little more sensitive and asked if we wanted the bus to stop at the seashore so that we could toss some of our flowers into the sea, which according to legend, the waves would carry back again to our loved ones. The bus also stopped at the Latvija sign on the border with Estonia and we left the remainder of our flowers on the stone letters honoring our homeland.

After a guided tour of Tallinn our group was served a fish dinner in a restaurant atop the Viro Hotel and then taken to board the Georg Ots ferry in the evening. The Soviet presence was very much felt as our ferry passed through the narrow ships channel. A whole fleet of warships appeared to be guarding the harbor. As the Georg Ots left the shoreline of the Baltic Sea behind in its wake and sailed into the sunset, I cried silently for a long time. My beloved Latvia still lay shrouded in a red fog that had enveloped the Baltic region since it was overtaken by the Soviets.

This second good-bye to our homeland was even more sorrowful and tearful than the first when we left Riga by train in 1944. This time we knew we would never be physically and financially able to establish a home in our native land again. Our brief, emotional return in 1989 gave proof that for us the refugee trains were meant to run only one way and our dream of returning home was just that—a dream. Reality and our home destination had been laid out for us along the railroad lines that initiated our odyssey into foreign lands. We had to follow the route God had planned for us when we originally were forced to leave our homeland in 1944. At that time, not knowing our destination and what was coming next made it easier for us then to believe that life held infinite possibilities for us along new pathways.

★★★

21

REFUGEE TRAIN DESTINATION UNKNOWN— FAREWELL TO LATVIA 1944

The weeks long, cold October 1944 train ride in drafty freight cars was anything but an autumn color tour. We did not know our final destination. Several families and all their belongings were jammed into each car. The piles of boxes and suitcases served as makeshift beds. To protect his children from the cold winds that blew through the thin, crack-filled walls of the train, my father wrapped his shearling "Father Christmas" fur coat around us and mother covered us with her own fur coat. The adults had to endure the cold as they huddled together with no room to lie down. After sitting in the darkness of the crowded boxcar it was an adventure to catch glimpses of the bleak scenery of war-torn Europe through the freight car's wide door. Whenever the rain slowed down, the men pushed the door back to allow some light and fresh air to freshen the pungent odor of unwashed people and buckets of excrement jammed into close quarters. What an interesting travelogue a description of this trip would make! It could be titled "Refugee Guide to a Free Trip through Eastern Europe" with a bonus section on "How to Survive Daily Bombings on a Freight Train".

While the train chugged its way through Latvia, Kārlis called out the familiar train stations to entertain the children. The country landscapes southward from Riga toward Lithuania still looked peaceful, wrapped in a pastoral cloak of autumn. When the meager portions of food brought along for the trip were gone, mother used her German language skills to persuade some of the military troops at the various stations to share some soup from the field kitchen with the hungry refugees. While riding through Lithuania, I anticipated arriving at Memel. Memel was a Lithuanian port city on the Baltic Sea, which had become an important German navy base when the territory was annexed to Germany. Since there had been frequent mention of Memel on newscasts, I was quite intrigued by the prospect of seeing this important historic site. When the train arrived at Memel late one afternoon, workers from a field kitchen greeted the refugees. Large kettles of thin broth had been prepared for the refugee train and we all lined up to receive our ration. The lukewarm, thin broth was as welcome to the cold and starving people as if it were a gourmet meal.

But as soon as we had received our cups of soup, the air raid sirens sounded their mournful warning that Soviet bombers were heading toward Memel. Everyone was quickly ordered off the train and into a crowded makeshift shelter of the railroad station. When there was no more room in the shelter, the remaining refugees crawled under the train as if the cars above them could offer protection from deadly bombs. At some point the officials decided it would be safer to pull the trains out of Memel rather than leaving them as ready targets. Everyone was ordered to return to the train immediately. The announcement that the trains would be leaving caused a chaotic stampede, as the refugees, fearing to be left behind, rushed back to their cars and belongings. As the mass of humanity shoved and pushed their way forward, I felt that I would suffocate as my small figure was being pushed and squeezed into the bodies of the adults in the surging crowd engulfing me. Father had picked up Mudite on his shoulders to keep her above the pushing mass of people. Mother, walking behind her husband who was trying to clear a way for his family, hooked her hands unto father's belt and squeezed me in the space between them. It took all of mother's strength to keep her arms outstretched to keep enough space between her and father so that I would have some breathing room without having my face pushed into my father's back. Linked together, the Gedrovics family made it back to their railroad car without mishap other than some feeling of terror remaining from the experience. This feeling of terror has a way of cropping up whenever I am in close quarters in a pushing crowd even decades later. Even an enthusiastic, happy crowd marching into the University of Michigan "Big House" football stadium can bring a flashback of the feeling of panic originating from being caught in the people stampede in Memel.

Some other refugees on the train were not so fortunate in escaping death. An elderly grandmother riding with her family in the same boxcar next to the Gedrovics' was too weak and traumatized by the incident at Memel to survive. She died that night with her family helplessly by her side, unable to offer any medical assistance. When the train made its next stop somewhere in Poland, the family, with the help of fellow travelers, buried the grandmother in a shallow grave next to the railroad tracks. Only a cross that was made by tying two sticks together marked her lonely grave in a strange land. Along the miles of railroad tracks in Germany and the lands the Nazis had occupied, many such shallow anonymous graves marked the route of death. Many refugees fleeing from the Russians, and Jewish families being forcefully taken to concentration camps, succumbed to the harsh rigors of the trip and had to be buried along the tracks with their final resting place never to be found again. Soldiers just took the dead bodies off the trains and buried them along the tracks without coffins. It was during this traumatic train ride into the dark unknown that the words to the old German hymn, "Lord *Take My Hands...*", got engrained in my memory. Nearly every day tearful strains of the melody drifted skyward as another person was hastily laid to rest next to the tracks. "Pie Rokas Ńem un Vadi..." I timidly joined in singing with the sorrowful mourners.

As the refugee train continued rolling through Poland, then Czechoslovakia, there were more air raids. The weather became colder and it was necessary to keep the doors of the railroad cars closed most of the time. Sitting in the dark and listening to the monotonous sound of the train chugging along the tracks seemed to have a hypnotic effect on the train's occupants. By then everyone had lost interest in watching the unfamiliar foreign landscape rushing by. The prevailing mood was as bleak and gray as the dark clouds of rain swirling over the bare branches of the trees shorn of their colorful foliage. Even the children could no longer be convinced that this type of tour through Europe was educational and something to be remembered. To be sure, the route took us through the magical city of Vienna, Austria. But there were no strains of waltz music filling the air. Instead of glimpses of magnificent palaces, cathedrals, and the famous opera house, there was only the rubble of what was left of the once beautiful city on the blue Danube. Vienna, like all the other railroad stations along the way, was to be remembered as a place of desolation and destruction. War had transformed the foreign lands that had been so vividly described in my geography books into foreboding and depressing mountains of rubble. On the train ride from Latvia, I lost the magic of childhood and became an adult with full awareness of death and how fragile life really is. The fear of separation from the family was always with us. At one stop, my father left our boxcar in search of food hoping to pick some apples in a nearby orchard. As the train whistle blew signaling departure, there was still no sign of father. The hiss of steam and sound of the train whistle no longer signaled a pleasant trip to me but rather a dark foreboding departure into the unknown. My sister and I started crying and mother must have been in a panic fearing we would be separated from father. The train started to slowly chug along forward when we saw father running to catch the moving train. He made a leap for the open door of our car and managed to land on the floor of the boxcar instead of under the moving train. The terrifying journey by train and the flames in Jelgava consumed my childhood. Yet, small parts of it remained in Livberze, wrapped in the package of treasures that were left behind in the attic, never to be recovered again.

When the adults spoke during the long, cold ride it was usually in whispers as the long unplanned journey by train continued. Nobody wanted to voice the troubling questions on all of their minds. What was the final destination of this refugee train as it made its way westward toward Germany? Everyone had been told they were needed for work in German labor camps when the train left Riga. Just what were these alleged "Labor Camps"? Was this a Nazi metaphor for extermination camps such as Dachau and Auschwitz? At last, the train arrived at its destination. It indeed was a labor camp, separated by barbed wire fencing from a POW camp of Russian soldiers. The complex was made up of rows of weathered grey army barracks near the railroad in the Austrian town of Knittelfeld. The austere accommodations in the labor camp were not like any the Gedrovics family had ever experienced. Approximately thirty people were crowded into one room. There was no furniture other than the bare wooden two-story bunk beds with straw in burlap bags serving as mattresses. Each person was issued a rough grey wool army blanket. Usually each family sacrificed one of the blankets to be used as a curtain between the bunks to offer some semblance of privacy for each family. Food was issued in a common mess hall, but there were no dishes. Each family picked up its ration of bread and soup in whatever tin cup or can they had used on the train.

Kārlis was immediately assigned to work on the railroad restoring bombed out tracks. With her language skills, Tatiana worked as a translator in the camp offices. One night Tatiana did not return on time to the barrack to which the Gedrovics family was assigned. Hour after hour, everyone waited anxiously. Suppertime came and went, but there was still no sign of our mother. As it was getting near midnight, I was crying quietly in my bunk imagining that my mother had been taken away like all the other people who had disappeared without trace. Just then some military guards carried her in and laid her still body on one of the beds. The guards had found mother, barely conscious, lying on the railroad tracks. Apparently she had been running back to the barracks after work and had tripped on the tracks in the pitch darkness of the night, as no lights were allowed in the camp due to blackout precautions against air raids. The fall had knocked the wind out of her. With our family anxiously praying for her recovery, God again was merciful and mother soon recovered from her injuries. But more trouble lay in store for us. The family had only been at the labor camp for about a week, when an air attack on the railroad burned down the entire camp. As lacking as the camp had been, now the refugees were in a worse situation with no roof whatsoever over their heads. We were completely homeless, left with only the meager belongings we had managed to carry out of the burning barracks before they were entirely consumed by flames.

Full of purpose and never lacking ideas for finding new homes for the people left homeless by the fire, my mother approached the camp commander and convinced him to appeal to the town people of Knittelfeld to come to the rescue of the refugees burned out by the Soviet bombers. The citizens of Knittelfeld proved that people of good will existed even in wartime. Several families volunteered to share rooms in their apartments with the homeless "Fluechtlinge", or refugees. The Gedrovics family was placed in the apartment of a prominent newspaper publisher in Knittelfeld. The Karasek family gave up their spacious living room in their apartment, situated on a hill overlooking the town, to provide shelter for Kārlis and Tatiana and their two daughters. Omi and Jānis Berzins roomed with another Austrian family on the other side of town. Kārlis was assigned work on the railroad in the nearby town of Zeltweg. The Karasek family, with their three daughters, was very gracious in sharing their home. At Christmas, the Karaseks surprised the Gedrovics' with the gift of a small tree and offered to share their holiday dinner with us. I became friends with the middle daughter, Ingrid, and Mudite found a playmate in the youngest daughter. The oldest Karasek daughter Edith often babysat for the entire brood of girls. I was enrolled in the third grade after the Christmas holidays and had no problem in resuming my studies as my mother had tutored me in German at home. The only roadblock was the requirement to learn the German script in a one-week time span when Hitler ordered all Austrian schools to conform to the German style of writing.

It seemed that Knittelfeld had stretched out its helping hands to the refugees and that the Gedrovics family could lead a somewhat normal life again despite the war. Knittelfeld was located in the foothills of an alpine valley on the Mur River in the province of Styria, or Steiern. It was known as the "Eisenbahnerstadt", or Railway Town, a hub connecting Vienna to all points west. It seemed like an appropriate venue for the family from the railroad hub of Jelgava. The beginning of the year 1945 arrived with the promise of a respite from the air attacks and war activity. Though formations of American bombers could often be seen flying high overhead in the blue skies, they seemed to be heading for destinations in Germany and did not appear to threaten the picturesque town of Knittelfeld which lay wrapped in fluffy white layers of snow. Although it was known that bombs cause death and destruction, somehow the American bombers were more admired than feared in Austria. Americans were said to bring freedom from dictatorship and the refugees from Eastern Europe looked to them for liberation from oppression although nobody dared to voice this sentiment out loud under Nazi rule. To me, the planes looked like silver eagles with the sun glistening on their wings. I enjoyed watching them gliding high overhead as if they were playing hide and seek among the fluffy white clouds.

Karasek girl on sled with Skaidrite & Mudite, Jan. 1945

January was filled with fun in the snow as the Karasek family included Mudite and me in sledding activities on the hills surrounding the town. On one such outing I learned what if must feel like when a football player gets the air knocked out from the chest by a hard tackle. Some sleds in Austria have a high iron bar across the front, presumably for the front rider of the sled to hang onto. On one fast ride down the hill, the sled hit a bump and I was thrown against the bar, knocking the air out of me. It was strange that I had the air knocked out of me just like my mother had a couple of months earlier when she fell on the railroad tracks. Unable to breathe, I was certain I was about to die. Thoughts of how grieved my mother would be rushed through my head. I could not believe that my death would come while having fun sledding rather than during the bombing attacks I had feared. Ingrid Karasek somehow managed to manipulate my chest so I could breathe again and the sledding fun resumed although my chest was painful for a few days.

But normal enjoyment of life is of short duration during wartime. Although most of the residents of Knittelfeld were not aware of it, the local ceramics factory in the picturesque hilly town had allegedly been converted to an ammunition factory. When this secret location became known to the Allied forces, the long shrill air raid warning sirens became part of the daily routine as reconnaissance planes flew overhead. They must have been trying to locate the target, as usually no bombers followed. One day I was at a clinic having a large abscess removed from my left arm. Malnutrition had lowered my resistance against infections and I developed several abscesses. Just when the surgeon was in the middle of the delicate procedure to excise the tumor, which was underneath the blood vessels on the inside of my arm just below the elbow joint, air raid sirens began to pierce the quiet of the operating room. Sometimes war creates heroes, but there are also times when the worst characteristics in people are manifested. This was one of the worst of times. The Sisters, or nuns, who were assisting the surgeon, were only concerned for their own safety. The nuns abandoned their patient on the operating table and, pushing everyone aside, rushed down the stairs to the basement bomb shelter. The surgeon, however, was true to his Hippocratic oath to above all else not to do harm. He showed kindness and courage as he picked up his patient and, with the wound still open, carried me in his arms to the shelter. The operation was finished only when the all-clear siren sounded and the surgeon again carried me back to the operating room. To this day, I still bear the scar inside my left arm.

Despite the frequent warning sirens signaling that low-flying American bombers had been sighted, activities in the town did not cease and school attendance was mandatory for the children. If the long warning siren sounded, children were sent home. If, instead of a warning the main alert actually sounded, the undulating wailing waves of the alert siren signaled for everyone to take immediate shelter. Sometimes there was no alarm if a bomber reached its destination unnoticed. One such incident happened sometime in February. There was just the droning of some planes, then a sudden explosion with clouds of smoke signaling that a bomb had been dropped. It was said that a bomb had been dropped on a farm near Knittelfeld and that six civilians were the first deaths in the area. Everyone wondered why a farm had been the target of the detonation. Perhaps it was a practice operation for the devastation to follow a few days later, but meanwhile life went on as usual.

I did well academically in the Austrian public school, but the righteous nature I had inherited from Tatiana asserted itself when orders were given that I considered to be morally unacceptable. Twice a day, at the beginning of school and at noon, the children were lined up and commanded to stand at attention and salute "Heil Hitler". The Nazi Fuehrer was expected to visit the town and the children were trained to welcome him at the railroad station with a perfect salute. On the fateful day when Hitler arrived, the school children were all lined up ready to salute him, but I had my own righteous agenda to follow. When the man with the funny little mustache appeared in the doorway of the train, the teacher gave the signal to salute.

I did not raise my arm with the rest of my classmates to salute Adolf Hitler, the unjust man who had caused so much death and whose greed for power had robbed me of my own homeland. Seeing Hitler face to face, I instinctively felt that this was not a man I could trust or respect. His eyes were piercing and cold, much like those of my nemesis, the deceitful Becis. The teacher again gave the order, her fierce eyes shooting daggers directly into my face. I stood very still, my arms dropped at my sides and my eyes afire with defiance. In a hissing whisper, the teacher threatened that the whole family could be arrested for such gross insubordination, but I, the little rebel, stood firm in my resolve not to salute the perpetrator of injustice.

But God is just. At this very decisive moment when my firm stand could have jeopardized the safety of my family, the air raid warning sirens started their earsplitting blaring. Hitler's train immediately pulled out of the station and everyone scattered every which way as the school children were once again dismissed to find shelter or run home. That evening our family pondered about our fate and what would happen if I were to return to school the following morning. We had always believed that if we cast our worries on the Lord, He would plan what is best for us. This possibly life threatening incident was no exception. God brought salvation in a strange way. The next morning dawned as a cold, clear winter day. Though I did not recall the date of the fateful day, I found out decades later with the help of the worldwide web publicizing a forthcoming book that it was on February 23, in the year 1945 that fortune smiled on me and put her seal of approval on my defiant act.[23] When it was time to return to school the morning following my daring silent protest, the air raid sirens started their ominous warning again. This time God's protecting angels came riding on the glistening silver wings of the U.S. Air Force which, unlike other times, zeroed in low over Knittelfeld and released their incendiary bombs to destroy the railroad hub and the ammunitions factory along with much of the town.

Before the actual alert signal could be sounded, there was the droning of low-flying silvery bombers with their deadly payload. Within seconds came earsplitting whistling and hissing sounds followed by deafening detonations as the bombs were released over Knittelfeld. The foundation of the house began to shake and windows shattered as my mother grabbed Mudite and shouted for me to follow.

"There is no time to reach the community bomb shelter. We have to hide in the cellar", mother exclaimed.

Bombs were bursting all around as mother quickly led us children to the basement coal cellar for protection. As the bombs detonated all around outside, the building shook so much that dust from the coal began to fill the air and everyone was in danger of suffocating. Somehow, my mother instinctively knew what to do in this emergency. Tatiana took leadership and tore the scarves from the heads of the other women who sat frozen from panic. She wet the scarves with a bottle of water and vinegar that she found on a storage shelf. Tatiana distributed the wet rags to everyone and told them to cover their faces to keep from smothering from the coal dust that was kicked up by the explosions. This fast action saved everyone from suffocating although we all later emerged from the coal cellar looking like minstrels with coal-black faces. The initial attack lasted but a few minutes. After a somewhat long pause, when everyone thought the bombing had ceased, a second wave of bombers brought new fear. It felt like the whole earth was shaking and the walls were trembling from the multiple bombs. It seemed unsafe to remain in the cellar. If there would be yet another wave of bombers coming, there was the possibility of being buried alive if the apartment building walls were to collapse. After a prolonged period of silence, mother decided we should run to the town's bomb shelter. When we emerged from the cellar, we were surrounded by an inferno. There had been no time to put on coats to protect us from the cold February weather, but the burning buildings put forth so much heat that there was a greater likelihood of burning than of freezing. It was unbelievable that our building was the only one left standing on the hill. Every building around us had been destroyed. With flames leaping from the buildings on both sides of the street, mother, Mudite, and I ran down the middle of the street. I was not afraid of the flames leaping and dancing all around us. I remembered that God would protect us like He had protected my father when Jelgava was burning. He had promised, *"When thou walkest through the fire, thou shalt not be burned; neither shall the flame kindle upon thee."* (Isaiah 43:2). When the three of us arrived at the bomb shelter, it was overflowing with people sitting on narrow benches and on the cold damp floor. Upon entering the shelter, mother, Mudite and I joined hands and we said a prayer thanking God for saving us from the bombs and the raging fires in the aftermath. We remained in the dimly lit shelter for hours as no all-clear signal was ever given.

Lone man, like my father, walks through rubble.[24]

This time it was Papuks who had to face hours of anxiety over the fate of his family. While working at Zeltweg, he learned that the entire town of Knittelfeld had been destroyed. He started running from his job at the railroad yard ten miles away to search for his loved ones. Mile after mile during his solitary struggle to reach Knittelfeld he saw nothing but smoke, fire, and rubble where familiar landmarks once stood. The church across the street from the apartment had been a landmark that could be seen from miles away. The steeple had disappeared from sight. As he finally reached the top of the hill, often having to climb over piles of debris where no streets remained, to his amazement, the Karasek house was still standing as the lone structure in the midst of destruction. The church across the street, where dozens of people had sought refuge, had suffered a direct hit and nothing but a pile of rubble remained. Kārlis silently prayed that his family had been spared, but he found the Karasek building empty. Where had his loved ones been when the bombing started? After a few hours of anxious searching, Kārlis was reunited with his family in the bomb shelter.

The Karasek and Gedrovics families eventually went back to the apartment to spend the night, but it was obvious they could not remain to live there. All the windows were shattered and the apartment was littered with pieces of fallen plaster and all sorts of rubble. There was no electricity and no heat. The scene was so eerie that I was afraid to fall asleep. Flames still flickered on the street two stories below. There were dead bodies inside the pile that had been the church and, directly in front of the Karasek apartment house, there was a cart with the dead bodies of a mother and her two little children lying next to her. Strangely, it was not the fire or the corpses lying within view that frightened me. It was the white curtains, fluttering in the breeze that came through the open windows where just a few shards of glass remained, that gave a spooky look to the room. Once again, war and death that had been stalking the Gedrovics family since the previous summer had again literally arrived in front of our window.

The only thought that comforted me was that with the town destroyed in the bombing attack, I would never have to return to school again. Although the air attack had dealt a deathblow to many people, the silver eagles in completing their mission had also saved my family and me from certain repercussions for my refusal to salute Hitler. The silver eagles over Knittelfeld must have been part of God's promise in Tatiana's Confirmation verse in Psalm 91:4, *"He shall cover you with his feathers, and under his wings shall you trust: his truth shall be your shield and buckler."* My family was not unique in having faith in the metaphoric protection under the wings of eagles as promised in Psalm 91. A Catholic priest, Father Michael Joucas, composed a hymn based on Psalm 91 in 1979. The hymn called "Eagles' Wings" has become a favorite in all Christian churches. Tatiana's confirmation verse accompanied her to the very end of her days. In 2008 the entire congregation of family and friends sang the hymn "Eagles' Wings" at the service to celebrate her life when her soul was carried up to dwell in the palm of God's hand.

The next day after Knittelfeld was bombed, Mr. Karasek made arrangements for both families to go to live with a farmer outside the town. The house on the outskirts of town where Omi and grandfather Berzins roomed had not been damaged. They stayed in town taking the chance that no further air attacks would come. Moving to the farm was another new and unique experience for me. The farmer came to get everyone with a huge farm wagon pulled by two immense oxen. Used to horses pulling carts, I was amazed by these large animals with their long horns. When we arrived at the farm, the Karasek family settled in at their friend's farmhouse. The Gedrovics family would live with the family of the farmer's shepherd who tended to the herd of cattle up the mountain from the farm. The small building where the shepherd's family lived consisted of two floors with one large room on each floor. The shepherd and his mother, wife, and daughter moved their beds to the first floor where the combination kitchen and dining room had been. The Gedrovics family got the upstairs room, which had been a bedroom. The upstairs room would serve as our bedroom by night and as the dining room for everyone by day.

Living in the mountain cabin from sometime in the winter when Knittelfeld burned until May of 1945, was another novel and exciting period for me. The hills were not exactly "alive with the sound of music" as the lyrics from the popular play, "Sound of Music" depict them. Life on the mountain was full of adventure, however. Father went down the mountain every day to work on cleaning up the rubble in Knittelfeld and neighboring towns that continued to be under attack. I stayed on the mountain to help my mother and the shepherd's wife with various chores. Mother also continued to home school me so that my education would not be interrupted. When there was free time, I was allowed to sled or ski down from the mountain cabin to the place where the clearing ended at the timberline below. The Karasek girls had lent some of their winter sports equipment for me to enjoy. On one attempt at skiing down the mountain, I decided I was expert enough to try the trail through the woods instead of stopping at the end of the clearing. Unfortunately, I did not know how to turn the skis to avoid the pine tree next to the trail and my skis straddled each side of the tree as I met the tree with a big hug. From then on I thought it wise to take off the skis when I reached the point where the trail went through the woods and continued down to the farm.

There was no running water at the mountain cabin. Water was carried up in pails from a mountain brook that ran through the woods below the cabin. During the winter, the men made the slippery climb down to the brook to obtain water. When spring came, I enjoyed playing by the brook and I often volunteered to go down to get water. On one bright spring day, I was merrily skipping down the hill toward the brook when a big bull got interested in my fluttering red dress. Snorting, he came running after me. Who would have thought the bull would choose the little girl in a red dress in the hills of Austria to make his charge as if he were fighting a matador in Spain! Terrified, I ran toward the brook with the bull following closely behind. Just before I reached the brook, I dodged behind a big tree and the bull kept charging full speed ahead until he landed in the brook with a big splash. The cold mountain water must have stunned him enough to forget about looking for the girl in the red dress. Soon, he ambled back up the mountain to the pasture. It was a long time before I dared to climb back to the cottage as I carefully darted from tree to tree so that the bull would not discover me again. The incident reminded me of the time in Rezekne when a big turkey had chased me when I had also worn a red dress. I never wore the red dress again while we lived on the mountain.

Another frightening experience on the mountain concerned the shepherd's daughter. Initially I had hoped the girl would become my playmate, but for reasons unknown to me, the quiet young girl was always kept inside the downstairs room and was rarely seen outside. One day I decided to visit the girl. I had been in the room where the shepherd family lived for a few minutes when the girl suddenly started thrashing her arms and fell to the floor. Fear filled me as I witnessed the girl's uncontrolled jerky movements and heard the strange guttural sounds. The girl's mouth was agape and it seemed to be foaming. The girl's mother rushed to her side and tried to hold on to her tongue saying that they did not want her to swallow it. Swallowing ones tongue was a concept completely foreign to me. Within a few minutes the seizures stopped and the girl was taken to her bed to rest. It was then that it was explained to me that the girl suffered from a disease called epilepsy. That was the reason the parents kept her inside to keep her in sight should she need help. The seizures appeared to come quite frequently, but I was allowed to visit the unfortunate girl and to play with her quietly for brief periods of time. I prayed that God would help the poor girl be healthy again.

For anyone to stay healthy during the last months of the war truly must have been through God's will and grace. There was no medicine and hardly any food. The Gedrovics and the shepherd families basically lived on bread, potatoes, some vegetables, and milk. Most of the time dinner consisted of root vegetables—potatoes, carrots, beets, and rutabagas with bread dumplings for variety. It was not too bad to eat just boiled potatoes. However, the shepherd family did most of the cooking and they preferred something called, "Kartoffeln Knoedel"–potato dumplings. The dumplings, shaped like big snowballs, were made from grated raw potatoes and boiled in water. Most of the time, the potato balls were not completely cooked. I had never been a fussy eater. As it happened, the only food I could not tolerate were beets, rutabagas, and raw potatoes. As hungry as I was, I tried my best to bite into the lukewarm, partially raw potato dumplings. However, my stomach won as it rejected the unpalatable food offering. From then on, mother gave me permission to just have a slice of bread for dinner when raw potato dumplings, rutabagas, or beets were on the menu. Even if there had been no bread, to me starvation would have been preferable to raw potatoes and cooked beets. The smell of cooked beets and raw potatoes drifts back from my memories when I recall life in the mountain cabin, although the cabin was surrounded by fragrant wildflowers and the fragrance of the pine forest.

On the morning of May 8, 1945, Kārlis came running up the mountain path unexpectedly early when he usually would still be working in town. His face was full of smiles as he excitedly told everyone that the war had come to an end. It was V-E Day! The Germans had capitulated to the Allied Forces. There was joy all around—no more war, no more bombs! Peace had come at last. But what lay ahead in the future? Peace had arrived, but no military forces occupied Knittelfeld. Who exactly was in charge? What was to happen to the homeless refugees? During the initial weeks following V-E Day, anarchy ruled. It was a time of every man for himself. If you had a home, you protected it. If you did not have a home, you found an empty one and moved in. My mother followed the official route and got permission from the provisional Austrian government in Knittelfeld to move into one of the empty condominiums at the edge of town where German army officers' families had previously lived. Omi and grandfather Berzins moved into the apartment next door. In the chaotic and lawless days following the end of the war, my uncle Janka abandoned his air defense unit and somehow made his way to Knittelfeld to join his parents and sister Tatiana's family. His cousin Ilmars had been injured and never got to return to his family. He contacted tuberculosis and died a few years later in a German veteran's hospital.

The apartment at the outskirts of town seemed too good to be true. It was the first time in over a year that the Gedrovics family actually lived in a private home all by themselves since they had left their sunny apartment in Jelgava. The German officer's family apparently had left their home in as much haste as the Gedrovics family had left theirs in Latvia. When the German military retreated from Austria, the family must have taken only their personal clothing. The apartment had been left completely furnished, including linens, china, and all kitchen utensils. There was a swing set in the back yard and benches among the flowerbeds in the garden.

Nobody knew what the future would bring once a government was formed and order was restored. My father continued to work in helping to restore the railroad system, but it was unknown if and when our family could return to Latvia. The summer of 1945 was a welcome respite from all the hardships the family had endured since leaving Jelgava. The days dawned sunny and passed as if in a dream. The hiatus between the ravages of war and the uncertainty of the future seemed unreal as if one were holding ones breath while waiting for something unknown to happen. Since it was summer, schools had as yet not opened since the fateful day when Knittelfeld had been bombed earlier that year. On weekends our family explored the hills and countryside surrounding the town. During our hikes in the woods, we discovered extensive patches of wild raspberries growing on the hillsides. It must have been July or August because the masses of ripe red raspberries made the hillside look as if it were cloaked in a red blanket. Our family returned again and again to the hillsides fragrant with ripe berries and carried home buckets filled with the delicious berries that mother cooked into jam. Little Mudite had never experienced such a bounty of fruit. She must have eaten so many fistfuls that her stomach rebelled and could hold no more. Life was good for a couple of months, too good to be true. Then the long arm of fate reached out again and emptied the hourglass that measured peaceful existence. The happy summer came to an abrupt end.

★★★

22

THE RUSSIANS ARE COMING AGAIN! KNITTELFELD, 1945

Sometime during the summer of 1945, the Allied forces decided to divide up Germany and Austria into Occupation Zones. The American, British, French, and Russian peacekeeping troops would each be responsible for restoring order in the zones assigned to them. Rumors ran rampant as everyone speculated about where the boundaries of the various Occupation Zones would be drawn and under which army's jurisdiction Knittelfeld would fall. Since the end of the war, there really had been no sign of any occupation forces. Soon there no longer was any doubt as to which army had won Knittelfeld when the spoils of war were divided. One afternoon a Soviet officer from an advance surveillance team barged through the door of the Gedrovics apartment. He seemed as surprised to find a family there as the Gedrovics family was startled by the intruder. He explained that his unit had been informed that the apartments had belonged to German officers and he had been interested in finding some war souvenirs. Tatiana thought that he had a polite way of describing his probable intent to do some looting.

Tatiana, although she had been ill that day and really felt weak, never lost her composure when facing the unexpected Soviet visitor. Her language skills again proved to be priceless. She took the Russian officer to the basement where the previous residents had stored some German SS uniforms and revolvers. Chatting nonchalantly in Russian, Tatiana offered to trade these war trophies for some information. She asked the officer when he thought the Soviet troops would arrive to occupy Knittelfeld and if he had any knowledge as to what would be the fate of any refugees they found. It must have been God's will again that this particular officer had a heart and that he wanted to help, instead of doing harm. The soldier explained that at this time, Soviet troops were already in Knittelfeld, but that the area actually belonged in the British Zone. Within a few days, when the town would be officially turned over to the British, the Soviets would leave and take with them anyone and anything that belonged to them.

The young officer looked at Tatiana meaningfully and stated, "Ti nasha!", or you are ours. He suggested that in the interim she immediately take her family to hide in the neighboring fields where some Hungarian gypsy families were camping on the way to a displaced persons camp for Holocaust survivors in the British Zone. The Soviets had orders to round up all refugees from the Eastern Bloc countries and put them on a freight train bound for Siberia before the area was turned over to the British. The officer left briefly and returned with some cheese and sausage links. Again he said, "Ti nasha", as if to let Tatiana understand that he wanted to take care of his own people. He told her to stay well and wished the family a safe trip into the British Zone. God had sent an angel, disguised in a Soviet uniform, to warn us of the imminent danger.

Once again, our family only took the few belongings we had brought from Latvia as we hastily left the apartment. I do not remember having to pack. Somehow my father must have managed to get our two boxes on one of the gypsy wagons. By now we were used to leaving on a moment's notice when our lives were in danger. Mother covered Mudite's and my heads with large headscarves so that our blond hair would not stand out and attract attention among the raven-haired gypsies, as our family merged in with their caravan. We were nomads on the move again, this time traveling with a band of gypsies! The gypsies did not seem to mind taking on new members. During wartime refugees had learned to look out for each other and to share whatever meager food supplies were available. We were thankful for the soup the gypsies shared from their communal kettle. For the next few days the Gedrovics family slept in the woods, although sleeping was difficult as I had constant nightmares of wild boars, wolves and, and other wild animals devouring me. The gypsy caravan moved by night to reach a safer place in the British Zone, in a town called Judenburg, or "Jewtown" in the Steirmark region.

★★★

23

SHALOM, JUDENBURG

Settled by Jewish merchants in the 11th Century, in 1945 Judenburg once again held a large population of Jewish people temporarily resettled from the nearby Mauthausen and other concentration camps. Jewish people of various nationalities filled several interim displaced persons camps in the Judenburg district on the Mur River. Somehow God's plan always led the Gedrovics family to a town where a river flows through with refreshing water, starting from the Lielupe in Jelgava, then the Daugava in Riga, and the Mur in Knittelfeld and Judenburg. The Gedrovics family was assigned to a camp called "Kaserne" which was a large gated quadrangular compound with a cobblestone courtyard in the middle. The structure resembled a fort or a prison, the living quarters were crowded, and I thought it could not be much of an improvement over concentration camps. Most of the people looked unkempt and emaciated and, due to their previous suffering in concentration camps, they seemed to behave in a savage manner. Fights constantly broke out over simple things like food rations and all sorts of swindling and stealing was commonplace with every man fighting for himself. Fortunately, my mother's language skills and experience as an educator came to the rescue again. She was assigned to be a translator for the British major in charge of the camp and given the responsibility for organizing a school for the refugee children. My father was given duties as Billeting and Housing Director. My parent's administrative duties gave them the privilege of having our family housed in a private apartment in a cheery yellow building across the street from the refugee camp. The Gedrovics family lived in Judenburg from late summer in 1945 until the spring of 1946, judging from dates entered in my book of memories where my classmates in various schools in Austria had entered their friendship poems and sentiments.

Judenburg was a picturesque town surrounded by hills and meadows and the Mur River. It was a town where one could imagine relaxing during a summer vacation. Yet, being assigned the label of a "Displaced Person", I felt like I lived in two different worlds at once, yet belonged to none. As Gentiles, the family did not fit in with the Jewish camp population, nor were we considered equals with the Austrian residents in Judenburg. While our family lived separately from the main camp, the Austrians still viewed us as being part of "the unruly rabble" of foreigners. Initially, the inhabitants of the "Kaserne" were indeed an unruly bunch and my parents prohibited me from going into the camp alone. Eventually life became more normal as people adjusted to being free again. The camp took on the characteristics of any organized community with weddings, births, celebrations, dances, and children going to the camp school.

From the outset, the British major ruled the camp with an iron fist. He was a small man but he carried himself with great dignity as if he were six feet tall. The major never walked, he marched as if to the beat of a drummer. The Hitler-like mustache he wore gave him a severe look of authority. Whenever he marched through the camp gates, he carried a large walking stick and had a huge German Shepherd dog heeling him. The major was always accompanied by his aide, a tall and handsome black man, for additional security. This was the first black man I had ever seen and I was fascinated by his exotic appearance, particularly because he had blue eyes in contrast to his dark hair and skin. The major always appeared to be in a rage over the antics of the camp population. One day he was particularly frustrated and told Tatiana, *"I can't stand these Jews!"* Surprised, Tatiana commented, "I thought you are Jewish yourself." The major clarified his view, *"I am a British Jew, not a lawless displaced person!"*

Some of the anecdotes of life among former concentration camp inhabitants were amusing, albeit somewhat sad. Coming from a life of starvation, these refugees used all sorts of ruses to get extra rations and clothing. People often went through food lines several times so that it seemed the population of the camp was three times bigger than the actual census. Whenever a room-to-room census was conducted, people ran from one room to another room on a different floor to be counted multiple times. The constantly fluctuating population census was problematic for my father, as he was responsible for billeting the refugees. The major decided to put a stop to this "multiple personality" syndrome by conducting a head count in the middle of the night to get an accurate count of the camp inhabitants. Tatiana was asked to go along to act as translator and the major's aide and Kārlis accompanied them for security. As the foursome entered one of the rooms, a woman on one of the top bunks jumped up in surprise and crashed through the bunk on top of the man sleeping in the lower bunk. The man on the bottom bunk stammered in embarrassment that they are not related and that he does not know this woman who was completely naked. Tatiana replied with a smile, *"You know her now."*

Tatiana's efforts in organizing a grade school for the children in the Jewish camp were quite successful. Initially the children, who came from several nationality backgrounds, had a hard time communicating. Tatiana wrote the curriculum with German as the common language and the young minds had no trouble in learning to speak the official language. Although she was not yet of school age, little Mudīte went along with mother when she was teaching. Sitting quietly beside her mother, Mudīte took in everything she observed. Before long, she had learned to read and do arithmetic all on her own. Turning from a teacher to a playwright and choreographer, Tatiana wrote a musical play for the spring convocation at the school. The children portrayed flowers and plants starting a new life in the warmth of the sun. The symbolism of the play, the children's language skills, excellent song and dance presentation, and the camaraderie existing in the school received praise from not only the parents, but also received notice from the camp administration and the Austrian school administration. Tatiana's play received an excellent, insightful, and poignant review in the May 4, 1946 edition of the Judenburg newspaper, "*Murtaler Volkszeitung*". Tatiana's greatest reward was that the school was granted full accreditation according to the Austrian standards of education.

| Nr.18 | Judenburg | *Murtaler Volkszeitung* | 4.Mai 1946 Seite 3 |

AN INTERNATIONAL SCHOOL IN JUDENBURG
THOUGHTS OF A FAREWELL PLAY AT FESTIVAL HALL

Judenburg 2.Mai

Recently the UNRRA School gave a farewell celebration in the Judenburg Festival Hall. Perhaps a few heard there for the first time of an UNRRA school in Judenburg. Surely, each Judenburger knows that in his hometown exist two elementary schools, two high schools, one secondary school, and one trade school. Certainly not everyone knows that besides these there exists a six-grade UNRRA school.

There is a school, established by UNRRA and its greatest assistance action that embraces all children and persons who were dragged away by the war and Hitler. Students of various nationalities attend this interesting school: Ethnic Germans, Croatians, Ukrainians, Slovaks, Serbians, Latvians, Lithuanians, and Poles.

How will one be educated in such a school? In what language? We find that out from the capable principal, Mrs. Gedrovics. Three teachers instruct in six grades arranged according to age. Education is compulsory. German is the language in which all subjects are taught. In addition, each nationality is also taught its own language. That means increased demands in teaching methods and language skills of the teaching staff.

With aroused interest, we sit in the Festival Hall next to the Director of the UNRRA, Mr. Rees, and the Welfare Officers, Miss Ruffon and Miss McRoberts and together with them we feel joy over the remarkable, noteworthy achievements of their charges.

The principal greets all attendees in several languages. We feel the homesickness from her unpretentious words and our hearts, hardened by war, concentration camps, and freedom fights, become tender when a woman, without gestures and without catch phrases, declares: " Spring has come. The birds turn homeward. Whither will we turn...? Where is our homeland...? We thank the UNRRA for the warm nest in the winter...."

And then we experience a charming round-song as children, dressed in Steirmark folk costumes, sing in an Austrian dialect: " In my homeland it is beautiful" and then "Cuckoo, Cuckoo".

A young girl recites a Polish poem. We do not understand the words, but it must be about spring and homesickness as the eyes of the foreigners in the audience become damp. Again a folkdance follows: " In the evening when the village music plays". How touching it is when these children, scattered from all over the world, form the words of our homeland; with what diligence they must have learned a language so foreign to them! A song for three voices: " A Little Bird sits in a Fir Forest", sung in German by children of three different nationalities. A Ukrainian song follows, then a solo on the accordion, a jolly, ingenious theater act in German: "The Model School" loosens universal merriment. "I am a Little Steirerin" is performed by one of the littlest children, a short German poem, a tap dance, a Ukrainian poem, a Russian poem follow. A difficult, complicated Russian dance performed by three girls gives us an understanding of the Russian soul, a Croatian poem follows, and in conclusion we are again entertained by a theater piece: "Spring Awakening". In homemade dresses constructed of brightly colored paper, butterflies and flowers dance and fluttor on the stage and wish us all a farewell.

I am pulled out from my dreamy state by the farewell words of the lady principal who with warm words gives thanks to the UNRRA for their generous and unselfish help, the county school superintendent Dienes for his support and cooperation, and finally the Director, Mr. Korinet, for his assistance.

But we go pensively and slowly home. The little children leave within us a peculiar somber mood. We will not write about it any further, we will only confess that our heart felt somehow heavy and somehow depressed. Why indeed....

RKB

(Translated by Rita Sparks)

By virtue of having completed the second grade in Latvia and two months spent in the third grade at Knittelfeld, I was too advanced to be with the beginners at the camp school. When school started in the fall, I was enrolled in the fourth grade at the Austrian public school in Feeberg, a suburb in the Judenburg district. I hardly remember anything about my experiences in the fourth grade, except that I felt like an outsider, being a refugee living in a Jewish camp and a Protestant in a Catholic school. Yet, in this friendly school my deportment was not a problem. My marks were excellent, as usual, and I must have been well liked by my classmates at the all-girls school. My memory book contains many beautiful poems and drawings dedicated to me by classmates and friends. Their excellent penmanship, calligraphy, and beautiful sketches bear witness to the superior standards of the Austrian schools where fourth graders by the name of Sieglinde, Hanni, Brigitte, Jendl, Lisl, Sophie, Lotte, Gerlinde, and others amazingly created artwork and writings equivalent to that of high school students.

The suburb where the school was located was quite a distance from the apartment where our family lived, so I did not have many opportunities to socialize with my classmates after school. One of the sad consequences of war and being a "displaced person", or a "DP" as refugees were commonly called, is that life-long friendships are rarely developed when families are on the move and do not have a home where friends can gather to create memories. Many of my friendships exist only as entries in my memory book that speak of friendships that will be ever blooming, lasting until the last breath is drawn, forget-me-nots along life's pathways. The images of the girls who wrote the sentiments have long been erased by the winds of change, but perhaps my life is richer from experiencing these brief friendships. Though a stranger in the land, I felt acceptance instead of discrimination during the four years spent in Austria. Discrimination is something that must be taught and the children in grade school did not have it in their curriculum.

When Christmas arrived in Judenburg in 1945, it did not enter the confines of the Kaserne. For the primarily Jewish population in camp, Christmas was not a recognized religious holiday. There were decorated Christmas trees at my school where I learned to sing German Christmas carols, but otherwise the feeling of Christmas did not fill the air at the Displaced Persons Camp. December 6, St. Nicholas Day, is the traditional day when the Austrian Santa Claus named Nikolas visits the homes to distribute gifts to the children who have been good during the previous year. A frightening creature called "Krampus" who resembles an evil red devil accompanies St. Nikolas, sporting a white beard and dressed in red. While St. Nikolas rewards the good children, Krampus stands by jiggling his chains as a warning that children who misbehave might get caught in his clutches. While walking home from school on the evening of December 6, I encountered a jolly pair of St. Nikolas and Krampus as they were joyfully running along the street carrying a bagful of presents to be distributed to some eagerly waiting children. The pair wished me a Merry Christmas, or "Frohe Weihnachten", as they disappeared into a nearby house. The encounter and the friendly greeting filled me with deep sadness and longing for the days long past when Father Christmas visited my family in Jelgava. As slowly falling snowflakes settled on my cheeks, they mixed with teardrops as I thought of how my little sister Mudite would not be able to experience the joy that had been brought by Father Christmas and all the happy events surrounding the Christmas holiday in my own childhood. There was no Christmas tree, no presents to open, no aroma of goodies baking in the oven. Yet, on Christmas Eve the family gathered and thanked God for sparing our lives and bringing peace to the world. Mother lit some candles and we all joined in singing "Silent Night, Holy Night". We were alive and had each other and that was the greatest gift of all.

By the beginning of 1946, the chaos that characterized the repatriation and resettlement of displaced persons had gradually come under control. The United Nations Relief and Rehabilitation Agency (UNRRA), which had been established with great foresight in 1943 in anticipation of the overwhelming numbers of displaced people who would need help in relocating at the end of WWII, had grown to be a vital organization for providing a smoother and orderly process for the relocation and resettlement of the refugees. While it was possible to repatriate some of the refugees to their country of origin, some 2,000,000 people required resettlement. The United States was the prime participant of the Allied Nations in assisting the "stateless" people whose native countries had been invaded by the Soviet Regime. Most of the refugees from the Baltic countries along with Poles and Ukrainians sought political asylum outside their native country, as they were afraid of persecution and reprisal by the Communist government. As a result, UNRRA started gathering the refugees in displaced persons camps according to their country of origin so that nationality groups would be together. Most of the approximately 250,000 Latvian refugees who had left their country to flee from their "liberators" ended up in displaced person camps located in Germany. In the early spring of 1946, Tatiana asked the camp administration at Judenburg that the family be transferred from the Jewish camp to a camp with a concentration of Latvians.

Thus started a complicated process of another migration for the Gedrovics and Berzins families, which involved moves that transcended two different military occupation zones. It was determined that it would be impossible to transfer refugees from a residence in Austria to any camps located in Germany. Furthermore, refugees could only be transferred within the military zone occupied by the British, since Judenburg was in the British Zone. A relatively small concentration of Latvians were gathered and transferred to a town called Spittal. Spittal, in the lower valley of the Drau River is an Austrian town in the western part of the federal state of Carinthia. Hills, meadows and forests surround Spittal. I spent many pleasant hours walking on various trails and hillsides. The surroundings were so beautiful that they awakened an artistic inclination within me as I attempted to draw the peaceful scenery on a sketchpad.

During the brief time spent in this displaced persons camp, my mother home schooled me so that I could catch up on the algebra and language skills required to enter fifth grade after only a month in the third grade in Knittelfeld and four months in the fourth grade in Judenburg. The lessons taught by my mother bring back very pleasant memories. Most of the time algebra lessons took place under some maple tree on the sun-splashed hillsides surrounding the camp. Except for some sentimental lines written in my memory book by long forgotten friends, I have virtually no other memories of the camp at Spittal. I remember just one brief encounter with a visiting French soldier. In passing, he smiled, touched his beret saluting me and offered me a candy bar; again showing that inside a soldier is the heart of a boy.

The most fortunate and strategic aspect of the Gedrovics family's stay in Spittal was the town's location on the railroad line between Villach and Salzburg which turned out to be the destination hub for the housing of thousands of refugees by the end of 1946. Many of the military camps surrounding Salzburg, first occupied by the Germans, and later the American forces, had been converted to displaced persons camps to house the many Holocaust survivors from concentration camps as well as the refugees from the Eastern bloc countries under Soviet rule after World War II. Over 36,000 refugees of 43 nationalities were gathered in barracks and fortresses where living conditions resembled prisoner of war camps. Indeed some of these camps had housed German POW's before being turned into refugee housing. One of the more desirable camps in the vicinity of Salzburg was Camp Glasenbach with the greatest concentration of Latvians. Tatiana devoted a great deal of research, strategic planning and scheming to orchestrate another train journey, a transfer from the Spittal camp to the DP Camp Glasenbach, near Salzburg in the American Zone.

Refugee train arriving in Salzburg[25]

At the time of the move from Spittal at the end of April in the spring of 1946, I was not aware of the major courses of historical events that controlled our lives and, indeed, our future. In the life of an eleven-year-old, the move was yet another journey that would take me away from the friends I had made for just a short period. I was beginning to wonder if the rest of my life would be spent as a nomad going from place to place on freight trains. Life in a permanent home and an entire year spent in one school was becoming just a sweet memory. It had become a known indicator to me that when conversations started about another train journey, it was a time for me to bring out my little orange memory book so that my friends could write more parting messages to record another set of friendships interrupted just as they were beginning to blossom. A friend named Rasma at Spittal expresses the philosophy of most of the Latvians who were forced to evacuate their homes and had to start over from scratch as refugees traveling from one camp to another in a strange country. On April 28, 1946 Rasma writes:

"Life is a battlefield,
Note it carefully, my friend!
There is no Happy Land anywhere, anywhere…
Sometimes life becomes so difficult:
The heart wants to break in two—
Nevertheless, we must endure, we must endure…."

It was impossible to imagine what the new camp near Salzburg would be like. It must have been a heavy responsibility for my parents to have their family answer the "All Aboard!" call of a train with a the destination unfamiliar to them. Just who were the people who would be providing another interim shelter for our family? God will guide us. Yes, Rasma, we must endure.

★★★

24

MILLENNIUM JOURNEY 2000— BACK TO THE PAST CENTURY

*A*fter a cruise on the Danube River through the historic Dachau Valley and visiting the Benedictine Abbey in Melk, the Collette tourist group from Michigan was approaching the "City of Music". Most of the people on the bus were anxious to see the City of Salzburg, one of the major stops on the way to Oberammergau, site of the historic "Passion Play". The citizens of Oberammergau perform the world-famous Passion Play every ten years, but this year seemed more special as it was the beginning of the new millennium. On this twelfth day of May in the year 2000, for me, or Rita as I was now called, the return to Salzburg after fifty-two years seemed like a journey back into time. My mind was racing with memories of familiar places and events long filed into the recesses of consciousness. Would any of the places be recognizable? It is said that "you can never go back"—you cannot relive history. But then again, our bus was passing the old railroad station where I had tearfully parted from my friends when our family left Salzburg in 1948. I wanted to shout, "I have returned", but all my friends were scattered throughout the world by now. Nobody awaited me.

Hotel Oesterreichischer Hof Sacher, Salzburg 2000

The bus stopped in front of the luxurious Hotel Oesterreichischer Hof Sacher, Salzburg. As my husband and I followed the tour guide into the lobby with the view overlooking the river Salzach, I had the feeling that I had been in this place before. Surely I had never visited such a grandiose place during my DP days, and yet, in the flashback I saw myself sitting at a table by the windows overlooking the river! How could this feeling be explained? Perhaps I was just tired from the daylong journey from Vienna and my mind was playing tricks on me.

The next morning our tour group walked across the bridge to the "Altstadt", or old historic portion of the town. Mozartplatz with the horse carriages, the Cathedral, Getreidegasse with its rows of merchants, and the birthplace of Mozart–those had remained unchanged for the most part over the more than half a century. From a viewing point at the Cathedral, I could see the well-remembered Gaisberg where I had gone on skiing outings and also searched for the rare blue Enzian flower. The 900-years-old fortress, the biggest restored fortress in Europe, looked more invincible than ever at the summit of Moenchsberg. In the afternoon, I decided to give my husband a tour of Moenchsberg and the fortress instead of joining the group tour to see the "Eagles Nest" which was said to be just a vacant spot where Hitler's fortification once had stood.

When our family had been living in Glasenbach, the fortress stood empty and in disrepair after the war. Now it had been restored to its grandeur. The gold room and hall with unique gold etchings, paintings, and massive marble columns were magnificent. The castle and fortress built in 1077 had once not only served as the residence of the archbishops, but also as a military garrison and a jail for prisoners. After a snack in one of the fortress dining rooms, we decided to walk down to the city along the many winding pathways through the park instead of riding down the funicular, a vertical gondola, which had brought us straight up the mountain and into the fortress. As we were walking along the pleasant paths that I had taken many times as a young girl and enjoying a view of the city below, I had no premonition that the paths would lead us back into history. The afternoon walk would lead to explanations of many of the historical events surrounding the Glasenbach DP settlement.

Dark clouds began forming over Moenchsberg by the time my husband and I had reached about the midpoint of the walk. When we were nearing the path going down into the city, rain began to pour. Luckily, there was a small souvenir store called "Souvenirs Fuer Jederman" just ahead and we quickly ducked in to get out of the rain. I enjoyed chatting in German with the owner Ulrike Kandutsch and with her help picked out two Austrian dolls to take back for our granddaughters. Fate must also been present during the conversation to motivate me to mention that I had once lived in the DP camp in Glasenbach. As if by magic, I had unwittingly stumbled upon Glasenbach being the password to take me from the year 2000 back fifty years into the twentieth century. Ulrike was astounded to meet a person who had actually lived in the camp. It turned out her husband had been acquiring historical memorabilia and information about the very same camp and had received his military training at the neighboring Camp Truscott! The shopkeeper wanted to take us right back home with her so that I could relate my experiences to her husband. Unfortunately the tour bus was leaving the next morning and the visit was not possible. Ulrike shared information with us about a history book written about the American occupation of Salzburg during the decade 1945-1955 which included information about the enormous number of refugees to be resettled after the war and their housing in the DP camps, including Glasenbach. A more personally meaningful souvenir I could never have found! Ulrike immediately called a friend at the Salzburg Museum where the book had been published and asked that he keep the museum open past the closing hour so that I could purchase the book, *Salzburg 1945-1955-Zerstörung und Wiederaufbau.* It was worth the rush down the mountain through the downpour to obtain this piece of history from my life.

The book was a wonderful compilation of previously unknown information about the destruction and restoration of Salzburg and all the influences that shaped existence in refugee camps during the decade following the war. My mother was even more excited to read

Tatiana, Mudite, Valiant Nichols, and Skaidrite at Camp Glasenbach

the book and to see a photo of the steps to the Officers' Club at Camp Truscott where my father had worked. The book contained maps of the surrounding area and the roads I had taken on my bicycle to shop for groceries and the pathways along the Salzach River where our family had left imprints of our footsteps. I was even able to share the book with a member of our church who had been stationed at camp Truscott at the same time I was at the DP camp. The book contained a camp map showing the barrack where our family had lived next to Camp Truscott along with many of the familiar places that had existed in the late 1940's. The most astounding revelation in the book[26] was that the American forces had appropriated the Hotel Oesterreichischer Hof Sacher during the fateful decade following the WWII for use as the U.S. Army officers club and PX.

The sudden flashback at the hotel was not a figment of my imagination. In 1947 a lady by the name of Valiant Nichols, the UNRRA officer with whom my mother worked, treated Mudite and me with a ride in her jeep and took us on a memorable excursion from Glasenbach to Salzburg. For a special surprise, Mrs. Nichols took us girls to the Officers Club and PX for an ice cream treat. Indeed I had been at the very same hotel and sat by the window overlooking the river at age twelve during the period the hotel had been used by the U.S. army. On a business trip to Dallas, Texas in the 1980's, I looked up Valiant Nichols and treated her to a lunch to thank her for her big generous Texas heart and all the help she had provided the

Gedrovics family when we were DP's. Mrs. Nichols fondly remembered Tatiana and the wonderful work she had performed in running the school in Glasenbach and as an assistant welfare office under Mrs. Nichols. What a pity that I was unable to share with Mrs. Nichols the feelings I experienced in being at the very same place again in the year 2000. Mrs. Nichols by then had joined the saints in heaven. The Hotel Oesterreichischer Hof Sacher also had the significance of being the location where the City of Salzburg formally surrendered to the Americans armed forces on the 4th of May 1945. Ulrike is to be thanked for being the hand of fate that connected our family to our past and gave me a better understanding of life in the "City of Music" which I had previously only seen through the eyes of a child from the confines of a camp for displaced persons. The information obtained through Ulrike has truly enriched my memories of Salzburg.

Danke, Ulrike!

★★★

25

THE SALZBURG EXPERIENCE, D.P. CAMP GLASENBACH, 1946

*T*housands of displaced persons had originally been forced into German Labor Camps in the vicinity of Salzburg to defend this strategic seat of German military power and to work on clearing and restoring the city that suffered heavy destruction during fifteen major air attacks by American bombers. Salzburg had been Hitler's strategic front in Austria as the city was the gateway, or his "Alpine Fortress", between western Austria and the Alps bordering northern Italy. Within the boundaries of Hitler's Alpine Fortress in the Salzburg region lay Berchtesgaden and Hitler's "Eagle's Nest" which Hitler had planned to defend even unto death. The repeated bombings by the Americans devastated Salzburg and the entire alpine region. When the American forces took over the Salzburg stronghold in 1945, their field of operations encompassed the awesome limitless range of responsibilities[27] for managing their own troops, the oversight of thousands of prisoners of war and countless displaced persons, assuming the policing of the district, and planning the restoration of the city and its transportation system which was in ruins.

After the initial invasion of Salzburg by the U.S. 3rd Infantry Division and the paratroopers of the 101st U.S. Airborne Division, the 42nd U.S. Infantry "Rainbow Division", under the leadership of Major General Harry Collins, became the military peacekeepers of the Salzburg region.[28] Gen. Collins initiated a strong affinity between the Salzburgers and the American people. Unlike the German military which had invaded Austria and taken away its freedom by annexing the country to Germany, the American Divisions that occupied Salzburg were respected by the Austrians as agents of change and rebuilding. In all the years of occupation, the Americans and Austrians not only learned to live and work in unity, they also established a good relationship between the two nations. American forces played a major part in the rebuilding of Austria and in resettling the hordes of refugees. When the final occupation forces left Salzburg, it was said that unlike it had been said about the German occupation, "Americans came as invaders, but left as friends". In 1955 there were many farewell parties when the final American troops left Salzburg. One of the last to leave was the Commander of all the U.S. troops in Austria, General William Arnold. When the General left Salzburg on a special train after one of many farewell receptions, it was said he had tears in his eyes.[29]

However, among the initial troops invading Salzburg there was also a certain unwholesome element of soldiers who were more interested in looting rather than protecting the civilians.[30] During the initial days of occupation, soldiers with rifles forced their way into houses and apartments and, under the pretense of looking for weapons, sometimes took everything of value that was not nailed down. The preferred bounty was jewelry, gold wedding rings, wristwatches, cameras, and radios. When citizens were stopped and searched on the streets, the soldiers also took everything that appeared to have value. Even the refugees living in Camp Glasenbach became victims of this criminal element among the occupying military contingent. Whenever something was missing at Camp Truscott, the military police would also search the adjoining refugee camp under the assumption that refugees were doing the stealing. Often some valuable items were missing from the refugee belongings after the search by the MP's.

While the relationship between the Americans and the Austrians for the most part was cordial and flourished, the displaced persons presented an unwelcome problem. The thousands of stranded refugees had become "stateless". Return to their homelands was impossible for political reasons. The Soviets considered everyone who had left their homeland with the Germans to be political enemies. The only remaining hope for the refugees was emigration overseas, as the Austrians did not welcome them to stay in their land, which already faced economic hardships after the war. Until they found another land willing to accept large masses of homeless people, the displaced persons, or DP's, were living, or rather waiting, in unfriendly surroundings in sixteen refugee camps. Because there were some criminal gangs, composed mostly of Russian deserters, who were responsible for criminal acts in Salzburg, the Austrians regarded the refugees from all eastern nations not as victims of the war, but as suspect criminal elements[31], or typical stereotypes of homeless drunks, criminals, and unemployed vagrants. Whenever crime occurred, it was easy to blame the DP's, as the Austrian officials thought the dispossessed would be more likely to steal and rob than some of the invading soldiers.

In May of 1945 there were over 66,000 refugees[32] in the Salzburg region. After the German refugees, prisoners of war, and refugees from nations friendly with the Allies were repatriated to their native lands, there were still approximately 11,000 foreign nationals in Salzburg awaiting resettlement at the end of 1946. In time, the Austrian government assumed a somewhat more accepting attitude toward the refugees who had proven to be worthy citizens through their hard work. In trying to bridge the discrimination gap between the citizens of Salzburg and the DP's, the *Salzburger News* tried to provide an objective investigative report on the refugee problem, though still wishing them to disappear elsewhere.

"The air surrounding the refugees is thick with worry. Some (citizens) worry that they are here at all, others worry over the difficulties that some of them present to their surrounding world, while the DP's themselves, among whom there are also many useful and diligent people, worry over their sad lot and over the fact that others are angered by them. Moreover now, most of the DP's would not like to remain here forever and always, they also want to get away so that they could find a peaceful stable stay with rights along with their duties." [33]

After the American military occupation in 1945, the DP camps in Salzburg were under the jurisdiction of UNRRA (United Nations Relief and Rehabilitation Administration), which was responsible for the welfare of the refugees throughout the Allied occupied zones. The DP camp at Glasenbach near the Salzach River, housed a large concentration of Latvian refugees. Tatiana convinced the administration at Camp Spittal that her teaching and language talents could best be utilized in the Latvian camp that already existed at Glasenbach instead of building a new school for the children at the interim Spittal camp. Her impressive credentials in establishing the school at Judenburg impressed the UNRRA officials at Salzburg. Tatiana was offered a position with the Glasenbach camp administration as assistant to the Director and Superintendent of the Latvian primary school with the responsibility to bring the curriculum up to Austrian accreditation standards. Later she was promoted to Welfare Officer when administration of the camp was taken over by the IRO (International Refugee Organization). Arrangements were made for the Gedrovics family and other Latvians housed at Spittal to board the train for Salzburg on the next portion of their amazing journey toward freedom.

The Salzburg destination was the refugee camp between Glasenbach and Elsbethen near the Salzach River. Camp Glasenbach[34], consisting of barracks that were split off from the Army Camp Truscott, housed 980 persons[35], most of them Latvians who developed a unique style of community life with educational and cultural institutions similar to those that had existed in their former homeland. The adjacent large Camp Truscott[36] housed part of the U.S. 5th Division, 62nd US Field Hospital, 63rd US Signal Operating Battalion, the 350th Infantry, Army Motor Pool, and Officers Club. The army camp, located on a hill, was separated by barbed wire fencing from the ten wooden barracks that had been allocated for the housing of DP's. A

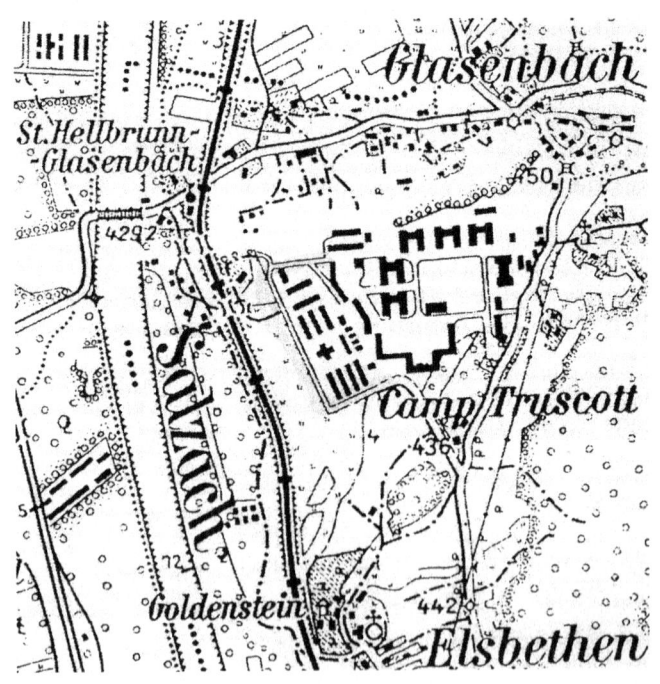

Map by US Army Map Service 1951 shows Camp Truscott and Camp Glasenbach barracks next to the road, + designates our mess hall/recreation center.

combination mess hall/recreation center was in the middle of the DP compound. Each of the barracks consisted of twenty rooms, each measuring about 100 square feet. Each family was assigned a single room. Single people often had to share the room with other singles. With the majority of the camp population being Latvians, they were allocated four barracks in the camp. One barrack housed Lithuanians, two buildings were assigned to residents of various nationalities and the UNRRA/IRO offices, and one building was set aside for the Latvian grade school and camp infirmary.

By the time the Gedrovics family arrived at Camp Glasenbach in the summer of 1946, there were no more vacancies in barracks #4 through #8, which were assigned to Latvians. Our family was assigned room #5 in the mixed-nationality barrack #1 located closest to the road. Omi, Mr. Berzins and uncle Janka were in room #8. In the same barrack were also a few more Latvians, some Estonian, Polish, and Yugoslavian families and even one rather exotic family of Gypsies. Although it was disappointing at first not to be with the main Latvian group, barrack #1 turned out to be the best location after all.

Sisters picking daisies, barracks in background

Gedrovics Family at Barrack #1, Room 5

Across the road, which ran along the first barrack, was a beautiful meadow full of wildflowers beyond which ran railroad tracks. The area was perfect for children to explore and the Gedrovics family enjoyed the beautiful scenery to the fullest. During the summer months, I enjoyed lying on my back in the field of daisies as I watched the puffy white cumulus clouds floating in the deep blue sky. I tried to figure out if any of the cloud masses represented some known figure and if there was a story in the cloud formation. Years later, blue skies full of floating white cumulus clouds would fill me with nostalgia as my imagination traveled back to the daisy meadow in the Alpine Valley in front of our barrack in Glasenbach. After crossing the meadow and the tracks, a path led through a patch of woods and then joined another path running along the beautiful Salzach River. In the distance the scene opened up to a range of snow-covered Alps. I was surprised a few decades later while watching the movie "The Sound of Music" that my hikes and bike rides along the Salzach River had led along the same pathways the Trapp Family had enjoyed until they left their homeland while fleeing from the Nazis. Fortune had really smiled on the Gedrovics family by bringing us to this idyllic setting, although the whole family being crowded within one small room in a drafty, noisy barrack had not improved our living quarters.

Sisters weeding garden plot at Camp Glasenbach 1947

Jelgava 1942-Tatiana, Mudite and Skaidrite watering seedlings in Vaļņu St.

A bonus at Camp Glasenbach was the garden plot each family was allowed to use to grow vegetables, berries and flowers. Gardening must be in the genes of Latvians. Wherever they live, soon garden spots develop. In Jelgava each family in our building on Vaļņu Street had space allocated in the backyard for planting flowers and vegetables. In Glasenbach, the strips of land between the barracks were spaded up and each family could plant their garden in a space as wide as the front of their room. Seeds were not readily available to most refugees. People who came from farms, however, placed a high value on the seeds upon which their livelihood depended. Farmers, who had learned from the famines during WWI years, had the great foresight to bring seed packets from Latvia. This treasure was shared, or bartered, with their countrymen so that everyone would have seed to start a garden.

The garden strip next to barrack #1 was the most productive of all, as no other barrack shaded it from sunshine all day. Just as the gardens flourished in the post-war period, so daily life, if not the substandard living quarters, began to return to normal civilized patterns even though the future was shrouded in a dense fog. Nobody knew if they would be around to harvest their garden of if they would ever see their homeland again.

When the families left Latvia, it was thought to be for a short period, but with the Soviets occupying the country, the Latvians were afraid to return to their home towns for fear of retribution as they would be perceived as enemies of the state and accused of working with the Germans. Even though people had been evacuated from Latvia by military orders and made to work in labor camps, the Soviets would perceive this to be treason. At the Yalta Conference in February 1945, it was decided between President Franklin D. Roosevelt of the U.S., Prime Minister Winston Churchill of Great Britain, and General Secretary Joseph Stalin of the Soviet Union, that the Baltic countries would become part of the Soviet Union. Furthermore, it was agreed that when WWII ended, citizens under the jurisdiction of the allied powers would be repatriated to their home countries.[37] The Soviets demanded that all their citizens residing in Germany after the war be turned over to the Soviet Union regardless of whether these people resisted repatriation. The people whom the Soviets considered to be their citizens included all the Russian POW's in German prison camps as well as displaced refugees from the Baltic and Slavic countries. The barbaric measures used in the forceful round-up of Soviet citizens who were sent back to their home countries for forced labor or execution are described in the book "The Victims of Yalta" by Nikolai Tolstoy, a distant cousin of the famous Russian author, Leo Tolstoy.

General Dwight D. Eisenhower and the Supreme Headquarters, Allied Expeditionary Forces, sought clarification as to who were considered to be Soviet citizens. As a result, the repatriation agreement, reached by the Allies in Leipzig-Halle in the spring of 1945, stipulated that citizens from countries that were outside the borders of the Soviet Union on September 2, 1939 could not be repatriated by force. This agreement was honored in the zones occupied by the western Allies.

In 1939 Latvians, Lithuanians, and Estonians were citizens of their respective independent countries and not of the Soviet Union. Thus, it was not compulsory for the Baltic citizens to be repatriated en masse by force to their homeland, as they no longer had a home country. The three Baltic nations no longer existed as they had been given to the Soviet Union when the occupied lands were divided at Yalta. The former citizens of the Baltic countries declared themselves "Stateless" with no home country to which they could return.

Despite protests by the refugees unwilling to return to countries under Soviet occupation, the American, British, and French military officials had to comply with the Leipzig directive to allow the Soviet Repatriation Commission to exercise the right to ask the former citizens of the Baltic countries to voluntarily come home. In the Soviet occupied zone, a number of people whom the Soviets considered to be their citizens were repatriated without the option for voluntary return. In the

American sectors, people were not repatriated by force, but Soviet delegations were allowed to come into the DP camps to exercise their right to "invite their citizens" to come home. Such a meeting with the representatives from the Soviet Repatriation Commission also took place at Glasenbach. The Soviets were full of smiles, welcoming "their citizens". A glowing picture was painted of the welcome that awaited people who returned to Latvia. Everyone would find a position suitable to his/her profession, children would be enrolled in schools, and the government would provide housing. The question of whether people would be persecuted and deported was answered with a laugh, "What a ridiculous question!" As a bonus, everyone who attended the meeting was given a package of meats and cheeses for their "journey home". The Gedrovics family did enjoy the treats, but did not sign up for the train that was supposed to carry them home. Most of the other families took an equally precautionary "wait and see" attitude. During the period when the Soviet Commission was active in Salzburg, it was determined that only one hundred and six (106) people voluntary signed up to return to "The Workers Paradise".[38]

Only a few elderly people and widows and children with no means of support signed the papers to return to Latvia. Among them was a family consisting of children Vija and Juris and their widowed mother. The husband was lost in the war and the mother did not think she would be accepted in any other country without a wage earner. Vija was one of Skaidrite's friends in the Girl Scout troop. Tatiana got the mother to promise that she would write and tell how they were really treated upon being repatriated. They agreed on some phrases to be used as a code. All letters from the Soviet Bloc countries were censored and all information the Soviets determined to be politically incorrect was stricken from letters with heavy black markers. If it would be written that they were tired from the long train journey, it would mean that the long ride in reality was to Siberia. If the children were taken away from the family and put in a state orphanage, it would be coded as them attending a "new" school. Tatiana wept as she read the letter from Vija's mother: "*We are so happy to be home again, though the journey was very long. The children are glad to be in their new school. They have so many friends now, I hardly ever see the children. Many people are watching over us now. I hope you reconsider coming home.*" Imprisonment, being under surveillance of guards, and separation of family was real indeed. Many of the people who agreed to go back to the Soviet occupied homelands did indeed meet with the hardships they had feared, including death and confinement to the Gulag archipelago. Many similar letters and postcards are on display at the Occupation Museum in Riga They bear witness to the real fate of the many victims of the Soviet occupation. One has to be familiar with the history to interpret the news on the seemingly cheerful postcards and letters. "*We are all fine, working hard now that we are settled after our long trip...the children like their new school surroundings...*"

When I returned for a visit to Latvia after it gained independence, I met Vija and her brother Juris and expressed thanks for their mother giving the coded warning. Vija confirmed the fact that the family had indeed been separated and her mother had spent many years as a prisoner in Siberia. A big wave of Latvians were arrested and sent to Siberia in 1949 in retaliation for what the Soviets perceived to be acts of treason against the regime. The most prominent act of treason was having been a refugee during the war.

It was a very difficult decision for the people who chose not to return to their homeland to declare themselves "Stateless" and no longer citizens of their beloved homeland, but giving up their "Soviet" citizenship meant they could stay at Glasenbach and wait for an opportunity to emigrate to a country where they could live in freedom. Glasenbach was not a final solution for a home, but at least the family units were preserved and everyone worked together to make the DP camp a vital community and a good neighborhood according to civilization patterns preserved from their home country. The stateless refugees still clung to the hope that someday they could return home when world powers like the United States and Great Britain would persuade the Soviet Union to recognize the independence of the Baltic countries. For nearly fifty years after the end of WWII Latvians in exile maintained unofficial Embassies in Washington and in Great Britain working toward the recognition of Latvia as a free country.

★★★

26

LIVING IN A MICROCOSM, OR CIVILIZATION RESTORED

While war can wreak havoc and destroy entire countries, cities, and populations along its wake, civilization seems to endure and resurface once people start working together to bring back their national heritage with all of its corresponding social, political, and cultural complexities. The Latvian community at Glasenbach utilized the education and professional skills of its residents to form a microcosm of Latvian culture, a miniature representation of national development analogous to the larger system previously existing in independent Latvia. Much like a miniature city, the displaced persons camp became structured with its own elected governing officials, school system, medical services, movie and theater venues, religious worship, music concerts, dances, festivals, and parades as well as fraternal and welfare organizations without anyone having to write a plan for a new society. Similar miniature Latvian cities developed in Latvian DP camps in Germany.

Latvian ladies in native costume on parade to welcome UNRRA official team to Glasenbach, leading parade is Janka Berzins

As a child living in the camp for displaced persons, I was not aware of the fact that the camp represented a subsystem of society that emerges wherever civilized people get resettled. Somehow society is programmed to rebuild itself even under unfavorable circumstances and people follow similar patterns of behavior to bring order out of chaos. This remarkable phenomenon become clear to me when I was invited to give a lecture on political refugees and civil rights to a class at Oakland University thirty years later, while I was a member of the faculty. The lecture was to be a commentary on the experience of the Japanese in America who were relocated to internment camps during World War II. The students were analyzing the psychological, cultural, and social effects of the internment experience as described in the book *"Farewell to Manzanar"*[39] by Jeanne Wakatsuki, who as a child had lived in the internment camp at Manzanar. It was surprising to note that the book could have been about the displaced persons camp at Glasenbach where the social structure and experiences were almost identical. It was evident from reading the book, that people in similar circumstances rebuild their lives by following the same pattern of behavior, as if using identical blueprints to save their cultural heritage.

The people living in both camps had left their homes with virtually no possessions. They had no home, no rights, and no control over their fate. The people in the refugee and internment camps were vulnerable and powerless to plan their lives. For the older generations, the experience of being homeless persons had a greater psychological effect than for the children. The children and youth were less aware than their parents of the profound changes and adjustments that would be required in restructuring their lives and starting all over again with no clear focus on what the future would bring.

Yet, nobody sat around in despair. They established schools, hospitals, churches, and pursued cultural interests. Couples celebrated weddings, gave birth to children, had them baptized and confirmed just as they had done when they lived in freedom. The only government department that was absent in the camps was the police department. There appeared to be no need for law enforcement. Stripped of worldly goods, everyone was on an equal economic level and people were busy building a new community rather than tearing it down. A play was produced in the 21st Century about the World War II Latvian displaced persons camp in Esslingen, Germany. As in Glasenbach and the Japanese camp in California, the script describing life in the camps followed a nearly identical formula and I could see my experiences mirrored in the lives of thousands of other refugees from Glasenbach to Esslingen and from Manzanar to Australia.

Compared to a typical small bungalow, or starter home in America, with an average of 1,000 square feet, the 10 by 10 foot room assigned to the Gedrovics family bore no resemblance to our home in Latvia. It took a great deal of patience, unselfishness and understanding for four people to live peacefully under such crowded conditions where privacy was a thing of the past. My sister and I slept in bunk beds along the outside wall. From my top bunk, I could look out the window at night to watch the moon over the snow-covered mountains in the distance. Mother's single bed was along the right inside wall and father's bed was across the room along the left inside wall with a small table and four chairs centered between the beds. At the foot of mother's bed were the two wooden trunks containing all our belongings. One of the trunks was used as a makeshift dresser for the entire family. The other trunk contained out-of-season clothing and the various albums and documents the family had brought from Latvia. The top of this trunk served as the "kitchen" where meals were prepared on a two-burner electric camping stove. Instead of a walk-in-closet, the family had a "walk-up wardrobe" which was one, twenty-four-inch-wide, metal locker at the foot of father's bed containing all of the family's clothing and footwear. I was too young to understand the stress that such cramped quarters could place on marital relations. With parents crowded into one room with their children and the thin walls separating each family's room certainly must have had a negative impact on privacy and intimacy.

Bathroom facilities in the barracks did give rise to nightmares for people who had been used to the comforts of civilization. Mudite and I and the rest of young girls and women in the camp dreaded the army-style latrines and open community showers, situated in a large room in the middle of the barracks. Similarly, the Japanese girls at Manzanar experienced the same feelings of disgust and dread when having to use the common bathroom facility that provided no privacy and lacked cleanliness. The toilets were mostly in open stalls with no doors and my sister and I usually went together so that one could stand guard outside the stall while the other took care of her personal needs. For the most part, daily bathing was done with a sponge bath from a metal washbowl kept in the room. Most people took showers once a week with the whole family going together so they could shelter each other for privacy. Going to the latrine during the dark of the night was out of the question for us girls. Our family kept a "slop" bucket, half-filled with water, behind a curtain in the corner of our room. This is where water was dumped after washing hands, washing dishes, and urinating during the night. It was my job to take the bucket to the latrine to dump it each morning, or whenever it got filled. Recurring nightmares of dirty public bathrooms have haunted my sleep throughout my life.

Mealtimes at the DP camp could generally be likened to chores rather than the enjoyment of a nourishing family experience. In the beginning, one warm meal was provided at noon daily at the camp mess hall located in the center of the camp. The meal usually was some warm soup or a stew, boiled potatoes, and bread. In the morning there was thin, runny oatmeal and the evening meal generally consisted of bread and cheese. People who have the privilege of living in a developed country where food is plentiful usually do not give thought to the psychological impact that a meager diet or hunger may have on a child. One Saturday afternoon I took Mudite to a movie matinee at the mess hall, which also doubled as a movie theater. The film was an old Charlie Chaplin still-picture comedy where Chaplin portrayed a hobo traveling the rails. In one scene Chaplin was cooking a hobo stew where he boiled his boots for added flavor and nourishment. Mudite ran crying out of the theater. When I caught up with my little sister, I asked her why she was crying over such a funny movie, the teary-eyed eight-year-old replied,

"*The man is even poorer than we are and had to cook his boots to make soup. When we rode the freight train, at least we got soup from the canteen when we were hungry. That poor man is not as lucky as we are.*"

Such sympathy, deep thinking, and wisdom came from the lips of a child. Mudite interpreted the comedy film to be a documentary of the difficult rail journeys we had experienced. The movie upset Mudite so much that father had to carry her back to our room in the barrack before she would settle down.

I considered my duty to line up at the mess hall to get the family meal portion poured into a metal army mess kit an unpleasant chore, especially if it was cold or raining outside and the meal got cold before I could carry it back to our room. After some time, the camp administration decided the refugees would be better off if they received the same ration coupons (something like our modern-day food stamps) as the rest of the Austrian citizens in post-war Europe. This allowed each family to purchase their rations at regular grocery stores.

Shopping for groceries at a regular store seemed to be a welcome change, but the nearest country grocery store was in the village of Glasenbach, some three miles from the camp. Car ownership was not one of the perks enjoyed by the DP's. The Gedrovics family was fortunate, since my father was given a bicycle to use for transportation to work. He chose to walk to work instead and the bicycle was left for me to use on weekly trips to shop for all the groceries, as our parents were both working. Riding the bicycle was not an easy task during the winter snow, but I liked the ice and snow more than the heat of the summer when the blacktop road became sticky and radiated heat. There was no bicycle path or shoulders separating the road from the ditches on both sides of the road. During the summer, snakes sometimes slithered from the ditches out onto the road, which added an element of fear to the journey. The return trip with the load of groceries was even more difficult. I had to carry a full knapsack on my back and steer the bicycle with one hand while balancing a metal gallon jug filled with milk in the other hand. Granted, the grocery rations were rather sparse and all fit in one large knapsack. The week's rations for the family included two loaves of bread, a pound of butter, half a pound of cheese, and only two pounds of meat in addition to whatever vegetables were in season. When the family needed their monthly ration of flour, sugar, cereal, and potatoes, I had to make an extra trip. Every bit of food was used. Solidified bacon drippings, flavored with salt and pepper, made an appetizing sandwich spread. During the summer, the family garden plot provided fresh produce to enhance the otherwise drab staple foods. Dried chamomile herbs from the meadow across the road were used to make a soothing home-brewed tea.

Once a month CARE packages were distributed to the displaced persons with extra rations of sugar, sweetened condensed milk, coffee, tea, canned corned beef, Spam, and sometimes even a box of Hershey bars and chewing gum. Usually I portioned out my share of the candy to my little sister, Mudite, who had not been able to enjoy such a luxury as her big sister had in Latvia. Children usually consumed the sweet condensed milk by the spoonful right out of the jar as a tasty dessert or candy. The CARE packages really made a big difference in providing nourishment for all the displaced persons. The day the packages were distributed seemed like a festival day. I have not forgotten the great difference that the CARE relief organization made in the life of my family. To this day, I continue to donate funds to CARE so that other impoverished people can get relief in times of disaster.

After two years of relying on food kitchens in refugee camps immediately following the war, both Tatiana and Kārlis were fortunate to find employment with pay when the family moved to Camp Glasenbach. A regular, though small, income enabled them to provide for our family's basic needs. Tatiana, reporting to the camp director under the jurisdiction of UNRRA, was appointed to serve as the Superintendent of the camp schools. Later she worked as Welfare Officer for the IRO. Kārlis and Jānis Berzins found employment at the neighboring military Camp Truscott, both working in the food service department of the Officers Club. Occasionally, the officers at Camp Truscott would give Kārlis a leftover piece of ham, cheese, or lunchmeat to take home to the family. The biggest feast ever was when my father was given a full five-gallon carton of rich vanilla ice cream to take home for a treat. Since there were no refrigeration facilities at our camp, the contents of the entire container had to be eaten at one sitting by the four Gedrovics', the three persons in the Berzins family, and some of our friends. That was a time when everyone was truly "stuffed to the gills" with the delicious ice cream. Even the subsequent frequent trips to the bathroom did not spoil the joy of the special treat of the family "Ice Cream Social".

While the family income was only at a sustenance level, the CARE packages supplemented the meager camp rations and shipments of donated surplus clothing from the United States allowed the family to have a reasonably normal existence. Although our family income was low, we were once more able to enjoy a reasonable standard of living with many cultural benefits largely due to a volunteer system of services that existed in the camp. Mudite and I were able to attend the Latvian grade school, which was fully accredited by the Austrian school system. Mudite, having learned to read with home tutoring, skipped kindergarten and started in the first grade. I was placed in the fifth grade after a combination of home schooling and one semester in the 4th grade. Both of us participated in the school choir and folk dance ensembles.

Opportunities for extracurricular activities were plentiful at Camp Glasenbach. Most of the displaced persons whom the Germans had deported from Latvia were professionals with advanced levels of education. These individuals were willing to volunteer their services in organizing various cultural activities at the camp. I had the benefit of

Swallows Troop, Skaidrite second from left in top row, Zigrida on her right, Ileane on her left

studying piano with two professional pianists, the twin sisters Karina and Ingrida Gutenberg, who organized piano recitals for their students. The Gutenberg sisters also gave numerous concerts for fourhanded piano at Camp Glasenbach and at venues in the musical city of Salzburg. They later became prominent piano and organ performers and educators in the United States and also in their native country of Latvia.

The Girl Scouts, or Girl Guides as they were called in Latvia, also became a prominent organization for the girls at Glasenbach, since the founder of the Girl Guides in Latvia, Vilhelmine Vilks, was one of the refugees living in the camp. After Mrs. Vilks organized the first troop at the camp, so many girls considered it a high privilege to be associated with the organization's founder that a second troop had to be started. I had the honor of being that troop's leader. The girls chose the name "Swallows" for our troop name and mascot because swallows are said to be "birds of freedom" which do not endure captivity. We likened ourselves to these migrating birds, which by some strong homing instinct are capable of returning to their place of birth. We hoped that we, like the swallows, would someday return to our native homes. Our uniforms consisted of a forest green skirt, white blouse with a swallow embroidered on the sleeve, and a yellow neckerchief. All the badges the Guides earned were hand embroidered by the girls themselves according to patterns the troop designed.

A Brownie troop was organized later and Mudite became a member of the troop "Bitītes", or honeybees. Having once belonged to the friendly group of "Honeybees", Mudite has always liked honeybees and their sweet honey and is not afraid of bees. The Brownie troop was led by one of the schoolteachers, Mrs. Meta Avens, who was one of the neighbors in Barrack #1. The Gedrovics family was fortunate to be able to continue the friendship with the Avens family after they emigrated to America and settled in Cleveland, Ohio.

Initially, the Girl Guides and the Brownies utilized the classrooms at the school for their meetings. At times this presented a conflict with school sports and extracurricular activities. When a residential room became vacant in one of the barracks, I got up the nerve to approach the camp administration for permission to have the room assigned for scouting activities. Impressed by my initiative, the camp director granted the request with the provision that the Guides be responsible for all cleaning, decorating, and maintenance of their facility. After countless hours of scrubbing, scraping, painting, sewing of curtains, and decorating with hand-drawn banners, the room was transformed into a comfortable lounge for activities. As a good deed and in thanksgiving for the new quarters, the Swallows' troop took on a project of giving assistance to physically disabled persons living in the camp. The girls took turns doing weekly cleaning of rooms for people with disabilities and assisted them with housekeeping tasks. The scouting motto of "Be Prepared" became a guiding motto for me even long after I left the DP camp. It followed me throughout my youth and into adulthood as the young "Swallow" of long ago continued in the scouting movement by evolving into a den mother of Den #5 when my three sons joined Boy Scout Troop 1607 in Royal Oak.

Nora, Skaidrite, Zigrida in folk costumes at graduation 1948

Skaidrite, Nora, Zigrida in Hamilton, Ontario 1998

Many lasting friendships were formed among the Girl Guides that transcended years and continents. Though everyone eventually emigrated to other countries, my closest friends and I kept in touch over the years. Reunions with some of my friends took on an international flair, as they involved travel from Australia to the United States and then on to Canada, from the U.S. to Australia, and from Venezuela and the U.S. to Latvia. Yet, when we met, the years seemed to fall away and we picked up where we left off half a century ago, as if time had stood still while we matured, got married, and even became grandmothers.

The miles and years fell away as I met Nora Rudzitis Pulciņš, who lives in Hamilton, Ontario, at Latvian Song Festivals in Toronto and Cleveland. In 1998, Zigrida Smilga Dimits came from Australia to visit me and we both traveled to meet Nora in Hamilton. As we three lined up for a photograph, it seemed like it had been just a little while since we had stood together for a similar photograph taken after our graduation in Glasenbach in 1948 fifty years ago. Zigrida also visited our Sparks' NortHouse and helped water some newly planted fir tree seedlings just like we had helped each other in watering the gardens at Glasenbach. In 2007, accompanied by my husband and our grandson Shawn, I visited Zigrida in Melbourne, Australia. What a blessing it is to have friendships that last so many years that friends can enjoy getting to know each other's grandchildren.

In 2001 when I traveled to Latvia with my two granddaughters, they got to visit the home of yet another former "Swallow" from Glasenbach, Vija, who had returned to Latvia and was living at Jūrmala after an exile in Siberia. I found Vija by responding to an advertisement Vija had placed in the Latvian "Laiks" newspaper searching for classmates from Glasenbach. An article in another edition of "Laiks" mentioned the e-mail address of a Peter Bolšaitis. Since the name Bolšaitis in not very common, I wondered if Peter was the little brother of another "Swallow" named Ileane. When I contacted Peter, I learned that he indeed had a sister named Ileane. At that time Ileane lived in Caracas, Venezuela but later moved back permanently to Riga, Latvia. After not seeing Ileane since 1947, and only a handful of e-mails to recapture significant events of sixty interim years in our lives, I visited her on a trip back to my homeland in 2009. Ileane Bolšaitis lives in Riga in a luxury apartment complex managed by her brother Peter.

Skaidrite with Ileane Bolšaitis in Riga 2009

Ileane and Peter welcomed my family and we caught up with the past decades by reminiscing through the pages of photograph albums. I shared the photos of the visit with Ileane with Zigrida and Nora. The sixty-year reunion through photographs across the continents turned out to be the last for the four classmates. At Christmas, 2009, I received the sad telephone call from Zigrida's daughter Karina in Australia that Zigrida had passed away on December 13, 2009, following a stroke at age 76. One of her last acts had been to mail Australian calendars to her Glasenbach friends for Christmas, as had been Zigrida's custom over the years. I had the sad duty to notify Nora in Hamilton and tears flowed over the phone just like they were shed when the friends parted sixty years earlier, only the parting from Zigrida this time was permanent. Yet, her friendship will remain in the hearts of the Glasenbach girls always.

My husband and I visited Nora and her husband Edmunds in Hamilton in 2010 and had a wonderful visit reminiscing about our lifetime of friendship. Nora underwent a complicated by-pass surgery a week later and she is convinced that the friendship angel statue, which I gave her as a gift protected her during her hospital stay. We vowed to get together again as long as we are able to travel. In 2011 I had the opportunity to visit Ileane again in Riga and thus the strong bonds of friendship established in Glasenbach will keep stretching across oceans our entire lifetime.

★★★

27

SCHOOL DAYS IN GLASENBACH

Latvian School children and staff, 1946, 2nd row middle: Mrs. Avens, Principal Raikovskis, & Rev. Reinfelds, unknown teacher, and Mudite

Since the majority of the Camp Glasenbach residents were Latvians, there were sufficient children there to have their own Latvian school, grades one through seven, taught by six teachers. Children of other nationalities attended an International School, which Tatiana Gedrovics organized to provide study opportunities for all of the various language groups in the camp. As Superintendent of both the Latvian and International schools, Tatiana was successful in getting the camp schools accredited by the Austrian government according to the educational standards of the land. For this achievement she received a commendation from the Chairman of the County School Board of the Salzburg Region for her exceptional knowledge of teaching objectives, ability to converse in four languages, and excellent leadership ability in establishing a friendly and disciplined learning environment for the multinational and multilingual student body. Among other documents, which I treasure even after my mother's death, are glowing references and written testimonials from the Glasenbach Chief Welfare Officer Valiant Nichols, the Camp Director of the UNRRA Team 191 Phillip Gullion, and several officials of the Church World Service where my mother worked as Emigration Officer.

The level of education for the children surpassed that of public schools due to high standards, small class size, and individualized attention to each student. The students were tested and their placement in grades depended on their achievement and the level of education they had reached after leaving their homeland during the war. Despite frequent moves and short periods of attendance in Austrian schools in Knittelfeld and Judenburg, I was fortunate as my mother had "home-schooled" me while we lived in the different Displaced Persons (DP) camps. Thus, in 1946, I was moved into the fifth grade although I had only had a total of four months of formal education in grades three and four. Mudite, only six years old, qualified to start first grade without having to complete kindergarten.

My only classmate in the fifth grade was a boy named Igors, who was two years older, having missed going to school during the refugee years. With only two students in grade five, it was almost like being home-schooled or tutored. However, this time the various subjects were taught by different teachers and not my mother. There were formal examinations and report cards documenting academic achievement as well as deportment in the classroom.

School assignments were always easy for me, but my free spirit and independent thinking inherited from my mother caused some problems in adjusting to a formal school regimen. I found it somewhat problematic to adjust from home schooling to a formal classroom, just like my mother had found the transition to a public school difficult after being taught by a governess. Whenever a teacher or the principal entered the classroom, we were required to stand up at attention until given the signal to sit down again. We were not permitted to speak unless we raised an arm and were recognized by the teacher. Following my mother's footsteps, my independence resulted in frequent trips to the principal's office where I was greeted by principal Raikovskis usually exclaiming, "You again!" when I was sent to be disciplined for talking back to a teacher when some assignment or order seemed unfair to me. Being a "Champion for Justice" constantly remained my goal, which often interfered with the teacher's orders. But as a young girl I did not as yet have the wisdom to discern which battles are worth fighting and which perceived injustices are not worth contesting, such as on whom a teacher called for an answer from the day's assignment.

With two students in the class, the science teacher had fallen into a pattern of calling on Igors and me on alternate days to stand up and answer questions from the previous day's science reading assignment. At some point, he must have started wondering if his two students were taking advantage of this pattern and were only doing their reading assignments on alternate days. I always did my homework every day and always knew the answers whether I was called upon to recite the lesson or it was Igor's turn. However, one day the teacher changed the order and called on me two days in a row. Deciding this was not "fair", I told the teacher that it was not my turn and that he has to call on Igors.

"I want you to answer my questions today," the teacher informed me sternly.

"I answered yesterday. It is not fair that I have to answer when it is Igor's turn," I stubbornly insisted.

"Then I must assume that you did not read your assignment for today", responded the teacher. "I will have to give you a failing grade for today".

The grading system ranged from a high 5 to the lowest of a 2, which was a failing grade, with 3 being an average mark.

"Fine", I responded. "All my grades have been a 5 or a 5+. It will make no difference over the semester if I get a 2 today. It is the principle of the thing and I refuse to answer when you already tested me yesterday and today is Igor's turn."

"Then we will let the principal decide whether you have to answer a teacher's questions whenever you are called upon. Go to the principal's office!"

I appeared at the principal's office as told. I explained to Mr. Raikovskis that my refusal to answer stemmed from the fact that it was unfair to always call on me just because I always knew the answers. In my opinion, Igors was not getting equal education if I had to take his recitation turns as well.

"Did you do the reading assignment and know the answers today?" the principal asked.

"Of course!" I responded.

I was instructed to go back to the classroom and to answer the questions so that my perfect record would not have even one "2" failing grade among all the 5's. The wise principal explained that sometimes a teacher might appear to be unfair, but that he is in charge and his orders are to be respected. It would be even more unfair to me if I took a failing grade just to prove a point even if I was right. Back to the class I went and answered all the questions correctly, thus earning a grade of 5, but in the behavior category for the day, a lone "**2**" stood out among all the 5's.

Boredom also tended to initiate problems for me, as I was a quick learner. When I got bored with repetitive explanations, I did not indulge in mischief. Rather, my mind started wandering and allowed me to turn off hearing the same material being discussed over and over "ad nauseam". During one Religion class, I started doodling on a drawing pad as entertainment during one seemingly endless discussion. Pastor Reinfelds noticed my doodling and took it as a sign of inattention.

"Put down your pencil and listen to the lesson", he sternly instructed.

"I am listening to the same thing being said over and over again. I listen with my ears and I understood the first time before you started repeating yourself. There is nothing wrong with me quietly drawing by using my hands to escape boredom."

"I am telling you to put down your pencil now!' the Pastor ordered.

"You are to teach religion", I impudently responded. *"You are not qualified to judge whether I can draw or not".*

"Principal's Office!"

"It's You Again!" exclaimed the principal.

This time the principal decided that since I enjoyed writing, I should write an essay on "Justice and Equal Treatment in the Classroom". I received a "5" for the extra-credit essay in my writing class, but the behavior grade in Religion showed a humiliating, but deserved "3".

At the conclusion of the school year and the fifth grade, the teachers decided that I, as a gifted student, needed more of a challenge than being promoted to the sixth grade to be its only student, because Igors had missed too much school and had to repeat the fifth grade. I was allowed to skip the sixth grade if I completed certain assignments and tests during the summer. This I did with ease and in the fall of 1947, I started the seventh grade as its youngest student at age twelve. My friends Zigrida, Nora, and Ileane were all fourteen. Mirdza and Victors were seventeen. The latter two were catching up after years of missed schooling when they had to work during the war. They did graduate from grade school at Glasenbach but both died at a young age. Victors died from tuberculosis in South America and

Mirdza lost her battle against cancer in Canada. Zigrida, Nora, Ileane, and I were fortunate to spend a memorable year together while we were in the Swallows troop of the Girl Guides, cementing our friendship for over sixty years. Ileane, however, did not graduate with the rest of us. Before we started the seventh grade, Ileane's days as a DP ended and she left Glasenbach and our friendship circle for a new homeland.

5th & 6th grades, 1947; Standing: Ileane, Nora, Igors; Sitting: Zigrida, Skaidrite, Principal Raikovskis, Mirdza, and Victors.

Ileane's mother received sponsorship for the Bolšaitis family to emigrate to Venezuela under the premise that she would be able to continue working in her profession as a dentist. In 1947 Dr. Bolšaitis, Ileane, and her brother Peter departed from Salzburg with expectations for a brighter future, though their mode of transportation had not changed from when they left Latvia as refugees. Loaded unto a freight train as if they were commodities instead of intelligent professional people, these future citizens of Venezuela left their friends behind and departed Salzburg in August. They arrived in Venezuela on October 1, 1947 to start a new life on a strange continent with unfamiliar customs and a strange language. Starting over did not come easy in Venezuela

Refugees departing in cattle car for Venezuela 1947; Ileane squatting in front row, right.

or any other country that accepted refugees. It took a great deal of hard work, self-sacrifice, and courage for Dr.Bolšaitis to support and educate her children while starting over again to regain her status as a dentist. Before she could practice her profession, she had to pass exams and get a degree in dentistry at the university in Venezuela again. The process took ten long years and a strong spirit to rise above all the obstacles before she could work in a full professional capacity. Ileane followed her mother's footsteps and also became a dentist.

The remaining five students in the 1948 graduation class of the Camp Glasenbach Latvian Elementary School were privileged to participate in the first, one and only, graduation ceremony ever to take place in this displaced person's camp. By the following year most of the inhabitants of the camp had been scattered through resettlement in various countries. March 14th, 1948, although it was not spring as yet according to the calendar, dawned bright, warm, and sunny as if heralding spring and a new beginning for the happy graduates. The four girls in the class–Mirdza, Zigrida, Nora, and I— all were dressed in traditional national folk costumes borrowed from some of the camp ladies who had brought the original hand-woven treasured costumes with them when fleeing Latvia. Victors looked handsome in a sports coat, also borrowed from the principal. The number of dignitaries at the commencement exercises exceeded the number of graduates.

Graduation class 1948 and teachers in front row, parents in the back, and Camp Truscott partially visible on top of hill.

The Latvian Lutheran Pastor Reinfelds gave the invocation. Phillip Gullion, the Director of the UNRRA/IRO Team 191 at Glasenbach, congratulated the graduates on behalf of the U.S. government. Valiant Nichols, the Chief Welfare Officer, presented flowers to the graduates. Superintendent Tatiana Gedrovics gave the graduation address, and Principal Raikovskis presented the diplomas. Director Karlis

Avens congratulated the graduates on behalf of the Latvian Association at Glasenbach and Vilhelmine Vilks, the founder of the Latvian Girl Scouts/Guides, was also present to greet the girls from the Swallows troop. Her wish for me was that I would grow as tall as my ideals and courage. Being the youngest and shortest person in the graduating class of '48, I had often been teased about my short stature. Mrs. Vilks' wishes did come true. Four years later, when I graduated from high school, I was one of the tallest girls in my class.

Following graduation, the students had the option of enrolling in a private high school in Salzburg, as there was no high school in the village of Glasenbach. The older students could enter the workforce. My parents decided they would keep me out of school for a year because their financial situation did not allow for tuition in a private school. Since I was still a year or two younger than other students in my class, it was deemed best if I just continued independent studies and took it easy for a year, as my health had not been particularly good. However, fresh air and wholesome food in summer camps returned my health. Somehow, sacrificing their own needs, my parents also found means to come up with the tuition and in late summer of 1948, I enrolled in a private girls' school in Salzburg. I only attended the Bundes-Mädchenrealgymnasium mit Frauen-Oberschule in Salzburg for less than one month before leaving the displaced persons ranks at Glasenbach. This period was too brief to build any lasting memories or friendships. The only memory remaining is that of the long daily trips into the city and the pathway through the woods, along the Salzach River, and over the bridge to reach the bus taking me to the high school.

The only mental picture I retained of these walks was of one shocking experience when a young man emerged from among the trees, and opening his tan raincoat, flashed me with complete nakedness. Shocked, my eyes stayed riveted to the youth's handsome face and I have no recall of any other details of his exposed body. If showed in a line-up, I am sure I could identify the young man with the blond curly hair and big brown eyes even to the present day. I later learned that former soldiers, traumatized by the war, sometimes wandered around naked, as if by shedding their clothing, they would also shed their atrocious memories of the war. As my sister Mudite and I would learn later in life, memories of some traumatic experiences are never completely erased. They continue to live hidden in the farthest recesses of ones mind and can suddenly appear later without warning. However, most of the time my friends and I enjoyed a relatively normal life in Glasenbach, as we were blissfully unaware of what represented a "normal" life of a teenager outside the confines of the DP camp.

★★★

28

THE HILLS ARE ALIVE WITH THE SOUND OF MUSIC

*A*s seasons changed, life for the adults at Camp Glasenbach went on from day to day with the usual worries about where to find work, a permanent home, how to support the family, and what the future will bring. For the children, the summers of 1947 and 1948 were a continuous "camp" experience, with "camp" taking on the meaning of a group summer vacation place, not a DP camp. It seems every organization with a mission to help displaced persons had a special goal to make summers particularly productive for the DP children. The Salzburg area is richly endowed by nature and excellently suited for summer outings with lakes, rivers, mountains, and miles of walking trails to explore. The YMCA, Scouts, UNRRA, and church groups all sponsored summer activities and camps and the children of Glasenbach and other area DP camps got to participate at least once or more times each summer.

Tatiana and daughters biking along the Salzach River

I remember several excursions to climb to the summit of Gaisberg, a mountain predominating the Salzburg scenery. This was a safe, yet demanding climb, popular with school groups. In the winter, the children were provided with surplus military skis in the white camouflage color and the foothills of Gaisberg provided a beautiful venue for daily skiing. I turned out to be quite expert at ski jumping and navigating moguls and even helped some of the G.I.'s from Camp Truscott learn how to ski. In the summer, Gaisberg provided the lucky climber with a special gift of rare alpine flowers. Though I never found the rare Edelweiss, which usually grew at higher alpine elevations, I had the fortune of discovering the Enzian several times. Austrians treasure the Enzian (gentian), a deep blue bell-shaped flower, nearly as much as the Edelweiss.

The Hellbrunner Palace[40] grounds in the southern district of Salzburg were another favorite destination for outings. The former summer castle of the Archbishop of

Salzburg, Markus Sittikus, was built in 1613 for entertaining his guests. The castle and its grounds, spared from destruction during World War II, were opened to the public and was a feature attraction for families and school children. It has become a permanent fixture for visitors in the 21st century, especially after the film "Sound of Music" was produced. In the movie, the pavilion where Liesl and Frank met is located in the Hellbrunner Park and is the site where the couple sang the song "You are Sixteen, I am Seventeen". The ornate buildings and beautifully landscaped garden architecture provided an attractive day's outing for the children of the Glasenbach DP camp.

The main attraction of Hellbrunn was the "Wasserkunst", or "Wasserspielen", a true children's paradise. The children and adults were always surprised and amused by this water art or mechanical water-play park. While the unsuspecting visitors were admiring some statue in the park, suddenly water would come shooting out of concealed openings in the statue and water fountains would come cascading over the surprised visitors. Not every statue contained the water plumbing, so one never knew where the surprise drenching would occur unless they had studied the activities in the water park on a regular basis. The Archbishop must have been a great practical joker. One stone banquet table with surrounding stools was used for entertaining royal guests at dinner. Unexpectedly, water conduits in the round stools would spray the seats of the astonished visitors. One can only imagine the bedlam it caused when the 17th Century ladies in their long dinner gowns got drenched! The children enjoyed the spraying water to cool them off in the heat of the summer. I never did find out whether someone operated the fountains by remote control upon observing people at a rigged statue, or if in the 1600's such inventions as motion controls already existed in some early form. The Bishops of Salzburg must have been a merry bunch indeed to incorporate the "Wasserkunst" in the statues as a practical joke for the amusement of visitors. The castle itself was not open for tours when my school group visited, but the Hellbrunn Palace website describes interesting new features, such as bird songs echoing from within the walls of the palace and a zoological garden next to the park for families to enjoy.

Salt mine tour in Hallein; Gedrovics family in the middle

Another natural attraction in the Salzburg lake region that the Gedrovics family and our friends visited during the summer were the salt mines near the village of Hallein. Visitors were provided with white pants, jackets and caps to protect their clothing and then driven deep into the mines on a ten-person trolley cart driven by a miner who acted as a guide. What an interesting experience it was to be driven through salt tunnels into caves where the walls were formed by rock salt glistening by lantern light. Since I have always had an appetite for everything salty, I could not resist touching the walls against the guide's instructions. It was a treat for me to lick my salty fingers. "Mmmmmm, what great refreshment!"

The summer day outings with classmates certainly provided great enjoyment for all the Glasenbach children, but the greatest experience during the summer of 1948 was actually getting away from the DP camp to spend a whole week at a real summer camp. The first such camp experience was near the village of Fuschl near Salzburg in a region called the Salzkammergut, or "Salt Chamber" which is not only the area where salt is mined but also the picturesque location of numerous lakes. Through the auspices of UNRRA, a large villa on Fuschlsee was made available to house the summer camp for the Girl Guides and Boy Scouts. I was able to attend the camp not only as a Girl Scout, but my entire family was also able to join me for a vacation. As the Superintendent of Camp Glasenbach Schools, my mother was also in charge of the Guides and Scouts. She was given the additional responsibility for procuring all food and camp supplies for the summer camp and had the privilege of having her spouse join her. Mudite was enrolled in the camp with the Brownie troop. Scouts from other DP camps were also at the camp and my sister and I made many new friends, participated in singing by the campfire every evening, and enjoyed nourishing meals thanks to the dietary expertise of our mother who planned all the meals for the entire camp population. Rowboats were available for rowing or fishing. Swimming in the cool mountain lake was a favorite pastime, but making a big splash by jumping into the lake from a diving board was perhaps the most fun of all. I learned the meaning of "Look before you leap" the hard way. Not particularly looking where I was jumping, I bounced particularly high one time and reached the bottom of the lake feet first. My foot landed on a broken jagged glass bottle and my heel was cut rather deeply, requiring a visit to the camp first aid station for stitches. This put an end to jumping in the water, but fortunately it happened next to the last day of camp. I received a great deal of sympathy from the other campers as I appeared at the campfire on crutches because the doctor did not allow me to put any weight on the injured foot. I got so much attention, I felt like a sports hero, injured in the heat of competition.

The injured foot had barely healed when I got the good news that I had also been chosen to attend the YWCA camp located in the same region. This camp was in the village of Strobl on the largest and most scenic of the Salzkammergut lakes, the beautiful Wolfgangsee. Again, my mother was chosen as one of the camp leaders and the entire family had an opportunity to rest and relax on the lake and in the surrounding hills. This time there were no injuries, but my swimsuit created an embarrassing problem for me. Swimsuits were a luxury that none of the DP girls could afford, nor were they readily available in the immediate post-war period. Latvians were good at improvising and also were skilled in sewing and handicraft. Some wool yarn was obtained by taking apart an old army sweater and I proudly wore a new brown two-piece swimsuit I had knitted into a beautiful pattern from the reclaimed wool. Perhaps there was a good reason why swimsuits normally are not constructed from wool yarn. Whenever the suit got wet, the wool would get heavy and waterlogged and the entire garment would start sinking down from the hips and over the thighs while the top stretched and threatened to roll down my midriff. I managed to exit from the lake quite demurely while hanging on to the top and bottom of the suit to keep them from completely sliding off. From then on the new bathing suit was worn only for sunbathing.

Numerous hiking trails wound through the lake region and up into the nearby hills. My father and I took many hikes together. When our mother had free time from her duties at camp, we girls also enjoyed riding in the boat with mother while our father cast his fishing line into the lake and often came up with plenty of fresh perch for a very delicious meal cooked over the campfire.

Kārlis at Strobl on Wolfgangsee

Skaidrite at Wolfgangsee overlook

Tatiana and daughters at Strobl 1948

The sunny, carefree days of summer were a blessed respite from everyday life in the DP camp, but it is said that all good things must come to an end eventually. As the earth moved further away from the sun's caressing warmth in 1948, along with the autumn rain also came tears of farewell not only in parting from the new friends at summer camp, but often also when separating from family members. Tears and farewells when parting from family and friends were a common occurrence during the war years and also the resettlement period. Arriving in a new place and making it your home was comparatively easy. As the refugee years unfolded, the dominant theme became the endless partings from familiar places, friends, and sometimes even family members because DP camps in principle are but temporary dwelling places for people displaced from their homes. A permanent solution had to be found to resolve the wandering refugee situation.

★★★

29

FAREWELL, SO LONG, AUFWIEDERSEHEN, GOOD-BYE...

*E*fforts to find new homelands for the refugees increased during the summer and fall of 1948 when the refugee question entered the third year of uncertainty not only for the people involved but also for the host countries and international organizations sponsoring the DP camps. The Allied forces in Europe had originally planned that the persons displaced by World War II were to be repatriated to their homelands as quickly as possible. Persons whose citizenship was easy to identify and who were willing to be repatriated were rapidly sent back to their country of origin. Of the Latvians at Glasenbach, only a handful of people, including my friend Vija and her family returned to Latvia voluntarily after the official Soviet Repatriation Commission's visit to the Camp to invite everyone to return home. The smiles pasted on the faces of the recruiting party and the familiar, all-inclusive slogan of "Vi nashi" tried to assure the former residents of the Baltic countries that they belonged to the Soviets. That was a line that people who had escaped when their country was invaded found hard to swallow. Everyone who had lived through the purges of 1941 instinctively knew not to trust these messengers trying to entice them with the proverbial "thirty pieces of silver" and hollow promises. The Soviets, being part of the Allies, had the right to conduct these "Informational Meetings", but they were not provided lists of Latvians, Estonians, and Lithuanians by the UNRRA/IRO administration. The agreement, reached by the Allies in Leipzig-Halle in the spring of 1945, stipulated that citizens from countries that were outside the borders of the Soviet Union on September 2, 1939 could not be repatriated by force. This agreement was honored in the zones occupied by the western Allies.

The situation was different in Eastern Germany, which was occupied by the Soviets. The refugees from the Baltic States of Estonia, Latvia, and Estonia, who found themselves in the sector occupied by the Soviets, were immediately rounded up and sent back to their home countries. From there, most refugees returning home ended up being banished to the Siberian Gulag archipelago as punishment for allowing themselves to be sent to German labor camps during the war. Only the refugees whose occupations were deemed to be essential to the Soviets were allowed to work in their home countries. My cousins, whose father was taken from Latvia in 1944 to work as a surgeon for the Germans, were in Eastern Germany at the end of the war. They were given no choice and were returned to Latvia immediately. They were spared being imprisoned in Siberia because Dr. Teodors Lācis was a prominent surgeon and was needed in Latvia, which had a severe shortage of physicians after the war. However, life for his family was not easy for the next forty-five years under the Soviet regime. Like in 1940 when Latvia was first invaded, people lived with a cloud of suspicion hanging over them constantly.

Upon declaring ourselves to be "Stateless", the Gedrovics family members had no hope of ever returning home to the Latvia we knew during its brief glory days when freedom still reigned. Our lot was now cast with thousands of other refugees who refused to be repatriated and had to wait for some foreign country to offer asylum from Communist persecution. As difficult as it had been to be labeled a DP, or "Displaced Person", it was even more heartbreaking to be "Stateless", as if all identity had been lost in addition to nearly all material possessions, the homes so lovingly built, and the professional paths successfully pursued. We were no longer Latvians, but rather faceless wanderers among thousands of other homeless people who had no government looking out for our safety and welfare.

Being stateless had different psychological effects on the older and younger generations. Though the children had lived through all the dangers of war and subsequent years of homelessness, they did not have to carry the heavy burden of making the decisions that would shape their future. Only in retrospect, as they reached adulthood, could the children appreciate their parents' valor, survival skills, boundless energy, determination, and strong religious conviction. The grandparents and parents were aware that in saving their family from death or imprisonment in Siberia, they had exposed them to new unknown hardships. One can only imagine the many sleepless nights spent in trying to make critical decisions in a vacuum. As adults, my parents were cognizant of the poverty, hard work and discrimination they would be facing as new immigrants wherever they ultimately found their home. They knew that challenges lay ahead in starting life all over again in exile with no resources other than their personal courage, inner strength, and reliance on God to lead them according to His will. God had protected our family throughout all the horrors of war, physical hardships almost beyond human endurance, and hunger when we often did not know where the next meal was coming from. The family had survived and our needs remained simple as long as we had each other.

Unaware of all the economic, social and political nuances, the children were more flexible, more tolerant, liked adventure, and mixed more readily with other nationalities. For Mudite and me, the new status of "Statelessness" held little meaning. We still had our parents and life was sweetened by occasional Hershey bars from some G.I. in the neighboring Camp Truscott as reward for our cute smiles. For me Hershey bars would always bring back fond memories of the American soldiers who often sacrificed their own rations or packages from home to share them with a poor refugee child. Several decades later, I found out that a fellow church member at Our Shepherd Lutheran Church in Birmingham was one of the soldiers at Camp Truscott when the Gedrovics family lived at Camp Glasenbach. Hoyt Centers remembered the children begging for candy at the fence and he admitted that he sometimes shared some sweets with them. Even when some incidents appear random and accidental, only God can arrange that people's paths cross years, miles, and oceans later. How else could it happen that I came to America and was able to personally thank one of the G.I.'s who in a Christian spirit helped some disadvantaged little children in our D.P. camp? The little begging arms stretching through the barbed wire fence that separated the two camps must have painted a poignant scene that the young soldiers, not many years past their own adolescence, could resist.

The refugee children in turn shared the handouts with their younger siblings and friends. Mudite and her little playmates were particularly fond of the chewing gum the G.I.'s passed to them through the fence. The girls soon developed a "recycling" procedure, which allowed one piece of gum to be shared by friends for several days until no trace of flavor remained. The girl who initially came in possession of a packet of gum would chew one piece for the first day. In the evening the ball of gum would be stuck to the metal post of her bed to preserve it through the night. The gum could only be attached to metal as sticking it to wood or fabric would make it adhere too firmly. The next morning the "gently chewed" gum would be passed on to a friend who would follow the routine until the next day, or whenever there would be no trace of flavor left to pass on or someone accidentally swallowed the gum. No modern day recycling enthusiast could match this gum recycling routine. Of course the girls made sure that the recycling was only done between good friends who could be relied upon to practice good personal hygiene.

Yet, at the same time our parents must have experienced severe anxiety over having to renounce their citizenship in order to provide food and safety for their family that was their only treasure. It was not a win-win situation. There was no immediate reward in sight. Where would they find a new country to accept them dispossessed as they were? Everyone was vulnerable and powerless to decide where the winds of change would carry him or her. The refugees had no rights, no home, and no control over their lives. This would leave a lasting impression on their personalities. Having had to prove their loyalty and worth as a human being to survive under the Soviets and the Nazis, now everyone had to prove again to be worthy of being accepted by some strange land with strange language and customs. The feeling of being looked upon as second-class citizens needing to prove their worth lingered among immigrants even after they were successfully assimilated in their new countries.

Latvians, for the most part, have always been industrious, taken pride in their work, and have not been willing to accept welfare either in their homeland or in the new countries adopting them. It is in their nature to work diligently and to place a high value on education to learn new skills and earn higher degrees in order to prove themselves as worthy citizens wherever they live. The new immigrants did not use prejudice as a crutch for failure. It is interesting to also note that the dispossessed refugees have always placed great importance on their appearance. As much as it was prudent economically, they tried to dress according to what they felt to be their true status in life, not the indigent, poor people the world perceived them to be. The World War II immigrants proudly followed the code that you are what you dress to be. Even at the gatherings in Camp Glasenbach, people came dressed in their good dresses and suits, though threadbare. Wrinkled pants and t-shirt garments commonly worn by a laborer were abhorred even when one did perform the work of common laborers. The meager wardrobes they had brought from Latvia had to last a long time, so they were kept neat and clean and often repaired and altered to be handed down to a child.

My mother, though regarded by her colleagues and supervisors as a highly educated and intelligent professional person, always had a lingering feeling of insecurity about being looked upon as "different" or less-qualified because she was an immigrant in America. Her daughters were taught to always look and behave their best because she had the impression that foreigners in America are profiled and "stick out like spotted dogs". She always strived for perfection in everything she did. Tatiana, knowing how humiliating it is to be discriminated against, always treated everyone with equal respect and never was too proud to befriend even the most unfortunate and least likeable people. Tatiana, like many Latvians, also never completely trusted any political propaganda and never lost the fear of reprisal from the Soviets even after Latvia was recognized as an independent nation again.

The older generations also found it difficult to exercise the right of freedom of speech. There seemed to be wariness in expressing a political opinion or giving out personal information lest somebody were listening and stood ready to betray their trust. Some of this cautionary attitude also rubbed off on the younger generation. Mudite remembers waiting at a bus stop on the way home from the university some ten years after arriving in America. A gentleman also waiting for the same bus started a friendly conversation with her and asked her what her destination was and where she was going to school. After Mudite answered the man, she was filled with panic because an old fear rose in her that perhaps some political official had found a devious way to interrogate her about her family. Perhaps last, but not least, the refugees acquired the virtue of patience as they stoically waited for some military power or bureaucracy to play with the wheel of fortune that determined their fate. Thus, 1948 primarily was the year of the "Long Wait" for the seemingly indestructible stateless people waiting to start a new life at a destination yet unknown.

While the resettlement issue ran its slow meandering course and took a prominent place in daily discussions, life in the DP camp continued along its usual pattern with the refugees living one day at a time and giving each other moral support while facing their unknown future. Initially it was uncertain whether the remaining DP's would ever find a home, but eventually many countries made the humanitarian effort to accept refugees providing they met the high immigration standards. Belgium was the first country to initiate an immigration program for 20,000 people who were willing to sign contracts as coal mine workers. Chile in South America also sought workers for the mines and the United Kingdom accepted 86,000 refugees for their labor forces. Canada implemented a bulk-labor program to accept qualified labor. In later decades, from these masses of hardworking laborers throughout the world rose prominent doctors, lawyers, architects, artists, musicians, professors, and engineers.

In an exceptional case, an immigrant child who had settled with her family in the Quebec Province of Canada became the first female President of the Republic of Latvia after it gained freedom in the nineteen-nineties. Vaira Vike-Freiberga, a professor of Psychology from Montreal, had never lost the love for her native country as she become involved in furthering the cause of Latvia's political freedom and cultural affairs. Following her election, President Vike-Freiberg became a most successful and admired leader not only in Latvia, but also the NATO and nations throughout the world.

The people at Glasenbach lived in a limbo of uncertainty while nations other than Belgium, South America, and the British Commonwealth debated whether to accept immigrants. Bulletin boards were anxiously checked daily and long lines waited for immigration authorities to hand out coveted applications for admission. All the countries that agreed to accept immigrants outside usual peacetime quotas wanted only able-bodied, skilled people with no medical problems. The highly restricted immigration regulations often required families to split up again. Often elderly parents would not be accepted for immigration along with their able-bodied adult children who could provide cheap labor in the mines.

Once again the Gedrovics family faced the tough decision of having to separate from Omi, her husband Mr. Berzins and my dear uncle Jānis or "Janka". Countries that accepted laborers allowed a limited number of dependents per each immigrant laborer. Large families generally found it difficult to find a sponsor. Thus Kārlis and Tatiana again faced the difficult choice of accepting asylum for only their immediate family of four, while young Janka, who was a strong and healthy single nineteen-year-old, looked for a sponsor who would allow him to declare his parents as dependents. Janka, whose parents were more difficult to place as both were close to age sixty, registered for emigration to all the countries offering asylum regardless of the labor he would be required to perform. Coalmines in South America were the most liberal in granting visas to the young and strong males, including their dependents.

Working in the mines was not an option for Kārlis for whom such physically challenging labor would be too taxing for his health at age forty-five. Kārlis hoped that he would be able to qualify as a farm worker with his many years of farming and forestry experience on his aunt's farm "Ziedoņi" in Livberze. He held out no hope for employment in his field of accounting due to lack of ability to converse in English or Spanish. Tatiana's American employers urged the family to request sponsorship for employment in the United States.

In May of 1948, the family had its last joyful celebration together as Pastor Reinfelds of the Latvian Evangelical Lutheran Church confirmed Janka at Camp Glasenbach. After the confirmation, Janka led the family to a stripped old Ford abandoned in the nearby daisy meadow. He joked that he was planning to restore the junked automobile and that he would proudly end his DP stateless status by driving in a style befitting a gentleman to the ship taking him to his new homeland. Janka had just received confirmation that he and his parents had been accepted by Chile in South America where he would be using his mechanical skills in a coalmine. It is an interesting coincidence that the abandoned Ford closely resembled the first used car Janka bought in Chile and also the Ford that the Gedrovics family acquired in the USA about the same time.

Jānis Berzins, Mudite, and Kārlis in front; Skaidrite, Tatiana, Janka, and Omi in back; Last family photo in May 1948

Parting from the beloved Berzins family members was no easier than having to see the lone, small figure of grandmother Gedrovics waving goodbye to her son and his family on the dark and stormy day in September, 1944, as she made the decision to stay on the farm in Livberze rather than face the unknown future as a homeless refugee from war. As in 1944, it was thought that the parting would only be temporary. Janka was quite excited about the adventure of moving to a country halfway around the world and located in a different hemisphere below the equator. Surely, when he and his parents had settled down or the Gedrovics family had achieved security in their new country yet unknown, there would be opportunity for the family to be reunited again.

On the evening of their departure, Janka came to his sister Tatiana's room to say good-bye as I lay sobbing in my upper bunk. I could not bear to come to Omi's room to part from my dear grandmother and my wonderful uncle Janka who had been like an older brother to me. As Janka hugged his niece so overcome by grief, he assured me that surely we would meet again as we were both so young and had our entire lives ahead of us. But I could not be comforted. A great sorrow and dark foreboding overcame me. I lay in my bunk bed and, sobbing uncontrollably, told my uncle, "No, this goodbye is forever. I will never see you again...." How could I bear to have part of my beloved family torn away again when everyone's efforts always had been to stay strong by being together? I wrote a poem after the last hug and the heartbreaking goodbyes.

"*We always need to stay together,*
Arm in arm through stormy weather.

Our embrace must remain ever tight
To withstand all danger and all might.
Can anyone tell me what our destiny will be?
When strong winds carry us across the sea?
The storms of change will blow us so far,
We'll only meet when wishing upon a star.

My intuition proved to be prophetic. Janka died in Chile at age thirty from pneumonia acquired in the mines without ever being reunited with his sister's family again. Janka did leave behind four cousins for me but, but much to my sorrow, I have never been able to locate them. A daughter named Ingrid was born from Janka's union with his first wife, Karina, a Canadian lady of German origin. After they divorced, Janka married a native of Chile by the name of Elena Alfero. They had three children–Juan, Gema, and Gerardo. After Janka's death, Elena stopped communications with Tatiana. Ingrid kept in touch for several years and I was fortunate to meet my cousin at the funeral of Mr. Berzins in 1969. Ingrid wrote several letters to her Aunt Tatiana for several years thereafter but never enclosed her return address. Ingrid reported that she had married a man named David (no last name provided) and was moving to England. Letters to her former address in Montreal, Quebec and to her mother Karina came back with the notation "Addressee moved, no forwarding address". In time Ingrid's letters stopped. Sadly, she must have believed that her aunt Tatiana either had also died or did not want to communicate with her. Ingrid apparently never realized that she had not provided an address. Without knowing even her married last name and city of residence, I could not trace her even with the help of the worldwide web.

It is painful for me to think of four of my blood relatives living in unknown places in the world, unaware of the love I carry in my heart for them and their departed father, my beloved childhood uncle and companion, Janka. Almost every displaced person's family can relate to stories of families torn apart by war. Wars produce many more victims than the soldiers felled in battles as families are separated for political, economic and medical reasons. My parents were thankful that their nuclear family remained intact as they still held out hope that they would be able to emigrate to the United States which the world considered to be the Land of Opportunity.

The United States was late in accepting displaced persons. Existing quotas that allowed entry into the United States for Eastern European refugees were completely inadequate. Facing great opposition in Congress, President Harry Truman was nevertheless successful in signing the first Displaced Persons Act on June 16, 1948. The Act allowed 200,000 DP's to enter the US in 1948, and another 200,000 in 1950 and made Harry Truman the hero for all Latvians seeking admission to America. Although the Act was the most idealistic of all Allied Immigration Programs, it was not meant to provide government welfare assistance to foreign nationals. All immigrants were required to have sponsors guaranteeing that they would never become a burden to the State and the nation and that they would not deprive any American citizen of a job.

The immigration rules were extremely strict and allowed only the ablest and the fittest to enter the country. The Gedrovics family, as all other immigrants, had to pass strict screening to determine that they had no ties with political enemies or organizations, had never had a criminal record, served in the military of the Axis powers, were free of any medical problems, and were guaranteed a job by their sponsors. President John F. Kennedy, a champion for immigrants, once remarked that U.S. immigration rules were so strict for the displaced persons that Emma Lazarus' poem on the Statue of Liberty should have an addendum to read: *"Give me your tired, your poor... as long as they come from Northern Europe, are not too tired, or too poor, or slightly ill, never stole a loaf of bread, never joined a questionable organization, and can document all their activities".*[41]

Kārlis had excellent recommendations from his supervisors at Camp Truscott and Tatiana had glowing references from everyone she worked for in the UNRRA and IRO organizations in addition to the Austrian Education Ministry in Salzburg. In 1948 mother was employed by Church World Services (CWS) in Salzburg, working as an Emigration Officer with responsibility for maintaining all case records and interviewing clients in preparations for their evaluation for CWS sponsorship. One of her supervisors, Mrs. Rice, was so impressed with the professionalism and quality of Tatiana's work, that she offered sponsorship by her Christian Science Church for the Gedrovics family to work in Wisconsin. Though thankful, mother declined the offer as one of the provisions of the sponsorship was to be converted to the Christian Science religion. Our family did not want to compromise our Lutheran beliefs. Valiant Nichols, Tatiana's former UNRRA supervisor and friend, also promised to investigate opportunities for the Gedrovics' in Texas upon her return home to Dallas. Tatiana's great concern was that perhaps the U.S. would deny an entry visa if she indeed was considered to be a Soviet citizen by virtue of her Russian birthplace and the family would be repatriated to the Soviet Union.

Strange as it may seem, Tatiana's Russian ancestry was exactly the prime factor in obtaining a U.S. sponsor. The Tolstoy Foundation, headed by the youngest daughter of the famous Russian novelist Leo Tolstoy, author of *War and Peace* and *Anna Karenina,* was one of the charitable organizations working with CWS in finding asylum for Russian orphans and other Russian nationals fearing Communist persecution. Hundreds of Russian expatriate refugees were sponsored by the Foundation. Sometimes Tatiana had to work an entire night to process the emigration papers for the Russian refugees the Tolstoy Foundation had chosen to sponsor. She worked without self-pity and without complaining about not having a sponsor for her own family. Alexandra Lvovna Tolstoy was impressed when she heard of Tatiana's selfless dedication. When she realized Tatiana spoke Russian, this time the exclamation "Ti nasha!" had a joyful tone as the Countess Tolstoy recognized

Tatiana as one of "her own". In addition to being a dedicated worker, Tatiana happened to have the exact education and language background that the Tolstoy Foundation needed for the director of their home for Russian orphans at Valley Cottage, New York. The orphanage was located on Reed Farm, a large poultry and egg producing facility owned and operated by the Tolstoy Foundation as a refugee resettlement center. Kārlis' farming experience was an additional bonus and he was also offered employment on the farm.

Ironically, in fleeing the Communist regime of Soviet Russia, the Gedrovics family was the only non-Russian family offered a sponsorship and shelter in the United States by a Russian organization due to a feeling of Christian kinship and recognition of shared ideals of freedom. Alexandra Lvovna Tolstoy was truly an angel sent by God to help the Gedrovics family. Not only did she sponsor us through her Foundation, she was also instrumental in passing the Refugee Act of 1948 by testifying before the House Judiciary Committee on the need for a change in immigration laws to facilitate refugee resettlement efforts. Thus began our long homeward journey in October of 1948—not eastward toward Latvia, but on a westward bound train with the final destination and destiny shrouded in uncertainty for the Gedrovics family.

★★★

30
PARTING IS SUCH SWEET SORROW

Once the United States passed the Displaced Persons Act of 1948 in June, the wheels that would carry the immigrants to their new homes moved with amazing speed. I had only been in an all-girls Austrian high school for one month, when our family was notified in late September that we would be leaving Glasenbach on October 4 for a holding camp in Germany where a group of refugees going to the United States was to be processed for departure on October 21. Packing up all our worldly goods in two wooden boxes and one suitcase would not be a problem with the one-week notice, but parting from all the people who had become close friends in the Glasenbach community would be more difficult. Even after hundreds of miles traveled and living in multiple temporary abodes, letting go of Glasenbach was perhaps one of the most emotionally traumatic experiences for me since leaving Latvia. Austria with its friendly people had become my second home country. The last week in camp was spent in an endless series of farewells. Every encounter ended in a flood of tears. Saying good-bye to the Swallows Girl Guide troop resulted in the entire troop sobbing. Nora and I hugged and cried together, but, of all the friends, we had the best odds of seeing each other again as Nora and her mother and brother had been accepted to emigrate to Canada.

Puppy love coming to an end at age thirteen was more difficult to handle when I had to say farewell to my "first love". There was a handsome dark-haired boy named Georg from Croatia whom I particularly liked. When I said good-bye to him in the middle of the camp square during a rainstorm, again the tears started to flow as if to supplement the raindrops falling down to drown the young couple in sorrow. Georg, at age fifteen, was amazingly sensitive to my feelings and found the perfect gentleman's way to console a girl. He took the desolate crying bundle in his arms and told me that he wished me much love and happiness in the new world. Then he dried my tears and gave me my first kiss. It was a bittersweet moment. My heart was happy to receive the first kiss from this handsome boy, yet the realization that this was also the last kiss for perhaps a very long time made the moment particularly poignant. I also had become friends with Josef "Seppi" Grifatong, a refugee from Serbia. He and his mother had also declared themselves as being "stateless" since his country had been taken over by the Communist leader, Tito of Yugoslavia. Seppi lived across the hall from us in barrack # 1 and we spent many hours together talking about the future. Seppi was eighteen and he often speculated that he would wait until I would become eighteen so he could marry me. On the October morning when the Gedrovics family had to board the train in Salzburg, Seppi came to the station to say good-bye to me. It broke my heart to see his figure looking so forlorn standing alone on the platform. Seppi's father had been killed during the war and the uncle he lived with died while at Glasenbach. The uncle's two sons became foster children of some distant relative in the United States. When Seppi gave me a parting hug, his last words were, "Now I have lost everybody dear to me."

The last and most difficult farewell, which I delayed until the last evening, was saying good-bye to my best friend, Zigrida. We both cried inconsolably thinking we had a zero chance of ever meeting again, because we would be living in different hemispheres. Zigrida's family had been approved by the immigration program launched by Australia, which accepted a total of over 182,000 refugees, principally of Polish and Baltic origins. I later learned from Zigrida's letters that the Australian program was a far cry from freedom for the refugees. The new immigrants were often put in work camps, separating men from their wives and children. It was mandatory for the immigrants to put in two years of labor as directed by the Commonwealth Employment Office before they were allowed to be reunited with their families and could start life anew as free people. Anyone over the age of sixteen was not allowed to continue their education but had to work the required two years. Zigrida was assigned to the position of a nanny in the family of a Lutheran Pastor and had to continue her education on her own when she had finished her contract and was allowed to rejoin her family in Melbourne. Had we known that Zigrida would have to spend the rest of her teen years under such undesirable conditions, the parting would have been even sadder.

Zigrida's father felt sorry for the two distraught friends and asked us to join him in celebrating our friendship instead of dwelling on the sadness of the looming separation. Mr. Smilga ceremoniously poured two glasses of red wine for us and made a toast to our good friendship and a happy reunion in the future. He declared that a toast was certainly in order to mark this important event and that there was no time to wait until the two friends were of legal age to have wine. Mr. Smilga's special toast transformed the sad occasion into a celebration of friendship and brought smiles among the tears. It was something Zigrida and I both remembered throughout our lifetime. Perhaps some guardian angels took notice of Mr. Smilga's toast to the girls and made the reunion a reality fifty years later. When Zigrida came to visit me in Michigan, she brought a bottle of red wine from Australia for the reunion toast but a reunion was hard for us to anticipate at the time we said goodbye to each other in Glasenbach.

The morning of October 4, 1948 dawned bright and unseasonably warm. The Gedrovics family and their meager belongings were picked up by an army truck and taken to the railroad station in Salzburg early in the morning. We were surprised to see Seppi Grifatong, Georg, Zigrida, Nora, and several members of the Swallows Girl Guide troop waiting for us at the station. The young friends had

Farewell to friends at Salzburg train station, 10/4/1948

taken an early morning bus from Glasenbach to give us a proper send-off. Tears were flowing without ceasing; even the boys' eyes became misty despite their stiff upper lips, which they tried to keep from quivering. A representative of the Latvian community in Glasenbach also came with his family to wish a safe journey and God's blessings to the Gedrovics' as we started our long journey to a new life in a foreign destination. The first stop was to be in Munich where refugees were gathered before being transferred to ships in Bremerhaven.

IN MUNICH LIES NO "HOFBRAUHAUS"

When the train pulled out of the Salzburg station, the initial destination of Munich did not have much meaning for the Gedrovics family. Whatever the displaced persons interim camp held in store was unimportant as it was but a temporary shelter. Any situation could be tolerated for a brief time because it had been indicated that by October 21 the refugees would be heading to the United States. I had only heard of Munich through stories about the Bavarian Beer Festivals and from a song, "In Muenchen liegt ein Hofbrauhaus", that I had heard in summer camp. As the train rolled through the Bavarian countryside, our family discussed how nice it would be to become acquainted with yet another German city before leaving Europe. But as the train pulled into Munich, it was shocking to see nothing but bombed out buildings with missing windows, church towers diminished into piles of rubble in the shell of a sanctuary, and partial walls standing as if they were ruins remaining from a previous period in civilization. The streets had been cleared of debris after the air raids to allow traffic to move, but there seemed to be few buildings left suitable for habitation and no music or singing filled the air from joyous Oktoberfest celebrations.

The refugees were taken to one of the remaining structures that must have been used for military quarters at one time. Three-story masonry buildings, arranged in a quadrangle, were to be our new living quarters. But before the family was shown our quarters, a humiliating experience lay in store for us. All the arriving refugees were herded into a huge hall, men were told to go into one room, women into another and everyone was told to completely disrobe for a health exam. I was mortified to have to stand in line completely naked amidst a rabble of strangers and to be examined by a strange doctor. The worst humiliation came after the examination. Everyone was told to raise their arms as they continued to walk the line so that they could be sprayed with a white powder during a "de-lousing" process. It was difficult to judge which experience was worse–walking naked among strangers or the offending assumption that we were some kind of dirty people harboring lice.

After the clothing also was sprayed, the refugees were allowed to dress and were taken to their assigned room. Having had a separate room in Salzburg, the Gedrovics family was shocked when we were led to a huge hall with approximately 15 bunk beds lined up perpendicularly along each long wall. We were issued four rough grey wool army blankets and assigned to two adjoining sets of bunk beds. The blankets were so scratchy that people made jokes about the fabric being so rough that it must have been intended for horse blankets, not to touch people's skin. The family occupying the area on one side of the Gedrovics' beds had already hung two of their blankets along the side of their bunks to separate their quarters into a blanket-enclosed cubicle. Kārlis and Tatiana did likewise. They hung their blankets lengthwise along the sides of their bunks to make a blanket wall offering some semblance of privacy for the family so that Mudite and I would not be further humiliated having to undress in public. It was yet another sacrifice the parents made without thinking of their comfort. Mudite and I at least had our scratchy blankets to keep us warm during the cool October nights while our parents used whatever clothing they had as cover. The blanket walls did offer privacy, but they also kept daylight out of the cubicle so that soon it was decided to take the blankets down during the day and put them up again at night. Sleep did not come easy during the night, however, as a baby's plaintive wailing would break the silence or multiple voices joined from every corner of the hall for a dissonant concert of snoring.

Though the stay in Munich was relatively short, it was quite uncomfortable to be cooped up in the huge, noisy hall with some sixty people. As often as the weather allowed, the Gedrovics family went out for walks to explore the city. No matter in which direction we chose to walk, the scenery never seemed to vary. The skeletons of crumbled buildings gave the city a ghostlike look, as if some human skeletons or skulls would emerge from the piles of broken concrete at any moment. Everyone breathed a sigh of relief when it was announced that the next trainload of refugees would depart Munich on October 14 for Bremerhaven where 826 of the over 1,000 refugees from the IRO Resettlement Center would board the first army transport ship for the United States on October 21 with the second group following about November 6. The refugees soon found out that in reality they could not count on any of the departure dates ever being accurate. Complications and delays became part of daily life. Only when their ship left port with them aboard, could everyone be sure they were going to the United States.

On October 14, four years and one day after the Gedrovics family left Latvia by train, they, along with nearly another thousand refugees from Munich and other cities in Germany, boarded the train for the long ride to Bremerhaven on the North Sea.

This time there were no farewell ceremonies, no cheers, and no friends waving good-bye. Only the heavens cried as sheets of rain came down when the refugees, carrying their meager belongings in worn containers, boarded the train. To sustain the people on the twenty-hour trip, refugee organizations handed out black bread and army rations from trucks parked beside the train. The hungry children had already devoured much of the food before the train even left the station. Belatedly, some families were taken off the train as officials discovered some visas were lacking when documents were checked. Only when the train's whistle blew and the engines slowly started chugging away from the station could everyone sigh with relief to be on the way at last on the next portion of their long journey.

The temporary refugee camp at Bremerhaven presented a dismal scene to the arriving trainload of weary travelers. The long rows of wooden barracks were separated by strips of mud with no grass or other vegetation in sight. One could only rationalize and take comfort in knowing that again this situation was to be temporary for perhaps a week or two. I do not remember much about the stay at Bremerhaven, having suppressed this unpleasant portion from my memories. The memory that remains for Mudite and me is of standing in multiple long lines for the required documents & health checks again. All the refugees were told to line up in an enormous hall and to bare both arms for mandatory immunizations. Clerks stationed at various checkpoints periodically called off individual names from long lists and then moved the refugees to the next station. Both of us worried that we might get detained or separated from the family at any given stop and never see each other again. Only grownups were allowed to speak or answer questions. In the interest of moving hundreds of refugees through the lines as efficiently as possible, children were just moved along without being told what to expect at the cost of creating emotional trauma for the little ones.

At age eight, Mudite had lived all her years in unstable times when people disappeared, were deported, or died, and children were left as orphans. Immense fear gripped her each time a clerk called out, "GEDROVICS, MUDITE" and she was led to another line or another immunization station. When Steven Spielberg's movie "Schindler's List" came out in 1993, it made Mudite and me relive the experience of being herded like animals in the long lines without being told where we were going or what was being injected into our arms. Forty-five years after experiencing panic while standing in the long lines at Bremerhaven, Mudite felt the same enormous fear again as she watched similar scenes in the film. She could almost feel the needles being stuck into her arms, as her mind was moving her along with the people in the long lines on the movie screen.

In addition to the injections, everyone was also vaccinated against smallpox even if they could show the scar from a previous vaccination like I had on my left arm. Nobody really knew against what diseases they were being immunized, but multiple injections were given to everyone, adults and children alike. The medical staff informed the people that there might be "side effects" from the multiple vaccines and this information was absolutely true. Many people, especially Mudite and other little children, ran fevers and experienced swelling and pain with no medications available to alleviate the side effects. Mudite's both arms became red, swollen, and hot to the touch from the many times she had been poked in both arms but there was no palliative treatment to make her more comfortable. The crowning touch added to the immunization ordeal was another round of pesticide showers. Just to make sure that the refugees had not acquired lice during their train ride from Munich, everyone again had to strip to be fumigated before they were shown to their quarters. In this camp no effort had been made to convert the army barracks to individual rooms and again, people had to share their living space alongside strangers in large halls.

Perhaps the first army transport ship with refugees bound for the United States did depart on October 21st, but the Gedrovics family was not among those sailing, nor were we among the second group leaving in early November. Evidently, the immigration process was more overwhelming than anticipated, and much confusion reigned in processing the thousands of people bound for various parts of the United States. With hundreds of organizations acting as sponsors, chaos was the overriding order of life. Many of the refugees lacked either the proper set of documents or did not pass the rigorous medical clearance. In the 21st Century America seems to be inundated not only with illegal aliens, but also with foreign diseases such as AIDS and unwanted species of plants, animals, fish, and insects from other lands. In 1948, however, there was such a paranoia about keeping foreign pests out of the United States, that a single nit in a child's hair or one missing signature on a visa could quarantine a family before they were allowed to board a ship.

There was no entertainment to break up the monotony during the long days of waiting. When the mud created by the autumn rain dried up, the wind from the North Sea gave rise to sand and dust blowing through the camp, only to give way for early December snow flurries. Finally, in late November, when Tatiana did the daily status check, the Gedrovics family was cleared to be on the third shipload. But fate had more frustrating delays in store to test our patience. Whether it was due to a dockworker or some other union strike, the departure of the third transport ship had to be changed to the port of Hamburg. At 8:42 a.m. the refugees left Bremen by train and two hours later arrived at the port of Hamburg. The change in ports meant there would be another interim "delousing" and document checkpoint. Finally, on December 10, 1948, the Gedrovics family bade good-bye to Europe and hand-in-hand the four of us walked up the gangplank of the army transport "Marine Flasher" with 545 other displaced persons. Standing at the ship's railing we prayed together that this would be the final leg of the journey toward a new home and away from being a stateless displaced person.

★★★

31

S.S. MARINE FLASHER

Photo courtesy U. S. Maritime Commission

MARINE FLASHER

Length, overall 523' 0"	Gross tons 12,420	Propulsion Turbine
Beam 72' 0"	Speed (knots) 17	Passengers 1,463
Draft 30' 0"	Radius (miles) 12,000	Cargo (cu. ft.) 51,000

Built in 1945 by Kaiser Co., Inc., Vancouver, Wash.
Operated in World War II by Matson Navigation Co.

There were many families who were brought across the Atlantic to the shores of the United States by this C4 type troopship. In New York the Marine Flasher was retrofitted from a troop ship to one with smaller cabins that would carry refugees from Europe to the United States. She sailed on the Bremerhaven-New York or Hamburg-New York routes until September of 1949.

On December 10, 1948, the send-off from Hamburg, Germany had a festive atmosphere for the 549 fortunate displaced persons emigrating to the United States. Colorful streamers and flags fluttered along the gangplank and the upper deck. The ship's accommodations differed from the last few crowded refugee quarters in Muenchen and Bremenhaven and were more befitting private passengers. Men and women had separate quarters, but each ship's cabin only housed four sets of bunk beds for eight people, instead of fifty or sixty people in one large hall. As soon as the assigned rooms were located, everyone returned to the upper deck to experience the departure from the port of Hamburg. The 12,000-ton Marine Flasher lifted anchor to the blaring of the ship's horn and a local band playing upbeat marches for a send-off. Small crowds of what must have been Hamburg residents, dock employees, and representatives of refugee organizations waved good-bye to the refugees lined up on the upper deck decorated with colorful streamers. I was a little afraid that the big ship would tip over with most of the 549 passengers all standing at the harbor-side rail of the ship.

It seemed like a light mist started to fall as the ship eased out of the harbor, or perhaps the mist was in the eyes of the departing refugees as they saw the shoreline of Europe fading into the distance. There was no turning back to the land where everyone was born and the land they loved despite all the hardships encountered. The ship slowly slid out of the harbor accompanied only by a few seagulls. I wished that one of the seagulls would someday return to the Baltic Sea to bring my greetings to the Amber Shores. The shimmering lights on the shore finally disappeared from view, as I, the former seagull Kaija, became shrouded in darkness and started my long flight to distant shores. The passengers, enveloped in the dark silence of the night, silently bid farewell to their fatherlands. Only an occasional sob and the lapping of the waves against the ship broke the oppressive quiet. My own sentimental feelings at the time were aptly described in a German song called "*Möwe, Du fliegst in die Heimat*"[42], or "*Seagull, fly to my homeland*". The song was probably written to commemorate the World War II soldiers and refugees sailing stormy seas away from their home. Translated, the lyrics bring tears to my eyes every time I hear the song.

"*Day after day, night after night,*
A lonesome ship rides over the seas.
Nobody sleeps, everyone wakes,
The heart is heavy in everyone.
Seagull you fly to the homeland,
Greet it warmly from me.
All my good thoughts
Go to my home with you."

Would we ever see the shores of Europe again? Floating on international waters, everyone indeed was stateless. It would be eleven days before anyone would set foot on any land again.

After the shore had receded and disappeared from view, the Gedrovics family went below deck to their assigned quarters. Though the three female members of our family shared a room with five other females, the space seemed adequate for the relatively short duration of the trip that was supposed to last nine days. Father was assigned to similar all-male quarters near the bow, or front part of the ship, which was more prone to heavy rocking as the ship climbed gigantic waves and then trembled as she fell into a deep trough before climbing the next wave again. The women's cabin contained four sets of bunk beds and no other furnishings. Shared toilet facilities were down the hallway. There were no windows or even portholes and, although some means of ventilation must have been present, the room seemed airless and in time became suffocating. It later became evident that I would only spend one night in the cabin. I spent the remainder of the trip sleeping on the floor in the hallway or up on the deck during daytime as I was too seasick to tolerate the close space and airless cabin.

Kārlis, Skaidrite, Mudite aboard SS Marine Flasher, Dec. 10, 1948

Dinner the first evening was an extravagant surprise for everyone. The dining room was as elegant as any found on luxurious cruise ships. There were white tablecloths on the tables and attentive uniformed waiters stood ready to serve anything one would desire from a complete gourmet menu. Imagine finding entrees featuring goose, roast duck, pork loin, or perhaps lamb chops and steaks after the meager rations served in DP camps! Desserts consisted of all sorts of tortes, pastries, fresh fruit, and ice cream. Beverages included a full compliment of juice, dairy, and soft drinks in addition to tea, coffee, and hot chocolate. The dining room was a Utopia and seemed too good to be true. Everyone looked forward to ten days of lavish gourmet dining, but, alas, our stomachs were not used to such rich diets. I could only eat the first dinner and the next day's meals in the dining room. After the ship left the relatively calm North Sea, I was forced to share anything I ate with the fish in the ocean. What irony, to have the best food selection of a lifetime at a time when ones stomach keeps heaving along with each rolling wave and the tantalizing aroma of food triggers the heaving mechanism.

Before starting the journey, our family had worried that perhaps mother and Mudite would have a difficult time at sea since they did not seem to have the strength and endurance father and I exhibited. But Neptune and all the creatures of the sea must have really had a good laugh when they churned up the sea to such fury that one morning, out of the 549 passengers, only little Mudite and mother were able to come to the dining room for breakfast that was served by the whole contingent of attentive waiters. The only problem for those two sturdy sailors was trying to keep the dishes and silverware on their table as the tables and chairs were tipping and rocking as the ship bobbed up and down on the mountainous waves. During most of the stormy days, meals were served on paper plates that Mudite remembers to be somehow fastened down to the tables so that they would stay in place during the meal. For the remaining duration of the trip I was unable to tolerate being in the dining room. My diet consisted of sipping 7-Up and nibbling on some crackers and fruit. Mudite, gleefully, would emerge from the dining room after stuffing herself and tease her sister by waving some gooey candy bar or a greasy sausage under my nose to make me sick as I sat on the deck cradling my churning stomach. Mother brought food back to the deck for my father, as he also felt sick inside the confines of his room in the bow of the ship.

The first day on the North Sea was calm and the Marine Flasher sailed ahead with good speed. The morning of the second day, the ship entered the English Channel and the seas became quite rough, making most of the passenger succumb to seasickness. The seasoned sailors stated that they considered the sea at this point to be peaceful and smooth as a mirror compared to what lay ahead on the Atlantic Ocean. Even though the air was misty, the shores of England could be seen in the distance shrouded by fog. I felt too ill to take much interest in the scenery. I was busy leaning over the railing and feeding my stomach contents to the fish. It was amazing that one could throw up without ceasing even without having eaten all day. On the third day the refugee transport entered the Atlantic Ocean. The waves looked like huge walls of water and the ship rocked heavily. Rope guardrails were put up on the deck so that people could grip them for balance while walking outside.

The sea was all around the tossing ship clad in her white foam. There was no end to the monotonous view. It was interrupted only by the wind whipping some gigantic ocean waves upon the deck or an occasional fish jumping high out of the depths of the water. The salt water spraying the deck eventually made everyone's shoes fall apart. The roar of the December gales and the height of the waves increased as the trip progressed and the buffeting sea grew angrier as the days went by. Finally, the ship's crew conceded, that this was not a smooth crossing, but rather one of the fiercest ones. Since I could not tolerate the confines of the airless cabin, I tried sleeping on my blanket in the long and roomy hallways, but I spent most of the time up on deck with my father even through high winds and rain. We tried to avoid sitting downwind from the large deck vents, which constantly poured out nauseating engine fumes.

Sometime halfway through the trip, a severe winter storm aimlessly tossed the ship for two days. All doors were sealed to the outside because of the danger of passengers being swept overboard by the gigantic waves crashing over the deck. People could not get help in the infirmary, as the ship's doctor had also become very ill and all the hospital beds were filled with people whose bodies had become dehydrated from severe seasickness and those who had been injured by falls. Two days in a row, the captain of the Marine Flasher announced that the ship had made no forward progress. It was actually pushed back by the storm while fighting to stay afloat as it was being tossed about by the ocean waves like it were a matchbox. Though its 12,000 tons of weight seemed huge at the time, the troop transport was just a lightweight compared to the cruisers of the 21st Century like the Royal Caribbean's "Freedom" which weighs in more than ten times heavier at 158,000 gross tons and is over twice the length of the Marine Flasher. The biggest liner in the 1940's, the Queen Elizabeth, was a hefty 83,000 tons by comparison. The 1912 Titanic had a gross weight of 46,000 tons and length of 882 feet compared to the 523 feet of the Marine Flasher. Physically, the crossing of the Atlantic was difficult for everyone, but the spirit of the refugees remained high as they considered the journey toward their freedom to be worth the discomfort.

I felt so weak that I just lay in the hall on my blanket. When I threw up on the floor, a very kind black steward stood ready to mop the floor and with a smile said, "Such a sweet girl, so sweet." This was my first personal encounter with a person of the Negro race and it gave me a very positive impression of black people. This caring man was filled with the kind of humanitarian spirit my mother always exhibited and he was trying to bring comfort to a homeless stranger in strange surroundings. The gentleman was from Harlem and, when he was not working as a ship's steward, he drove taxis in New York. He promised to give the Gedrovics family a tour of the city. This could have been the first friendship the Gedrovics family established with a New Yorker, but this never came about because our family moved to Michigan before the kind man finished serving on the ship.

Finally, on the tenth day of the stormy voyage, the sea became calmer and people were allowed back out on the deck. The captain announced the Marine Flasher would dock in New York the next day, with a two-day delay from the originally estimated nine-day trip. Weak and hungry after the weeklong struggle with nausea, I decided to join my family for breakfast in the dining room. At the very moment the steward brought my meal, the sight and smell of the scrambled eggs called forth a wave of nausea again. With my stomach threatening to explode, I made a mad dash for the stairs leading to the deck hoping to delay the inevitable projectile dumping of my stomach contents. The kind steward misinterpreted my stricken look and quick escape as a desperate girl's intention to jump overboard. He ran after me and managed to grab me just as I reached the middle of the stairway, only to throw up at the steward's feet. His kind comment was "Poor, sweet girl". I was too embarrassed to venture into the dining room again and continued my 7-Up and fruit diet until my feet were on solid ground.

After eleven days on high seas, the transatlantic journey came to an end. It had been a difficult journey with much of the time spent outside on the deck come wind or rain. Besides debilitating seasickness and some injuries, most passengers also suffered from lack of sleep. Throughout the journey, the clock had been turned back one hour every other day for a total of six hours to acclimate the European people to the Eastern Standard Time in New York. The time change resulted in people feeling like they were ready for a night's sleep at 4:00 p.m. and then rousing everyone at 4:00 a.m. before the break of dawn. In an interview by the New York Times, Capt. Stanley Thompson, master of the ship, described the crossing as "a rough, lousy trip all the way". He said the Marine Flasher had docked thirty-six hours behind schedule, ten days after leaving Hamburg.[43]

On December 21, 1948, land was finally in sight and the raging sea had at last become calm. The Gedrovics family thanked the Lord that He had protected us on the stormy seas through all the gales and had brought us to the sunny shores of our new homeland. The countryside shone bright and white under the cover of a new snowfall. No longer did we have to worry about our lives being in danger. The Land of the Free was opening its gates to us. The Marine Flasher passed some fishing boats peacefully casting their nets and some dolphins and whales rose out of the water as if to welcome the refugees. Cars could be seen driving by on a small island outlined by vacation cottages. An aura of peace seemed to come forth from the wintry landscape. America looked like an imaginary land depicted in a fairy tale.

The ship dropped anchor at noon. She was not allowed to enter the Port of New York until the completion of one more credential and health check. This last checkpoint was symbolic of hopes for a new homeland or the alternate final rejection of some unfortunate refugees. From one side of the deck the Statue of Liberty could be seen standing tall and welcoming the weak and the weary travelers. The statue was impressive as it stood its silent watch with the torch of freedom in her raised arm greeting the new arrivals to a new life. From the other side of the ship one could see Ellis Island shrouded in fog waiting to engulf those souls whose papers were found to be lacking even some minor phrase or who failed to pass the final health exam. I worried that my emaciated condition due to seasickness might cause me to be rejected, held on Ellis Island to be deported again. Some agonizing minutes passed as everyone had to stand in line again to be fumigated for whatever parasites one could have acquired since boarding the ship in Hamburg. Finally, the examining doctor and the immigration official each stamped "Approved" on our documents. New York City and a New Life awaited us as soon as all the passengers were processed and the ship was allowed to dock at the pier.

FREE AT LAST!

★★★

32

NEW YORK, NEW YORK…WHAT A WONDERFUL TOWN!

*T*uesday, December 21, 1948, 2:25 p.m. marked the arrival of 549 prospective U.S. citizens when the Maritime Commission ship Marine Flasher docked at Pier 62 North River in New York Harbor. 44 Loud cheers, tears of joy, and the babble of no less than ten different foreign languages filled the air as the newcomers were met by representatives of various relief agencies associated with the International Relief Organization of the United Nations. The arrival of the DP ship was reported in the New York Times, Wednesday, December 22, 1948 issue with the headline reading "549 MORE DP'S LAND AFTER ROUGH TRIP". An accompanying photo showed Santa distributing gifts. It did not take long for the children aboard the ship to recognize the world-famous person who had come especially to greet the arriving youngsters. Santa Claus paid a visit to Pier 62 and brought a special note of Yuletide merriment as he distributed small gifts to the Catholic children at a Christmas party planned by the Catholic Welfare Conference.

By the time the refugees and their meager belongings were processed through customs and they could leave the ship, night had fallen. In contrast to the winter darkness, the skyline of New York City was lit up with millions of lights shimmering from skyscraper windows, street lights, flashing neon advertising signs, and Christmas decorations in all colors of the rainbow. The refugees, who had become accustomed to the darkness of blackouts during the war years, stared in amazement at the wondrous display of illumination. Even fireworks displays during 4th of July celebrations in subsequent years could not rival the skyline of New York all decked out in bright splendor. The Gedrovics family was met by the President of the Tolstoy Foundation, Countess Alexandra Lvovna Tolstoy, from the Reed Farm in Valley Cottage. It turned out that there was another family, the Kozlovs, from Salzburg going to Reed Farm although the Gedrovics' had not met them on the Marine Flasher. It was quite helpful for everyone to be greeted in the Russian language by Madam Tolstoy and Marta Andreyevna, one of the supervisors from Reed Farm, since only Tatiana was able to communicate fluently in English. Throughout the refugee years, Tatiana had been designated by our family to be our interpreter and spokesperson because of her foreign language skills.

After welcoming the new families, the two Russian ladies asked if anyone would like something to eat as we walked past some of the fast food vendors at dockside. Father only knew basic phrases in English, but the few words he knew caused sudden consternation as he read the neon sign at one of the food stands. There in bold flashing red neon letters was the marvelous culinary offer of **"Hot Dogs"**! Father stopped in his tracks and, with his voice expressing loud outrage, demanded to go back to the ship. He said he had preferred going hungry during the war years instead of eating horsemeat, but he refused to allow his family to live in a country that flagrantly advertised the consumption of **dogs**! Had the sign advertised **"Grilled Frankfurters"**, the shock could have been even worse if one understood Americans to be engaging in cannibalism by grilling citizens from Frankfurt. There was a lot to learn about the peculiar colloquial expressions in America. After a good laugh, everyone decided to just relax and rely on the Russian instructions of Alexandra Lvovna and Marta Andreyevna so that we could speedily arrive at the destination where we would spend the first night on American soil. The hour had arrived at long last when we could look forward to living in peace after four years of being tossed about in different countries under the siege of warring enemy powers.

★★★

33

THE LAND OF MILK AND HONEY

From the time the Gedrovics family left the harbor where the Statue of Liberty stood a silent watch welcoming the refugees to a new life, we rode in deep reverie through the peaceful snowy countryside until Alexandra Lvovna brought the car to a stop at the Tolstoy Foundation Reed Farm in the Village of Valley Cottage. She welcomed the newcomers to our new home and led us to the community dining room where Marta Andreyevna set out our first meal in the United States on a long wooden table. Whether it was by symbolic forethought, or due to the late hour when no kitchen workers were available, amazingly the table was laden with large pitchers of cold fresh milk, loaves of white bread, and jars of honey. What a fitting welcome it was to the "Land of Milk and Honey", as its immigrants had often described the United States. Our family had not had such delicacies as farm milk, white bread and pure honey since leaving Riga. It seemed we were insatiable as we consumed this basic meal that to us seemed like a gourmet dinner. The Countess Tolstoy assured us that we could have unlimited refills and, indeed, everyone ate until we could eat no more. Our family of four consumed three large, half-gallon, pitchers of milk, three whole loaves of bread and several jars of honey before we felt completely sated for the first time in over four years. Physically and emotionally exhausted, our sleepy family was then led to our new home, a private residence next door to the Tolstoy estate. Everyone was too stunned after the long voyage to realize that we had said no more than "Please pass the milk" and "Thank you " to the famous Countess Tolstoy who was the angel sponsoring our coming to America and had also so humbly served our supper.

The next day Marta Andreyevna introduced us to the Reed Farm staff including a Russian Orthodox Priest and took us on a tour of the large estate. Among the many buildings were the commercial chicken farm, greenhouses, and cottages housing many immigrant families. The main house contained dining rooms and a chapel. A portion of the house was used as a shelter for care of the elderly. The orphans were housed in a dormitory where mother would work as Director and Housemother. After the holidays the Gedrovics family would move into the orphanage so that mother could be close to the children she supervised. Since Christmas Eve was only two days away, Marta Andreyevna informed Kārlis and Tatiana that they could start their duties after the holidays. She gave my parents five dollars each as an advance on wages and told them to buy whatever the family needed to celebrate Christmas.

The small village convenience store seemed like a treasure trove with shelves filled with all sorts of colorful goods. Father found a small Christmas tree to bring back to our new home along with some red apples for decorating the tree. Mother decided that she would bake some traditional Christmas breads and cookies for Christ's birthday to thank the Lord for His mercy. While my sister and I for the most part could not understand the English labels describing the contents of all the bright packages, mother had no trouble finding flour, sugar, yeast, raisins, and shortening for her baking needs. Mudite and I were each given a dollar to pick out a little gift for ourselves. It did not take me long to spot an unmistakably familiar brown package with silver lettering spelling out Hershey. There were six bars under the cellophane, enough for a special treat for the entire family. Mudite was drawn to the produce aisle where fresh fruit was displayed. How amazing to see such luxury items in the winter! Four big oranges and a bunch of bananas was Mudite's choice of a Christmas gift for the family that first wondrous celebration of Christ's birth in our new homeland. Everyone trudged back to the new home with our arms full of the simple edible gifts we had selected for the family. Our hearts were filled with joy over the wonder of Christmas Eve when our gifts would grace the celebration table on this Holy Night. The thankful family felt as rich as the ancient magi bearing their gifts to honor the Baby born in Bethlehem.

24.12.48–*"Silent Night, Holy Night...",* so starts the notation entered in my diary on Christmas Eve. *"Our first Christmas Eve in America has arrived. Although we have only been here a few days, Mamite and Papitis have managed to put up a Christmas tree. We also have the small gifts we got each other. We sit in the light and warmth of the Christmas tree and think about the wonder of God's grace. He has been merciful in giving us, refugees, who were wandering homeless and without a country, the most beautiful present in the world–a new homeland. It certainly is a gift that is priceless. On this silent night, the words of the old Christmas carol 'Every Year the Christ Child' comes to mind...'He would with his blessing in each home abide and on every pathway travel by our side".*

Skaidrite, Tatiana, Mudite at Valley Cottage, N.Y. 12/25/48

1 January 1949, my diary continues..."*Happy New Year! Joyous greetings fill the air. This year will certainly be*

happy for us. Previous years were spent living in war-torn areas, in underground bunkers trying to escape from killing bombs and bullets. This year we will be able to live in peace and security. We will no longer have to be afraid that a bomb will take our lives; we will not have to listen to piercing sirens warning of another air attack that may end thousands of lives. We hope that in our new homeland the New Year with its happiness and joy will have driven away the Old Year, full of worry, pain, tears, sad farewells, and fearful nightmares."

The next notation in my diary from 6 January 1949 again is translated from Latvian..."*Today I started attending Nyack High School. It is very difficult to understand anything as everyone speaks English. I hope that soon I will be able to study and learn as well as any of the American students. The Latvian school at Glasenbach must have been quite advanced. After graduating from the 7th grade and only one month in the Salzburg High School, I was placed in the 2nd semester of the ninth grade at Nyack High although I was a year younger than most of the 9th graders. I will be carrying a heavy load. I was told I would have to take the N.Y. State Regents exams for the 8th grade subjects when I learn sufficient English and also to take the required 8th grade American History class along with all my 9th grade subjects in order to satisfy State requirements. The teachers are very kind and help me in getting accustomed to the new school, new subjects, and a new language."*

The transition to the English language turned out easier than expected for me. My knowledge of German and Russian came in handy. The high school assigned a German girl by the name of Stella to act as my "Big Sister" and interpreter during the initial weeks. Stella was very helpful in giving me a tour of the school and in explaining the routines for ending up at each class at the right place and time. Each day the school bus picked up several of the Russian orphan children and me to take us to Nyack High. Although I did not like hearing some of the high school students yelling, "The Ruskys are coming!" when the bus from Valley Cottage arrived at the school, it was helpful to have some of the older Russian students to help me get oriented. Particularly helpful were a brother and sister team, Peter and Lydia Penkrat, who became my good friends. Lydia was also in the 9th grade and she helped me keep track of daily homework assignments when I found it difficult to understand the instructions given by some teachers. Peter was a senior and he acted like a big brother and always gave me an encouraging smile or a wave whenever we saw each other passing in the hallways or in study hall. However, before these supportive relationships were established, the first day in the Algebra I class was perhaps the most confusing of all. Yet, on this day I learned how friendly my American classmates could be in helping a new foreign student.

On that first day after the Christmas vacation, the Algebra teacher announced there would be a quiz to see how much the students remembered after the holiday break. I had never had formal instruction in Algebra before and I had not yet been given any textbooks when I registered upon arrival at this big Nyack high school. The subject of Algebra had been touched upon briefly during the summer before the fifth grade at Spittal when my mother tutored me before moving to Camp Glasenbach. Neither did I, full of first-day jitters, have any clue as to what the word "Quiz" meant. A kind black girl must have observed my look of confusion and lack of any books or supplies. She brought some sheets of loose-leaf paper and pencils from her desk and with a smile offered her personal supplies so that I would have something to write on. Amazingly, though I did not pass this first quiz, I did know the right answers for almost half of the problems by just using some logic. After the quiz, a boy named Bill told me not to worry. He promised to help me catch up until I could master the subject all by myself. Bill, who was very bright in mathematics, sat in the seat next to me the remainder of the semester and was always ready to explain more complex concepts in simpler language on a level that I could understand. Thank you, Bill, wherever you are. Hopefully life has rewarded you for your kindness and understanding.

The German language class was really a fun subject in the 9th grade. I used the daily instruction "in reverse" to learn English from the German words I understood quite well. This class also gave me a boost of self-confidence as I was looked upon as the most advanced student in the class because of my fluency in German. The teacher also often called upon me to ask for help in pronouncing some German words that were not familiar to him. With the help of my teachers, Russian, German, and American classmates, by June, quite unnoticed, I had become fluent in the English language. One would not realize from reading my autobiographical term paper written in June, 1949, that the writer could not speak English five months earlier. Although there are a few awkward sentences grammatically, my paper earned a final grade of B+ in English for the semester. My experience of rapidly learning the English language by direct immersion in the regular classroom contradicts the modern-day thought that schools need to accommodate the native languages of immigrants by offering them instruction in their native tongue. Foreign students at Nyack High did not require or get any special concessions or affirmative action academically. The school made an effort however to assure that the new students were introduced to the entire student community to facilitate their socializing needs. New students were welcomed and assimilated in the student body, but it was up to the foreign students to learn the English language, to ask questions if something was not understood, and to study hard. One month after I started classes at Nyack High School, I was photographed and interviewed for the school newspaper. On February 3, 1949, an article introducing me to the student body appeared in the school newspaper. The article described my journey to America on the same ship with Michael Koslov, another new student from Austria who also lived on Reed Farm. After the article about my interests and background as a refugee from Latvia appeared in the paper and quoted me as saying that I found American students to be friendly, it seemed that wherever I went, I was greeted by someone who recognized me and made a special effort to welcome me and to invite me to some activity or club. The only invitation that turned out to be a disaster of major proportions for me was being asked to try out for the girls' softball team in early spring. One would think that participation in a high school sport would help new students open more doors of friendship. This was not the case for a girl who had always been more of a spectator than a participant in sports. Baseball and softball were still unknown sports in Europe at the end of WWII. It was explained that all I had to do was to simply swing the bat and hit the ball as it was thrown toward me and then start running around the bases. Hitting a fast-moving ball as it was coming directly at the batter seemed quite hazardous to me. Every time the ball was pitched and flew directly toward me, I instinctively ducked instead of attempting to hit the fast-moving missile, which threatened to knock me down and out upon impact. Despite all the efforts of my teammates to help me when I was at bat, I decided that perhaps it would be best if I could be "Americanized" by some means other than through the All-American sport of softball or baseball.

While I was becoming accustomed to all the new experiences at Nyack High School, the rest of my family also carried out their assigned tasks. Mother, as Director of the Russian orphan home at Reed Farm, soon became loved by all her charges. One little girl, Tonia, kept begging mother to adopt her so she could become part of the Gedrovics family. She desperately clung to mother and said she would be a very good girl if she could become a sister to Mudite, who was her constant playmate. My parents discussed the matter and their loving hearts could not resist such a request from a little orphan. Our family had always been closely knit; one more mouth to feed would not be a problem. My mother and father petitioned the Tolstoy Foundation to let them adopt little Tonia. The adoption request was denied by the State of New York on the grounds that the couple had no home of their own at the time and did not have United States citizenship. Bureaucratic rules do not always take into consideration what would be best for an unfortunate child. The legal machinery ground up Tonia's hopes and dreams and filled her days with sorrow and tears when she had to say goodbye to us when the Gedrovics' relocated to Michigan.

Father was assigned various duties at the poultry growing operation at Reed Farm. The job certainly did not utilize his professional expertise in accounting, but he enjoyed working on the farm as he

Father and Mudite tending to chickens on Reed Farm

had done during the summer on his aunt's farm in Livberze. Since father spoke Russian, communicating with the staff at Reed Farm was not a problem for him. After school Mudite and I often joined him and helped with the feeding of hundreds of chickens. Mudite especially enjoyed working with father, as she got to pet and feed the little baby chickens and to help in gathering eggs every day. Mudite would have preferred to work with the chickens all day instead of going to the local grade school in Valley Cottage.

She was initially filled with fear and apprehension about being among students whose language she did not speak or understand. For someone who had always been a quick learner, it was difficult for Mudite to understand that it would take time to become proficient in a new language and that she would learn best by being in school with other children. Separation anxiety probably also contributed to Mudite's fear of going to school. The poor little girl cried and cried when mother walked her and the other grade school children to the primary school in Valley Cottage. The school had put her in classes according to her ability in a subject. In mathematics Mudite could keep up with the third grade students, but in English she was assigned to the first grade group so that she could learn to speak and read in English. As in all schools, there were some mean kids who made fun of her for being bigger than the first-graders, yet not being able to speak English. It was so traumatic for Mudite to let go of her mother every morning that it was decided it would be best to have another person walk the children to school in the morning. Of course, Father Time proved to be right. Mudite absorbed the new language like a sponge. Within a few weeks Mudite was yelling back in English at the kids taunting her so there was no reason to laugh at her. Mudite not only learned to speak, read and write in English by the end of the spring term, her intelligence and ability to excel in studies led her on to graduate from high school as valedictorian of her class and to earn honors and a diploma "With Distinction" from the University of Michigan.

It did not take long for the Gedrovics family to get accustomed to the new life at Reed Farm, although living in a Russian compound in America seemed like being in two different worlds. While living among Russians we also had to fulfill the obligations of immigrants to the United States. The regulations pertaining to immigrants were strictly enforced and being "illegal immigrants" was not an option when we arrived in America. Immigrants were expected to make a "Declaration of Intention" within ninety days of coming to America that they would become citizens after fulfilling specified requirements. On March 21, 1949, exactly three months after arriving on the "Marine Flasher", my father had to sign such an affidavit for our family. The head of the household had to list all members of the family on the declaration and sign it in front of officials at the Supreme Court of the County of residence, which for us was Rockland County in New York. The declaration read in part:

"It is my intention in good faith to become a citizen of the United States and to reside permanently therein. I will before being admitted to citizenship, renounce absolutely and forever all allegiance and fidelity to any foreign prince, potentate, state, or sovereignty of whom or which at the time of admission to citizenship I may be subject or citizen. I am not an anarchist; nor a believer in the unlawful damage, injury, or destruction of property, or sabotage; nor a disbeliever in or opposed to organized government; nor a member of or affiliated with any organization or body of persons teaching disbelief in or opposition to organized government...I do swear (affirm) that the statements I have made and the intentions I have expressed in this declaration of intention subscribed by me are true to the best of my knowledge and belief: SO HELP ME GOD."

It must have been very difficult for father to sign the declaration promising to give up "absolutely and forever" his Latvian allegiance which he had already given up once declaring to be "stateless". From this day on, there was no looking back or hoping to return to our native land. He prayed that God would continue to guide the family according to His will. Latvia did not exist and we were compelled to become American citizens.

It was Alexandra Tolstoy's firm goal to help new immigrants in adapting to life in their adopted country and to become productive citizens through education and practical training. Programs were offered at the refugee compound for learning new skills for obtaining new jobs and instruction was available to learn the English language. Father joined the language classes and also gained some valuable experience in poultry farming. The family participated in various social functions and attended the Russian Orthodox Church services since there was no Lutheran Church within walking distance. The fragrance of burning incense was quite pleasant and I became quite adept at chanting "Gospage Pamiloy", or "Lord Have Mercy", during the church services. For the Gedrovics girls, being Lutheran, but living in a Russian Orthodox community, presented the unique opportunity to celebrate church holidays such as Christmas and Easter twice. Two weeks after the family celebrated Christmas in December according to the standard Gregorian calendar, the second celebration of Christmas came to Reed Farm in January according to the Julian calendar used by the Eastern Orthodox Churches. At the celebration in January all the children at Reed Farm received gifts and sweet treats distributed by Father Christmas from the Tolstoy Foundation. My sister and I had learned to sing Christmas carols in Russian in the short time span of two weeks. I had fun switching from Latvian, to German, then English, and at last to Russian as I sang "Silent Night" with the Reed Farm children. Yet, it seemed to me at times that I was learning more of the Russian language and customs than being acclimatized to American ways. However, celebrating holidays twice and learning two foreign languages at the same time did not present any major problem and I considered it a bonus in my process of education. Just how involved this process would become did not become evident to me until later in the spring.

When Easter came, our family colored a few eggs and celebrated the holiday quietly by ourselves since the official Easter at Reed Farm was still two weeks away. During the Easter Spring break from school, Alexandra Tolstoy approached me and complimented me on my Russian language skills. She said that a special theater presentation of Aleksandr Pushkin's most famous poem "*Eugene Onegin*" was planned for the Orthodox Easter and she had decided that I should perform the lead female part of the beautiful peasant girl, Tatiana. This was quite an honor to be asked to play the lead role in a theatrical production of a famous poem that had served as the basis for a Tchaikovsky opera by the same name. The Countess gave me the script and said she was confident that I could learn the part in two weeks.

"But..." I stammered upon glancing at the script.

"No but about it", responded Alexandra Lvovna. "*You are a bright girl and I know you can learn the scene in two weeks.*"

"But, I do not know how to read with the Russian Cyrillic alphabet", I managed to respond when I had regained my voice.

"Slushai, listen to me, your mother can teach you." Thus the Countess closed the subject.

Mother began immediately to teach me the Russian alphabet after school. Besides my Nyack High School classes in English and German, Russian was now added as an extra curricular language course. The additional assignment was not just learning plain conversational Russian phrases either. It was also a cramming course on the literary masterpiece of Aleksandr Pushkin. I did learn to read in Russian and memorized the part in the two week time period. It was thrilling to play the role of Tatiana because the male lead of Onegin was to be performed by Misha Verdun, a tall and handsome Russian orphan who was a couple of years older than I and on whom I had a giant teen-age crush. Much of the "Eugene Onegin" poem dealt with the love relationship between the weak scoundrel Onegin and the beautiful, sincere, and devoted Tatiana. I fantasized that Misha would not be able to resist my charms once I looked into his eyes and with all sincerity declared my lasting love for him. On the night of the performance, I was dressed in a long sky blue taffeta gown and had my hair styled in princess curls as would befit a real princess. The performance was a success. Everyone congratulated me on a fine performance. However it had seemed quite natural for me to get immersed and identify with the script declaring my love for Onegin as personified by Misha. Evidently, expressing his disdain for the young love-struck girl also came quite naturally for Misha when he played the role of Onegin. Much to my chagrin, he paid no attention to me afterwards.

What a pity that real opportunities and real blessings are not sometimes recognized by the young. While I enjoyed my acting debut at Reed Farm, I did not grasp the true meaning of this experience until years later while reminiscing about some of the significant happenings in my coming to America. I was mortified realizing that as a love-struck teen I completely missed the meaning of the opportunity presented to me by Alexandra Tolstoy. Here was a prominent philanthropist known throughout the world, a champion of human rights, and the daughter of Russia's most famous novelist recognizing my ability and encouraging me to stretch to reach new heights and all this girl thought about was the crush on Misha! I should have felt honored that I achieved the high goals set by the Countess who believed I showed promise and could learn to read in a new language and memorize a challenging script in just two weeks. While I completely failed to appreciate the advantage of performing for the esteemed benefactor, the potential of my family did not go unnoticed by the Priest at Reed Farm. Our future was about to change.

The Russian Orthodox Priest always greeted Mudite and me with a friendly smile when our family attended the church services at Reed Farm. He was very complimentary in congratulating both of us girls on our performances at the Russian Easter festival and our acquisition of the Russian language. Shortly after Easter, the Priest approached mother and informed her that since her girls were doing so well in learning the Russian language and getting assimilated into the Tolstoy community, it was time they received instruction to join the Russian Orthodox Church. Tatiana politely declined to have her daughters change religions, since the whole family had been baptized and were practicing Lutherans. The Priest was quite adamant in insisting that the family could not attend his church services indefinitely unless they intended to become members and receive Holy Communion. He also informed Tatiana that she should set an example to the children in her charge about the importance of being an active church member. Whether the Priest genuinely was concerned for the welfare of our souls or just wanted to see his church membership grow, his insistence that the Gedrovics family convert to the Russian Orthodox beliefs presented a serious dilemma for us. While my parents were grateful to the Tolstoy Foundation for sponsoring us and giving us the opportunity to get our family settled in America, they were not comfortable with the idea of becoming a part of the Russian subculture instead of following the American way of life.

Tatiana consulted with Alexandra Lvovna and explained the paradoxical situation facing our family. The Countess Tolstoy, whose goal had always been to facilitate the rapid integration of refugees into American society, was helpful in resolving the conflict in a fair manner. It was her opinion that Tatiana and Kārlis were valuable members of the Reed Farm community and performed their jobs commendably. However, it was not her intent to convert us all into Russians and keep the family on the farm permanently. She suggested that mother contact the Church World Services office in New York to seek a re-assignment to a different sponsor through Lutheran Charities so that our family could go on with our lives as new Americans. Within a few weeks, word came that the Gedrovics family application for a change in sponsors had been approved. The new sponsor was a Lutheran gentleman by the name of Leo Kuhlman, who was interested in having Kārlis work on his dairy and produce farm near Armada, Michigan.

After prayerful consideration, Kārlis accepted the offer though Michigan was another totally unfamiliar territory to him. It did not make much difference to him whether he worked with chickens on Reed Farm or would be milking cows as long as he was able to provide for his family. Mr. Kuhlman had requested that father be ready to start work on June 1, 1949. He promised to assist mother in finding some employment through his network of friends in Armada. The imminent move caused more consternation, as Mudite's and my education would have to be interrupted once again before the end of the school term. Finally it was decided that Mudite would travel to Michigan with our parents the end of May, as she could make an easier transition in catching up in the lower grades. The Countess Tolstoy agreed to have me stay on Reed Farm by myself to complete the last month in the ninth grade. As scary as it was for a fourteen-year-old to be left alone for nearly a month, finishing the school year seemed like the wisest decision after all the changes and interruptions in my education since leaving Latvia. At the end of the ninth grade, I had completed a total of four complete school years in grades one, two, five, and seven. A few months in grades three, four, and eight, with a semester in the ninth grade added up to five years of school attendance for me by the time I would enter the tenth grade. Despite interruptions in education and several changes in the official teaching languages, I successfully completed the ninth grade in Nyack and passed all the compulsory New York State Regents examinations. At long last I could look forward to a normal uninterrupted educational experience when I would start my sophomore year in Armada.

★★★

34

MICHIGAN, "LAND OF COWBOYS AND INDIANS"

June 26, 1949 seemed like it would never come while I stayed by myself at Reed Farm to finish the ninth grade at Nyack High School and to take the New York State Regents exams before I could rejoin my family in Armada, Michigan. Mother and father had written many letters in the interim praising me for being very capable and mature in living independently of them, but I never divulged how lonesome and frightened I really was. When I told my Nyack classmates that I would be moving to Michigan at the end of the school year, everyone seemed to have the opinion that the State more than six hundred miles west of New York City must still be quite uncivilized. I could not be sure if my classmates' opinions were based on Western movies or lack of knowledge in history and geography, but I had real reservations about traveling that far westward alone, if indeed the train was in danger of being attacked by robbers on horseback. The Indians did not worry me, since I had become accustomed to live peacefully with people of all nations, but outlaws and cattle rustlers with six-guns was a totally unfamiliar threat to overcome. Although my parents only wrote about the peaceful life on the farm and the very small town nearby, I really had no concept of what small-town and farm life in the Midwest would be like.

Living alone in the shelter of Reed Farm did not present any real problems for me after my parents left with Mudite. Though I missed my family, school kept me occupied and I managed to finish the year with a B+ average. The B+ that I earned in my English class seemed like the highest achievement after starting with zero knowledge in English. The daily routines flowed effortlessly except for two incidents that caused me some grief. On one sunny June day, I passed a fruit vendor on the way to the school bus that was to take me home to Valley Cottage after school. I spied a watermelon on sale and decided to buy it with some money I had left over from lunch so that I could treat the kids in the orphanage. The vendor put the watermelon in a brown paper sack and I joyfully skipped to the bus while happily anticipating tasting this rare delicacy myself. As I stepped off the sidewalk, the watermelon rolled out of the sack and broke into several pieces. Not wanting to waste this precious commodity, I gathered up all the pieces, put them back into the paper sack and placed the bag under my seat on the bus. Never having had watermelons while I was growing up, unfortunately, I was not familiar with the ways of watermelons and their propensity to leak vast amounts of fluid once they are cut. It was not long before I became aware of the other students snickering while their eyes were riveted in my direction. When I followed the angle of their stares, I was horrified to see that a puddle was spreading under my seat. This moment would remain fixed in my memory as the most embarrassing instance in my life. When the bus stopped at Valley Cottage, I stood up and walked off the bus without a backward glance and left the leaking melon behind, as if I had no knowledge of it and why everyone was laughing. I swished my skirt to show the snickering students that my skirt was dry and that I had not wet myself. I could not distinguish if I felt worse from my embarrassment or my failure to share the watermelon with the orphans at Reed Farm.

The second incident scared me to the point where I feared that I might die before being united with my family again. The day before I was to leave on the train for Detroit, the weather was extremely hot and humid. I developed a severe headache from the heat and decided to splash my face with cold water before I went to bed. As I leaned over the washbasin, the water started turning bright red. Frightened, I realized blood had spontaneously started flowing profusely from my nose. It was quite late at night and nobody was available nearby to help. As I watched the blood pouring from my nose, I had visions of all the blood draining out of my body, just like the blood that I had seen pour from the dead and the wounded during the war. In my vivid imagination, I pictured myself being found lying dead on the floor of the bathroom and my parents' deep sorrow upon being notified of my lonesome passing from the earth. Not knowing what else to do, I pinched my nose shut as tightly as I could to keep the blood from spurting out. Instinctively, I had come upon the solution to apply pressure to the bleeding vessels. This was probably what doctors would have recommended and the bleeding stopped within a few minutes. I thanked God for letting me survive the bleeding episode, which did not recur again. Instead of a lonesome death ending my journey, I was able to take the train to yet another unknown destination in Michigan the next day.

At last on the bright and sunny morning of June 26, I said good-by to the Countess Tolstoy. Alexandra Lvovna wished me all the best for a bright future and gave me a bountiful lunch basket, which had been prepared for the daylong trip to Michigan. Marta Andreyevna drove me to the Grand Central Station on 42nd Avenue in New York City and made sure I boarded the right train. The gigantic structure and bustle of Grand Central itself was enough to frighten anyone, let alone a teen traveling alone into strange territory. There seemed to be no end to the cavernous inside of the station. Hallways led into all directions and masses of rapidly moving people were hurrying all about. Frightening scenarios flashed through my imagination as I wondered how I would ever find my parents if the station in Detroit would be even half as big and busy as the overwhelmingly busy and noisy one in New York. After boarding the train, a new fear rose and grew to dramatic heights in my mind. How would I be able to recognize the station in Detroit where I must get off? What if I just kept on riding into the wild, wild West never to connect with my family again? Marta Andreyevna spoke to the train conductor and had him promise to warn his frightened young passenger when the train was approaching her destination at the Michigan Central Station in Detroit. After giving me a warm hug and reminding me to be sure to eat my lunch, Marta Andreyevna said "Dasvidanya" and I was left alone with a bundle of fears larger than my one big suitcase.

As the skyline of New York City receded in the distance, the reassuring familiar click-clack of the wheels on the rails lulled me into a more peaceful state of mind and a calmer inner feeling. The journey would be long, so I decided to sit back and relax. By closing my eyes I journeyed back in memories to the many times I had ridden on the train in the secure presence of my father. Mile after mile the changing countryside should have been interesting to observe. In June the passing scenery was robed in the fresh bright greenery of spring. Yet, I do not remember anything of the farmland, towns and villages along the way. All the names of the stops the conductor called out were foreign and unknown to me. The only familiar thing on the entire trip was the lunch that had been packed for me at Reed Farm. As I opened the little basket, the fragrance of the fried chicken made me think I was back again in the dining room at Valley Cottage. The lunch basket contained several pieces of crunchy golden brown chicken, home baked rolls, pickles, an apple, some cookies, and a carton of milk. Somebody had even thought of sneaking in a few magazines into the basket as a surprise so that I would have something to read. As the train was not expected to arrive in Detroit until late in the evening well after suppertime, I saved part of the lunch for later in the day. I wished I could thank the cooks at Reed Farm for preparing the delicious food that Alexandra Tolstoy had been thoughtful enough to order for the trip. Shortly after lunch, I started asking the conductor how many more stops there would be before Detroit. Though I had always been patient, this time anxiety moved me into the childish mode of "Are we there yet?" The conductor kept reassuring me that he would not forget to tell me when my final destination was approaching.

The kind conductor was true to his word. He gave plenty of warning for me to be ready when the train approached the outskirts of Detroit. The Michigan Central Station was indeed a magnificent edifice that would have been difficult to miss. Though this grand structure was abandoned some years later and is no longer in use, it would remain in my memories among all the railroad stations that played a prominent role in the journey of my life. The conductor helped me carry my suitcase off the train and when I got into the arrival hall, there were my father, mother, Mudite, and a kind-looking grey-haired gentleman waiting for me. The distinguished looking gentleman was introduced as the family's sponsor, Mr. Leo Kuhlman, who owned the farm in Armada where father worked. Without further delay, everyone got into Mr. Kuhlman's car. With everyone happily chatting simultaneously, we were together again and on our way to the new home.

Time passed quickly while there was so much catching up to do and before I knew it, we had arrived at the farm. The family had already settled in at the white two-story farmhouse at 430 Omo Rd., just north of 32 Mile Road in Armada Township. Though the farmhouse was ordinary among old farmhouses, it seemed like luxury quarters for the family to have an entire house for themselves. Shaded by big elm trees, the house remained cool in the summer. The downstairs had a kitchen with a dining area, one bedroom and a large living room. There was also a large walk-in closet near the front door. During summer thunderstorms, the closet provided shelter for mother and Mudite who hid there, as they were both very much afraid of thunder and lightning. I liked the wild raw power of storms and spectacular lightning flashes and wanted to watch them from the front porch. I had always been in awe of God's majestic power and creative beauty of the earth and liked to observe His great handiwork. Inevitably there was an argument between the mother, who wanted to gather both daughters in the closet to protect them, and the eldest daughter, who wanted to stand her ground and watch the stormy skies illuminated by flashes of lightning. Usually nature's spectacular show won and I got to watch the dramatic illumination followed by rolling waves of thunder.

There was a large wood-heated cook stove in the big kitchen. If the house actually had a furnace, it was not in working order while the Gedrovics' lived there. With no central heating, the stove in the kitchen also had to provide heat for the downstairs rooms. The upstairs bedrooms were never used by the family as they were too hot during the summer and would have been really frigid in the winter had the family continued living there. Mudite played upstairs during the cooler days of summer and I liked to go upstairs to read. Fortunately, the family did not have to live in the drafty farmhouse during the coldest months when frigid air was blowing through the cracks. When the tenant farmer Oscar Fistler, his wife Frieda, and children moved out at the end of the summer from the newer cement block ranch home on the Kuhlman property across the road, the Gedrovics family moved to the newer, though smaller living quarters with central heat.

The old house also had an attic where the family stored the wooden boxes that had contained all our belongings during our treks through war-torn Europe. The family's most precious possessions like photo albums and diaries did not get unpacked but remained in the boxes in the attic so that they would not get lost and be ready if the family had to move again. I liked to sit on the attic stairs and recall my childhood from the pictures in the photo albums and entries in the diary my mother had kept for the first five years of my life. There was an identical green leather diary for Mudite in one of the boxes. Mudite's diary was bought as a present from her big sister for mother's birthday in 1940 so that the new baby would also have a precious record of her life. The diary held the dedication Karlis had written for Mudite in my behalf. Many loose sheets of notes about Mudite's early childhood were tucked in among the pages of the diary. Father had written the notes marking important events in Mudite's early years when mother was ailing and could not keep up with the diaries. Father had lovingly made notes for mother to transcribe into the diary later. Somehow during all the moves, there was never any free time for the parents to incorporate the notes into the pages of the diary. Unfortunately,

Mudite's priceless diary somehow got lost and was never found after the family moved to the Village of Armada when father's work contract with Mr. Kuhlman ended. If the diary was somehow accidentally misplaced in the attic, it must have been destroyed when the old farmhouse was razed when Mr. Kuhlman sold the property after natural gas was discovered on his land.

★★★

35
BLOOD, SWEAT AND TEARS

The work that Kārlis was contracted to do on Mr. Kuhlman's farm demanded a great deal of stamina and long hours. During the summer of 1949 Mr. Kuhlman also had a tenant farmer family living across the street. The tenant farmer, Oscar Fistler, was responsible for most of the work with farm machinery such as plowing, seeding, and combining. Mr. Kuhlman also owned a dairy herd and among Kārlis' duties was taking care of the dairy operation, including the feeding and milking of the cows and keeping the barns clean. Kārlis performed the manual labor from dawn to late at night. In order to paint the large barn, father had to climb high ladders to paint it entirely by hand while Tatiana constantly worried that he would fall off the high ladder. Evidently paint sprayers were not available at this time, at least not at the Omo Road farm. The hardest work for dear Papuks who never complained was the clearing of some ditches and woodland by hand. During the winter, when there was no other work to be done outside, Kārlis labored in chopping down trees and bushes entirely by hand using an axe, as chain saws were also not available.

Kārlis' wages for the hard labor were very minimal, as Mr. Kuhlman considered that the housing he provided for the family counted for a large portion of the wages. Mr. Kuhlman helped Tatiana find work in the town of Armada as a waitress and housekeeper in the Armada Hotel owned by the Dheygere family. Until Tatiana could re-qualify for certification as a teacher in Michigan, she had to resort to performing manual labor as well. Only when my sister and I became parents ourselves did we realize the tremendous sacrifices our parents had made in order to provide a secure home for us in the United States where we would have an opportunity to live in freedom. Freedom had not come easily as an entitlement, as a prize won in a lottery, or a privilege bought on credit. Freedom for my parents as immigrants had to be earned by hard work with their own hands, with their own intellect, and their own sweat and tears. The price of freedom for immigrants was the loss of their professional status when they became laborers in their new homelands. Not once did we hear our parents complain about their hard lot in life or having to work in menial jobs to assure that the family's basic needs were met.

When mother first started to work at the Armada Hotel, a kind bartender gave her rides to and from work. This arrangement was only temporary and it was evident that the family needed a car for getting to work and for basic transportation. Mr. Dheygere gave mother an advance on her wages and recommended a Ford dealer in Richmond where used cars were sold. The family selected a grey 1942

Ford and the salesman assured them the car would serve them well. The proud new owners of the seven-year-old car could not have been happier if they had bought a shiny new luxury car. My parents used the circle drive in front of the house to learn to drive by going around in circles. During one of father's practice driving times, a duck ran under the car and met its death. Father was very much afraid that he might lose his job over the loss of Mr. Kuhlman's duck, so he threw the duck into the stove and cremated it. It is a wonder people did not come by to inquire about the source of the odor. When mother started driving to work, however, it became evident that the car salesman had not been honest with us, for the car turned out to have multiple problems. Mother never knew if the car would take her all the way to work when she started out, or if the temperamental vehicle would decide to stall after going a short distance. If there was a mechanical or electrical problem a car could have, the Ford was sure to develop it. The car dealer was unwilling to repair the obvious "lemon". Finally, Mr. Dheygere got so mad that his acquaintance had knowingly sold such an unreliable car, that he threatened to broadcast all over Armada that the Richmond dealership is not one to be trusted and patronized. The dealer then made some necessary repairs, but the Ford remained temperamental and required a great deal of tender loving care and understanding until our family finally was able to buy a new 1954 Ford five years later.

Mother and Mudite with 1942 Ford at Omo Rd. farm in September 1949

After mother taught herself to drive with some instruction from the bartender, she bravely drove to work every day. Never having owned or driven a car before, she was not familiar with driving regulations. The bartender inquired one day if she had her permanent driver's license. Tatiana replied that she did not know that private people needed licenses, since she was not a chauffeur.

"You better go to the Richmond Police Station to get a license right away, or you could be arrested for driving without a license", advised the bartender.

"I certainly hope the police do not find out that I don't have a license before I can get one!" exclaimed the really worried Tatiana.

"The police already know", replied the kind and helpful bartender as he grinned and displayed his deputy sheriffs' badge. "I will drive you to Richmond myself so you do not get stopped by someone else."

Mother carefully studied the booklet of driving regulations the bartended gave her so she could prepare for the written test. She passed the written test with ease. The examiner, who was supposed to give the road test, then asked Tatiana in what

State she had lived before and she replied, "*New York*", which was indeed the truth. At this, the examiner exclaimed,

"*If you can drive in New York, you can drive anywhere. You certainly do not need a road test!*"

He proceeded to issue her a Michigan driver's license. Had he known that mother was only comfortable driving forward and had never even tried parallel parking the outcome would have been different. The bartender quietly sat with a knowing smile on his face. Only he knew that he had to park the car for mother when she got to work every morning until she learned how to do it herself. The lesson to be learned from this is that one should only truthfully answer the questions asked and not volunteer additional information if such is not required.

While the Gedrovics family lived on the farm, Mr. Kuhlman required that my sister and I also do various chores. There was a large garden on the farm where produce was grown for sale at the Eastern Market in Detroit. When Mr. Kuhlman came to the farm on weekends, he always told me what my chores would be the following week. In the spring I was instructed to pull weeds from the endless rows of beans. Mudite was too young to be assigned jobs, but the sweet little honeybee always volunteered to help her big sister so that the work would go faster. Just like we had weeded our small garden plot at Camp Glasenbach, a year later the sisters were weeding again in America. Even in the Land of Plenty, weeds had to be eliminated for the plants to develop their full potential. As the vegetables ripened, we picked bushels and bushels of green and yellow beans and what seemed to be tons of cucumbers and pickles. Though we, like our parents, worked hard during the summer, we were free to enjoy Sundays.

Sisters picking cucumbers 1949

On Sundays our family attended Our Savior Lutheran Church in Armada where the Rev. Dwain Gade and his lovely wife Marcia helped us to be integrated into the church family. Mudite and I were often asked to sing and mother substituted as the church organist when the former organist retired. I also taught Sunday school and accompanied the children's choir on the piano. After I was confirmed, I also taught Vacation Bible School. The members of Our Savior readily accepted the Gedrovics family into their midst and found various ways for helping us with advice, material gifts, or helping with home repairs.

Mr. Kuhlman usually made his visits on Sunday afternoon and often took our family to town for a treat of banana splits at the Simpson Pharmacy soda counter, or for cool drinks at the Armada Hotel. Sometimes Mr. Kuhlman brought along some member of his family and some food for an evening picnic. After school started and the vegetables were harvested, I no longer had to do farm chores. Upon the recommendation of a lady from the church, I started working on Saturdays cleaning the house of a teacher to earn money for high school activities. The families at Our Savior also often had me baby-sit for their children, especially the Bambach children. It was interesting for me to find out years later that Mrs. Eleanor Bambach not only helped me get involved in church activities, but was also dedicated in helping other disadvantaged and orphan children as a member of the Lutheran Child and Family Service Auxiliary, or Children's Friend Society, as it was called at the time. When I became State President of the Auxiliary, I found Eleanor's name on the membership roster of the organization's founders.

Another church member who took particular interest in helping the Gedrovics family was Hilda Schraeder who with her husband lived on a farm not too far from the Kuhlman property. Hilda often came by with some home baked goods, vegetables, or helped to provide transportation when one of us needed to get to town. Mrs. Schraeder also made sure my sister and I had some fun during the summer. During the Armada State Fair she arranged for me to sell pies at the church's refreshment stand so that I would be admitted to the Fair Grounds for free. One delightful summer day was particularly enjoyable for Mudite and me. Hilda took us along to Fenton to visit a friend who lived on the lake and we got to swim all day.

The couple who lived at the neighboring farm on Omo Road also became very good friends of the Gedrovics family. William and Clara Manska had never had children of their own and they treated Mudite and me as if we were their grandchildren. Mudite, in particular, spent a great deal of time at their farm. Will and Clara took pleasure in showing Mudite any newborn animals and always had some treat ready for her. Mudite has never forgotten Mrs. Manska's kind gestures like baking large batches of cookies—enough to fill the large metal New Era Potato Chip cans as a treat for Mudite to take home. Since Mudite was separated from both her grandmothers at an early age, she loved Mrs. Manska as if she were her real grandmother. Will and Clara's hearts returned the love and let it multiply. The Gedrovics family was often invited over for dinner, to celebrate a holiday, or to go on some special outing.

A visit to the Detroit Zoo in Royal Oak with the Manskas was a special surprise for the entire family. We all spent the entire day walking through all the pathways to be delighted by the amazing collection of animals from all over the world. When I took my own sons to the same zoo and later took photos of my grandchildren there, I always told them about the dear couple who had taken my photo at the very same location at the fountain when I was a young girl. The Manskas would be delighted to know that the same fountain they showed us Gedrovics girls would delight our children and their families through four generations. The Manskas remained close friends of the family throughout their lifetimes and were often invited for a holiday dinner with the Gedrovics'. When I got married, both Will and Clara attended the wedding. Some years later, Clara was delighted to meet my sons and treated them as if they were her own grandchildren.

In the fall of 1949, I enrolled in the 10th grade at Armada Rural Agricultural High School, since I had successfully completed the 9th grade at Nyack. Somehow, even with missing and interrupted years of schooling, I had advanced to the status of a sophomore although I was a year younger than my classmates. Mudite, now fluent in English, was happy to be at the proper level in the fourth grade with the children in her age group. My sister and I were happily looking forward to the 1949/50 school year when at long last our studies and newly formed friendships would not be interrupted by another move to a different city, country, or continent. The only travel we would have to experience was by the yellow school bus that transported us from the farm to the school in the Village of Armada.

In transferring credits from Nyack High School to Armada, I did encounter a problem due to the differences between the subjects that were required for study in the ninth grade in New York and Michigan. In Armada the subject of Biology had to be completed in the ninth grade. I had missed this requirement, as Biology was offered in the 10th grade in Nyack. Thus, the Armada school required that I take the additional subject of Freshmen Biology along with all the 10th grade subjects. The dilemma was that Biology was offered the same hour as Geometry. Since I had become accustomed to completing entire grades after brief part-time attendance, I did not think it would be a problem to study two subjects simultaneously. I convinced the Biology teacher, Mr. Lee Dimon, and the Geometry teacher, Mr. Thomas Stacey, to allow me to attend their classes on a rotation basis every other day. It was wonderful to be at a school where teachers were really interested in individual students and their learning ability rather than insisting on regimentation. Both gentlemen agreed to try to schedule exams on the days that I would be present in their classroom. This arrangement worked well, as I managed to do the homework in

Gedrovics family with Will Manska at the Detroit Zoo in Royal Oak, 1950

both subjects every day. Though I did well in both subjects, Geometry in particular was my favorite. There was one unusually difficult and tricky problem in the Geometry textbook. Mr. Stacey claimed he did not know how to solve the problem. He offered to give an A+ to the first student who could find a correct solution and proof for this challenging problem. I did not rest until I discovered the solution and was the first to proudly present it to Mr. Stacey and the class, thus earning the A+. I find it rather hard to believe that after many years of teaching Mr. Stacey could not figure out the solution to a problem in a textbook he had used for years. This wise teacher no doubt created this challenge to motivate students to try to do their best, but I did not realize until years later that Mr. Stacey had used his great sense of humor and all sorts of creative tactics to make learning fun and challenging.

It was during one of Mr. Stacey's classes that I decided I needed to change my first name of Skaidrite to something more common and easier for Americans to pronounce. I really liked the easy Latvian name my parents had chosen for me. My name is the Latvian counterpart of the German "Klara" and French "Claire", meaning clear or pure. By sheer coincidence, when my great-granddaughter was christened in 2007, her mother chose the name "Claire" for her. It is my prayer that sweet little Claire will grow up to be pure in thought and heart in keeping with her name.

Mr. Stacey's version of "Skid" as my name, however, did not particularly appeal to me at all. Mudite was not happy either when Mr. Stacey jokingly called her "Skid's sister". Most of my classmates, though good-natured, either used the name which Mr. Stacey's had bestowed upon me or used a variety of other even less appealing nicknames, such as "Skid-Rite" or "Reet". My Latvian first name had not been a problem at Nyack High, as students were addressed by their last names. Not having a middle name, I decided to take the ending of "rite" from my first name and change it into the new middle name of "Rita". Thus, as of the fall of 1949, I acquired a dual personality known as Rita Gedrovics by all Americans while continuing to be Skaidrite in legal documents, and among family and other Latvians. When I received my citizenship papers, the name "Rita" was officially inserted as my middle name for legal purposes. Once the name issue was resolved, I got accustomed to being called Rita, though I did not like the new name nearly as much as the one given to me at my Christening, or the nickname "Kaija" my family always used.

For the "new" Rita Gedrovics and her family, the New Year of 1950 proved to be difficult. The winter did not bring much snow, but there was a great deal of freezing rain, which made driving to work difficult for mother on the icy roads. With the rain freezing on the windshield and the car skidding all over the road, she would grip the wheel so tightly that her arms ached by the time she got home. New Year's Eve was particularly traumatic for her. She had to spend the evening away from her family, as she was needed to work at the hotel where the revelers were enjoying a big holiday bash. The party guests, filled with benevolence, gathered a kitty to give mother a fifty-dollar tip to make up for her having to work when everyone was having fun. Mother's supervisor noticed that she received the tip and informed her that all tips belong to the hotel and would not let my hard-working mother keep the money she had been given and which her family really needed. Mr. Dheygere, who had always been fair, heard about the incident and presented mother with a whole case of beer for her to take home for a belated celebration with her family. When mother left work in the wee hours of the morning, everything was shrouded in a thick fog and the roads were as icy as glass. She started to drive home, but she was so tired and so disappointed over the unfair treatment, that she pulled the car over to the side of the road and had a good cry to start out the New Year. She sat shivering in the icy cold, surrounded by fog and the rain freezing on the windshield, until she could compose herself and drive home to greet her loving family with a smile and wish everyone a Happy New Year.

The icy winter was followed by a wet spring. Heavy rains following the spring thaw changed the unpaved Omo Road into a river of mud, making it impassable for vehicular traffic. Mother had to leave the car a quarter of a mile away on 32 Mile Road and had to walk to and from the house on the muddy shoulder to get back and forth to work. The muddy road was also impassable for the school bus, which only picked up children on the main roads. On the days when most of the rural roads on the bus route were impassable, the Armada schools closed for "Mud Days". Mudite and I also had to trudge through the mud wearing high boots to get to the bus when school reopened. At times it seemed like we would get sucked into the depths of the earth as our feet got stuck in the quagmire. I held my little sister by the hand to make sure she did not fall into the oozing mud. The only respite from the mud came during the Easter school break when we could stay at home for a week. However, the family did not get to enjoy celebrating Christ's Resurrection as I became ill. Early Easter morning, April 9, as I arose to get ready for church, I suddenly started hemorrhaging, leaving a large puddle of blood on the floor. The problem was far beyond a normal menstrual period, as the blood flow was severe every time I moved or tried to stand up. Dr. Bower, the wonderful country doctor who never hesitated to make house calls, could not drive up to the farm through the mud either. This dedicated physician trudged quarter of a mile through the mud on Easter morning to check on his young patient. He prescribed a strict regimen of staying in bed as I was very weak from the blood loss. I could not attend classes for two weeks after school resumed.

Despite feeling weak, I could not help laughing when my classmate and good friend, Shirley Priestap, drove a huge farm tractor through the sea of mud from her house a mile south on Omo Road to deliver homework for me. For several days Shirley had been giving piles of my homework books for Mudite to carry from the bus stop on the main road to our house a quarter of a mile north on Omo Road. Poor little Mudite struggled valiantly under the heavy load to extricate her legs from the mud only to have them mired again with the next step. On some days walking home alone without her big sister and carrying a heavy load of books overwhelmed the little girl and she stood in the mud up to her ankles and cried forlornly. Perhaps Shirley noticed the desolate scene as she was walking from the bus to her house in the opposite direction and took pity on Mudite. Shirley continued the unique homework delivery by tractor for another week until I was well enough to go back to school or the road dried up. Whichever came first has become "muddied" with the passage of time.

Though still weak, I was well enough by April 23, to attend my confirmation at Our Savior Lutheran Church. Being past the normal age when children get confirmed following the 8th grade, I had attended adult instruction classes taught by the Rev. Dwain Gade. I wrote in my diary that becoming a communicant member of the congregation was one of the most significant events in my life. I prayed that I would be able to follow God's word and live my life like a true

Confirmation Day, April 23, 1950

Christian woman. On my confirmation day, the sun was bathing the countryside with the warmth of springtime, the roads had dried up and were graded, and father had lovingly washed the mud off the old Ford for his daughter's big day. I dressed for this festive occasion in a navy blue suit ordered from the Montgomery Ward catalog. I wore a corsage of white carnations presented to me by my parents and all white accessories. My parents, with the help of some money sent by Omi from Chile, gave me a gold ring with two red garnet stones, my birthstones. The Ladies Aid of Our Savior gave a small reception for the nine adults joining the congregation. Among the confirmands was one of my classmates, Dick Enberg, who became an internationally known sportscaster. In later years I joked that it is my claim to fame that I drove the celebrated Dick to all the confirmation classes at church.

In June, I finished my sophomore year at Armada High School and received a silver medal for my scholastic achievement. Despite my heavy load of carrying Biology and Geometry in the same time slot and missing several weeks of school during my illness, I achieved the second highest grade average in my class. By this time, father had fulfilled his contract to work on the Kuhlman farm. The family decided to move to the town of Armada after the difficult winter and spring on the farm so that we would be closer for the school and mother's work. It had become obvious to the townspeople that Tatiana was far too educated to keep on working as a hotel maid. She was offered a clerical position in the Kresge 5 & 10 ¢ Store where she worked for a Mrs. Staudenmeier. Some months later, she advanced to a cashier's position at the Kroger grocery store.

Due to limited English language skills, Kārlis was not able to obtain work as an accountant, but he was offered a job working on line at Armada Products, an automotive parts manufacturing plant owned by a Mr. Conrad. The plan that God has charted for each of His children may not ever be fully known to anyone, but for Kārlis to be placed with Mr. Conrad could not have just "happened" spontaneously if one is a believer in the Almighty. When Kārlis had a major heart attack in the spring of 1954, Mr. Conrad's oldest son Don, an Osteopathic Physician, was there to treat him. Although angioplasty was not an available procedure at this point in medical history and Kārlis' heart muscle was permanently damaged, Dr. Conrad's treatment did save his life. While working at Armada Products on Ridge Road, father also befriended a man by the name of Carl Reiter who was like an angel sent by God. This good man drove father to work every day and was also willing to help out with any home repair work that needed to be done at the Gedrovics' residence.

Before school started in the fall of 1950, the Gedrovics family moved to a furnished apartment on Spencer Street where we had to share the one bathroom with the family living on the opposite side of the house, which was divided into two apartments. The neighbors, Dick and Loretta, and their young son were nice and friendly, but the lack of sound proofing in the house at times became intolerable. Dick seemed to be crazy about the popular song, "Goodnight, Irene", that was on the "Hit Parade" for several weeks. When Dick came home from work, he started playing the record over and over again at the loudest volume and highest decibels of sound that could be produced by his amplifier and speakers. When the radio program, "The Lone Ranger", was being broadcast, I would then in retribution turn up the volume to the highest level as well. The sound of galloping horses and the command "Hi-Ho, Silver, Away!" would then echo and resonate through the thin folding doors separating the two apartments, no doubt infringing on Irene's goodnight's sleep. Eventually both sides capitulated and the sound war ended with neighborly cooperation.

The apartment was located only a few blocks from the school and it was convenient for Mudite and me to participate in after-school activities without worrying about missing a bus ride home. Though small and simple, the apartment was also the venue in 1951 for my Sweet Sixteen birthday party attended by many of my classmates. Mother was also pleased to host a bountiful brunch at the apartment for her former supervisor, Mrs. Rice, with whom she had worked at Church World Services in Salzburg. Mrs. Rice visited the Gedrovics family in Armada while she and her husband were vacationing in Michigan. She again made an offer to help mother re-establish her teaching career if the family would agree to join the Rice's Christian Scientist church in Wisconsin. Though appreciative of the offer, mother declined as she had previously done in Salzburg. Compromising our religious beliefs by leaving the Lutheran Church in order to improve job opportunities was not an option the Gedrovics family was willing to consider. If it were God's will that Tatiana teach again, surely He would show her the way when the proper time came.

Meanwhile, the family was content with the opportunities God had provided. Economically our family certainly could have been classified as impoverished, but it did not take material possessions to make us feel blessed when we had God's love and a loving family. At last we could enjoy being on our own and having the freedom of choice of where to live and where to work without being obligated to any more sponsors. However, while enjoying our freedom, our family never forgot our sponsors and appreciated the assistance we had received in getting established in the United States. Just like I looked up Valiant Nichols while visiting Dallas, mother and Mudite stopped at Valley Cottage on a trip to New York and were able to express their appreciation to some of the people we had known at the Tolstoy Foundation's Reed Farm. Interestingly, I also re-established contact with Leo Kuhlman when I discovered that one of my sons' teachers at Our Shepherd Lutheran School in Birmingham was Mr. Kuhlman's niece. It was a small world after all. We were grateful to have an opportunity to thank the people who had helped us.

While living in Armada, the Gedrovics family established a reputation as conscientious and reliable workers. When I tried out for a part in the Junior Class Play in April 1951, it seemed to me that this reputation of "faithful servant" automatically typecast me into the role of the housekeeper, Mrs. Fitzgerald, in the play "Cheaper by the Dozen". Dick Enberg was cast in the lead role as Frank Gilbreth, the head of the household, and I, one of the class brains, had to be satisfied in being chosen to play the servant. In my young vain mind, I could not understand why I was not picked for one of the lead roles to either play the part of Mrs. Gilbreth, Dick Enberg's wife, or at least the lead role of the daughter Ernestine. Enlightenment came many years later when I realized that my teachers had really been very astute in assigning me the housekeeper role. It was only logical to have the housekeeper portrayed by someone who spoke English with an accent. The twelve offspring of the Gilbreth family and both parents, of course, would have all spoken perfect English without an accent. The wisdom of the casting choices had escaped the sixteen-year-old motivated by pride and vanity. In the Senior Class play, "Meet Me in St. Louis", the following year, I felt vindicated as I was chosen for the romantic role of a flirting coquette, Lucille Ballard, competing for the attention of one of the male leads.

Despite feeling slighted by not being chosen to play a lead, I thoroughly enjoyed being part of the Junior Play cast and had fun at all the performances as well as the rehearsals. After the last performance Ron Juip, who had played the part of Dr. Burton, hosted a dinner party on his farm. Filled with pride over the successful performance and the ringing of applause in my ears, I arrived at the party in the '42 Ford showing off how I was allowed to drive by myself. My little bubble of pride burst with a bang, however. As I was leaving, the car had to be backed up along a long dark drive. Instead of doing it slowly and with care, I backed up with a flourish. When I turned just short of the road, the rear bumper caught on a metal guide wire on a telephone pole next to the driveway. I was stuck for good until Ron got out a tractor and pulled the car loose. When I visited Ron and his wife at his home in Imlay City over fifty years later, he reminded me to back out of the long drive carefully. Tongue in cheek, he said he did not have a tractor available to rescue me again. Why is it that embarrassing moments seem to stick in people's memories forever? At least I was spared such a repeat performance at the Senior Play cast party the following year. Fortunately, painful or embarrassing moments were but a minute part of my high school years in Armada.

Armada was a good place for children and youth to grow up and develop their abilities. In this small friendly town people cared for each other and were supportive and proud of the accomplishments of the young people. Since studies came easy for me, I had plenty of time to participate in various activities. In addition to having parts in class play productions, I also was a writer for the school yearbook, Regit. Regit stood for the school tiger mascot spelled backwards. As a member of the Regit staff, I had fun interviewing people and writing articles for the yearbook. My English teacher and advisor on the Regit staff, Mrs. Noreen Johnson, always gave me encouragement to develop my writing abilities. Mrs. Johnson and her husband, who was the coach and driving instructor at the high school, lived in the house next-door to us on Spencer Street and both were willing to answer questions even outside the classroom. Mrs. Johnson had the great ability to give a critical evaluation and to help improve a student's work in a positive way without finding fault in a disapproving manner.

Mrs. Johnson recommended me for a part-time job at the local weekly newspaper, *The Armada Times*. Initially the owner and publisher, Mr. Walter Schultz, taught me how to do typesetting for the articles but later I was given writing assignments as well. Working at the Armada Times was more fun than work. I got along well with the publisher's twin sons, Walter and Willard who also worked for the newspaper. The young men were just a few years older than I and we three always kidded around and teased each other which made the time fly quickly while we were working. The twins were so identical, that unless they were standing side by side, it was impossible to tell them apart. This proved to be quite embarrassing as time went on. Willard became interested in dating me and invited me to see the movie "South Pacific" in Mt. Clemens. We stopped for a meal afterwards and it was one of the most interesting dates I had experienced. The next day I met one of the Schultz boys on the street in town. But was he Walter or Willard? What a difficult situation for me to be facing when I could not tell if I was talking to the same fellow with whom I had been on a date the previous night!

The young man inquired how I was and in return assured me he was feeling fine. I then politely asked the unidentified twin how his brother was, hoping he would answer including the brother's name. No such luck. The brother apparently was also fine. Just in case I was talking to Willard, I mention that I really enjoyed the movie "South Pacific", but he just answered, "I'm glad", without divulging if he had also been there the night before. After a few more awkward moments of exchanging stilted niceties, I excused myself indicating I was in a hurry to do some errands. Since I never learned to distinguish who was who when either of the guys came in to work alone without the brother, I was always uncomfortable addressing either one by his name. I also avoided further dates with Willard though I really enjoyed being with him on that first date. I could never be sure whom I was with if the boys decided to switch places just to fool me on some future date. Identical, as if they were both cloned, they surely must have realized my predicament and my fear of being fooled just like they had confused the townspeople and teachers on multiple occasions.

I continued to work at the *Armada Times*, however, and Mr. Schultz always was delighted to see me even after I went away to the University. Some years later, I stopped at the *Times* offices with my three sons while visiting my parents in Armada. Mr. Schultz took a photograph of us all and published it on the front page of the *Armada Times* under the headline: "*Remember Rita*", as if I were some celebrity visiting my hometown. Armada really gave its people a sense of belonging. Mr. Schultz even managed to mention in the article that I came home to care for my mother who was recovering after major surgery for breast cancer. Consequently, mother received many get-well cards from the concerned citizens in Armada. The people showed they cared. The Gedrovics family had become assimilated as one of their own and not looked upon as "spotted dogs" as mother had feared.

Front-page photo in The Armada Times, Feb. 18, 1960

The merchants in Armada also showed they cared for their customers. People were trusting in those days. When the Gedrovics family first came to town, everyone knew that money was tight for our family. Mr. Doggendorf, who owned the grocery and meat market, allowed the family to run a tab for our groceries. He trusted that the bill would be paid whenever the family was able to do so on payday. When Mudite became ill with a fever of unknown origin and had to stay home alone while recovering, the owner of the hardware store sent over a television set so that Mudite would have entertainment during the days she had to spend alone. Mudite's recovery proved to be lengthy. She was taken to Henry Ford Hospital in

Detroit when her fever would not relent. It was discovered that though her tonsils looked normal, they were severely infected and growing inward into the throat. When she was brought home after the tonsillectomy, she started severe hemorrhaging and the kindly Dr. Bower came over during the night to pack the bleeding cavity. When mother told the hardware store owner that the family really could not afford the modern luxury of a television set in addition to the medical bills the family was facing, the owner replied,

"Consider it a loan, I know I will be paid when you can do so."

Similarly, Dr. Bower did not request payment when he made the house calls. He relied on us paying the bills when the family could afford to pay. Meanwhile, Dr. Bower considered his house calls to be just neighborly visits since he lived on the same street only a few houses away. Mother and father kept careful tabs of all their debts and made sure they were all paid in full in a timely manner.

Mr. Conrad, the owner of Armada Products where father worked, was especially considerate of the welfare of his employees. He always treated them with respect, was fair in adjusting work schedules when a special need arose, and provided turkeys for holiday dinners. For the Gedrovics family, Mr. Conrad turned out to be a financial angel as well. Mr. Conrad suggested that perhaps the family should invest in a home of their own when a suitable place became available. My parents could not dream of having enough savings for a down payment to qualify for bank financing. When a nice two-story home went on sale on Fulton Street, Mr. Conrad offered to buy the house for the Gedrovics family and re-sell it to us on a land contract with favorable credit terms for repayment. Praise the Lord for all His blessings and sending an angel to guide us to a new home! The Gedrovics family prayerfully considered the offer and father gratefully signed the land contract with Mr. Conrad. Three years after our family came to the United States as immigrants with no money and no possessions, we would finally have a beautiful and spacious permanent home of our own. Mudite and I, and later our families, had a home where we were always welcome. After seven years of wandering from country to country and one temporary abode to another, we had the security of our own home and the joy of being able to unpack our boxes at last.

★★★

36

HOME, SWEET HOME, 1951

Sometime in the early spring of 1951, the Gedrovics family moved again. Once more my sister and I had to find a different route to walk to school, but this time the path to school led from a home of our own in the very heart of Armada. It seemed unbelievable that three years after arriving in the United States, we now could call the big two-story white frame home our own. When we first entered the vacant house, our family bowed their heads and gave thanks to the divine presence, which, though unseen, had always been with us and had led us to this place. Later the Pastor of St.Paul's Latvian Evangelical Lutheran Church, the Rev. Valters Liventals, was present at a housewarming where he prayed for God's sheltering arms to protect this house and all who dwell there and for the Holy Spirit to abide at the home always. According to an old Latvian custom, the first items the Gedrovics family brought into the house were bread and salt. The bread was a symbol for an abundance of food to fill the house and salt signified prosperity in our lives, as salt in ancient times had been a valuable instrument in trade transactions.

74065 South Fulton St., Armada 1951

Our family unpacked and settled into the rooms on the first floor. The previous owners had converted the upstairs into a separate apartment, which the Gedrovics' later rented out to another Latvian Family. The downstairs had more space than our family had ever enjoyed previously. The first floor had a large living room, dining room, a kitchen with lots of cupboards, and a bathroom. Having a private bathroom meant a lot to the family, especially Mudite and me. After having to share the bathroom at the apartment on Spencer Street and at all the displaced persons camps, we could now take a bath without worrying about someone disturbing our privacy. Our parents used the large parlor adjoining the living room for the master bedroom. Mudite and I shared a bedroom next to the master bedroom. A third bedroom served as a den or guestroom. Even the temperamental family car seemed to like its new home and performed better when it did not have to stay out in the cold. The old 1942 Ford rolled merrily into the driveway and its engine seemed to chuckle upon seeing that there was an attached garage as well as a free-standing garage where it could find shelter from the elements and keep rust from attacking its creaking body.

The lot was of a generous size. The lawn in the back ran down to a small, bubbling creek. Father was delighted to have plenty of garden space to resume his fruit-growing hobby. As soon as the weather would allow in the spring, he planted apple, peach, and pear trees in the back yard as if to assure that his family would again be permanently rooted. He also added a long hedge of grape vines and several raspberry bushes which in future years yielded an abundance of berries for juice and jam. In later years after moving to a new house built in Ann Arbor, father expanded his gardening activities and also planted black currant and red currant bushes and learned how to use the berry juice in brewing his own brand of delicious wine and brandy. The raspberry brandy had an especially excellent aroma and taste. This "Aveņu" brandy was a prized elixir treasured by the entire family for three generations. Mother turned the flowerbed next to the house into a blooming rainbow of colorful flowers that decorated the house from spring through fall. Next to the back porch stood a still functioning water pump supplying cool, clean well water for irrigating the Gedrovics garden. The antique water pump proved to be a major attraction for my three sons a few years later. The boys enjoyed many happy times when their small arms proved to have enough strength and endurance to make the water come forth from the well. "Pump Grandma and Pump Grandpa" were the names the grandsons bestowed upon Tatiana and Kārlis.

Having always lived in furnished homes and apartments since coming to Armada, our family initially had no furniture of our own to place in the new home. Our dear neighbors from Omo Road came to the rescue. Mrs. Manska, who had inherited a houseful of furniture from her mother, gave our family everything needed for the home. Some church members also donated many items. At last the albums, photos, and diaries could be unpacked from the box father had constructed during the war so that priceless family memories could be preserved. From then on, the box remained empty, stored in the basement of the Armada home. The family could never discard the treasured box, as it had preserved the irreplaceable mementos of the Gedrovics

Steven and David at grandparents' house, Easter 1958

family throughout the war and through the storms our wind-tossed ship had endured while crossing the Atlantic ocean. When Kārlis and Tatiana moved to Ann Arbor many years later, the box went along to the new house. Kārlis painted it a bright red to celebrate its vital importance to the family. It was placed in the basement of the new home and was used for storage. After the death of Kārlis, I asked to be given my father's handcrafted container in remembrance of him. Without the pictures and documents that Tatiana had with so much thought and foresight thoughtfully packed into this simple wooden box, my family biography would be woefully incomplete and fragmented. The photo albums and diaries are vital segments in re-constructing our family's journeys on the pathways charted for us in God's Book of Life. The red wooden box presently occupies a prominent place in my family room.

Becoming homeowners and moving into a place of their own is a major event in anyone's life. For our Gedrovics family home ownership brought new responsibilities and made life considerably busier. It only seemed natural for the older house to start complaining so that the new owners would fix some problems that come with age. The heating system and the plumbing always called for father's attention. Often his co-worker, Carl Reiter lent his helping hand and knowledge to tackle the emerging do-it-yourself challenges. Plaster needed repairs, old wallpaper had to be removed, and touches of paint had to be applied to make the walls and ceiling sparkle and shine. There were hardwood floors throughout the house, though their true beauty was obscured by years of wear. I volunteered to sand the old dirt and grime from the floors and for days the house was filled with flying particles of wood dust as the beautiful grain on the parquet floor began to emerge and every board was sanded smooth. Father then carefully applied several coats of varnish and the shining floors gave the old house a bright new appearance.

Meanwhile, mother had received an offer to work in a clerical position at the Macomb County Library in Mt. Clemens. Mrs. Margaret Montgomery, who served on the Library Board, had noticed mother while she worked as a cashier at the Kroger store and the two ladies became friends. Mother's hard work, integrity, intelligence, and ability to relate to people was apparent to Mrs. Montgomery and she arranged for mother to be interviewed for work at the Macomb County Library where her education could be better utilized. The Macomb County Librarian, Dorothy Hyatt, was equally impressed with mother's credentials and recommendations and she was hired.

Although father performed strenuous manual work at Armada Products, he used his bookkeeping and accounting skills to keep the family finances in order. Even though Tatiana had received a pay increase with the move to work at the Macomb County Library, it took a great deal of thought, planning, and juggling of their combined incomes to keep up with mortgage expenses, home and car repair and upkeep, and expenses for their girls' education in addition to meeting everyday needs for food and clothing. My parents canned bushels of tomatoes, beans, apples, pears, peaches, and Concord grape juice to save on food costs. Her full-time work also did not keep mother from making her own jam, doing a lot of baking and sewing clothes for her girls.

When I got invited to my Senior Prom and there was no extra money for a new gown, mother took apart a gown that an older lady from church had donated and altered it for me into a younger halter-top style. I felt like a princess in the swirling sky-blue dress with minute gold dots shimmering like stars on the taffeta material. Mother also made a black velvet cape from one of her skirts to complete the exquisite outfit for her daughter's mid-winter ball. If my eyes were shining when I looked at my reflection in the mirror, it was partially from tears of gratitude for the late hours into the night when my mother had lovingly sacrificed her own sleep to fashion the beautiful prom wardrobe.

Omi came to the rescue with her fashion design skills from far-away Santiago, Chile for another prom. I only had to airmail my measurements to my beloved grandmother and back came a gorgeous cream colored full-length skirt embroidered with golden swirls and an elegant jacket in rich golden crushed velvet. Another form-fitting tunic jacket with narrow long sleeves was made of eggshell satin and featured what must have been about two dozen small round self-fabric covered buttons down the entire length of the jacket. Again my eyes filled with tears of gratitude as I pictured Omi covering the buttons and making the loops for the buttonholes with her loving hands.

Every payday, father sat down at the table with several rows of envelopes, each marked with a specific budgeted category such as "House Payment", "Food", "Church", "Car Expenses", "Repairs", "Clothing", "Medical" and "Savings" among others. No matter how tight the funds, there was always something set aside in the "Savings" envelope for an emergency or future needs. He carefully distributed the cash into each envelope according to the amounts he had calculated for the budget. When an expense arose that was not budgeted, such as piano lessons or a gift for a special occasion, he would check all the envelopes and calculate from which envelope the needed cash could be borrowed until the expense could be worked into the budget. Accountants are sometimes nicknamed "Bean Counters". Kārlis, our loving and caring head of the household, never counted beans. He counted every penny, however, and made sure it was put to the best use. He was never extravagant when it came to spending for his own needs, but was always generous in giving to his family and others who were in need. Somehow he managed to budget so that his beloved daughters would not feel that they were impoverished at any time, but would learn the virtue of being thrifty.

When father needed something major like a new suit or a new pair of shoes for himself, he carefully chose the item that seemed to promise the longest wear. He would then announce with conviction,

"*This will last me until the end of my life. I will not need another suit (or shoes) in my lifetime*".

Fortunately, such a pronouncement turned into an amusing anecdote over the years. The Lord blessed Kārlis with several more decades of life and several more suits and new pairs of shoes were purchased until the faithful father was called to his eternal rest. Yet, it was father's strict adherence to a budget and careful use of funds and mother's thrifty housekeeping that allowed the Gedrovics family to establish itself in a new country, buy new homes and cars, and help both daughters achieve higher education.

Kārlis and Tatiana taught their daughters well. Both of us girls grew up to be industrious and hardworking. Mudite and I both started working while still in school to provide for some of our own needs. I worked after school for the Armada Times and Mudite later worked at Simpson's Pharmacy. Mother also taught us how to sew many of our own clothes to stretch our meager budget. Feed for farm animals in the 1950's came in dual-purpose, recyclable cotton bags in various colors and flowery patterns. When farm friends gave these bags to Mudite and me to use as fabric for clothing, we artistically designed and sewed the material into pretty summer skirts. We felt quite fashionable wearing these feedbags. When we had families of our own, Mudite and I designed and sewed all our children's clothing while they were young. Mudite became quite an expert at sewing and could even tailor suits for her husband. The clothing she designed and tailored became welcome gifts to all family members.

Working as "European Nannies" also provided additional income. Some of the neighbors on Fulton Street were particularly pleased to have Mudite and me as baby-sitters. The Ulrich family that lived across the street often asked me to watch their two little boys, Harvey and Robert. The boys were well behaved, but very active and curious. They constantly wanted me to play active games with them. During the encounters with the Ulrich brothers I learned that the "Cowboys" my Nyack classmates had warned me about apparently were quite active right there on Fulton Street. It did not matter that there seemed to be a shortage of Indians. I was assigned the role of running around the yard yelling what I thought was quite a passable Indian war chant, while the two little cowboys pursued me on imaginary horses with toy pistols clicking away. The boys were also curious about my Latvian background and were very eager to be taught the Latvian language, except that they confused it with "Latin" and told their friends they could speak Latin. I got quite attached to these little guys and hoped that if I had sons, they would be just as charming.

The Schnell family, living next door to the Ulrich's, also found it to be convenient to have me as a baby-sitter as I could just walk across the street and not require transportation home. The Schnells had five daughters, ranging from newborn to age eight and I babysat for the four oldest ones. If I thought the girls would be easy to care for due to my experience with my younger sister, it soon became apparent that taking care of four girls is quite a major challenge, perhaps requiring military experience as a drill sergeant. No doubt the girls must have been used to playing with each other while their mother was at home and busy with the baby. When I was in charge, the girls changed their routine and employed different tactics. Each girl wanted to be entertained in a different way. Three eager voices called out, "Can you read me a story?", "Let's sing a song,", or "Let's play with my dolly!", while I was trying to change the diapers on the shrieking newborn. It turned out that the newborn had colic and would not stop crying all evening. Being afraid that I was doing something wrong, I called my mother for advice. Upon learning that some newborns are colicky, my mind was put at ease and I was able to cuddle and comfort the baby while doing some of the activities the three older sisters requested. Evidently the parents were satisfied with how I handled the "Fearsome Four" and the Schnell family relied on the Gedrovics girls to watch their daughters for several years. When I went away to the University, Mudite took on the task of caring for the expanded "Fearsome Five", but by then the youngest ones had outgrown the colic stage and the other girls had lost interest in testing the new babysitter. Mudite was closer in age to the oldest of the Schnell girls, and they became friends in the ensuing years.

The townspeople of Armada took notice of the how industrious and hardworking the Gedrovics family was. The ladies of the Armada Literary Guild decided to also sponsor some displaced persons and thought that another Latvian family would make a positive addition to the town. Thus Žanis and Herta Vizulis came to work on the dairy farm owned by the Day family on Ridge Road, just outside of Armada. The Vizulis couple lived in a small old house meant for itinerant workers. The kind ladies of the Literary Guild had cleaned and furnished the home and were on hand to welcome the couple as they arrived in Armada. They also provided transportation when the couple needed to go into town. Žanis and Herta were older than Kārlis and Tatiana and soon the long hours of working on the farm became too strenuous for them. Upon Tatiana's recommendation, Žanis and Herta were hired for work at the Armada Rubber Company. Kārlis and Tatiana renovated their upstairs apartment and welcomed the Vizulis couple as their first tenants. Several months later Herta's brother, Paul Zelmenis, also obtained work at the Armada Rubber Company and came to live at the Vizulis apartment. Žanis and Herta along with Paul became lifelong friends of the Gedrovics family. The home on Fulton Street became a Latvian gathering place where my parents entertained many of our friends from St. Paul's Latvian Evangelical Lutheran Church in Detroit. Besides the camaraderie that was fostered by sharing the home with fellow countrymen, the rent income from the apartment also helped my parents meet their financial obligations.

Though the Gedrovics' were frugal in their spending, it was not at the expense of giving up cultural activities. When we moved into our big house, an old upright piano that the previous owners had left in the house was moved into a prominent place in the living room. The cabinet showed its years and was not as shiny as the piano that flames had consumed in Jelgava, but mother was delighted to be able to play again and to make sure I resumed piano lessons I had started in Glasenbach with the Gutenberg sisters. The sound quality of the piano improved considerably after it was properly tuned and once more happy notes filled the air. A piano teacher came to the house weekly to give lessons. I participated in my first piano recital on May 28, 1951 in New Haven, Michigan, where I played Scherzo #1 by Schubert. What a joy it was to hear music in the house again! Whenever our Latvian friends gathered at the Gedrovics' home, it was customary to celebrate by singing folk songs. Mother always accompanied her guests on the piano. In good times or bad times, whatever the circumstances, Latvians never gave up singing. When mother's talents on the keyboard became known at Our Savior Lutheran Church, she was often asked to accompany the congregation on the organ.

I was chosen to accompany the Sunday school children's choir on the piano and to lead the singing at Vacation Bible School. Mudite had been gifted with a good singing voice. Accompanied by mother, she was able to practice her singing for a performance at the Romeo Peach Festival and to audition for a children's "Auntie Dee" talent TV program. Mudite and I also played around on the piano with our arrangement of a song called *"Oh Ducky, Ducky, Please Don't Go Away."* The manuscript regretfully has never been published for the music world to enjoy. Mudite had composed the song while on the Kuhlman farm as she watched the ducks parading in the yard. No doubt the composition would have become an American Standard had it ever gone on the air, but alas, Armada lacked a radio station, and sophisticated audio equipment like digital recorders, MP3 players, and YouTube were not yet invented to record our masterpiece. Though the "Ducky" song began and ended our careers as composers, Mudite and I were fortunate to perform on stage in class plays, however, and both had the honor of delivering speeches at our Armada High School Graduation Ceremonies.

My senior year at Armada High School flew by at record speed. Football games, decorating the Homecoming float, dances, the Senior Play, putting together the school yearbook REGIT, learning to develop photographs in Physics class, and working at the Armada Times–all became part of the constantly moving stream of activities in the 1951/52 school year. That I would go to college was a given, an established fact, only subject to the choice of the college. Since Tatiana and Omi had university degrees, the same was expected of the Gedrovics sisters. Initially, I wanted to study nursing and considered the Harper Hospital School of Nursing. I encountered a roadblock in being accepted into a nursing program because there was an eighteen-year minimum age requirement. I, being seventeen at graduation time, did not qualify. I then applied at the University of Michigan and Michigan State College, which in 1951 had not yet attained University status. I applied for tuition scholarships, as it was impossible for my parents to fund university education no matter how carefully they budgeted. Scholarships at MSC were awarded on the basis of grade averages at the end of the first semester of the senior year. The University of Michigan required that applicants for the Regents Alumni

Scholarship Award take a long and comprehensive examination. Two of my classmates, Shan Renton and Nancy Simon, and I were registered for a regional examination given at Port Huron High School. Though I had never had problems in taking examinations, the U-M version was very difficult and contained a great deal of unfamiliar subject matter. I quickly answered the questions to which I knew the answers and let logic guide me on unfamiliar grounds. When even logic failed to point to the right answer among the multiple choices, I sometimes had to resort to the "Eeny, meeny, miney, moe" method of choice. At the end of the grueling three-hour exam, when I compared my answers to those chosen by Shan and Nancy, we discovered that each had chosen a different answer for many of the questions. There was a long wait until we received the results of the scholarship examination.

The Senior Class did not have to wait long, however, to find out individual grade averages for our four years of high school classes. The principal, Mr. Stanley, was very prompt in calculating each student's grade average immediately after the close of the first semester. I was ill with the flu and had stayed at home on the day in January when the grade averages were posted and the two top winners for the Valedictorian and Salutatorian honor were announced. My friend, Shan Renton, stopped at the house to bring me my homework assignments and gave me the news that Bea Ann Drinkhorn, the class beauty and brain, had won the honor of being Valedictorian. I assumed that if Bea Ann had earned the highest grade point average, then surely Dick Enberg must be the Salutatorian with the next highest average. Dick had always excelled in all subjects and had almost made it a competitive academic game each time he took an exam and then compiled the statistics to see if he had beaten all his classmates.

"Don't you want to know who will be the Salutatorian?" Shan asked me.

"Well, I guess it is Dick Enberg, he's the smartest guy in our class", I responded.

Shan broke out in a big smile. "*Congratulations, Rita, you are the Salutatorian!*" My grade point average had bested Enberg's by 0.01! When I returned to school, I was congratulated by all my classmates, all except Dick Enberg, who teased he would never forgive me for keeping him from achieving the honor he had coveted. Of course, in professional life Dick's intellect, drive, and high motivation led him to be honored throughout America and known throughout the world as the voice of professional and Olympic sports broadcasts. I was, of course, pleased that studying had paid off and brought me this honor, but I was also apprehensive about having to give the welcoming speech at the graduation ceremonies. Mrs. Johnson, my English teacher, promised that she would be my mentor and coach me on preparing and delivering the speech.

My class standing evidently impressed Michigan State College. When I went to pick up the mail at the post office one day early in May, I found an official envelope addressed to me. The envelope bore the green logo of MSC. Eagerly, but with trepidation, I tore open the envelope right on the spot and did not have to look much beyond the first lines before my face broke out in a big grin as I read, "We are pleased to inform you that you have been admitted to Michigan State College." The letter went on to congratulate me on my scholastic achievement, which qualified me to receive a full academic scholarship. I was so excited that I skipped all the way home. Nobody was there during the day to hear the great news, but I was too excited not to share my good fortune with somebody. I ran over to the home of Dr. Bower who lived a few doors down and shared my good news with his son, Earl, who was washing his car in the back yard. The young man must have been surprised to have the excited girl come skipping into his yard, waving a paper and yelling, "I did it, I did it!" Later that evening our entire family was in a happy mood hearing my news and we all went to the drug store to celebrate with a round of ice cream sundaes. MSC had requested that an acceptance letter be sent within two weeks.

   I still had not heard from the University of Michigan. I decided to delay the decision as long as I could, hoping to hear from U-M so that I could evaluate my options if both institutions were to accept me. The University of Michigan kept me on pins and needles for nearly the full two weeks. My heart started beating faster when I received the business envelope with the blue block M on the letterhead. "Congratulations", the letter began. "You have been selected as a recipient of the University of Michigan Regents Alumni Scholarship".

I praised the Lord for making it possible to have two of the top institutions in the State of Michigan willing to pay my tuition in full. The decision as to which scholarship to choose was not easy to make. Both schools were among Michigan's best educational institutions. I consulted with Mrs. Johnson, who had always given good advice and who knew my strengths and weaknesses. Mrs. Johnson offered the opinion that a degree from the University of Michigan might be considered more prestigious, because it was the only institution of higher education in the State of Michigan accredited as a University at that time. Michigan State, on the other hand, had accreditation as a college. For this reason, Mrs. Johnson seemed to prefer U-M. I also asked the principal, Mr. Stanley for advice. It was his opinion that I should get my education at whatever college or university offered the best program to fit my vocational interests. When I asked Mr. Stanley to share the results of my interest and aptitude tests with me to determine what line of studies I should pursue, Mr. Stanley responded that he had no idea how to advise me on the basis of my test scores. I was shocked by this answer. Could it be that I was not suited for anything if even the principal did not know how to advise me? Mr. Stanley then smiled and explained that I had scored high in just about any field of interest.

"You are a very smart girl, Rita, and your scores indicate a high interest in every field of endeavor. Someone who is interested in all aspects of life will do well in whatever she chooses to do. I know you will always do your best in whatever occupation you choose. You will be a winner if you continue to follow your own quest for excellence. I wish you success in any university or vocation you choose."

I decided to enroll in the pre-medicine curriculum at the University of Michigan to fulfill my dream of helping the sick and injured, a dream that had been born during the war when as a young child I had wished I could help the many people I had seen dying from illness, starvation, and war injuries. As long as I kept up a B+ average, the Regents Scholarship would continue to pay my tuition which in 1952 amounted to ninety dollars per semester for a full load of fifteen credit hours. To the Gedrovics family this seemed like a fortune. Today such an amount would not even cover one credit hour.

The joy over the impending graduation day and being accepted at the U-M was mingled with tears of nostalgia during the month of May as preparations began for "Class Night" when the seniors say goodbye to their classmates and turn the leadership baton over to the Junior Class. For me it was another painful time in the series of farewells. I had to part from classmates and good friends again as we all would be scattered to pursue different pathways in adult life. During the last weeks of school Larry Mahaffy and I had become closer friends and he always picked me up for all the Class Night rehearsals. Every time the class practiced the song "Memories", I would look at my friend Larry and become all choked up at the words *"Memories, memories, dreams of love so true. O'er the Sea of Memories I'm drifty back to you..."*. Larry and I remained life-long friends and we were able to recall memories from high school when I brought my grandchildren to pick apples at Larry's family orchard in Armada. Yet, while memories gave rise to tears and a nostalgic mood, there was also happy anticipation of what lay ahead in the future when the class sang *"There's a long, long trail a' winding into the Land of my Dreams...."*. For me the beginning course on the long trail would lead me to the University of Michigan, and I was eager to start my journey following graduation.

At long last, the anticipated day arrived. I donned the gray gown and cap with the tassel in the blue and white colors of the senior class. I proudly displayed the silver honors cord presented to the class Salutatorian. The thirty-two graduates were evenly divided, sixteen men and sixteen women as we solemnly walked into the auditorium together in pairs to the music of *"Pomp and Circumstance"*. It was time for me, in the role as Salutatorian, to give the welcome speech. I had practiced it several times with my mentor, Noreen Johnson, and I was not nervous being on stage with the School Superintendent, Mr. Kitson, Bea Ann Drinkhorn who was the Valedictorian, and John B. Swainson, who was to deliver the graduation address. I had a great admiration for the U.S. military and considered it to be an honor to be on the same stage with John Swainson. Later, in his address he told the graduates that if we tried hard enough, anything was possible. Mr. Swainson had served in the U.S. Army Infantry during World War II and lost both legs to a land mine. He had been awarded France's Croix de Guerre, the Presidential Unit Citation with two stars, and a Purple Heart–all before he reached the age nineteen. The loss of both legs never stopped Mr. Swainson. His spirit and determination lifted him to the heights of becoming the 42nd Governor of the State of Michigan some years after he delivered his challenging address to our class.

As I faced the audience of parents and guests, I felt humble in addressing these people who had so many years of experience in the real adult world our class was about to enter. Filled with emotion, I began the welcome speech:

"How many, many times in life we are forced to admit the inadequacy of mere words to express the deepest sentiments of the soul. Our hearts fill with emotion; and we learn when our tongues falter and our lips refuse to say what we wish them to, something of what Tennyson had in his heart when he wrote: 'I would that my tongue could utter the thoughts that arise in me!'

Dear friends, one and all, this occasion is one of those times. I cannot possibly put our thoughts into words, and to any degree make you feel as we do. And yet, men and women who know what it means to be wanderers over the face of the earth tell us that there is really no sweeter word in the English language than the word WELCOME.

My classmates have conferred upon me the great honor of speaking the words that shall bid you welcome here tonight, and I, in the warm inspiration of your presence, am most sincere in telling you, in their name, how truly glad we are to have you here. But the voice could never convey to you all that the heart would say, and there are many other ways in which it expresses itself to those who can understand, even better than the words we try in our weak way to speak. So I feel that you must already have felt your welcome, without any of our assurances. You must have seen it in our eager eyes and in our smiles; you must have caught it from the very air you breathed; you must, through the charged atmosphere in the room, have sensed the thoughts in our minds.

Tonight, we as a class are just pushing out from tiny seeds to grow upward into a mature form of life. All these years we have been sheltered in the tiny sphere of the seedling, protected by the shell from the rougher elements of our environment, and warmed by every nourishing force that was necessary for our enfolding. It has been a safe, snug, happy season of growth to us–this period of our High School germination. Here, we have learned many lessons of life in God's universal garden–lessons that only a practical growing experience can prove. This, then, is the hour of our transplanting, when we must test in other soil the theories we have gathered; and it is to this–the great moment of our first pushing forth into the full sunshine and air of life's infinite expression–that we give you greetings.

I am very grateful for the privilege of welcoming you tonight, but still, as I look around upon your faces, so much more marked with the lines of wisdom and wider experience than ours may be for many years yet to come, I cannot but feel that the words of welcome should come from you. To be sure, you have demonstrated your interest in us by coming to listen to all that we may have to say during this important hour in our lives, yet, it is we who are passing into your midst, we who are joining you in the larger school of progress outside these doors, we who are entering into your pursuits and pleasures, and becoming one with you in the social and business centers that make up active life.

Is it not we, then, who should ask for the glad hand of welcome? Is it not we who are the outsiders, seeking your favor and admission into your greater society? Is it not we, who, though we have now the pleasure and privilege of entertaining you for an hour at this turn of the road, must yet step forth and demand our share in all that has been yours for so long?

Then, while we do truly thank you for coming, and trust you may have every reason to long remember with a thrill of pleasure the fellowship of this hour, we yet feel that we must also ask your forbearance and kindly sympathy while we crave from each of you, as we step forth into your midst, the warm handshake and cordial smile that will assure us of your joy in bidding us welcome.

We hope that you may all feel that is has been good to be with us tonight, and may see in all that we do an say some assurance of your welcome this hour, even while realizing that as a class, we cannot well ask you to 'Come again'."

Valedictorian Bea Ann Drinkhorn and Salutatorian Rita Gedrovics, May 29, 1952, Armada High School.

As I bowed to the audience following my address, the rising warm applause sounded like a symphony welcoming the former stateless refugee to the New World. Six years later my sister Mudite stood on the same stage as she delivered an address as the Valedictorian of her class. She stood proud and tall as she was honored; gone was any resemblance to the fearful little waif who cried on the way to school when she first arrived in the strange land that now was our home.

A TRIP BACK TO NEW YORK

There was not much time to bask in the warmth of the congratulatory comments and well wishes after the diplomas were awarded and my class of 1952 was officially introduced as "Alumni of Armada High School". Many of the graduates hosted open houses and parties after the ceremonies and nostalgia gave way for music and merriment as I went from party to party with my friends until the wee hours of the morning.

The Senior Class left Armada for their senior trip two days later on Memorial Day, May 31, 1952. This was an especially exciting adventure for me as I had not been away from Michigan since arriving in Armada three years earlier. The first stop was at Niagara Falls, Ontario, where the majesty of the Horseshoe Falls was truly a wonder to behold. Although everyone had their picture taken as they sat on the stone fence along the edge of the falls, no photo could do justice to the thunderous roar and cascades of spray and mist that filled the air as tons of water came rushing down. God truly had created a natural wonder that would astound people from generation to generation.

After the school bus crossed the Rainbow Bridge into Niagara, New York, the tour hit a roadblock at U.S. Customs when everyone had to reveal their country of birth. I presented my Alien Registration Card, which was the required document for border crossing at that time, so I did not anticipate any problem. The Customs Agent, however, had never seen such a card and asked the bus to pull over and I had to go into the Customs Office so that the validity of my identification could be verified. One of the class sponsors, who had come along on the trip as a chaperone, showed that even teachers can be prejudiced. Instead of trying to resolve the problem and help me to deal with the customs authorities, as one would expect a class advisor to do, I was made to look as if I was to blame for the delay. As I started to follow the Customs Agent, the teacher exclaimed in frustration,

"*I knew we would have problems if we took that foreigner along on the trip!*"

Despite the fact that I had done well in school and was salutatorian of the class, I wondered if people would ever stop thinking of me as a foreigner. Where was my real home? Would I ever find it again?

It turned out that the supervisor in the Customs Office was also not familiar with the regulations that had been issued regarding new identification cards for aliens traveling into the United States. A call was made to Washington, D.C. to get confirmation that my registration was indeed valid. The Customs Agent showed understanding in recognizing how the advisor's comment must have offended me. He escorted me back to the bus where he publicly stated that I certainly had the proper documentation and apologized for his mistake in not recognizing the alien registration card, which identified me as a person eligible for US citizenship in the future. No apology came from the teacher for the demeaning foreigner "profiling" remark.

After Niagara the trip proceeded smoothly as the class visited beautiful Watkins Glen. The next stop on the trip was like a homecoming for me, as the classmates rode a ferry from the Port of New York to the Statue of Liberty. What a contrast this visit was from the time I had passed the Statue of Liberty on the Marine Flasher in 1948! There was no fear of being detained at Ellis Island or deported, no uncertainty of whether I would remain stateless, and certainly no more embarrassing nude line-ups for delousing! This time it was a lovely spring day and everyone got to climb to the top of the Statue of Liberty. I felt like I was on top of the world with the harbor of New York across the shimmering water spread out in front of me. Perhaps the other students did not feel such strong emotions when they stood on the very top of this symbol of freedom, but for me the Statue of Liberty stood for the gift of liberty and a new homeland that had been given to my family. Tears filled my eyes as I thanked God for bringing my family to the United States. My family now had a home where we felt secure. I had completed my high school education with honors, and could look forward to getting a university education on a scholarship. God Bless America!

Sadly, for two of the students in my class, the trip to New York meant a new kind of freedom. Two girls found the freedom to legally drink alcoholic beverages at age eighteen in New York to be their "liberating experience". When the class advisors discovered that the girls had become intoxicated on their first night in NY City, the girls were suspended from participating on the remaining portion of the trip and were put on a bus back to Armada. They were chaperoned on the bus trip back home by the same advisor who had made the derogatory statement about me causing problems because I was a "foreigner". It seemed poetic justice that the teacher had to miss the rest of the trip due to two misbehaving American-born citizens.

Washington, D.C. was the next stop on the senior trip where the students saw the entire city spread out at their feet from the Washington Monument where the young people managed to climb the hundreds of steps leading to the top. Though man-made, the various monuments in Washington were as awe-inspiring as the Niagara Falls and made history come live. It was amazing how many places the class was able to visit in just one week, but then we were strong young people who did not tire from walking for hours. We toured the FBI, visited George Washington's home in Mt. Vernon, and watched solemnly as the guards changed at the Tomb of the Unknown Soldier at Arlington National Cemetery in Virginia while a carillon played hymns in the chapel during the ceremony. Scenes, monuments, and artifacts of The Civil War made history come alive on the battlefields of Gettysburg in Pennsylvania. It seemed eerie to be walking on the hallowed ground that had been soaked with so much blood. The trip served as a climax for bringing together the historical facts the class had read about in history books and the unforgettable experience of being on the actual sacred grounds ourselves.

At the end of the trip, when the bus was within a few miles from Armada, most of the students were dozing after the hectic travel schedule. Everyone suddenly awoke from the sound of a big bang as we were passing through the small township of Ray Center. One more adventure, though unplanned, was in store for us. A car came through the main intersection with North Avenue without stopping and the bus was broadsided. The last adventure for the Class of '52 had ended with a loud bang. Fortunately, the bus driver had the vehicle under control and nobody on the bus was injured. The woman who had crashed her car into the side of the bus seemed to think that this was an interesting experience for her and asked that her picture be taken next to the bus. She kept laughing and making jokes about having attacked the big yellow bus and conquering it without a scratch on her. Evidently, and tragically for her, she must have suffered an unseen injury to her brain–she died a week later. After this last incident, I was glad to be safely back home and thanked God that all my classmates and I were protected from harm. The accident served as a reminder how unexpectedly plans can change and lives come to an end, but God had spared us and now it was time to get ready for the next new adventure on the next segment on the road to adulthood.

In real life, "adulthood" evidently did not come with graduation from high school. When I interviewed for some temporary secretarial positions in Mt. Clemens, I was told I was highly qualified but, at age seventeen, I was too young to be hired for any position where the minimum age was arbitrarily set at eighteen. Having a caring mother with many friends helped me in finding summer employment. Mother put in a good word with her supervisor Dorothy Hiatt, the Director of the Macomb County Library, and I was hired to work as a Library Page for the summer. The summer job was a crucial factor in the family budget if there were to be sufficient funds to pay for my room and board at the University of Michigan when the fall semester started. Tom Cook, the son of another library employee, was also hired for the summer. Having a young co-worker changed work into fun for me and the days passed quickly. We mended books, did filing, shelved books according to the Dewey Decimal System, and performed various clerical duties together. Only occasionally did we hear the warning "Ssssh" from our mothers to maintain silence in the library when our teen exuberance got too noisy.

Sometime during the summer, I received a letter from the University of Michigan Housing Office, informing me that I had been assigned a room at Prescott House in the East Quad and my roommate would be a Dorothy Davis from Bridgeport, Michigan. An announcement also came inviting me to "Freshmen Rendezvous" a camp that was offered for a minimal fee during the week preceding the start of the fall semester. The orientation camp was set up with the new incoming students assigned to small groups of eight that were housed in cottages on a lake near Ann Arbor. Upperclassmen acted as counselors to acquaint the new students with various aspects of campus life and what to expect once they arrived at the University. There were plenty of opportunities to ask questions about class schedules, what to wear, the weather in Ann Arbor, social and religious organizations, clubs, sororities, and work opportunities. Plenty of time was allowed for get-acquainted activities and recreation while at the camp so that the new students would not feel lost among the thousands of complete strangers once they arrived on campus. During the first few days on campus, these same small orientation groups continued to meet with their counselors for a tour of the campus and its facilities. In addition to the friends I met at Freshmen Rendezvous, I knew that two students from Armada would also be on campus and I could count on them when I needed a friend. Shan Renton had also received a Regents Alumni Scholarship and was enrolled in the Nursing School. Bob Beckett, the brother of my friend Audrey, was already a sophomore at the University and had promised me a ride home to Armada during school breaks.

I was filled with happy anticipation as time was drawing near for Freshmen Rendezvous and the beginning of my new role as a coed at the University of Michigan. I knew I would miss my family, but they would always be there for me when I needed them. When I left Armada for Ann Arbor, unlike in previous moves to unknown places, this time there were no parting tears, no sad farewells, no home lost, or bridges burned. U-M held the promise of membership in "The Victors" circle. My days as a stateless "Displaced Person" were over, but in my heart I would always feel a longing for my homeland and its golden amber shores.

★★★

37
HAIL TO THE VICTORS VALIANT

September 12, 1952 dawned as a sunny day full of promise of new adventures. I stood in line with the other freshmen women waiting for their name to be called out for a group and cabin assignment for "Freshmen Rendezvous", orienting students to the University of Michigan. One by one the girls joined their respective groups until only I remained standing alone waiting for my name to be called. The call never came and the counselors started calling the men for their groups. With the letter confirming my registration, I approached the counselors to inquire about my group assignment.

"No, your name is not on the list", came the answer.

When I showed my acceptance letter, somebody thought of checking the main registration list and found my legal name Skaidrite Gedrovics on the men's list! The counselor explained that they had thought that "Skaidrite" was a man's name and promised to assign me to a women's group immediately. It appeared that my given Latvian name would continue to give me problems at U-M as it had in Mr. Stacey's class in Armada. Perhaps I was no longer homeless and stateless, but in America I would remain nameless and have to use the shortened version of "Rita", a name I did not like, because the beautiful Latvian name my parents had given me was too foreign for people to pronounce. This latest incident with my name was amusing, however. It would have been interesting if I had waited until my name was called for a men's group. It would have been quite amusing to have seven guys for roommates and to see how the counselors handled this unique situation.

Freshmen Rendezvous proved to be a good transition to college life for students coming from smaller high schools, like Armada where I was one of thirty-two graduates in my class. The freshmen class of 1952 was a hundred times larger with over three thousand students entering the University. It was optional for students to participate in the weekend get-acquainted program, but I was glad I took advantage of this opportunity. The three days were spent in a whirlwind of activities including instructional meetings, games and swimming, and evening song and dance sessions. I met several nice young men at the camp and never lacked dates for the evening dances and some of the on-campus "mixer parties" held at various residence quadrangles.

After I arrived on campus on September 14, my roommate Dorothy Davis and I decorated our room 305 at Prescott House in the East Quadrangle. The extent of decorating was limited to getting matching bedspreads and a few personal belongings. In those days bed linens were furnished in the dormitories and most students arrived with only their clothing, books, and perhaps a radio if they were fortunate enough to own one. The rooms were sparse by 21st century standards. The institutional furnishings in each room were identical with each student having a bed, a desk, and a small closet with built-in dresser drawers. Each room had its own washbowl but showers and toilet facilities were in a separate central area. The girls found it amusing to have urinals in the toilet area left over from when Prescott was a men's dormitory. Someone decorated the urinals with artificial flower arrangements. The furniture, appliances and electronic devices that students of later generations brought by the truckload were unheard of in the post-war decades. Personal phones and cell phones were nonexistent. There was a pay phone on each end of every floor and each student had a special buzzer ring-tone similar to a Morse code signal assigned to her for incoming calls received through the operator-assisted switchboard in each quadrangle. Phone calls were limited to five minutes. Though some of the students who came from luxurious homes found the accommodations in the dormitories to be too sparse and confining, I had no problems in adjusting to group living. U-M was certainly an enormous step up from camp life in post-war Europe.

Prescott House was one of four dormitories grouped in the East Quadrangle on the corner of East University and Hill Streets. There was also an all-male West Quad and an all-male South Quad on the central campus. The North Campus did not exist at this time in history. Most of the female dormitories were grouped on what was called "The Hill" near the University Hospital further away from the campus. For the first time in history, the University opened Prescott as an "experimental" residence for freshmen women among the men's dormitories in the East Quad. In prior years there had been a mix of students ranging from freshmen to seniors in all residence halls, thus providing upper-classmen in each house as mentors for the freshmen. Due to the growing influx of female students, Prescott was opened to freshmen women only on the premise that freshmen were old enough to govern themselves. It did not take very long to disprove this experimental theory.

The entire first week of the fall semester was devoted to orientation and registration for classes. Each morning I met with my group from Freshmen Rendezvous at the meeting place we had agreed upon next to the lion statues in front of the Science Museum. By the end of the day my legs were aching from walking all over the big campus and from standing in lines to register for classes, pay for various fees, purchase books, and locating the multiple buildings where classes would be held. There were forms, forms, and more forms to be filled out to register for classes. My hand felt all cramped up by the time I filled out the same information over and over again. In those pre computer days there was a separate registration form to be filled out for each class session. If the student reached the registration window and the class for the desired time slot was already filled, another form had to be filled out for a different class session. The convenience of pre-registering for classes by using a computer was yet to be invented. Acting on the advice of my orientation leader, I requested early morning classes that were less popular with many students. By starting my classroom schedule at 8:00 a.m., I was usually finished with classes by 2:00 p.m. on most days, which left the afternoon open for part-time work I hoped to find on campus.

I did not waste any time in looking for work. Although I was on an academic scholarship, I had to work because our family's budget did not allow for the room and board expenses, which amounted to $335.00 per semester. Enough had been saved from working during the summer to cover the first semester, and my parents sent me five dollars every week for books and miscellaneous expenses. In order to save for the next semester, however, I knew I have to start working immediately. During a break from the orientation sessions on the second day on campus, I filled out an application for work in the U-M General Library. Apparently my experience at the Macomb County Library was a positive factor in getting an interview with the Library Director. After the interview, he explained that I certainly was qualified to work as a Student Library Assistant, but that it was not advisable for freshmen to combine work and study during their first semester.

"You should concentrate on studies this semester to maintain your scholarship. If your grades remain high, you can come back next semester and we can talk about your work schedule."

I did not have to think about my response, it was work now or never!

"If I do not get a job immediately, I will not be back next semester and you will never see me again. I have to earn my room and board if I want to stay at the University. I know I can handle both work and school if you only give me a chance."

The Director must have liked my determination.

"Stop at the Circulation Desk on your way out and talk to Mrs. Connie Dunlap. She will arrange your work hours and tell you when to start."

"Hail to the Victors..." I felt like I was walking on air after receiving the good news. As I left the Director's office, I paused briefly to say a silent prayer of thanksgiving to the Lord for guiding me in a successful job search. Mrs. Dunlap assigned me to working in the stacks shelving and retrieving books and "reading shelves" to make sure all the books were in their proper places. I was scheduled to work fifteen hours per week at eighty cents an hour. With my weekly allowance of five dollars from my parents added to my pay, I could save close to eighty dollars a month and by February my room and board for the next semester would be assured. I would have to budget my money and time wisely in order to get good grades and earn enough to return for the spring semester. I started work on September 17 in the middle of the orientation week, which left me tired but quite determined to take advantage of the opportunities offered by the University.

Depending on the class schedule, my work hours varied between afternoon and evening assignments when I was responsible for closing duties at 10:00 p.m. In 1952, the General Library served all campus students before the Undergraduate Library (UGLI) was built a decade later and the General Library became the Graduate

Library. The book storage stacks consisted of several floors, plus an attic and a basement. Only graduate students and the Library staff were allowed to enter the stacks. If an undergraduate student wanted to borrow a book, it had to be retrieved from the shelves by a Student Library Assistant, who was assigned to work on one or more floors. Orders for the books came to each floor through pneumatic tubes. Working the late evening hours was sometimes a scary experience for me, especially when I was assigned to work on the top floors. Study carrels, where graduate students did their research, surrounded the book stacks on the lower floors, and generally there was enough activity for me not to feel alone and vulnerable. Since access to the book storage stacks was denied to undergraduate students, the top floors and the attic had virtually no activity and the library workers were alone with only creaky floors, long shadows, and their fertile imaginations to keep them company in the oppressive silence. Nobody had ever encountered any problems during the evening shift or any other time in the library. Campus crime was not an issue at universities in the 1950's, but being alone was eerie enough when one was surrounded by seemingly unending walls consisting of row upon row of bookshelves. It seemed strange for me to be afraid within the secure walls of the library when I had never felt afraid when faced with all the existing real dangers that surrounded me during the war. One night, while reading the titles on a shelf filled with fiction books, I came across a book titled "Murder in the Library". This was enough to get my imagination working overtime. I was trembling by the time I went off duty and ran all the way to my dormitory through the shadowy darkness and silence that surrounded the library and classroom buildings.

As the semester progressed, I became more accustomed to working all floors and was familiar with the noises coming from the creaking floors and various pipes and shafts in the ceiling. I made sure I did homework assignments every day so that I would not fall behind and did not have to cram at exam time. When many students asked for time off from work so they could study for exams, I was able to take on even more work hours because I had kept up with my reading assignments all along.

UNIVERSITY LUTHERAN CHAPEL

By Friday, September 19, 1952, the official orientation week and the first two days of working in the Library were finally over and the evening was left open for "church night". The last evening of orientation week was designated for the students to get acquainted with the church of their respective religious affiliation. In the "Age of Nondiscrimination" in the 21st Century, it is deemed discriminatory and illegal to ask anyone about his or her religious preference. Students are left on their own to find a church group that shares their interests or to disregard religious activities altogether. In the 1950's, however, the students could state their preferred religion when registering to make it easier for them to find a church affiliation of their choice. Each campus church or chapel received lists from the University with the names of students who claimed a preference for a certain religion. Thus, the various religious organizations could invite new students who shared their faith to events welcoming them to the campus.

I had received an invitation from the University Lutheran Chapel (ULC) to the Friday night party to welcome new students. It was just a short walk of two blocks up Hill Street to Washtenaw Avenue where the Chapel was located. When I met Pastor Alfred Scheips and his wife Winifred, or "Ma Scheips" as the students affectionately called her, I immediately felt like I was at home. The Scheips had never had children of their own, but they treated each student as if he/she were their own son or daughter. I was met with welcome smiles and hugs and I could feel the warm fellowship surrounding me and filling the air with joyful sounds. God had blessed me again by leading me to the ULC and I could now joyfully *"Sing to the Lord a New Song"* (Psalm 96:1)

University Lutheran Chapel
1511 Washtenaw, Ann Arbor, MI

Besides all the new freshmen, I met many upper classmen who were on hand to welcome and get acquainted with the incoming students. Everyone seemed to be genuinely friendly. The basement of the Chapel was set up for games, fellowship, and refreshments. Though I had never played Ping-Pong before, it looked like fun and I decided to try joining the people playing the game. Though I had no idea of the significance of this decision, it set the course for the remainder of my life. Just as I was picking up my paddle, a senior by the name of Norman Sparks walked through the door. He looked friendly and had a nice smile, which motivated me to ask him if he would like to play a game of Ping-Pong with me, or rather would he teach me how to play? Another couple came up who seemed to know Norman and said,

"Come on, Sparky, let Rita be your partner, and we can play doubles."

The game turned out to be fun, though I could not contribute much during this initial session. I thought if was rather funny how Norm wanted to make sure that I held the paddle correctly and had to hold my hand in his to show the proper moves. I did not mind at all being instructed by this tall senior with the bright smile and clear blue eyes. Time passed quickly as we played another game, which I naturally lost. However, I gained a great deal of information about this charming senior who turned out to be also a saxophone player in the U-M Marching Band. I was pleased to learn that Norman also lived in the East Quad at Strauss House while he was completing his last semester in the College of Engineering. At the end of the evening, Norm and I walked back to East Quad together. When we stopped in the courtyard to say goodnight, Norman invited me to a dance at the Michigan Union the following night. I felt honored to be asked to a big dance by a senior and happily accepted. Later, when I got back to the third floor, all the girls were out in the hall telling each other of their experiences at the get-acquainted parties they had attended. There were happy shrieks when someone told of meeting an interesting fellow. When I told them that a handsome senior had invited me to a dance at the Union on Saturday night, they all congratulated me on the biggest achievement of all in the "Boy Meets Girl" game. Imagine, a freshman bringing back the top prize of a handsome senior on her first weekend on campus.

The Saturday dance at the Union Ballroom turned out to be quite pleasant. I had felt quite insecure while getting ready for my date with the senior I had just met the evening before. How could I a seventeen-year-old, inexperienced former "DP", show enough sophistication to be of further interest to this charming male? Would the stigma of being a refugee follow me at the University and would I stick out like a "spotted dog"? I decided to let my happiness filter through my eyes and do the talking for me. Norman was an excellent dancer and I found it easy to follow his lead when he taught me how to do some fancier moves and the big dip. After the dance, we walked hand in hand over the Diagonal and through the Engineering Arch on the way to the East Quad. When we reached the Engineering Arch, Norman asked me to stop. He explained that, according to engineering tradition, a girl could not become a real coed unless an engineer kissed her under the arch. I decided that perhaps I would check into the validity of this "tradition" when I had a chance, but that night under the stars I was not about to counter U-M tradition, and willingly let myself be initiated by Norman's kiss. It felt good to be kissed by such a nice guy, and what a great story my rite of initiation to the status of a coed would be for the replay and debriefing session with my dorm mates on the third floor.

Engineering Arch, site of coed "initiation"

The Saturday night dance was but a preview of the many formal ballroom dances to which I was invited. Swing dancing to the sounds of Big Bands was a popular form of entertainment on university campuses in the fifties. The very next Saturday after the football game with Michigan State (MSC beat Michigan) Norm took me to the" Golden Rule Ball", jointly sponsored by U-M and its sister college in Lansing, to promote the spirit of sportsmanship among the universities. The venue for this dance again was the Michigan Men's Union where the tradition still held that women were not to enter the sacred enclaves of this men's domain through the front entrance. Women were allowed to enter only through the side door and, though this rule seemed silly, nobody ever questioned it. This rule was not abolished until decades later as a result of the Civil Rights movement.

I felt like my guardian angels had smiled on me and turned me into a princess when I was dancing in Norm's arms again two weeks later at the "Blue Horizons" Ball at the Michigan League Ballroom to the music of the Paul McDonough Orchestra. This time I had invited Norman as the League dance was "girl bid" and the coeds got to ask their favorite fellow to the dance. Though I initially dated other men on campus, Norman soon became my favorite dance partner. It seemed I fit perfectly into his arms and we both enjoyed dancing in synchronization to the Big Band music. During my first year at U-M, Norm and I attended thirteen ballroom dances. Dressing for all the formal dances soon became a problem, since few girls had a formal wardrobe extensive enough to wear something different to every dance. However, living with scores of "sisters" in Prescott, gave me the opportunity to exchange gowns with my friends so that I could wear a different outfit every time as if I were a Hollywood celebrity.

At Frosh Weekend Ball 1953; Rita is wearing the white satin jacket made by Omi in Santiago, Chile

The "Autumn Nocturne " Ball with the Tommy Dorsey Orchestra was my first experience in dancing to the music of a famous Big Band. When Sam Donahue, the tenor saxophonist with the Dorsey orchestra, was featured in a solo, I imagined it was Norman serenading me on his saxophone. The Dorsey Orchestra returned to play at the J-Hop a few months later and once again Norm and I got to enjoy the familiar melodies at this "Grand Baroque" Ball. Whenever a major event was observed on campus, there was a dance to go with it. "The Snowflake Ball" at the East Quad started the Christmas season. Norman looked handsome in a navy blue suit and I wore a light blue strapless formal. At midnight when the music drifted off into the winter night, I felt like Cinderella having to leave her prince. However, I did not have to worry about my chariot turning into a pumpkin as I only had a few steps to walk to my room at Prescott and Norm' s dormitory was next door. There was a blurb in the University Lutheran Chapel "*Courier*" newsletter stating that "*Norm Sparks has the shortest walk after a date*" to the neighboring Strauss House. "Santa's Fantasy" a week later featured a beautiful Christmas tree in the ballroom. During the Christmas break from classes, as if we needed more practice for our dance routines, Norm took me to the "Winter Wonderland" dance at the Bancroft

Hotel in Saginaw where I was a guest at his parents' home for New Year's. At the end of the first semester in January, "The Bluebook Ball" gave everyone an opportunity to have a last merry fling before the start of exams.

In early March, although spring had not yet arrived, the "Emerald Enchantment" ball, decorated in the green finery of St. Patrick's Day, marked the debut of the spring series of formal dances. It seemed that when I arrived in Ann Arbor, I must have worn dancing shoes on my feet. Even my class schedule allowed for dancing as I chose "Ballroom Dancing" for the mandatory Physical Education class. I could not help but be starry eyed and feel like I was floating on a cloud whenever I was dancing with Norm. When Paul McDonough's Band played the popular song, "Don't Let the Stars Get in Your Eyes", I decided to ignore this admonition. Paul, a law student, also lived in the East Quad and I often listened to him play the piano in the Greene House lounge and we frequently chatted. Paul had noticed that I was at all the campus dances, where his band was playing. He enjoyed teasing me about getting Norman to take me dancing just so I could be with Paul.

Another student whose piano music I also enjoyed hearing at Greene House was Jerry Bilik. Jerry, a music virtuoso since his teen years, was a member of the Michigan Marching Band. While at the East Quad, Jerry often entertained his fellow students with his own multiple arrangements of "The Victors" fight song as he played the tune in multiple different styles. Jerry could transform the march beat to sound like a waltz from Vienna, a lively polka, an Oriental melody, or a heated Latin dance. From the humble sessions at East Quad, Jerry went on to be an arranger for the U.S. Military Band at West Point[45] and the Marching Band at the University of Michigan for which he composed the famous "M Fanfare". He has had an illustrious career in music as an arranger, composer, songwriter, conductor, director of stage productions, and music writer for the "Disney on Ice" shows and TV series including "Charlie's Angels". It has been a pleasure for Norman and me to watch Jerry's brilliant successes and to be able to say, "We knew him when..."

Since Norman was an engineer, he invited me to the "Black Magic" slide rule ball sponsored by the Engineering College. The ball took place on Friday, March 13, 1953. My co-workers in the Library had given me the nickname "Bewitching Witch" and they urged me to accept the invitation so I could work more magic on Norman. I was delighted to accept. Paul McDonough's Orchestra was playing again and it was fun to tease Norm and Paul about which of the two was my favorite Michigan music man. This Friday the 13th turned out to be unlucky, however. The slide rule ball became a rather riotous affair when a rowdy group of law students staged an invasion at the dance as part of the friendly rivalry that had traditionally existed between the lawyers and engineers. What had originated as a harmless prank as the lawyers tried to steal the eight-foot slide rule decorations, went awry when students from both sides got overly enthusiastic and an engineering professor broke his ankle in the melee. That incident put an end to further staged invasions at subsequent events. Paul's orchestra continued to play throughout the faux attack by the law students. We danced again to Paul's music at the Frosh Week Ball in April.

On the first Saturday in May, Norm and I boarded the mystical U.S. Terpsichorde docked at East Quad for a "sail" to the Orient though I had vowed I would never take a ship voyage again after the travails on the Marine Flasher. The cost of the passage was $3.60 per couple. Paul McDonough and his band entertained in the fantasy ship's ballroom, decorated with Japanese lanterns. Apparently young people and their imaginations can relocate from one continent to another within the span of a week. On the second Saturday in May Norman decided to take me away from Paul and we used dance programs resembling passports to board the "Cruise Continental" while it was anchored at the Intramural Building where the bandleader was the well-known Ralph Flanagan. My passport dance program from this grand dance cruise was personally autographed by Ralph Flanagan and it remains among my treasured university memorabilia. If I had been floating on air at previous balls, the "Cruise Continental" exceeded all previous encounters and I wrote in my diary that this dance was "marvelous". The venue was grandiose with beautiful decorations and Norman looked so handsome in his white dinner jacket. As the last strains of the music were fading away, I could still hear the tune "Tenderly" drifting through my mind and my heart was filled with tender love. Since that magic night in May, the tune "Tenderly" became my favorite song.

"THE BIG HOUSE"

Michigan Marching Band in formation in the overflowing "Big House"

But college life was not all about dancing. In addition to enjoying dancing with each other, Norman and I also attended every Wolverine home football game together, but separately. I was among the spectators rooting for my favorite player Tony Branoff and the team captain Lowell Perry. Though Norman had told me that the Michigan Stadium was the largest college football stadium in the country, I was totally unprepared the first time I entered it. After all, I did not entirely consider myself to be a small-town girl having crossed the ocean with over 500 people on my ship and mingled with the busy crowds of people in New York City. But when I entered the U-M Stadium, it was like landing on a strange planet with a mass of some 90,000 blue and gold aliens shouting and cheering while standing on rows upon hundreds of rows of bleachers, arranged in a huge bowl-shaped theater without a roof. I could remember only one other occasion when I had been totally overwhelmed by the scene in front of me. That was in my childhood when I first saw the magnificent Baltic seashore from atop the dunes. I was really astounded by the Michigan Stadium. Overhead, small airplanes were in a holding pattern circling around with banners streaming from their tails with strange threatening slogans like "Wolverines Bury Badgers!", "Stomp Out Hoosiers!" or "Gophers are Dead Meat!" The same type of slogans depending on the featured "dead meat" opponent of a particular week, were featured on the imaginative floats and displays in front of all the dormitories, fraternities, and sororities at Homecoming. Some decades later, the Michigan Stadium was enlarged and became known as "The Big House", seating over 109,000 spectators, but with fewer students being able to afford the high-priced tickets. In the fifties, all full-time students received season tickets at no cost, as admission to sports events was included in the tuition of ninety dollars per semester.

Norman was performing with the Michigan Marching Band and when the booming voice of the announcer gave the order " *BAND, TAKE THE FIELD!!*" one hundred and thirty men came high-stepping from the tunnel at 220 steps per minute. The shivers that ran up and down my spine felt as if they were in step with the band and my heart rate seemed to increase to match the rate of the drumbeat. I found the half-time shows even more exciting, especially when I watched my favorite man going through the complex dance routines, like the "*St. Louis Blues*", while playing his saxophone. The Marching Band had to learn new marching formations and dance routines every week under the direction of Dr. William Revelli and George Cavender. Sometimes, Norm practiced some new dance step while walking with me across the campus and it was amusing to watch people's reactions when they noticed Norm doing some high-stepping legwork while walking beside me. After the game I always came down to the field and stood near the saxophone section during the post-game show and then kept in step with the band as they marched through the tunnel and back to Wines Field. It is said that women cannot resist men in uniform. This was certainly true for me.

Norman in U-M Marching Band uniform, Homecoming 1952

As I marched next to the saxophone rank while the Band played "The Victors", I could not keep my eyes off the tall and handsome senior. Entry into the tunnel is now restricted and only athletes and band members are permitted to enter and exit the field through the tunnel. For me it was an exciting part of the Saturday football experience to march beside the band and be enveloped by the thundering echo of the drums reverberating throughout the tunnel.

On October 25, 1952, just a month after meeting Norman, I again went down to the field after the Homecoming game where Michigan defeated Minnesota and won the traditional Little Brown Jug from the Gophers. Norman's parents, Anton "Tony" and Eleanor Sparks, along with his sister Edith, had come from their home in Saginaw to watch the Marching Band perform. When Norman introduced me to his parents, I felt right away that they were a very nice and caring family. The day had turned quite chilly after sundown and I was shivering from the cold. Tony wrapped me in the lap blanket they had brought to the game and I was touched by his kind gesture. When I went back to the dorm in the evening, I announced at the ritual debriefing that I had met my future in-laws and really liked them! Norm, of course, still had no clue about the plans I was weaving for his future.

Music and dancing, of course, were not the primary interests that Norman and I shared. The University Lutheran Chapel (ULC) where we met was the main bond that kept us together. Every Sunday morning we walked hand in hand up Hill Street for services at the Chapel. We returned to the Chapel again every Sunday evening for supper prepared by the Lutheran Gamma Delta (ΓΔ) student organization. No meals were served in the dormitories on Sunday evening and the supper at the Chapel, followed by fellowship, was a popular Sunday activity. On October 5, 1952, I was initiated during a candlelight ceremony into membership in ΓΔ. As I received my pin, I felt like I was a part of a large family of brothers and sisters, all children of God the Father, and I could feel love surrounding me. This feeling of kinship prevailed even after graduation when everyone went on separate ways. The friendships formed among the members of the ULC continued for a lifetime. Many marriages took place between the Chapel students and "Ma" Scheips liked to take credit for being a great matchmaker. It was a joy for her to see her Chapel children fall in love, get married, and establish a family in a house that served the Lord. Even after retirement, the Scheips' shared news about their Chapel children in Christmas newsletters and thus kept the ties of fellowship strong among the alumni. Every time Mrs. Scheips introduced Norman and me to someone, her face lit up in a joyful smile as she remarked, "*I introduced them, you know!*"

The Scheips after retirement at a Chapel reunion

When Norman graduated and went to work for Chrysler Engineering in Highland Park just four months after meeting me, the Chapel still remained a common ground for us. We continued to attend the Sunday worship services and evening suppers. In January, of 1954, we both attended the Gamma Delta (ΓΔ) Winter Camp with the UM Tau Chapter. The camp provided religious, social, and winter sports activities for fostering fellowship among Gamma Delta members from Michigan and neighboring state universities. The 1954 ΓΔ Camp sponsor was the Ohio State Chapter with attendees from U-M, Michigan State, Wayne State, Western Michigan, Central Michigan, Cleveland Area, and Kent State. A never-to-be-forgotten prank played at the ΓΔ Winter Camp was perpetrated by some unnamed U-M students who confiscated a pair of Pastor Scheips' pajamas and hoisted them up the flagpole to flutter in the wind in full view of everyone at the camp. To keep the Chapel gang connected during the summer, picnics at a lake near Ann Arbor were also on the agenda. These picnics turned out to be the first of countless summer beach days throughout the years with good friends from the Chapel, their spouses, and families living in the Detroit area.

All the extra-curricular activities, of course, had to fit in without interfering with the high academic standards of the University. Being a student at the University of Michigan meant setting a high priority on the scholarly portion of college life. I was determined to not let my working hours and fun weekends interfere with the high level of grades required for maintaining my scholarship. Many of the freshmen women in Prescott let themselves be distracted by the social whirl created by the hordes of eligible males surrounding them. When the grade point averages were calculated for all the residence halls at the end of the first semester, Prescott had the lowest average on campus at 1.9 out of a possible 4. The experiment of housing freshmen women in a men's quadrangle proved to be a failure from an academic viewpoint.

Norm and I always gave studies the highest priority and spent many hours studying together in the library, study halls, and even at the Arboretum. Besides being a beautiful nature preserve, the Arboretum was also known as a "Lovers Lane" for couples. My diary bear witness that Norman and I actually took books to the Arboretum and appreciated its beauty while studying. Classes in German Literature and German Conversation courses were a delight for me. I enjoyed the opportunity to sharpen my German language skills and decided to declare German as my minor. Mathematics classes were a different story. Though I had received an A+ in all mathematics courses in High School, College Algebra proved to be difficult for me. With Norman's tutoring, I managed to pass the course with a C+, the lowest grade I ever received for any course anywhere. The grades in the rest of my subjects were high and the Prescott House Director, Mrs. McCoy, suggested that my high scholastic achievement and participation in campus activities qualified me for admission to the elegant honors dormitory, Martha Cook. Only women above the rank of freshman were eligible to apply at the time I was at the University. Now the dormitory is open to incoming freshmen as well as upperclassmen and graduate students.

THE MARTHA COOK BUILDING

Martha Cook Building, 906 South University, Ann Arbor

Portia Over the Doorway

Known to outsiders for its English Gothic Renaissance architecture, beautiful gardens and magnificent blooming magnolia trees, Martha Cook, the first women's residence built on the U-M campus in 1915 is unique among dormitories. The building is considered unusual among dormitories not only due to its grandiose architectural style but also the elegant, genteel style of living of its residents. William W. Cook, noted University of Michigan Law School graduate and philanthropist, donated funds for the Martha Cook Building in honor of his mother, Martha Wolford Cook. Cook's motivation was to provide a safe place where *"women could live while learning social graces and pursuing an education"*.[46] Cook had strong feelings about the concept of "Home" being at the foundation of a strong nation. With this in mind, he had the words *"Home the Nation's Safety"* carved over the main fireplace in Martha Cook.[47]

As the residents and alumnae of Martha Cook look forward to celebrating the one hundred year anniversary of the building, the structure remains as magnificent as ever. Although some interior decorations have been changed over the years, time has enriched the beauty of the brick, stone, marble, and the walls of oak. The brickwork on the outside of the building exemplifies old-world quality, not often equaled. Two different colors of brick were used with a contrasting mortar to shape a diamond pattern within a second larger diamond to create a tapestry effect.[48] Mr. Cook later donated funds to build the Law Quadrangle out of stone according to the same Gothic style.

After the completion of the building, Mr. Cook also donated splendid statues to be placed in the building. Rejecting all proposed statues of saints and angels, Mr.

Cook commissioned the statue of Portia for above the front entrance because she represented the most intellectual of Shakespeare's heroines. Portia, created by the famous Picerilli brothers, was placed "o'er the doorway" in 1918.[49]

A large statue of Venus was donated in 1917 to reign over the main hallway. Another valuable artifact bequeathed by Mr. Cook in his last will was a spectacular Steinway grand piano which has been the centerpiece in the main floor Gold Room, or Blue Room as it was called when my sister and I lived at Martha Cook. It took a year for the custom-made piano to be built, with some four hundred people contributing their artistic skills.[50] The piano consisting of forty-two species of wood from seventeen countries contains twelve thousand moving parts. The cover has inlaid figures of mermaids, flowers, vines, and musical symbols. Inscribed in Latin above the keyboard in gold lettering is the year 1913 and the phrase "*Music is medicine to the troubled soul*".[51] The piano was restored to its original magnificence over two years in 2002-2004 and the spectacular musical instrument still entertains the residents and guests whenever a talented "Cookie" pianist reverently makes the keyboard come to life.

Rita and Mudite visit Venus at Martha Cook Spring Tea 2012

In providing a residential atmosphere of beauty and harmonious living for the development of "*Cultured American womanhood*"[52], Mr. Cook linked the beauty of the house with the beauty of the character of Martha Cook inhabitants. According to Mr. Cook, the residence "*must be a college home, inspiring cultural courtesy, sincere friendship, devoted service, integrity of character, industry, self-reliance, sound scholarship, and an appreciation of the finer things of life*"[53]. Martha Cook residents over the years have embodied a spirit of friendship, devotion to service, high scholastic achievement, participation in campus life, and willingness to contribute to group living. Martha Cook residents as a group also achieve a diverse student body representing the races, religious creeds, nationalities and economic classes comprising the entire campus population and also different States and countries of the world. The approximately 150 residents in the 1950's were expected to take on responsibility for the governance of the building and hosting a number of social events including musicales, formal teas, and dances. Many of these traditions continue to this day as new traditions take root.

With the passing of time, regulations have been modified, but my contemporaries in the 1950's were governed by what we considered to be a strict Constitution and By-Laws which specified the decorum the women had to follow, including quiet hours to be observed, the sanctions imposed by a Judiciary Council when curfews were not observed, responsibilities for guests, regulations for the use of the formal dining room, lounges, and the grand piano. The rules included even details about dress codes, prohibitions of the wearing of hair curlers on the main floor, where outer garments and lounging clothes were not permitted and by what time all beds were to be made. But life in the 50's was simpler and less complicated. Now the *Resident Handbook* includes an "Honor Code"[54] which covers an even broader base of responsibilities. Rules have been added for when male guests can be present in resident rooms, the use of computers and electrical appliances like microwaves, and modern conveniences like meals-to-go. More casual dress codes now allow the wearing of slacks, jeans, shorts, and tank tops except during formal dinners. In my day, slacks were permitted only on Saturdays and during examination times. There was no excuse for being ignorant of any regulation as *"All residents are responsible for a knowledge of the contents of this book and of all actions taken at any House Meeting."*[55] The rules in the 21st Century have added sanctions for more serious infractions should a "Cookie" succumb to emerging social problems such as the use of liquor or drugs, theft, assault and battery, harassment, and possession of weapons.

When I was interviewed by Mrs. Leona Diekema, the House Director, I felt I had entered a new world of gracious living comparable to royal residences with gleaming silver, shiny marble floors, rich oak walls, elegant drapes, and beautifully crafted furniture. I was bold enough to imagine that now I would finally be living under conditions suitable for the granddaughter of the nobleman Fyodor Petrovs. The building had a special aura of graciousness where all residents reflected an attitude of gentility, group cohesiveness and friendship. My high scholastic average, participation in campus life by working at the Library and as a volunteer on the editorial staff of the *Michigan Daily* campus newspaper, being chosen to be on the Freshmen Rendezvous counselor staff, and my status as a political exile from Communism, must have contributed to the diversity sought at Martha Cook.

During the second semester of my freshman year, I received a letter of acceptance from Martha Cook. It was thrilling to be considered qualified for this elite honors residence. Yet, when I read the list of the room and board fees, my heart sank. My work at the Library could not possibly cover the higher cost of the amenities. I made an appointment with Mrs. Diekema to personally thank her for the honor and to tell her the reasons for having to decline it. When I mentioned my financial situation, Mrs. Diekema thoughtfully commented,

"Is that all that is keeping you from being a "Cookie?"

She further wanted to know the amount that I needed to cover the additional fees that were above those I had included in my budget for living in the East Quad. When I told her the approximate amount of my funds shortage, Mrs. Diekema lifted up her telephone receiver and asked to be connected to the Dean of Women, Deborah Bacon. After a brief conversation with Dean Bacon, Mrs. Diekema instructed me to appear at the Dean's office immediately for an interview after which I was assured that the needed sum would be available to me from some special grant funds. Two University administrators were able to meet a student's need through an immediate direct grant based on a simple telephone conversation. Those could really be called "The good old days".

In addition to writing thank-you letters to Mrs. Diekema and Dean Bacon, I also joyfully thanked the Lord for His merciful intervention. I did not learn until over ten years later at the Martha Cook 50th Anniversary that I also owed thanks to Mr. Cook who had set the tone for allowing poor students to live at Martha Cook by providing jobs in the building and also monetary grants. In a letter written in New York on February 10th, 1914 to the Regents of the University of Michigan, Mr. Cook stated the conditions under which the Martha Cook Building is to be governed. He stated that any surplus from income from the room and board fees is to be used by the occupants for furnishings and improvements "*and the remainder, if any, at the end of each year shall be set aside as a fund to be used the following year to give lower or free rates in the building to such undergraduates or post-graduates as the President of the University and the Dean of Women may designate from time to time.*" 56 Mr. Cook's concern to "*let the poor girl have some of the luxuries of life which the daughters of wealthy parents can have in their homes*"57 evidently provided the earliest guidelines for the grant Dean Bacon was able to make available to me. In 1923 Mrs. Frederic Beckwith Stevens (Anne E. Shipman), who served as a governor on the Martha Cook board from 1915 to 1932, gave the first funds for the Scholarship Loan Fund to help Martha Cook women who are working their way through the University.58 In 1933 the fund was renamed the Anne E. Stephens Scholarship Fund. Apparently Mrs. Diekema and Dean Bacon in the spirit of Mr. Cook considered me worthy of receiving a small grant to assist me in my financial situation. This grant, although I do not recall the name of the exact funding source, made all the difference in providing me the special opportunity to become a member of the "Cookie" family.

In the fall of 1953 I moved into room 413 on the fourth floor of the Martha Cook Building. My roommate was Myrna Cohen from New York City. Mrs. Diekema had made a wise choice in pairing us off as roommates as we became close friends and shared many memorable moments together.

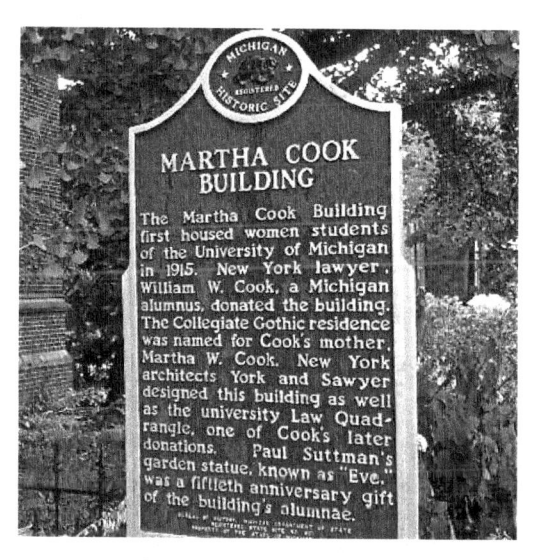

Martha Cook Commemorative Plaque

Not only did I feel honored to be accepted at Martha Cook, I also received an invitation from Mrs. McCoy to the Spring 1953 East Quad Recognition Night for scholastic achievement and the Honors Dinner that followed a few days later. I felt humble to be recognized as a freshman for my high grade point average and for being chosen as a freshmen counselor for next fall's incoming students. I felt insignificant among the upperclassmen from all the other East Quad Houses who had attained excellent standings for several years. It was sad to think that many of my friends at Prescott would not be able to return to the University for the next semester because they were among the students with the lowest scholastic standing and many had lost their scholarships by failing to apply themselves to all the diverse demands and multiple nuances of campus life. In my nightly prayers I always thanked God for guiding me on the paths He chose for me. I was so blessed to be in such favorable circumstances with doors opening to new interesting opportunities.

One extra-curricular opportunity that especially intrigued me was the student-run newspaper, *The Michigan Daily*. The divining rod must have searched out the printer's ink portion in my blood and intuitively led me to apply for a staff position on the *Daily*. Although normally freshmen were not considered for any staff positions, my experience at *The Armada Times* and the Armada High School yearbook, gave me an advantage for being accepted as part of the Night Editor staff. Initially my assignment was to write the headlines for all the articles before they went to press. It seemed to be an easy assignment, but it became apparent on the first night that writing a clever and catchy headline to fit a specified font size and column width required a great deal of imagination and skill with words for everything to fit perfectly. There were no computers in those days to automatically adjust articles and headlines within given margins.

Within a few weeks, having proven my skills in headline composition, I was given a reporting beat of my own. As "Society Reporter", I interviewed sponsors of various social events and then wrote articles promoting the event. With my own name appearing in the by-line, I had become a real reporter. At times some fraternities wanted to remain so exclusive as to not allow reporters to interview them about their events. I was fortunate that I had many friends among the Frosh Rendezvous counselors and usually could find a "contact" wherever I needed information access. During the spring term of my freshman year, I was assigned to the prestigious beat of the International Center. My first assignment was to interview the Ambassador from India, His Highness Ambassador Mehta, who was making an official visit to the campus. The complete interview, with my by-line, was printed in the *Daily* and I received compliments from campus leaders for the extensive coverage of the Ambassador's visit.

The International Center proved to be a very interesting beat for me as my experience of living in multinational displaced persons' camps had prepared me for interacting with people of different languages and cultures. For the most part, the students who participated in the activities of the International Center were quite open to friendship. Perhaps being alone and far away from their native country made them appreciate opportunities to make new friends. On the other hand, students who were not afraid to leave their families to study abroad were generally quite independent and gregarious and possessed the social graces to "mingle with the natives". Thus, the International Center was an ideal venue for meeting new friends at the various social functions, though I could not decide if I wanted to be considered as one of the international students, or a new American reporter.

While covering my beat for the *Daily*, I went to the Spring International Tea and met a charming student named Franco from Italy. He was quite handsome and glamorous and exhibited the charming manners allegedly possessed by Italian men. After the tea Franco invited me for a Coca Cola at the Union and asked for my phone number when he chivalrously escorted me back to the East Quad. True to his word, he called several times inviting me to dates and dancing, but his charm failed to work on someone already bewitched by Norman's magic. I could not get romantically interested in anyone else, though for a few fleeting moments I did fantasize that a man from Italy could one day bring me back across the Atlantic and thus closer to my beloved Latvia.

Yet, while it had not taken long for me to become starry-eyed over Norman, I had to be patient in waiting for him to express his feelings to me. I was doing well academically, had been promoted to be secretary to the Library Director, writing for the *Daily* was interesting, but my relationship with Norman was not progressing as rapidly as I would have liked. It looked like no commitment was coming from Norman in the near future. He considered me to be too young for any serious relationship. Toward the end of May, I began scheming about what magic I could weave to encourage the man "Ma Scheips" and I had chosen as my "Intended" to take our relationship to a higher level of commitment.

★★★

38
IN PURSUIT OF HAPPINESS

"Indefatigable" was the word a colleague once used to describe my character traits. I had to look up the word in the dictionary to understand its meaning. In thinking about my usual mode of operation, I had to admit that I could indeed be described as tireless when pursuing my goals. From early childhood on, I, like my parents, had always relied on God for guidance, but I also firmly believed that I had the responsibility to do my part and always put forth my best effort in carrying out the Lord's will. I could not thank the Lord enough for protecting my life throughout the tumultuous war years, for giving my family freedom and a new home, and guiding me through the first year at the University of Michigan in my quest for higher education. Though I had to work for my room and board and budget my time wisely to keep up with my studies and extra curricular activities, life for me, an eighteen-year-old girl, was nearly perfect. I felt I was at the top of the world, lacking nothing. Unlike some of the coeds in the early nineteen hundred and fifties, I had not come to U-M expecting to meet my future husband and to earn my "MRS" degree. My education came first and finding a suitable husband could wait as there were plenty of "fish in the blue ocean". Then I met Norman Sparks the very first weekend on campus in September of 1952 and my life took a new turn down another new and unfamiliar path.

My intuition, or call it a sixth sense, had always been on target in judging people when meeting them for the first time. When I saw Norman at the University Lutheran Chapel, it was as if some magnet was drawing me toward him and his bright smile that held the promise of a bright future. Though I doubted that what I felt was "love at first sight", there certainly was something about the man that attracted me like a magnet and told me that he was "a keeper". I instinctively felt that if I hoped to find lifelong happiness with Norman, time was of essence and I would have to be as indefatigable in pursuing him as I was with all other important goals in my life. Standing at the fork of this unpredicted road detour, reminded me of my favorite poem by Robert Frost, "The Road Not Taken". I had initially charted my course to follow the path leading to a diploma and a medical career. Unpredictably, my life's journey was again taking me along new twists and turns and I had to decide which fork in the road to follow. Would a detour via the matrimonial route bring me happiness and still allow me to complete my education and career goals? Perhaps it would be *"somewhere ages and ages hence,"* in the twenty-first century, that I would be recalling the words from Robert Frost's poem I learned in high school:

*"Two roads converged in a wood, and I,
I took the one less traveled by.
And that has made all the difference".*

Norman was finishing the last semester as a senior and would graduate in February of 1953. He had been accepted at the Chrysler Engineering Institute in Highland Park, Michigan, to study for his Master in Automotive Engineering degree while simultaneously being offered a position in the Research Division developing the Chrysler gas turbine engine. Norman assured me that he would continue to visit me on campus every weekend, but I knew that it would be difficult to keep our romance blooming while we were apart. I knew when I met his family in October that God meant us to be for each other. Even "Ma" Scheips, the ULC matchmaker, approved of us as a couple and I was so sure of my feelings for Norman that it never occurred to me that he might be more cautious and not fall in love so easily. One month before Norman graduated, I went to a photo studio and had my portrait taken to give to him as a graduation present. I figured that if he had a large picture of me in his apartment, I would be on his mind and he would not be likely to forget me. For the portrait session I wore a delicate silver filigree necklace Norm had given to me for Christmas. I hoped that the necklace would serve as a further symbol of the affection between us.

On February 1st Norman's parents had a party in Saginaw in honor of his graduation. The home was literally filled with Sparks'. I enjoyed meeting so many of his relatives, especially his dear paternal grandmother, Clara. She was beaming with pride over her grandson's achievement. Though Norman got many gifts, my portrait was not among them. Unfortunately, in my haste of getting ready to drive to Saginaw, I forgot to bring along his present. The presentation would have to be delayed for when Norm came to Ann Arbor to take me to my first J-Hop with music by the Tommy Dorsey and Ralph Martiere orchestras. I felt like I was floating on air to the strains of the music while being held in Norm's arms. Many years later, when I first heard the words of the song *'It Only Takes a Moment'* from the musical "Hello Dolly"[59], I realized that the song was

Portrait of Rita in 1953, Norm's graduation gift

exactly describing my feelings for Norman that long ago starry evening at the J-Hop when I was dancing in the arms of the man I loved.

"He held her for an instant
But his arms felt sure and strong.
It only takes a moment
To be loved a whole life long."

When I gave my picture to Norman, he thanked me and remarked that he liked it very much. Afterward we went for a ride and I whispered that I love him very much to which Norm replied that he could not believe that I could learn to love him in such a short period. What is there to learn, especially for a fast learner? Love comes naturally when the right person comes along. That night I wrote in my diary: " *If I keep on waiting patiently, maybe I'll get him in the end. I never give up easily and I'll try my best to get him. Let it never be said women don't make plans to get their men. I'll weave millions of webs around Norman!"*

For the next few months I did wait patiently. If God meant for us to spend our lives with each other, Norm would realize it on his own. My patience came to an end on May 24 when Norm and I attended a banquet at the Chapel. I had taken great care in dressing to look pretty for Norman, but when he saw me, he said that I looked like a cute little girl and too young for him to date. My hopes were dashed and there was nothing I could do to quickly mature to an age more suitable for this twenty-two-year old man. It was not like I wanted to hurry him to the altar. All I wanted was some assurance that he shared my feelings and that our relationship would become exclusive. I was certain that I was in love with Norman, but there was nothing I could do to overcome the four-and-a-half year difference in our ages. Without telling Norman of my plan, I unilaterally set a one-week, perhaps unrealistic, deadline for him to fall in love with me when he asked to take me on a date Memorial Day weekend before the end of the spring semester. If the preparations for my last strategic maneuver did not bring victory by Memorial Day, I would move on with my life and let Norman find someone more mature. The old "Pate" or 'Self' from my childhood was emerging again, but I was totally unaware that I was actually acting like a child to prove I was an adult.

The next few days were filled with activities geared to assist me in giving myself a makeover to a sophisticated, mature lady. Why did there always have to be some reason for discrimination? Apparently at U-M, where students came from all over the world, being a foreigner was not a disadvantage. Being too young was definitely a barrier that would be difficult to overcome. I decided against wearing any of my "juvenile" dresses for the dinner date on Memorial Day weekend. After my classes on Monday of the previous week, I withdrew some money from my savings account and walked over to the fashionable *Mademoiselle* boutique dress shop on State Street. I tried on several dresses to find one that held promise of a simple lady-like, yet romantic look. I opted for a black and white print sleeveless dress with a full skirt and fitted bodice with a low boat neckline. The dress cost twenty dollars, a fortune in those days, but the store manager said that the dress seemed to be made for me and gave me a twenty-five percent discount! In terms of my weekly earnings, the dress cost me twenty hours of work, but I thought it was well worth a lifetime of happiness if my strategy succeeded. The dress came with a wide red leather belt and a romantic stole in matching fabric to keep the chill away on cool spring evenings. The next stop was a shoe store where I found a pair of red high-heeled shoes to match the belt and the outfit for my transformation was complete. I hoped my new look would satisfy the more mature taste of the man I loved when he came to escort me to an upscale dinner at the Michigan Union with Phil Boston, a distant cousin of Norman's. Phil asked that I bring along a friend for a double date. My roommate Dorothy agreed to be Phil's dinner date and the evening promised to be an interesting interlude for us all. Only I knew that according to my war plans to capture my "prisoner of love", this was to be the D-Day in my life.

May 30th dawned bright and sunny and matched my happy mood. I took time in shampooing and styling my hair in a curly fashion favored by the popular movie stars of the day. I carefully applied mascara to my long eyelashes to make them look even more glamorous as they shaded my blue eyes that would sparkle with the look of love in gazing at Norman. It never occurred to me that my whole scheme to bedazzle Norman would seem juvenile as I looked back in amusement years later.

As we walked hand in hand along South University Street from the East Quad to the Michigan Union on State Street, Norman could not take his eyes off me. He seemed to be lost for words, but it did not take words for me to know that my efforts in transforming myself from a teen-age freshman girl to a sophisticated lady had met with success. We had a very nice dinner with Phil and Dorothy and my pleasant mood seemed to envelope us all. At the end of the meal Phil, who was a little older than Norman, complimented Norman on having such a "lovely young lady" for a friend and invited us to his home for the party to continue. On the way to the car, Norm whispered in a voice full of wonder and apparent surprise,

"Honey, I think I sort of love you!"

How does a girl respond to such a qualified declaration of love? I had been waiting for Norm to return my love, but I was not sure if his whispered statement was the effect of the black and white dress with red accessories or the culmination of a long build-up of true feelings. I thought it best to respond with just a tender smile and wait to see if Norm's feelings would last and if a

Rita modeling new black & white dress in Martha Cook garden, June 1, 1953

"sort of" love would turn into something real and permanent. While we were watching television at the Boston's, Norman again leaned over and whispered, "I love you" as he encircled my waist with his arm. Memorial Day, 1953, was truly a day to be remembered. Of course it was the day when people paid tribute to veterans who had shown their valor and love for their country by giving their lives. For me the day had the additional meaning of Norman declaring his love to me for what I hoped would be for our entire lifetime.

Although the events of that far-away Memorial Day remained forever bright in my memory, the glow of that special evening dimmed the next day. When Norman and I arrived at the University Lutheran Chapel for the usual Gamma Delta Sunday supper, Pastor Scheips greeted us at the door. His somber look gave indication that he was about to give bad news. Pastor Scheips informed Norman that his grandmother, Clara Anschutz Schmidt, had died that Sunday morning as a result of a stroke. As regularly as we experience the rising and setting of the sun and the earth revolving around the sun, our journey in life by contrast can seem capricious and change without notice according to God's scheme for us. Without warning, yesterday's joy had changed into tears and both Norm and I were jolted back into reality having to face our real adult responsibilities.

Norman drove to his parents' home in Saginaw for his grandmother's funeral, which was scheduled for Wednesday, June 3. This day again turned what was planned as a joyous high school graduation day for Norman's sister Edith into a day of mourning for the Sparks family. I felt fortunate to have met Norman's grandmother at his graduation party in February and tried comforting him with the knowledge that the grandmother and I had the opportunity to get acquainted and the grandmother had the knowledge that her only grandson had found a mate. Though I would have liked to stay with Norman and his family during their time of sorrow, duties called me home to Armada at the same time. Norman and I had to lay our personal interests aside to help our families when they needed us.

I had to return to Armada for the summer to help with the family household duties while my mother was studying at Western Michigan University in Kalamazoo. Mother was determined not to let her education as a teacher go to waste by being locked in an unskilled clerical position. Long before the slogan was coined as a motto for the United Negro College Fund, Tatiana had followed a similar personal view that "A mind is a terrible thing to waste" and stressed its importance over the years to her daughters and students as well. After presenting her credentials from Latvia and passing rigorous written and oral tests at the University of Michigan to have her undergraduate degree in teaching validated, Tatiana was accepted into the Master's in Library Science Program at WMU.

Being away from her family and having to make up work at the Library took a great deal of effort from Tatiana and support from her employer and her family. She used the two weeks of annual vacation time from the Macomb County Library to cover part of the six-week accelerated summer graduate-level course program. She had to earn the remainder four weeks of time away from work by working additional hours throughout the year. This meant not taking any vacations at all and working an extra 160 hours in the fall to make up for the time owed to the Library.

While mother was away from the Macomb County Library, I filled in doing her clerical work at the library for one summer. Father, Mudite and I made sure the household ran efficiently in mother's absence. Even Norman extended his helping hand and drove the family to Kalamazoo on some weekends to have a picnic with mother so that she could be with her beloved family and have a break from studies. Mudite was only fourteen years old when she took over the cooking duties during mother's absence. Mudite was determined to continue cooking our father's favorite recipes although she had never attempted cooking the meals all by herself. Her biggest challenge turned out to be a type of a meat-filled crepe called by the German name of "Komm-Morgen-Wieder", or "Come-Again-Tomorrow" referring to the leftover ground beef roast used to fill the square crepes. Mudite was so frustrated, tears flowed in perfusion as she struggled, but her self-taught cooking skills were the *sine qua non* in transforming Mudite into an excellent gourmet cook and baker.

Working full time, taking care of household duties, and spending free weekends with Norman should have made time fly quickly, but I always needed to work on a new challenge when things were running smoothly. Knowing that Norman loved me, made me wish even more that we could get married and live together as soon as possible. The summer of 1953 happened to be a popular venue for weddings in the circle of our friends. Every month there was another gala wedding celebration, which left me wishing I were the bride. I started dreaming of the next step in the relationship and hoping that Norman would present me with an engagement ring before the year ended, perhaps as a Christmas present.

Agreeing that a wedding was definitely in our future, we accelerated our efforts in getting acquainted with each other's families. Norman's parents had access to a friend's cottage in the Huron National Forest near Tawas City. I was invited to come along several times during the summer. Walking through the forest was like being transported back to the forests surrounding Livberze in Latvia. Unhindered by city lights, the skies at night displayed millions of glistening stars and the night air was filled with the fragrance of pines. The ground in the forest was covered with huckleberry bushes and it did not take long to pick kettles full of the ripe berries. The Sparks family had a favorite site for a picnic next to a cool stream at the nearby Silver Valley. For me picnics were a somewhat new experience as our family barely had enough food to survive the war years and their aftermath and my parents could not afford to take time off from work. The chicken, potato salad, lemonade from real lemons, corn on the cob, and homemade cookies prepared by Norman's mother were a real feast for me.

Sand Lake, summer 1953

The cottage was just a short ride away from Sand Lake, a small inland lake where the warm water allowed everyone to swim without getting goose bumps. Just a few miles further was Tawas Point, a peninsula jutting out into Lake Huron. This became a favorite swimming spot for Norm and me. The shoreline was undeveloped and relatively undiscovered by crowds of tourists. There were miles of dunes just waiting to be climbed and countless sheltered coves in the dunes where one could lie down in the sea grass and just watch billowing white puffs of clouds gently floating in the azure sky above. The shores of the Great Lakes in Michigan always made me feel as if I had come home to the Baltic Sea. I walked barefoot with the white sand squeaking beneath my feet and the tall pines in the sand dunes stretched out their sheltering branches to welcome me. At the lakeshore I could feel the wind blowing through my hair and caressing my skin. If I closed my eyes, the rhythmic sound of the waves breaking on the shore could lull me into such a peaceful trance that that I felt myself transform into the little seagull Kaija frolicking on the shore. But big girls who want to get married cannot stay entranced in memories. Norman had other activities planned for the weekend and I reluctantly had to leave the beautiful shoreline reminding me so much of my beloved homeland.

However walking along the lakeshore and feeling the gentle breeze gently swaying in the pine trees apparently also inspired Norman to feel connected with me in this peaceful setting. On the way back to the cottage the song "Tenderly"[60] came floating over the radio airwaves. This song had been my favorite since I first heard it at the various balls we had attended in Ann Arbor. After immersing in the lyrics, Norman asked if my favorite song could become our private theme song. From that moment on, whenever the tune is heard over the airwaves or played by a band, Norman comes to my side to hold my hand to connect with our beautiful memories...

"The evening breeze caressed the trees tenderly,
The trembling trees embraced the breeze tenderly.
Then you and I came wandering by
And lost in a sigh were we.

The shore was kissed by sea and mist tenderly.
I can't forget how two hearts met breathlessly.
Your arms opened wide and closed me inside.
You took my lips, you took my love, so tenderly..."

That magic summer of 1953 wove many bright patterns into the quilt of memories for Norman and me. Fishing, swimming, berry picking, hiking, and picnics near a brook were all activities that I enjoyed immensely. I felt that I really fit in with the lifestyle of Norman's family, and felt comfortable participating in all their fun activities, particularly the water sports available in the Tawas area.

The Au Sable River was a popular place for canoeing. Norman introduced me to this pleasant activity also and we spent many hours floating down the river and enjoying the beauty of the surrounding forest. Occasionally we would see a deer peeking through the trees and observing us with its gentle and soulful brown eyes. Not feeling threatened, the deer continued to graze as we continued our peaceful journey on the Au Sable River.

Au Sable River, 1953

Another vacation that would stay in my memories of the summer of 1953 was the one I was invited to take with the Sparks family to the Smoky Mountains and other points of interest out East. It seemed like I had become one of the family and my imagination was full of scenes I had woven in anticipation of the happy moment when Norman would ask me to be his wife and would present me with an engagement ring, but the scenes remained shrouded in fog in some yet too distant future. Throughout the trip, I had been assigned the role of the navigator who had to map the route that Norman drove to the next chosen destination. When we returned home, there was no doubt in my mind that it was time to start charting and navigating our route to matrimony.

Norman's thoughts must have run along parallel lines. One week after we returned home, he mentioned that perhaps we should plan on getting married the following summer. He hinted that he would like to give me a special gift for Christmas. Could this be the ring I was so eagerly awaiting? This would mean I had to start planning transferring to Wayne State University (WSU) if I wanted to live as Norman's wife in Detroit. Commuting daily to Ann Arbor would not be possible. The plan was to attend Wayne State as a guest rather than a matriculating student and to take only courses that would be acceptable for transfer back to U-M. After one year Norman would have his Master's Degree in Engineering from the Chrysler

Institute. He was then planning to enlist in the U.S. Navy for two years to fulfill his military obligation, since the draft still was in existence at that time. Under the military draft rules, if a man voluntarily enlisted, he could serve in the branch of his choice. Men who waited to be called by the draft had to serve in the military branch chosen for them, which usually meant the Infantry. It was my plan to then return to the University of Michigan to complete my studies while Norman was serving in the Navy.

With less than a week left before the start of the fall semester of my sophomore year, I consulted with academic advisors at WSU and at U-M to make certain that all my WSU course credits would fully transfer when I returned to U-M. I was told that if I did not actually enroll at another University but only attended WSU as a guest for a year, I would still be eligible to keep my U-M academic scholarship by taking a leave for a year. Even though I would have to pay tuition at WSU, it was important for me to maintain my U-M scholarship eligibility. Having made the arrangements for attending WSU as a guest student following our marriage, it seemed nothing stood in the way for us to be married and to still graduate from the University of Michigan while Norman completed his military duty.

Though I had looked forward to living at the Martha Cook Residence as a privilege, having Norman for a future roommate possibly might outweigh the amenities at the honors dormitory. Mrs. Diekema, the Director at Martha Cook, was most kind in helping me sort out my future plans before I had even moved into Martha Cook. She assured me that I would be eligible to return to the dormitory for my senior year while Norman was away in the Navy. In assigning Myrna Cohen to be my roommate during my first year at Martha Cook, she saw to it that I had a wise young woman for my mentor. Myrna was a senior in the College of Education and was studying to be an elementary teacher. Everything seemed to be working in my favor. At this particular time in my life I was looking at the world with stars in my eyes.

Phyllis, Myrna, Marcia, unnamed Cookie, and Rita in Martha Cook garden 1954

As expected, life at Martha Cook was truly an enlightening experience for me. I had never had the privilege of living in such elegant surroundings. After years of deprivation during the war and as a DP, I felt like Cinderella living in an atmosphere of beauty and harmony with so many exceptional women. From high teas with elaborate silver services to formal sit-down dinners served at tables covered with white tablecloths, it seemed like a dream to be in the midst of this gracious and talented group of "Cookies". The myriad cultural, educational, governing, social, and entertainment activities taking place at Martha Cook fostered the growth of its residents into accomplished, responsible, and well-versed citizens of the world. Over the years and with changing times, some of the traditions, songs, and events have changed with new generations of women passing through the famous portal with Portia in the doorway, but one tradition that has remained steadfast is the singing of grace. The *"Martha Cook Grace"* composed[61] nearly a century ago continues to echo through the formal dining room and at Alumnae events even today. At all sit-down dinners when I was at Martha Cook, the residents rose to their feet as the House Director, Mrs. Diekema, entered the room and on cue from the Chorister raised their voices in unison singing,

"Oh Power of Love, all-knowing, tender, ever near
Our thanks for bounty now we render, gathered here.
Oh guard our friendship's circle ever,
See that naught its firm bonds sever,
From year to year."

The Christmas, or Holiday Breakfast is another tradition that has continued to be enjoyed by Martha Cook residents throughout the years. When I was at the University, the Christmas Breakfast was celebrated on the morning after the last day of classes before the holiday break. The Breakfast was a very festive affair with carols, candlelight, and good fellowship, but, as I remember, it was unfortunately held very early in the morning, which seriously infringed on our sleeping time. All the girls had been warned not to be late and to be sure to set their alarms for 6:00 a.m. According to rules in effect at the time, unexcused latecomers were barred from events. To be sure, Martha Cook women are known for their charm and gracious behavior. At the ungodly hour of 6:00 a.m. on a cold morning in December 1953, charm took a brief flight from room 413 and was replaced by very unladylike protest. As the two roommates were still snug in their warm beds, a loud knock on their door disrupted their last precious winks.

"*Shut Up!*" exclaimed one of the sleepy girls.

"*Go away and leave us alone,*" shouted the other atypically inhospitable resident.

"*Sorry, girls,*" responded the polite and cultured voice of Leona B. Diekema, the very gracious Director of Martha Cook. *"I was just making sure all my girls were awake for our most festive event. See you downstairs"*.

If there ever was a time when one wishes to be able to crawl under a rug and hide, this was it. Of all the people to offend with our early-morning grouchiness we had to pick our respected and loved Director who cared for us like her own daughters. Myrna and I would have rather pulled the covers over our heads and stayed hidden in bed, but sleep had also flown from our room along with our temporary loss of manners. We quickly joined the others to enjoy the beautiful traditional holiday breakfast. We need not have worried about our rude outburst. When we apologized to Mrs. Diekema, she very tactfully wished us a Happy Holiday and remarked that she does not judge a person by what they say in their sleep. Myrna said she agreed with that. Evidently Myrna had often heard me screaming in the night when I had a flashback to some wartime nightmare, but she did not take such outbursts of terror as indicators of my character.

Living in the midst of friendship and security, I could not anticipate the alternate plans life held in store for me. I was not familiar with the truth that lay behind the popular saying of the poet Robert Burns, *"The best laid schemes o' mice an' men gang aft aglay (often go awry)"*[62]. When the 1953 fall semester began, I felt I was ready to change from the lifestyle of a coed to that of a mature woman about to assume the responsibilities that came with marriage the following summer. Myrna had become like a big sister to me and we shared many common interests. Myrna also had met the love of her life and was planning to marry Navy Lt. Hyman Levinson after her graduation. We shared many significant discussions about our men, plans for our marriages, and our expectations for the future.

During the coming months, however, thinking about all the changes that would happen in my life in the year ahead did not always come easy for me. Though I did not realize it at the time, perhaps Norman had been right when we first met and he considered me to be too young for a serious relationship. Just like I had skipped many grades in school, I also was forced to skip a large part of my childhood during the turmoil of the war years and the years in refugee camps when time seemed to stand still and everyone lived in a state of oblivion. During the times of unavoidable crises, like most refugees everywhere, I could meet adversity head on and be flexible in adapting to new situations. However, when faced with having to skip many of the college experiences of my coed years, I had many moments of doubt and regret. Although I was the instigator of the accelerated march into matrimony, I found it difficult to relinquish all the freedom, experiences, fellowship, and privileges I enjoyed as a coed living on the multicultural U-M campus. Riding the bus to the urban campus of WSU would never equal the fun of walking across the Ann Arbor Campus. Living in a small, furnished apartment in an industrial city would never replicate the grandeur and gracious living at Martha Cook. A small voice within me kept whispering, "Will love conquer all? Am I ready for marriage? Why must I give up my college life and freedom again?"

The academic part of transferring credits from one University to another in my junior year had presented no barriers to future plans, but re-arranging my social life did not come as easily. I was excited to come back to the campus in September of 1953 as a sophomore to be a counselor at the Fresh Air Camp for incoming freshmen. Returning to the camp as a counselor, I felt more self-assured. I welcomed the additional responsibility of mentoring the younger students and the extra privileges and activities available to the camp counselors. While at the camp, I met several interesting male counselors with whom I enjoyed the evening activities like dances and campfire sings. I did not have qualms about having fun with my new friends though I loved Norman exclusively. After all, he had not proposed to me nor given me a ring to signify an engagement. It did occur to me that in choosing to walk a shorter route to matrimony, I was skipping the socializing and dating years on my road to adulthood just like I had previously skipped grades in primary school. I came to the conclusion that perhaps dating was not a vital period in the stages of a lifetime.

Despite the fact that I had enjoyed all the fun and attention heaped upon me by various male students, I knew in my heart that Norman was the man God had chosen for me and that no other man I had met could measure up to him in my eyes. I had started and even accelerated the campaign to win Norman for my husband and I fully intended to honor my commitment to this man. Cutting short my dating years by getting married in my junior year did not seem like it would be a huge sacrifice. I had learned during the turmoil of war that a loving family relationship had prime importance in life and I was ready to share my life with Norman.

By contrast, giving up my position at the *Michigan Daily* newspaper upon transferring to WSU created an emotional turmoil of major proportions. Working as a reporter on the *Michigan Daily* staff was one of my favorite campus activities. Perhaps some printers' ink or journalism bug had entered my bloodstream when I worked at the *Armada Times*. I not only enjoyed writing, but it was also satisfying to see my name in print as a byline on the many articles I eventually saved in a scrapbook. I was proud of my achievement. But most of all, I enjoyed meeting and interviewing people and being able to share interesting stories and events with the readers. My writing ability and style was recognized and praised by the chief editors. I was to be promoted to the position of a night editor in the spring term in training for an even more responsible position of a feature editor the following fall. I did not think it was fair for me to take the position as an assistant to an editor when I knew I would not be at the U-M the following year. I also needed to add more hours at my work in the U-M Library to save for the upcoming wedding expenses.

This time I could not invent an alternate solution and made the painful decision to resign from the *Daily*. After I submitted my resignation, I returned to my room at Martha Cook and had such a long sobbing spell that my roommate Myrna was concerned that something serious had happened to my family or me. I explained that I was crying over the lost opportunity to be part of the publishing world. Myrna had become like an older sister to me and we often shared discussions about the men we loved and Myrna's wedding after her graduation in 1954. This time she wisely commented that if it hurt that much to give up the activity that had been so very important to me, then perhaps I was not ready to be married. According to Myrna, marriages should be based on love, not sacrifices. Of course, I knew that, but Myrna's comment helped me clarify my thinking. There was no question about sacrifice. I loved Norman and he came first over any editorship or any other activity.

Toward the end of October, Norman and I went home to Armada so that he could have that all-important talk with my father to ask him for his daughter's hand in marriage. The whole family was happy to hear the good news that Kārlis had agreed to his daughter's marriage. I kept teasing Norman that my father had probably not understood correctly what Norman was saying in English, but had nodded his head in agreement only to be polite.

Yet, it never seemed to fail that with every good event, something happened to cast a shadow on the rejoicing. My mom drew me aside later and told me that she was glad that the wedding would take place earlier than anticipated. The family doctor had informed Tatiana that Kārlis' heart was failing and that the prognosis was not good. The doctor's opinion was that my dear father's life could not last longer than five years even if he led a very careful lifestyle and did not exert himself. All the years of fear, tension, worry, hard labor, and lack of proper nutrition had taken a toll on the man's loving heart. This time there was no solution that anyone could offer to alter the dark prognosis. Big concerns needed to be taken to the Almighty God himself in prayer. That night I prayed for a long time asking God to be merciful to my father. The Lord had protected Kārlis from danger previously when his life was in jeopardy, as when Jelgava was burning. Kārlis had just celebrated his 50th birthday two weeks previously. If it was the Lord's will, I prayed that my father be granted many more years to enjoy his family and that the family be blessed with the father's love for more generations to come. With rivulets of tears cascading down my cheeks, I fell asleep while softly humming the familiar age-old hymn that had brought comfort to the family at so many times of danger or distress: *"Lord, take my hand and lead me…For when your hand is guiding, in peace I go… "*. This time everything was in God's hands, all I, "Pate", could do was pray.

Before I went back to the University after this eventful weekend in Armada, I considered every aspect of how my future plans fit in with the family situation and my future marriage plans. On the way to the bus station to return to Ann Arbor, I told my mother I had made another decision regarding my future and asked for her opinion. It was clear to me that my father could not continue doing the strenuous manual labor at the Armada Products factory. It was just a question of time before his heart would give out and he no longer could work to support his family. I decided that I needed to complete my studies quickly and enter the work force so that I could help the family if needed instead of expecting them to cover the cost of my education. I had come to the conclusion that by changing my major from Medicine to Business Administration I could graduate in a shorter time and at a considerable savings in tuition costs. Staying with the pre-med curriculum would require additional years of study upon being admitted to a medical school and more years of internship and residency before I could become productive. Whatever the future had in store for me, I was convinced that a Business Administration degree could be used in just about any field of endeavor. Perhaps if I could not work as a doctor, I could administer a medical office or hospital. I recalled how my high school principal, in advising me on career choice, had indicated that my interests were so widespread, that I could be a success in any career I chose. I was counting on Mr. Stanley's advice to be right. Mother said she agreed with my logic, but did not want me to think that I had to sacrifice my plans for the good of the family. I explained that, as always, I made this choice on my own, "Pate", out of love for my family and Norman, not as a sacrifice.

Changing majors was easy. When I was back on campus I made and appointment with an advisor at the School of Business Administration to discuss the possibility of applying the credits I had already earned to the basic requirements of the School of Business Administration. There was no conflict in my credits satisfying the Bus. Ad. Pre-requisites. It did not take me long to get my course schedule all outlined for the next semester and the next year at Wayne State University, but the wedding plans remained in limbo.

After my father gave his approval for Norman to take his daughter as a bride, it was taken for granted that the two of us would marry. Yet it was impossible for me to anticipate when the actual proposal would be forthcoming. Norman was very secretive and would not be pinned down as to when he would actually put the ring on my finger and the engagement remained elusive. Norman came to Ann Arbor every weekend to be with me and every time my heart beat faster from eagerness as my mind expectantly wondered, "Will this be the day?" Although a marriage proposal is usually planned as a surprise for the girl, I wanted to be ready for when the magic moment happened to me. Every weekend I took off my Armada class ring from my left hand to make sure that my hand was ready for the once-in-a-lifetime moment when a girl receives the ring signifying the eternal circle of love. On weekends when Norman came to see me, I was floating on a cloud. It was so wonderful just to be together, that we did not particularly seek out entertainment. We went to occasional dances, studied together, took long walks in the arboretum and attended the Sunday church service and Gamma Delta supper at the Chapel. The residents at Martha Cook got to know Norman quite well as he was always my dinner guest on Sundays. Before taking me back to Martha Cook on Saturday nights, we often enjoyed driving up a hill overlooking the Huron River. The hill, just off West Huron River Drive, where the Bird Hills Nature Area now stands was undeveloped at the time and the view of the city, the ravine and the river from the higher elevation was most beautiful at night.

One Saturday night after a movie, Norman and I went for a ride to enjoy the crisp autumn weather and we stopped once again at our favorite spot atop the hill. That particular night we had extra time to be enthralled by the beauty and the peace encircling us because, due to some major campus function, the curfew time at the women's residences had been extended to 1:30 a.m. With no city streetlights obscuring the beauty of the night skies, we could see millions of stars twinkling in the clear dark firmament. The distant buildings in the valley below us resembled a Christmas Village with lights reflecting from the windows. The Huron River was shimmering by the light of a full moon and tiny white clouds floated below the stars. The picture painted by nature was too magnificent for words.

Norman and I sat in silence because we did not want to break the evening magic with words. After letting the quiet magic work for several minutes, Norman took my hand in his and brushed my lips with a gentle kiss. That is when it happened as if by magic—it was just after midnight on November 22, 1953. I thought I saw a shooting star, but it was the diamond in a beautiful sparkling ring reflecting all the colors of a rainbow in the moonlight. Norman's voice shook with emotion as he asked me to be his wife. The girl who had been preparing for this moment and waiting for this moment was caught by surprise nevertheless. I was so overcome by love, sentiment and wonder of the beauty around me that I could only nod and whisper my joyful acceptance as Norm placed the ring on my waiting ring finger. No words were needed to express the happiness that both Norm and I felt that night. I spent the rest of the time on the hill admiring the rays from my diamond dancing in the moonlight. I never stopped smiling that night and Norman said it was more fun to watch the beauty of my face beaming than seeing the stars twinkling above.

My face was still beaming when Norm took me back to Martha Cook. Even if the girls at Martha Cook did not immediately guess why I was so radiant, the multi-faceted reflections from my ring sent out an unmistakable signal as I kept waving my left hand in the air while I was signing in at the front desk and walking down the hall to the elevator. The news of my happy event reverberated throughout the entire residence within minutes and soon nearly every girl on the fourth floor heard the happy shrieks and came out of their rooms to hug and congratulate me. My roommate Myrna helped to spread the news on our end of the fourth floor by knocking on doors to wake those friends who had not yet heard the news.

It was a tradition that when a "Cookie" got engaged, that all the girls serenade her when they are all gathered at some subsequent dinner. However it was also in the rules not to serenade anyone at the formal Sunday dinners. Since most of the girls were acquainted with Norm, they wanted him to be present when I was serenaded. This presented a problem because Norm lived out of town and he was only a guest at Martha Cook dinners on Sundays. Evidently someone got special permission from Mrs. Diekema, the House Director, to sing the traditional engagement song when my fiancé and I were seated for dinner. How wonderful it was to be able to call Norm my fiancé at last! It was a beautiful and touching surprise for both of us to have over one hundred women join voices to congratulate us with the traditional engagement song. It was difficult to say which sparkled brighter, the diamond on my ring or the tears of joy glistening on my eyelashes as the strains of the traditional Martha Cook Engagement Song[63] filled the air.

" Someone says 'I love you',
Someone says 'I do'—
That's the happy moment
Every girl looks forward to
We all love our Rita,
Someone stole her heart.
Now we know that happiness
And Rita will never part!"

★★★

Rita and Norman at Martha Cook Christmas dance, 1953

39
EPILOGUE

*T*he love that Kārlis and Tatiana gave their daughters was a gift that grew and multiplied from generation to generation. Family ties remained strong between Mudite and me and our parents until their golden old age and beyond because true love never ends. Mudite and I both entered marriages that have lasted a lifetime.

In 1956 our family had a joyful reunion with Omi and Mr. Berzins who came to live with my parents in Armada. The reunion was bittersweet, however. Doctors in Santiago had diagnosed that Omi had terminal cancer. She wanted to spend her remaining days with her beloved daughter whom she had not seen in eight years. Mother prayed that with excellent medical care available in America, doctors would find a way to at least prolong Omi's life. Doctors at the University of Michigan Hospital confirmed the diagnosis and gave us the sad prognosis that there was nothing else that could be done to arrest the deadly disease. Dr. Bower, our wonderful neighbor, agreed to provide terminal care to keep Omi comfortable in her last days.

Omi and Mr. Berzins settled in the upstairs apartment in my parents' home and we spent as much time with her as we could so that she could experience the love of her daughter and granddaughters and the joy of meeting her two precious great-grandsons, Steven and David. We had the traditional four-generation

Rita and Norman's wedding 1954

Mudite's and Ivars Sipols engagement 1960

photo taken with her first great-grandson. The second great-grandson was born a month later when Omi was too weak to sit up for a photo, but she did get to cuddle David in her arms and felt his little hand twine around her finger. She died on February 26, 1957 at age sixty-seven, exactly one year before the birth of her third great-grandson, Andrew.

Four generations: Omi, Tatiana, Stevie, and Rita on Thanksgiving 1956

We never did get accustomed to calling Mr. Berzins "grandfather", as this term seemed to belong to our two real grandfathers with whom we never had the privilege of sharing childhood memories, but who always lived in our hearts. We called Mr. Berzins "Onkulis Žancis " though he lovingly filled the role of our only grandfather and Mudite's godfather. He left me his legacy of a song he composed especially for me with music and words that came from his heart when I reminded him of dear Omi.

"How strange that you should be
Some deep and haunting part of me.
That in your clear blue eyes I see,
The one that is most dear to me."

He also wrote a beautiful touching tribute to Omi in her funeral memorial album and his words aptly describe our Omi as she was in life.

"Asja Berzins was a rather pretty, charming and intelligent woman, spiritually and physically well endowed, with a sharp mind and a thankful outlook on life. Admirable is her great faith and reliance on the Almighty God and the great patience and peace with which she endured her pain and suffering.

On February 24, two days before her death, the Pastor was preparing her for the imminent parting from this world. He asked her if she felt secure in her faith. Her answer was filled with such great strength that lived in her heart and soul that the minister was astounded. Smiling joyfully she said that she is not sad about leaving her earthly bonds because she is approaching something clear and bright. She asked the minister to comfort her husband and daughter who were sorrowfully weeping beside her deathbed."

Omi asked my mother to promise that she would look after Mr. Berzins as if he were her own father if the need arose. After Omi's death he decided to go back to Chile to live with his son. Very soon upon my uncle Janka's untimely death, Mr. Berzins wrote to mother asking her if he would be welcome if he moved back to live with our family. Without hesitation, mother and dad invited him to come back and Mr. Berzins lived with my parents until the end of his life in 1969. Not willing to retire, he spent a few interim years living at the University of Michigan Law Quadrangle where he was invited to work as a "House Father" and custodian for the young lawyers. He joked that since I had been so happy living in the luxury of the Martha Cook Building, he wanted to live in equally high style in the other magnificent Cook edifice across the street.

The young men enjoyed his wit and his musical ability and nearly every evening he was asked to join the law students in playing the piano and group singing. Upon his death the young lawyers insisted on honoring him with the music they had shared together. Hour by hour during the visitation at the funeral home, the men took turns playing the piano tunes they had shared with their old friend so that music would follow him into eternity. Mr. Berzins was also honored as "Senior Citizen of the Year" in Ann Arbor for volunteer work with senior citizens. He was laid to rest next to Omi in the Armada Cemetery while great-grandsons David and Andrew played taps on their trumpets in a musical tribute.

With her unrelenting diligence and cooperation from the family, Tatiana earned her MSLS degree in five hot summer sessions and, at age forty-five, proudly received her Master's diploma from Western Michigan University in August of 1957. It took Tatiana eight years since immigrating to Michigan to climb the long road back from working as a waitress to being a professional educator again. In addition to the Library Science degree, Tatiana's teaching certificate also qualified her to teach languages and mathematics to students from the elementary through the high school levels. She restarted her professional career at Fraser Public Schools as the Head Librarian and teacher of remedial reading and mathematics. At the request of the Ann Arbor Public Schools, our very gifted mother assumed the position of Head of the Media Center at Pioneer High School. Later she was asked to plan and establish the Media Center at the Huron High School as it was being built and to organize the collection of audiovisual resources and library materials to meet the requirements for high school's accreditation. She also supervised student teachers from the University of Michigan. Mother took an early retirement to care for our father when his heart began to fail in his last year of life.

Tatiana celebrating her MSLS degree from WMU, August 1957

Tatiana & Kārlis 50th Anniversary 1981

Tatiana with Pastor Saveljevs and great-grandchildren Jessica, Adam, Andy, and Stephanie (in front) at her second marriage 1991

The doctors' prognosis in 1953 that my father's heart would beat for only a few more years proved to be wrong. God's plan for him on earth was not yet finished. Our father Kārlis and Tatiana celebrated their golden wedding anniversary in the midst of their growing family circle in 1981. They continued to live together in the new house they built with love in Ann Arbor until our beloved Papuks went home to be with God on November 30, 1989. After the death of our father, Tatiana continued to exhibit her compassion and caring for people by volunteering as a nurse's aide at St. Joseph's Hospital.

In 1991 mother married a longtime family friend, John Eglis, who was a widower. It was significant to us that God's hand was instrumental in sanctioning this marriage. When mother visited Pastor Uldis Saveljevs at New Gertrude's Church in Riga in 1989, she could not imagine in the wildest of dreams that he would become a visiting minister at the Latvian church in Detroit and would officiate at her marriage ceremony with John Eglis. It was even more astounding to have her grandchildren participate in the wedding ceremony. Four of her great-grandchildren sang "Love is a Very Special Thing", accompanied by grandson Andrew on the guitar, as a surprise to her during the wedding rituals. Grandson David, accompanied by his wife Laura, played the "Trumpet Voluntary" for the wedding march, granddaughter Lara honored Tatiana and John with a violin solo, and grandson Steven was the wedding photographer.

As her Confirmation verse had promised, God blessed Tatiana with a long life. It enabled her to set the precedent for experiencing the span of five generations in her family. Before Tatiana went to be with God, she was able to add to her treasury of love the great-great-granddaughter Claire and was able to pose for a historic five-generation photo. As mother had raised Mudite and me with love, she continued to bestow her love on her five grandchildren and their spouses, ten great-grandchildren, and one great-great-granddaughter throughout her lifetime, remembering everyone in her prayers and always making the sign of the cross as her symbol of protection when she parted from loved ones. The loving matriarch of our family was blessed to meet all her great-grandchildren in her lifetime. She followed the lives of Andy II, Adam, Jessica, Stephanie, and Shawn Sparks, as well as Grace and Ransom Sipols with great interest. She was thrilled to cuddle her grandson Tim & Jessica's youngest son Theo Sipols shortly after his birth and met granddaughter Lara's twin adopted daughters Arianna and Katja. Our dear devoted mother left the bounds of earth at age ninety-six on May 21, 2008 following a complex hip fracture, but her love will reign in our hearts forever.

Five Generations: Grandson Andrew, daughter Skaidrite, Tatiana, great-grandson Andy, and great-great-granddaughter Claire, April 20, 2008

Tatiana sitting in the middle surrounded by grandchildren and great-grandchildren 2002; Granddaughters Jessica & Stephanie on top, Grace Sipols with teddy bear; Grandsons Andrew, Steven, David standing, Tim in front holding great-grandson Ransom; Great-grandsons Adam on Tatiana's right, Andy on left, Shawn in front middle.

Mudite and I followed our family tradition in seeking higher education. Mudite was Valedictorian of her high school class and graduated from the University of Michigan with Distinction. She worked in the Finance Department of Ford Motor Company until the birth of her children Timothy and Lara. God must have needed another little angel as He called Mudite and Ivars' middle child, a daughter named Karina, to Heaven in her infancy. Karina was the first member of the family to be buried in the family plot in the Latvian section of Woodlawn Cemetery in Detroit where our parents were subsequently buried.

Tatiana with youngest great-grandson Theo in January 2008

Four generations: Mudite with Katja, Tatiana, Lara with Ari, March 2008

Rita with her little graduation honors, Steven and David, and BA With Distinction from WSU, January 28, 1958

I obtained my BA degree with Distinction from Wayne State University one month before the birth of my third son, Andrew. Fortunately my academic robe made my advanced pregnancy inconspicuous. Further advanced degrees followed requirements of a diverse career as my interests changed over the years. Working as a librarian in a public library I obtained an MSLS degree and then added an MBA degree to serve on the faculty at Oakland University Libraries as Business Librarian. This position led me back to the familiar College of Education building adjoining the Martha Cook gardens at the University of Michigan where I obtained the status of PhD Candidate in Higher Education in 1978.

It was my MBA degree and work with Affirmative Action and Upward Bound programs at Oakland University, however, that led yet to another career change after I accepted an offer from the University of Detroit to fill the position of Affirmative Action Officer and Assistant to the Personnel Director. As my high school principal had predicted, I enjoyed all my professional work experiences, but I never ceased hearing the call from my primary interest, medicine. It must have been God's plan to keep focusing me, despite many detours, toward finally bringing together all my education and experience into the field of medicine.

One day in 1980 I stopped to pick up some *Portals of Prayer* at our church. I chatted a while with the Rev. Howard G. Allwardt and suddenly, totally out of the context of our conversation, he said,

"*Rita, you have an MBA degree. One of the doctors in our congregation is looking for a manager of his physician group at Hutzel Hospital. Would you be interested?*"

It seemed to me this question coming out of the clear blue sky from my spiritual advisor must be inspired by God guiding me to return to my first love, medicine. Following a brief interview with Dr. Robert Stanhope, I had another interview with the president of the medical group, Tommy N. Evans, MD. I expected to have to talk about my education and experience that would qualify me to direct the business operations of the medical practice. Instead he noticed that I had been a Cub Scout den mother among the personal interests I had listed on my resume.

"*I see that you have been a Den Mother for several years. If you can keep eight active boys focused together as a group, you can manage a group of doctors. We are all just Boy Scouts doing good deeds. I trust my colleague has already gone over your credentials and your pastor has recommended you. You are now officially the manager of our OB/GYN group.*"

Thus, I finally became part of the medical world I loved. It was interesting to be part of the OB/GYN Department at Hutzel in Detroit when it became renown as the first hospital in Michigan to have a baby born after an in-vitro fertilization. I never doubted that it was God's plan to guide me to Hutzel Hospital. When I needed surgery a few years later, Dr. Stanhope performed the operation and I felt as if God was present and working through this Christian physician. The day before the surgery, Dr. Stanhope, who was an Elder of our church, served me Holy Communion. Before I received anesthesia at the time of surgery, Dr. Stanhope took my hand and offered a prayer to God that the Lord would guide his hands to a successful surgical outcome. I went to sleep completely at peace knowing that healing hands would be restoring me to health.

From Hutzel Hospital I advanced to Administrator of the Internal Medicine Department and the ER at Sinai Hospital where I worked with many subspecialties. Since Sinai was a Jewish hospital, it served most of the Jewish immigrants from Russia in the Detroit area. At times I was called upon to translate for some of the patients who came to the ER and could not speak English. This was an interesting challenge as my basic knowledge of Russian never extended to medical terminology. When Sinai closed, I served as the manager of several Ambulatory Care Centers at North Oakland Medical Center in Pontiac until my retirement. At each medical center I was privileged to work with many fine physicians and it seemed that God always put me in the right place at the right time. Whenever a member of the family had a medical crisis, I was at the right place to find the best specialist. Many of the dedicated physicians from the former Sinai Hospital still take care of our family's medical needs.

Sinai Hospital Internal Medicine physicians 1990; Rita at right wearing dark jacket

Dr. Aris Lācis with Mudite & Skaidrite during visit with Physicians Without Borders 1990

Working in hospitals also enabled me to make connections to facilitate opportunities for my cousin Dr. Aris Lācis to participate in seminars and in-service training at the Cleveland Clinic and the University of Michigan Hospitals when Latvia was reorganizing its medical system upon obtaining freedom from the Soviet regime. My family also got to enjoy hosting Aris as our houseguest when the Physicians Without Borders organization sponsored three members of Aris' pediatric heart surgery team from Latvia to come to Detroit on an exchange visit. Being a pioneer in performing surgery on children with congenital heart defects in his own country, Aris has became world-renown for the first successful pediatric heart stem cell transplant and has traveled throughout the world to lecture and share his knowledge and surgical expertise.

Mudite, Zigurds Lācis, and Skaidrite in Royal Oak 1989

Skaidrite & Mudite with Edite Lācis Pašeiko in Latvia 2011

Aris has devoted his entire career to develop new methodologies for raising the standard of care in pediatric cardiac surgery. He was decorated with the Three Star Order of the President for his efforts in advancing medical care in Latvia. He also received a gold medal from the Latvian Science Academy for his contributions to medicine. I am thankful that Aris is just an overseas phone call away and is always willing to give a "transatlantic" second opinion when we have questions about diagnoses and treatments.

Mudite and I enjoy a close relationship with all three of our three Latvian cousins and feel blessed to be reunited with them and their families. In 2011 Mudite and Ivars celebrated their 50th anniversary by going to Latvia with son Tim and his wife Jessica and their three children. Though an ocean stands between us and keeps us from frequent visits, both Aris and Zigurds have visited us in our homes in the United States and we in turn have crossed the seas to be embraced by Edite's love in Riga.

Mudite and I treasure our Latvian relatives and I think of them daily and communicate with them frequently. Latvia will always remain in our hearts as our beloved homeland, but our roots have become so deeply entrenched in American soil and generations of children and grandchildren that it would be impossible to be uprooted and transplanted back to Latvia.

My husband Norman and I were blessed to reach the milestone of our Golden Anniversary, the weddings of our three sons, the birth of our five grandchildren, and our first great-granddaughter. We are fortunate to have our three sons Steven, David, and Andrew establish lasting marriages with loving Christian women, Kathleen, Laura, and Suzanne respectively. Our children and their offspring are a vital and major part of our lives.

Mārupe, 2011 with Mudite's family, Zigurds & Sandra, and Drs. Indars & Inga Lācis and family

Steven, David, Andrew, and Norman at Tatiana's 90th birthday celebration 2002

Our family celebrating the New Millennium at Bavarian Inn in Frankenmuth, January 1, 2000

By marrying into the Sparks' family, I have also become a part of a very large clan of enough Sparks to light up my entire universe.

Sparks Family and friends reunion at cottage in 2003 for Adam and Jessica's graduations from high school

God has been good in guiding our family through His grace along life's journey. Our future shines brightly. I know what lies ahead. It was revealed to me when I was confirmed and given the Bible verse to live by: *"Be thou faithful unto death, and I will give thee a Crown of Life"* (Revelation 2:10). The Lutheran Child and Family Service Auxiliary motto gives further assurance that God will always hold us in His hands.

★★★

I will not forget you....
I have carved you on the palm of my hand.
-Isaiah 49:16

APPENDIX I

THE NEW YORK TIMES, WEDNESDAY, DECEMBER 22, 1948.

SANTA GREETS DISPLACED CHILDREN FROM EUROPE

Youngsters arriving here yesterday on the Marine Flasher receive a merry Yuletide reception at the pier.
The New York Times

549 MORE DP'S LAND AFTER ROUGH TRIP

Christmas Party for Children Held on Pier—Sikorsky Relative in Group

Badly buffeted by high seas but eager to build their lives anew in this country, 549 displaced persons from American-sponsored camps in Europe arrived here yesterday afternoon aboard the United States Maritime Commission ship Marine Flasher.

Admitted under the Displaced Persons Act of 1948, the group included men and women from many lands, a number of whom had been victims of German forced labor camps, and ninety-eight children under 10 years of age. Their transportation to this country had been arranged by the International Refugee Organization, an agency of the United Nations.

As they disembarked at Pier 62, North River, the prospective citizens were met by representatives of four relief agencies responsible for their resettlement in this country. The 187 passengers of Protestant and Orthodox faiths were taken in hand by Church World Service, the 155 Roman Catholics by the War Relief Services Committee of the National Catholic Welfare Conference, and the 72 Jews by United Service for New Americans and by the Hebrew Sheltering and Immigrant Aid Society.

A feature of the afternoon was a Christmas party on the pier organized for the children by the Catholic Welfare Conference. A Santa Claus, scheduled to be on hand when the ship docked, was delayed, causing some confusion at first. He arrived, however, bringing with him a note of Christmas cheer.

Thomas J. Culhane of the Catholic Welfare Conference said the processing of the new arrivals was proceeding well and that the passengers under his supervision would have been on their way to their new homes by 1:30 A. M. today.

"In order to qualify for admission to this country," Mr. Culhane explained, "each displaced person must have a sponsor who will provide a home and a job. Our task is to clear the passengers on their arrival here and to arrange inland transportation to their final destinations. We also provide them with food and a little money for the remainder of their trip."

Voyage Called 'Lousy'

By nationality, the largest group among the Marine Flasher's passengers was Polish, with 252 persons. Other nationals represented were Lithuanians, Latvians, Czechs, Yugoslavs, Rumanians, Russians, Hungarians, Germans and Estonians. Eighty-five were classified as stateless. The newcomers will settle in twenty-eight states, with New York receiving the largest number.

Capt. Stanley L. Thompson, master of the ship, described the crossing as "a rough, lousy trip all the way." He said the Marine Flasher had docked thirty-six hours behind schedule, ten days out of Hamburg. Many of the passengers had been sick, he reported, and two had been injured slightly.

Among the arrivals was Thilda Sasko, Czechoslovak coloratura soprano and a daughter of Gustav Sasko, well-known Chicago pianist and composer. She said she planned to live with her father and hoped to sing with American opera companies.

Dr. Alexander Sikorsky, 46 years old, arrived to live with his nephew, Igor Sikorsky, aviation expert and a resident of Stratford, Conn.

Leiba Winekur, the sole European survivor of a family that once had numbered eighty persons, was another arrival.

This was the third shipload of displaced persons to enter the country under the 1948 act. A fourth group, numbering 339, now is on the high seas aboard the United States Maritime Commission ship Marine Marlin, due to dock here on Friday. The Marine Flasher is scheduled to sail again for Europe on Monday, but there was some doubt as to whether the crew would be available that soon because of Christmas.

FLANDERS BACKS ECA CARGO SHIFT

Senator Asserts American Charges Are Higher Than Market Rate

WASHINGTON, Dec. 21 (AP)—Senator Ralph E. Flanders, Republican, of Vermont, endorsed today a decision by Economic Cooperation Administrator Paul G. Hoffman to waive temporarily a requirement that 50 per cent of foreign aid shipments move in American ships.

The Vermonter said that 12 per cent of all European recovery funds now are used to pay freight costs. Shipments to France and Italy, he said, require 20 per cent.

REFERENCES

1. Photo of steam engine by permission of photographer Bill Merlavage Images, Image #5584 "Snow & Steam". Cumberland, Maryland
2. "Nowhere is it Good like at Home", Text used by permission of lyrics author Guntars Račs @ MicRec Publishing, Riga, Latvia
3. "*I am but a Stranger Here*", Commission on Worship Lutheran Church-Missouri Synod, Lutheran Worship Hymnal, #515. Concordia Publishing House, St. Louis, 1982. Text by Thomas R.Taylor1807-1834.
4. "*Going Home*", Lyrics by William A. Fisher, www.Wikipedia.org/wiki/Symphony_No._9_(Dvorak)#The song.
5. "*Lo, How a Rose is Growing*", Lutheran Church-Missouri Synod, Lutheran Worship Hymnal, #67. Concordia Publishing House, St. Louis, 1982. Text from German, 15th Century; Tune: Alte Catholische Geistliche Kirchengesaeng, Koeln, 1599
6. Caucasian Knot Encyclopedia. http://eng.kavkaz.memo.ru/encyclopediatext 2006
7. www.wikipedia.org/wiki/Grand_Duchess_*Tatiana_Nikolaevna_of_Russia 8/14/2006*
8. Wikepedia.org/wiki/Nicholas II of Russia, p.2 8/14/2006
9. Ibid. p.4
10. Ibid. p. 4
11. Wikipedia.org/wiki/ "October Revolution", p.1, 8/14/2006
12. Ibid., p.2
13. www.historyguide-org/europe/lenin, "The History Guide Lectures on Twentieth Century Europe", Vladimir Ilyich Ulyanov (Lenin) 1870-1914. 8/13/2006
14. www.Answers.com/topic/jelgava, Jelgava Information, p.3; 7/30/2006
15. Grosmane, Elita. Senā Jelgava (Ancient Jelgava). Publisher Neputns, 2010 p.57
16. "Laiks" Latvian Newspaper, Vol. 38, Number 24, Saturday, June 16, 2001, page 1
17. Lines written by Valters Nollendorfs, Ph.D., based on notes left by a deportee. "*Latvia under the Rule of the Soviet Union and National Socialist Germany*". Museum of the Occupation of Latvia. Riga: OMF, 2002, page 57.
18. "Laiks" Latvian Newspaper, Vol.62, Number 45, Saturday, November 26, 2011, page 1.

19. Jewish Holocaust Museum Photo Archives
20. Composer Gerald Plato, Lyrics by Herbert Ernst Groh
21. Harper Collins, "Atlas of the Second World War" 1989, p.104
22. Nollendorfs, Valters, PhD. Essay from Manuscript "Trimda un Neatkarība", 2012, p.1
23. www.knittelfeld.at/druckvorschau April 2007 "Geschichte", Preview of a book by Ilse Stubenberger, "Als Grossvater in den Krieg ziehen musste".
24. Photo Courtesy of Salzburger Museum, Jahresschrift des Salzburger Museums Carolino Augusteum 40/41, 1994/1995, *Salzburg 1945-1955, Zerstoerung und Wiederaufbau*, p.20
25. Ibid. p.14
26. Jahresschrift des Salzburger Museums Carolino Augusteum 40/41, 1994/1995. Salzburg 1945-1955, Zerstoerung und Wiederaufbau, p.297
27. Ibid. p.68
28. Ibid. p.53
29. Ibid. p. 75
30. Ibid. p. 45
31. Ibid. p.142
32. Ibid. p.139
33. Ibid. p. 143
34. Ibid. p.293, U.S. Army Map Service 1951.
35. Ibid. p.43
36. Ibid. p. 304
37. Harper Collins "Atlas of the Second World War", John Keegan, Ed., c.1989, p.188
38. Jahresschrift des Salzburger Museums Carolino Augusteum 40/41, 1994-1995, p.145
39. Houston, Jeanne Wakatsuki and Houston, James D. "Farewell to Manzanar", Bantam Books, 1973
40. www.Hellbrunner Palace, 2011
41. Kennedy, John F., "A Nation of Immigrants". Harper Perennial, 2008, p.45
42. Composer Gerhard Winkler, Lyrics by Günter Schwenn
43. Appendix I, The New York Times, Wednesday, December 22, 1948, p.14
44. Appendix I from New York Times, December 22, 1948, p.14
45. www.wikipedia.org/wiki/jerry_Bilik
46. Leary, Margaret A. *Giving it All Away; The Story of William W. Cook & his Michigan Law Quadrangle. The University of Michigan Press, Ann Arbor, 2011, p.92*
47. Ibid. p.93
48. Ibid, p.94

49. Board of Governors of the Martha Cook Building, *The Martha Cook Building Fiftieth Anniversary 1915-1965. Ann Arbor, 1965 p.2*
50. Leary, Margaret A., *Giving it All Away, p.105*
51. Ibid. p.106
52. *The Martha Cook Building Fiftieth Anniversary 1915-1965, p.1*
53. *Martha Cook Building Resident Handbook, 2010-2011*
54. Ibid., p.2
55. *Constitution, By-Laws and Regulations of Martha Cook Building, University of Michigan, Ann Arbor, 1952, Constitution—Article 9*
56. Ibid. Preface
57. Leary, Margaret A. *Giving it All Away, p.94*
58. The Martha Cook Building Fiftieth Anniversary1915-1965, p.7
59. *"It Only Takes a Moment"* from "Hello, Dolly!", Music and lyrics by Jerry Herman, 1964
60. *"Tenderly"* composed by Walter Gross, lyrics by Jack Lawrence, 1946
61. "The Martha Cook Grace", Music by Ellen Sargeant (class of 1916); Words by Hilda Hagerty (class of 1919)
61. From the poem "To a Mouse", *Burns Poetical Works,* Collins Clear-Type Press, London and New York. P.92 -94
63. Text as written in my diary on November 22, 1953 when the Martha Cook residents serenaded my fiancé and me upon our engagement.